NEW VOCABULARIES IN
FILM SEMIOTICS

SIGHTLINES
Edited by Edward Buscombe, The British Film Institute and
Phil Rosen, Center for Modern Culture and Media,
Brown University, USA

Cinema Studies has made extraordinary strides in the past two decades.
Our capacity for understanding both how and what the cinema signifies
has been developed through new methodologies, and hugely enriched in
interaction with a wide variety of other disciplines, including literary
studies, anthropology, linguistics, history, economics and psychology. As
fertile and important as these new theoretical foundations are, their very
complexity has made it increasingly difficult to track the main lines of
conceptualization. Furthermore, they have made Cinema Studies an ever
more daunting prospect for those coming new to the field.

This new series of books will map out the ground of major conceptual
areas within Cinema Studies. Each volume is written by a recognized
authority to provide a clear and detailed synopsis of current debates within
a particular topic. Each will make an original contribution to advancing
the state of knowledge within the area. Key arguments and terms will be
clearly identified and explained, seminal thinkers will be assessed, and issues
for further research will be laid out. Taken together, the series will
constitute an indispensable chart of the terrain which Cinema Studies
now occupies.

Books in the series include:

NARRATIVE COMPREHENSION AND FILM
Edward Branigan

NEW VOCABULARIES IN FILM SEMIOTICS
Structuralism, Post-structuralism and Beyond
Robert Stam, Robert Burgoyne and Sandy Flitterman-Lewis

CINEMA AND SPECTATORSHIP
Judith Mayne

UNTHINKING EUROCENTRISM
Towards a Multi-cultural Film Critique
Ella Shohat/Robert Stam

NEW VOCABULARIES IN FILM SEMIOTICS

Structuralism, post-structuralism and beyond

*Robert Stam, Robert Burgoyne and
Sandy Flitterman-Lewis*

London and New York

First published 1992
by Routledge
11 New Fetter Lane, London EC4P 4EE

Simultaneously published in the USA and Canada
by Routledge
29 West 35th Street, New York, NW 10001

Reprinted in 1993, 1994, 1995, 1996

Typeset in 10 on 12 point Baskerville by
Intype, London
Printed in Great Britain by
T J International Ltd, Padstow, Cornwall

British Library Cataloguing in Publication Data
Stam, Robert
New vocabularies in film semiotics: structuralism,
post-structuralism, and beyond. – (Sightlines)
I. Title   II. Burgoyne, Robert
III. Flitterman-Lewis, Sandy IV. Series
791.43

Library of Congress Cataloging in Publication Data
Stam, Robert
New vocabularies in film semiotics: structuralism, post-
structuralism, and beyond / Robert Stam, Robert Burgoyne, and Sandy
Flitterman-Lewis
p.   cm.–(Sightlines)
Includes bibliographical references (p.   ) and index.
I. Motion pictures-Semiotics.   I. Burgoyne, Robert.
II. Flitterman-Lewis, Sandy.   III. Title   IV. Series:
Sightlines (London, England)
PN1995.S674   1992
791.43′014–dc20   91–21530

ISBN 0–415–06594–1 (hbk)
ISBN 0–415–06595–X (pbk)

To Christian Metz

CONTENTS

CONTENTS

CONTRIBUTORS

Robert Stam is Professor of Cinema Studies at New York University. A Guggenheim as well as a Fulbright Fellow, he is the author of *The Interrupted Spectacle* (Paz e Terra, 1981), *Brazilian Cinema* (with Randal Johnson, Texas, 1982), *Reflexivity in Film and Literature: From Don Quixote to Jean-Luc Godard* (UMI, 1985), *Subversive Pleasures: Bakhtin, Cultural Criticism and Film* (Johns Hopkins, 1989), *Bakhtin* (Attica, 1991), and *Unthinking Eurocentrism* with Ella Shohat (forthcoming from Routledge in 1992). His work has been anthologized in collections such as *The Media Reader, Regarding Television, The Cinematic Text, Literary Theories in Praxis* and *Postmodernism and its Discontents*.

Robert Burgoyne is an Associate Professor of English at Wayne State University, and Director of the Film Studies Program. He has published extensively on narrative theory and film, including an important article on cinematic narration entitled "The cinematic narrator: the logic and pragmatics of impersonal narration," published in English in *Journal of Film and Video* and in French in *Poetique*. He has also published several texts on historical representation and film, including the book *Bertolucci's 1900: A Narrative and Historical Analysis*.

Sandy Flitterman-Lewis is the author of *To Desire Differently: Feminism and the French Cinema* (University of Illinois Press, 1990), as well as numerous articles in such journals as *Screen, Wide Angle, Enclitic, Literature and Psychology*, and *Discourse*, among others. Her work is anthologized in eleven collections, including *Theories of Authorship, Regarding Television, Channels of Discourse, Dada and Surrealist Film, French Film: Texts and Contexts, Visibly Female*, and *Framing Feminism*. A co-founder of *Camera Obscura: A Journal of Feminism and Film Theory*, she remained with the journal until 1978. She is currently Associate Professor of English and Cinema Studies at Rutgers University in New Jersey.

PREFACE

The founding premise of this text is that film semiotics has constituted one of the signal advances in arts criticism in recent years. Ever since film theory broke free from the impressionistic debate about auteurism and "realism" which had dominated film-critical discourse through the early 1960s, film semiotics and its developments have been at the center of the analytic enterprise in film. In a first stage, Saussurean structural linguistics provided the dominant theoretical model, followed by a second phase in which Althusserian Marxism and Lacanian psychoanalysis became the preferred conceptual grids, followed in turn by a more pluralistic period in which movements such as feminism, already a formative presence in film studies, both incorporated and critiqued the antecedent theories and schools. Although post-structuralism "buried" the scientist dreams of early structuralist semiology, currently semiotics, conceived in a broad sense, continues to form the matrix, and provide much of the vocabulary, for approaches ranging from the linguistic, psychoanalytic, feminist and Marxist to the narratological, reception-oriented and translinguistic. Although film semiotics has partially retreated from its earlier totalizing claims, what Guy Gauthier calls the "semiotic diaspora" remains a dynamizing presence within reflexion on film.

While film-makers and critics had always made sporadic attempts to theorize the cinema – one thinks of the work of Eisenstein, Kracauer, Bazin – it has only been in recent decades that film semiotics emerged as a powerful and comprehensive movement. The growth of semiotic theory and the presence of its vocabulary in a variety of intellectual fields confirms the importance of "the science of signs, sign systems and signifying practices" as a tool for addressing the semantic riches of extremely diverse cultural forms, while semiotics' cross-disciplinary thrust constitutes an antidote to the fragmentation and compartmentalization of intellectual disciplines. But semiotics has constituted a highly specialized language, fecund in neologisms, in borrowed and even resuscitated terms, and despite the wide dissemination of semiotic theory and its vocabulary, the absence of precise definitions and pertinent guidelines for use has made the teaching of semiotics a confusing and difficult task. The vocabulary has become familiar, while the concepts, and their interrelations, remain obscure.

New Vocabularies in Film Semiotics responds to the felt need, on the part of teachers and students, for a book which would define the critical terms in semiotic film theory and survey the ways the concepts have been employed. The terms here defined, it should be pointed out, range considerably in their status, moving from quasi-technical terms, such as "bracket syntagma," to much broader and inclusive terms, such as "reflexivity," which evoke whole constellations of interrelated concepts. The terms vary as well in their disciplinary provenance. Some terms, such as _langue_ and _parole_, have long been "consecrated" as fundamental terms within semiotics generally, quite apart from any reference to film, and are included here both because they provide essential grounding for understanding and because they have been appropriated for use by film semioticians. Terms such as "autonomous shot" and "cinematic apparatus," in contrast, are "film-specific"; i.e. they are expressly designed to pertain to film. Other terms, such as Barthes' "hermeneutic code," meanwhile, although originally imported from literary theory, have taken on specific "accents" in relation to film. Still other "imported" terms, such as Genette's "transtextuality" or Bakhtin's "chronotope," have only now begun to be deployed within film analysis. Terms such as "acousmatic," meanwhile, have circulated in French film-critical discourse but remain relatively unknown in the English-speaking world. The terms defined here vary widely, furthermore, in their degree of theoretical "trendiness." "Binary oppositions" have fallen from favor, while "dialogism" and _différance_, at the time of this writing, remain fashionable.

Post-structuralism reminds us that mere definitions cannot ever completely discipline or corral the anarchic dissemination of meaning. Signification cannot be "fixed" by the fiat of lexical assertion. The more complexly and contradictorily nuanced a term is, as Raymond Williams points out in _Keywords_ (1985), the more likely it is to have formed the focus for historically significant debates. We are also aware that semiotic language can be abused and become a jargon, deployed to furnish a patina of scientificity – part of what Metz has called "sausage-link semiology" – or an aura of post-structuralist sophistication. In any case, definitions can serve as signposts pointing in the direction of those issues that have engaged theorists and analysts at a given point in intellectual history; they exist to be used, questioned, revised, rejected, subverted.

This text is organized into five major parts, each centering on a key set of concepts or area of inquiry. The introductory part, "The Origins of Semiotics," provides a general overview of the historical roots of semiotics within intellectual history, with emphasis on the impact of structural linguistics and of specific movements such as Russian Formalism, Prague structuralism, and the Bakhtin Circle. This opening part foregrounds the common provenance and conceptual interdependence of all the terms under discussion, while simultaneously preparing the overall movement that structures the book as a whole, i.e. the movement that takes us from structuralism to post-structuralism and beyond. The second part, "Cine-Semiology," deals with linguistically oriented terms within film semiotics, and specifically those having to do with "film language" and "textual analysis." The third part, "Film-Narratology," traces developments in narratology (Propp, Genette, Greimas) as they have inflected film theory and analysis. The fourth part, "Psychoanalysis," deals with "second phase" semiotics, focussing on the psychosemiology of the cinema, treating both classical psychoanalytic terms and concepts (e.g. identification) and their extrapolations into cinematic theory. The fifth part, "From Realism to Intertextuality," charts the overall trajectory from the initial emphasis on "realism" in the theory of the 1950s, to the foregrounding of "discourse," "intertextuality" and "transtextuality" in the 1970s and 1980s.

Each lexical entry follows the same overall scheme. The basic definition of the term in question and a brief history of its disciplinary origin and historical evolution are followed by a brief appraisal of the term's actual or potential "productivity" in relation to film. Filmic examples serve both to illustrate the semiotic concepts, and to provide a kind of field-test of their applicability.

The sequence of definitions is organized conceptually, rather than alphabetically, emphasizing the linkages between the terminological groups which form part of a particular paradigm. Terms are thus generally defined both individually and in relation to larger "clusters" of interrelated concepts forming part of larger "problematics." When possible, the definitions are organized in terms not only of logical priority but also of their chronological insertion into film-theoretical discourse. In so far as possible within a lexicon format, the book also indirectly charts the successive transformations of film semiotics through diverse theoretical paradigms: the linguistic, the narratological, the psychoanalytic and the "translinguistic." The text in this sense incorporates a kind of subliminal, embedded history of semiotic theory, conveyed indirectly in the form of a sequenced series of problematics. The overall trajectory from structuralism to post-structuralism, meanwhile, is recapitulated, in diverse ways, in all the sections. The implicit chronologies are not linear nor consistent, however, nor could they be. Narratology traces its roots to the late 1920s but gains full force only in the 1970s and 1980s. Bakhtin did much of his work in the late 1920s, yet his conceptual categories, introduced into western Europe only in the 1960s, anticipate and go beyond the structuralism and post-structuralism which came much later.

In general, we have tried to assume very little, having the terms logically build upon one another. Thus a discussion of the Freudian sense of "identification" leads easily to a discussion of Metz' discussion of "primary" and "secondary" identification in the cinema, and Bakhtin's views on "dialogism" segue to Kristeva's formulations concerning "intertextuality" and Genette's concerning "transtextuality." This format will hopefully enable the reader to use the book either as a reference guide for individual entries or as a compact survey of the field. Thus the book can be read selectively item by item, part by part, or even from beginning to end. For those preferring to use the book only as a lexicon or reference guide, the defined terms are listed in the index, or can be found, set off by small capital letters in bold, at the point of initial definition. In cases where readers encounter terms that seem to require definition, we suggest that the readers turn to the index to see if the term is defined elsewhere.

As a multi-track sensorially composite medium, heir to all the antecedent arts and discourses, the study of cinema virtually compels a multi-disciplinary approach. Film semiotics has been inclined, furthermore, to what Gauthier calls disciplinary "polygamy," a tendency to "mate" with other disciplines and approaches. Although especially geared to the needs of film students, consequently, *New Vocabularies in Film Semiotics* is also relevant to students and scholars in neighboring fields. (The members of the editorial group, although currently teaching film studies, are also trained in comparative literature and visual arts.) Hopefully, the book will be useful for students in all areas of the arts, philosophy and literature, all disciplinary sites where an awareness of semiotic terminology and methodology has become indispensable to serious theoretical work. The discourses of the various disciplines should, ideally, interanimate and cross-fecundate one another. Thus our discussions of film-specific terms will perhaps provoke thought on the part of literary analysts, just as literature-specific concepts have already triggered reflexion on the part of film analysts.

We are highly aware of our own rather dense intertext, i.e. the diverse lexicons, dictionaries and survey texts which have preceded our own, and for which we feel only respect and gratitude, and which are in no way superseded by our own since they were conceived at a different time and in the pursuit of distinct goals. We are thinking especially of Kaja Silverman's *The Subject of Semiotics*, of the Laplanche-Pontalis *Language of Psycho-Analysis*, of the Ducrot-Todorov *Encyclopedic Dictionary of the Sciences of Language*, of John Fiske, Tim O'Sullivan, Danny Saunders and John Hartley's *Key Concepts in Communication*, of the multi-authored *Lectures de Film*, of Jacques Aumont, Alain Bergala, Michel Marie and Marc Vernet's *Esthetique du Film*, of Jacques Aumont and Michel Marie's *L'Analyse des Films*, of Rick Altman's *Cinema/Sound*, of Dudley Andrews' *Concepts in Film Theory*, of David Rodowick's *The Crisis of Political Modernism*, of Robert Lapsley and Michael Westlake's *Film Theory: An Introduction*, and of the Greimas/Courtes *Semiotics and Language*. The didactic texts of Jonathan Culler and Christopher Norris on issues of structural linguistics and deconstruction have also been indispensable to our endeavor.

The specific "difference" of this book, however, lies (a) in its inclusive-
ness – almost six hundred terms and concepts are defined – (b) in its
methodological range, its incorporation of a wide spectrum of theoretical
grids and disciplinary discourses and (c) in its attempt to reconcile diachrony and synchrony, history and system, through a history of semiotics
embedded in what is fundamentally a conceptual lexicon. We should clarify
that our emphasis throughout is less on the grand "debates" of film theory
than on their lexical fall-out. The book is intended as a didactic introduction to the vocabulary of the field, not as a series of interventions in film
theory. We do not generally evaluate or criticize the work we summarize
– for example, we do not explore the diverse theoretical objections raised
against Derridean deconstruction – although we do from time to time point
out tensions or inconsistencies. As a rule, we treat theoretical movements,
and individual theorists, not in terms of their ultimate value or importance
but rather in terms of their *terminological* fecundity and influence. Those
movements or individual theorists whose contribution has not been fundamentally terminological will of necessity seem under-represented here.
Although we will at times linger on the work of specific thinkers of crucial
importance to the development of film semiotics – figures such as Christian
Metz, Stephen Heath, Mary Ann Doane, and Julia Kristeva – in general
we do not attempt to perform an exhaustive survey of figures or of work
done. That any specific analyst or theorist is nowhere mentioned in no
way reflects on the value of the work; it simply suggests that the analyst
was not regarded as a major source of *terminological* innovation.

Although we generally try to survey the semiotic field impartially, our
own views inevitably come into play in the very selection of the terms to
be defined, the degree of emphasis placed on them, and the working out
of their implications. Occasionally, we depart from a dispassionate stance
to become more personal and essayistic. While we usually synopsize the
work and theory of others, we also at times speak in our own voice. It
should be pointed out, finally, that this text, although a collaboration,
also interweaves three distinct "voices." Robert Stam was fundamentally
responsible for Parts I, II, and V, as well as for the overall conceptualization of the structure of the book; Robert Burgoyne was fundamentally
responsible for Part III, and Sandy Flitterman-Lewis was fundamentally
responsible for Part IV.

We would like to thank Jill Rawnsley for her impeccable work as an
editor. And we would like to thank, finally, the various people who have
read the manuscript, in part or in whole, and who have made useful
suggestions: Richard Allen, John Belton, Edward Branigan, Joel Lewis,
Christian Metz, David Nelson, R. Barton Palmer, Tova Shaban and Ella
Shohat. We would like to express special appreciation to Bertrand Augst.
We would like to thank the editors of this series, Ed Buscombe and
Phil Rosen. We could not have asked for more sympathetic, alert and

discriminating readers. Finally, due to his undeniable importance to the field, and due to his peerless personal generosity, we have dedicated this book to Christian Metz.

I

THE ORIGINS OF SEMIOTICS

The emergence of **SEMIOTICS*** as the study of signs, signification and signifying systems, must be seen within the broader context of the language-haunted nature of contemporary thought. Although language has been an object of philosophical reflexion for millennia, it is only recently that it has come to constitute a fundamental paradigm, a virtual "key" to the mind, to artistic and social praxis, and indeed to human existence generally. Central to the project of a wide spectrum of twentieth-century thinkers – Wittgenstein, Cassirer, Heidegger, Lévi-Strauss, Merleau-Ponty and Derrida – is a concern with the crucial shaping importance of language in human life and thought. The overarching meta-discipline of semiotics, in this sense, can be seen as a local manifestation of a more widespread "linguistic turn," an attempt to reconceptualize the world "through" linguistics.

SEMIOTICS AND THE PHILOSOPHY OF LANGUAGE

Human beings have never ceased reflecting on their own language. The Hebrew Bible suggests a linguistic theory by claiming that God brought the beasts of the field and the fowl of the air to Adam "to see what he would call them: and whatsoever Adam called every living creature, that was the name thereof" (Genesis II, 19–20). Here name-giving is seen as the spontaneous exercise of a natural faculty, but we are never told the precise principles which ordered Adam's activity. The Babel story, mean-while, points to the problem of language difference, the origins of the diversity of human languages and their mutual incomprehensibility. At Babel, God deliberately confused the correlations between name and thing which had obtained when all the world was "of one speech." Linguistic speculations also dot the classical texts of Greek, Indian and Chinese culture, and arguably form part of *all* cultures, including oral cultures. Semiotics proper, however, traces its origins back to the western philosophi-

---

* When a term is first defined, it appears in small capitals in bold. See the index for location of definitions; the page numbers appear in bold type.

1

cal tradition of speculation concerning language and the relation between words and things. The Greek pre-Socratic philosophers explored the issue of the **MOTIVATION** of signs, i.e. the question of whether a direct inherent relationship links words and the objects they designate or whether the relationship is only socially determined and consensual. Heraclitus maintained that names and signs enjoyed a "natural" connection with the objects named, that the link between word and thing was, in contemporary parlance, "motivated," while Democritus saw names and words as purely conventional, or in contemporary parlance, "arbitrary." The argument in Plato's dialogue "Cratylus," the earliest record of any extended debate on linguistic questions, revolves around this same issue of motivation or "the correctness of names." Cratylus argues the "inherent correctness" of names, while Hermogenes argues that no name belongs to any particular thing by nature, but only by "habit and custom." (In *Mimologiques*, Gerard Genette traces the attempts, ever since the "Cratylus" to posit relations of motivation or resemblance between linguistic signifiers and their signifieds.) Aristotle conceived of the sign as a relation between words and mental events. In his treatise *On Interpretation*, Aristotle defines words as "significant sounds" (*phone semantike*) and argues that spoken words are "symbols or signs of affections or impressions of the soul," while "written words are the signs of words spoken" – a view later to be criticized by Derrida as logocentric and phonocentric. Aristotle sees particular languages as essentially nomenclatures, sets of names by which its speakers identify different persons, places, animals, qualities and so forth.

The classical period also introduced debates revolving around the concept of realism, debates with long-term implications for the semiotic discussion of the nature of representation. Although it is scarcely possible here to elucidate these long and intricate debates, we can distinguish, within classical philosophy, between **PLATONIC REALISM** – the assertion of the absolute and objective existence of universals, i.e. the belief that forms, essences, abstractions such as "humanity" and "truth" exist independent of human perception, whether in the external world or in the realm of perfect forms – and **ARISTOTELIAN REALISM** – the view that universals only exist *within* objects in the external world (rather than in an extra-material realm of essences). The term "realism" is confusing because its early philosophical usages often seem diametrically opposed to what one might call **NAIVE REALISM** – the belief that the world is as we perceive it ("seeing is believing") or **COMMON-SENSE REALISM** – the belief in the objective existence of facts and the attempt to see these facts without idealization. (We will return to questions of realism in Part V.)

Subsequent to the classical period, the Stoics also showed interest in the process of symbolization. The Stoic philosopher Sextus Empiricus distinguished three aspects of the sign: the signifier, the signified and the referent. But the first truly rigorous semiotician, according to Todorov, was Saint

Augustine, who took as his province the whole variety of sign phenomena. In *De Magistro*, Augustine saw linguistic signs as only one type in a broader category which would include insignias, gestures, ostensive signs. Apart from individual philosophers, one can also point to widely disseminated "proto-semiotic" metaphors. The trope of "the world as a book," prevalent in the literature of the Middle Ages and the Renaissance, for example, implies that all social and natural phenomena can be seen as "texts" to be read. It was also in the Middle Ages that William of Ockham (1285–1349) questioned whether words signify concepts or things, and proposed a dual classification of signs into "manifestive" and "suppositive."

The first modern philosopher to use the term "semiotic" was John Locke, who in his *Essay Concerning Human Understanding* (1690), referred to "*semiotike*, or the doctrine of signs ... the business whereof is to consider the nature of signs the mind makes use of for the understanding of things, or conveying its knowledge to others" (4.21.4). Locke also argued for the arbitrariness of the sign, claiming that words were signs of ideas, "not by any natural connexion ... but by a voluntary Imposition, whereby such a Word is made arbitrarily the Mark of such an Idea" (3.2.1–2). The German philosopher Gottfried Wilhelm Leibniz (1646–1716), in the wake of work by the English philosopher Francis Bacon, studied the syntax of sign structures and proposed a universal system of signs, while the French philosopher Etienne, Abbé de Condillac (1715–80) argued for "natural analogy" as the "first principle of signs."

If all these thinkers addressed the question of signs and signification, one might ask, wherein lies the innovatory nature of contemporary semiotics? The truth is that before the contemporary period, linguistic speculations merely formed part of the broader currents of philosophy, while contemporary semiotics proposed the inauguration of a new and comprehensive discipline based on linguistic methods. Semiotics must be seen as symptomatic not only of the general language-consciousness of contemporary thought but also of its penchant for methodological self-consciousness, its tendency to demand critical scrutiny of its own terms and procedures. When language speaks of itself, as in the case of linguistics, we are dealing with a **METALANGUAGE**. The term "metalanguage" was first introduced by the logicians of the School of Vienna, such as Rudolf Carnap (1891–1970), who distinguished between the language we speak and the language which we use to speak about that language. Linguistics, in this sense, is the higher-level language used to describe language itself as an object of study. The term **METALINGUISTICS** has been used to refer to the overall relation of the linguistic system to other systems of signs within a culture. Semiotics might be regarded as a metalinguistics, although Barthes argued in *Elements of Semiology* that linguistics itself "includes" semiotics, since the semiotician is constantly forced back into language to speak of the semiotics of any non-linguistic cultural object.

3

THE FOUNDERS OF SEMIOTICS

The two source thinkers of contemporary semiotics were the American pragmatic philosopher Charles Sanders Peirce (1839–1914) and the Swiss linguist Ferdinand de Saussure (1857–1913). Around the same time, but without either knowing of the researches of the other, Saussure founded the science of **SEMIOLOGY** and Peirce the science of "semiotics." In Saussure's *Course in General Linguistics* (1915), a book posthumously compiled by his students and based on notes drawn from three series of Saussure's lectures, we find his classic definition of semiology:

> A science that studies the life of signs within society is conceivable; it would be a part of social psychology and consequently of general psychology; I shall call it *semiology* (from Greek semeion 'sign'). Semiology would show what constitutes signs, what laws govern them. Since the science does not yet exist, no one can say what it would be; but it has a right to existence, a place staked out in advance.
>
> (Saussure 1966: 16)

Language, for Saussure, was only one of many semiological systems, but it had a privileged role not only as the most complex and universal of all systems of expression but also as the most characteristic. Linguistics, consequently, provided the "master-pattern for all branches of semiology" (Saussure 1966: 68).

Peirce's philosophical investigations, meanwhile, led him in the direction of what he called "semiotic," specifically through a concern with symbols, which he regarded as the "woof and warp" of all thought and scientific research. In a letter, Peirce wrote: "It has never been in my power to study anything – mathematics, ethics, metaphysics, gravitations, thermodynamics, optics, chemistry, comparative anatomy, astronomy, psychology, phonetics, economic, history of science, whist, men and women, wine, metrology – except as a study of semiotic." (Peirce uses the term without "s"; Margaret Mead reportedly initiated the use of the plural "semiotics" on the analogy of "ethics" and "mathematics".) That there are two words for the semiotic enterprise, "semiotics" and "semiology," largely has to do with its dual origins in the Peircean and Saussurean traditions. Although some theorists such as Julia Kristeva have argued that "semiotics" studies the signifier, while semiology studies the signified, the two terms have often been used interchangeably. In recent years, however, "semiotics" has become the preferred term, seen by its partisans as connoting a discipline less static and taxonomic than "semiology."

Like Saussure's, Peirce's papers were collected and published posthumously, between 1931 and 1935. Peirce's ideas on language are scattered throughout the eight volumes of his *Collected Papers* as well as in a body of unpublished material. For Peirce, language constitutes the human being:

"the word or sign which the man uses *is* the man himself . . . thus my language is the sum total of myself" (1931: V, 189). For our purposes, Peirce made a number of essential contributions of relevance to the semiotics of film. One is his definition of the **SIGN** as "something which stands to somebody for something in some respects or capacity." This definition, as Eco points out, offers the advantage of not demanding, as part of the sign's definition, the qualities of being intentionally emitted or artificially produced, thus avoiding the mentalism implicit in the Saussurean definition, which envisions the sign as a communicative device taking place between two human beings intentionally aiming to express or communicate (Eco 1976: 15). Eco, following the Danish linguist Hjelmslev, substituted for "sign" the term **SIGN FUNCTION**, which Eco defines as the correlation between an expression (a material occurrence) and its content. The process of **SEMIOSIS**, or the production of meaning, for Peirce, involves a triad of three entities: the sign, its object and its interpretant. The **OBJECT** is that for which the sign stands, while the **INTERPRETANT** is the "mental effect" generated by the relation between sign and object. There has been some confusion about the notion of the "interpretant," which refers not to a person, the interpreter, but to a sign, or more exactly, the interpreter's conception of the sign. The status of the real in all this, as Kaja Silverman points out, remains somewhat unclear, in that at times Peirce suggests the possibility of a direct unmediated experience of reality, while elsewhere implying that it can be known only through representations whose signification is established by social consensus. But since the conversion of sign to interpretant, in Peirce's system, occurs not within the mind but within the sign system, he manages to anticipate a post-structuralist vision of **INFINITE SEMIOSIS**, i.e. the process by which signs refer endlessly only to other signs, with meaning constantly deferred in an infinite series of signs, without any direct dependence on any object or referent.

Peirce's second major contribution to semiotics was his tripartite classification of the kinds of signs available to human consciousness into icons, indices and symbols. Peirce defined the **ICONIC SIGN** as "a sign determined by its dynamic object by virtue of its own internal nature." The iconic sign represents its object by means of similarity or resemblance; the relation between sign and interpretant is mainly one of likeness, as in the case of portraits, diagrams, statues, and on an aural level, onomatopoeic words. Peirce defined the **INDEXICAL SIGN** as a "sign determined by its Dynamic object by virtue of being in a real relation to it." An indexical sign involves a causal, existential link between sign and interpretant, as in the case of a weathercock, or of a barometer or of smoke as signifying the existence of fire. A **SYMBOLIC SIGN**, finally, involves an entirely conventional link between sign and interpretant, as is the case in the majority of the words forming part of "natural languages." Linguistic signs, that is to say, are symbols in that they represent objects only by linguistic convention.

The iconic sign, then, exhibits the same configuration of qualities as the represented object. In a photograph, the person pictured resembles the actual person in the picture. Diagrams that reproduce or represent analogical relationships – for example, between rising sales and rising profits – are also, for Peirce, iconic signs. The three types of signs are not mutually exclusive, however. Although a language like English is largely composed of conventional symbols, onomatopoeic words like "buzz" and "hiss" display an iconic dimension in that they function through resemblance between the actual sounds and the sounds of the phonemes evoking the sounds. Non-phonetic languages based on hieroglyphs or ideograms mingle the iconic with the symbolic to a much higher degree. Iconic signs, meanwhile, can also deploy an indexical or symbolic dimension. Photographic signs are iconic in that they function through resemblance, but indexical in their causal, existential – Bazin would say "ontological" – link between the pro-filmic event and the photographic representation. One must assume a certain relativity, then, in defining signs as forming part of one category or another.

It is Saussure, however, who constitutes the founding figure for European structuralism and semiotics, and thus for much of film semiotics. Saussure's *Course in General Linguistics* ushered in a kind of "Copernican Revolution" in linguistic thought by seeing language not as a mere adjunct to our grasp of reality but rather as formative of it. Before we introduce some of the fundamental concepts of film semiotics, it is essential to outline some of the principal Saussurean linguistic ideas on which much of semiotics was based. Saussurean linguistics forms part of a general shift away from the nineteenth-century preoccupation with the temporal and the historical – as evidenced by Hegel's *historical* dialectic, Marx's *dialectical* materialism, and Darwin's "*evolution* of the species" – to the contemporary concern with the spatial, the systematic and the structural. Saussure argued that linguistics must move away from the historical (diachronic) orientation of traditional linguistics, an approach deeply rooted in nineteenth-century historicism, toward a "synchronic" approach which studies language as a functional totality at a given point of time. A linguistic phenomenon is said to be **SYNCHRONIC** – etymologically "same time" – when all the elements it brings into play belong to one and the same moment of the same language. A linguistic phenomenon is said to be **DIACHRONIC** – etymologically, "two times" – when it brings into play elements belonging to different times and states of development of a single language. Synchronic linguistics, according to Saussure, "will be concerned with the logical and psychological relations that bind together coexisting terms and form a system in the collective mind of speakers" (Saussure 1966: 99–100). For Saussure, it is a serious mistake to confuse synchronic facts with diachronic facts, since the contrast between the two points of view is "absolute and admits of no compromise." Synchronic linguistics, furthermore, takes

6

necessary precedence over diachronic linguistics, since without synchronic systems there could be no diachronic developments.

In fact, it is often difficult to separate the diachronic from the synchronic, especially since there are differing definitions of what constitutes the same moment of speech interaction – a generation? a century? – or the same language – are Castilian Spanish and Latin American Spanish the "same" language? (The semiotically oriented film historian is confronted with analogous ambiguities. Does the "same moment" mean a period of a year, a decade, a half-century? Is *Breathless* part of the "same moment" as *Citizen Kane*? Does the "same language" include "dialectal" variations such as the industrial film, the animated cartoon?) In fact, it is difficult to define synchronic relationships without reference to history; history and the state of the language are mutually imbricated. The qualifiers "synchronic" and "diachronic" apply less to the phenomena themselves, therefore, than to the perspective adopted by the linguist. What matters is the shift in emphasis from the historical approach to language – preoccupied with the origins and evolution of language, with etymologies of words, with "sound shifts" over time, and with the comparative evolution of languages – to an emphasis on language as a functional system. How does the English language function at the present moment? For Saussure, it would be a mistake to over-emphasize the question of origins and evolution. That the pronoun "you" once existed in opposition to the more formal "thou" (now used only in a religious context) is "non-pertinent" to the study of the system of contemporary English where that differentiation no longer operates. Diachronic study, while valuable on its own terms, does not help us disengage the nature of a language as a functional system. Saussure compared the situation to that of a game of chess: the successive moves are comparable to the successive synchronic states of a language in evolution. What matters is that the chess game has reached a certain point, not that one trace all the moves that preceded that point.

In his book on Russian Formalism, *The Prison-house of Language*, Fredric Jameson deconstructs Saussure's chess analogy, arguing that in language it is the very rules that change, while in chess the rules stay the same; only the positions evolve. The structuralist affinity for the synchronic, Jameson argues, makes it ahistorical, unable to account for historical change: "Once you have begun by separating the diachronic from the synchronic . . . you can never really put them back together again" (Jameson 1972: 18). Saussure's defenders, on the other hand, see Jameson's critique as unfair, since Saussure saw the splitting off of diachronic and synchronic as a heuristic device or methodological fiction intended to reassert the importance of the synchronic as a corrective to a purely historical study. In any case, the interventions of the Prague School and of the Bakhtin Circle can be seen as attempts to heal the rift between the synchronic and the diachronic opened up by Saussure.

Saussure was also dissatisfied with linguistics as practised by his contemporaries because it never constituted itself as a science in the sense of determining the precise nature of its **OBJECT**, i.e. the aspects of the field of investigation of interest to the investigator, aspects potentially forming an intelligible system or totality. Saussure's answer to his own methodological question concerning the object of linguistic study was that it should first of all be synchronic, and that within the synchronic, secondly, it should focus on *langue* rather than on *parole*. **LANGUE**, in this context, refers to the language-system shared by a community of speakers, as opposed to **PAROLE**, the individual speech acts made possible by the language, i.e. the concrete utterances performed by individual speakers in actual situations. Saussure thus saw the object of linguistic investigation as disengaging the abstract signifying procedures of a language, its key units and their rules of combination, rather than tracing its history or describing individual speech acts.

Saussure also provided the most influential definition of the **SIGN** within the semiological/semiotic tradition; he defined the sign as the union of a form which signifies – the signifier – and an idea signified – the signified. (The impossibility of cutting a sheet of paper without simultaneously cutting recto and verso symbolized for Saussure the fundamental inseparability of the phonetic and the conceptual dimensions of language.) The sign is for Saussure the central fact of language, and the primordial opposition of signifier/signified constitutes the founding principle of structural linguistics. The **SIGNIFIER** is the sensible, material, acoustic or visual signal which triggers a mental concept, the signified. The perceptible aspect of the sign is the signifier; the absent mental representation evoked by it is the **SIGNIFIED**, and the relationship between the two is signification. The signified is not a "thing," an image or a sound, but rather a mental representation. The signified of "cat," for example, is not to be equated with the referent – the animal itself – but rather with the mental representation of a feline creature. (The non-referential nature of the verbal signified becomes more obvious in the case of interjections such as "but" or "however," words lacking any clear physical referent.)

Central to the Saussurean definition of the sign is the **ARBITRARY** relationship between signifier and signified in the sign. The linguistic signifier is not related in any analogical way to the signified; the sign "cat," in the disposition of its letters or the organization of its sounds, does not resemble or imitate the concept, but has an arbitrary and unmotivated relationship to it. (The exceptions to this include onomatopoeia as in "buzz" and cases of "secondary motivation" in which the combination of words is motivated, as in "type-writer," even though the individual signs are not.) For Saussure the relation between signifier and signified is "arbitrary," not only in the sense that individual signs exhibit no intrinsic link between signifier and signified, but also in the sense that each language,

8

in order to make meaning, "arbitrarily" divides the continuum of both sound and sense. (It is this non-coincidence of the divisions of the conceptual field that renders computerized word-for-word translation so problematic.) Each language has a distinctive and thus arbitrary way of organizing the world into concepts and categories. The color spectrum of Russian, for example, does not exactly coincide with the spectrum as organized by English. The sign, then, is social and institutional, existing pragmatically only for a well-defined group of users for whom the signs enter into a differential system called a language.

Signs, for Saussure, enter into two fundamental types of relationship: **PARADIGMATIC** (Saussure actually used the word "associative") and **SYNTAGMATIC**. The identity of any linguistic sign is determined by the sum total of paradigmatic and syntagmatic relations into which it enters with other linguistic signs in the same language system. The **PARADIGM** consists in a virtual or "vertical" set of units which have in common the fact that they entertain relations of similarity and contrast – i.e. of comparability – and that they may be chosen to combine with other units. The alphabet is a paradigm, in that letters are chosen from it to form words, which can themselves be seen as mini-syntagmas. Paradigmatic relations can be posited at all levels of linguistic analysis, for example the section of /p-/ as opposed to /b-/, or "a" as opposed to "the" or "this." The **SYNTAGM**, and syntagmatic relationships have to do with the sequential characteristics of speech, their "horizontal" arrangement into a signifying whole. Paradigmatic operations involve choosing, while syntagmatic operations involve combining. Roland Barthes was among the first to discern these kinds of relationship within apparently non-linguistic realms such as cuisine – the diner chooses from a paradigm of possible soups but then combines the chosen soup syntagmatically with other items chosen from other paradigms, for example, meat dishes or desserts – and fashion – one chooses between hats, but combines the hat syntagmatically with tie and jacket. Jean-Luc Godard's *Two or Three Things I Know about Her* (1967), in this sense, highlights not only the general semiotic wealth of human culture but also the paradigmatic and syntagmatic operations involved in film-making as a "linguistic" practice. Godard's whispered commentaries – "Should I focus on the leaves, or the sign? . . . Am I too close? . . . Is my voice too loud?" – point to the precise kinds of selecting and combining involved in making a film.

RUSSIAN FORMALISM

Another important source-movement for contemporary semiotics was Russian Formalism. The origins of the movement, which flourished roughly from 1915 through 1930, date back even before the Russian Revolution to the activities of the Moscow Linguistic Circle, founded in 1915, and to the

Society for the Study of Poetic Language (OPOJAZ), founded in 1916. Roman Jakobson was a leading figure in the Moscow Linguistic Circle (and later founded the Prague Linguistic Circle in 1926), while the major figures in OPOJAZ were Victor Shklovsky, Roman Jakobson, Boris Eikhenbaum and Yury Tynianov. (Todorov's publication of French translations of key Formalist texts in *Théorie de la Littérature* in 1966 indicated not only the importance of Formalist theories for literary critics but also further solidified the already significant relationship between Formalism and structuralism.) The Formalists rejected the eclectic and belletristic critical approaches which had dominated previous literary study in favor of a scientific approach concerned with literature's "immanent" properties, its structures and systems, seen as independent of other orders of culture and society. The subject of this science was not literature as a whole or even individual literary texts but rather what the Formalists called **LITERARINESS (LITERATURNOST)** i.e. that which makes a given text a work of literature. Literariness, for the Formalists, inheres in the form of a text, its characteristic ways of deploying style and convention, and especially in its capacity to meditate on the qualities of its form.

The earlier phase of Formalism was dominated by the Futurist-influenced polemical writings of Victor Shklovsky, whose 1916 essay "Art as Technique" (Shklovsky, in Lemon and Reis 1965) was among the first to outline major Formalist tenets. According to Shklovsky, it is not the "images" that are crucial in poetry but rather the "devices" deployed for the arrangement and processing of verbal material. The Formalists generally downplayed the representational and expressive dimensions of texts in order to focus on their self-expressive, autonomous, uniquely literary dimensions. They saw poetic speech as involving a special use of language which achieves distinctness by deviating from and distorting the "practical" language of everyday life. (Later, in the work of Jakobson, the opposition between poetic and practical language was to give way to a less rigid distinction between poetic and practical *functions* of language.) While practical language is oriented toward communication, poetic language has no practical function but simply makes us see differently by "defamiliarizing" ambient objects and "laying bare" the artistic device.

Shklovsky coined the term **OSTRENANIE** or **DEFAMILIARIZATION** (also "making strange") and **ZATRUDNENIE** ("making difficult") to denote the way that art heightens perception and short-circuits automatized responses. The essential function of poetic art, for Shklovsky, was to shock us into awareness by subverting routinized perception, by making forms difficult, and by exploding the encrustations of customary perception. Defamiliarization was to be achieved by the use of unmotivated formal devices based on deviations from the established norms of language and style. Shklovsky cites the example of Tolstoy, who describes the human system of ownership through the eyes of a horse. (Subsequently, Bertolt Brecht gave a highly political meaning to the notion of "defamiliarization," reconceiving it as his *Verfremdungseffekt* (variously translated as alienation effect or **DISTANCI-ATION**), the procedure by which a work of art, in a politically conscious way, simultaneously reveals its own processes of production and those of society. Unlike Brecht, however, the early Formalists were, as their name implies, rigorously aestheticist; for them, art was largely a means for experiencing what Shklovsky called the "artfulness of the object," for feeling the "stoniness of the stone."

The Russian Formalists are crucial to any discussion of contemporary filmo-linguistics partly because they were the first to exploit Saussurean formulations in order to explore, with a modicum of rigor, the analogy between language and film. Their consistent emphasis upon the *construction* of artworks led them (particularly Jakobson and Tynianov) to an under-standing of art as a system of signs and conventions rather than as the registration of natural phenomena. In their 1927 anthology *Poetica Kino* (*The Poetics of Cinema*, in Eikhenbaum 1982), with contributions by Eikhenbaum, Shklovsky, Tynianov and others, the Formalists stressed a "poetic" use of film analogous to the "literary" use of language they posited for verbal texts. Despite the influence of Saussure, the Formalist aesthetic was "anti-grammatical" and anti-normative in that it stressed deviation from aes-thetic and technical norms; thus it looked with favor on the avant-garde. (We will discuss in Part II the ways in which Christian Metz expanded and synthesized the insights of Saussurean linguistics and Formalist poetics.)

But even if the Formalists had not written about the cinema *per se*, their conceptualizations would have been invaluable in the sense that film semiotics later "took over," as it were, Formalist formulations concerning literary specificity and extrapolated them into cinema theory, as in Christ-ian Metz' emphasis on the "specifically cinematic." The distinction between "story" (*fabula*) and "plot" (*syuzhet*) – discussed in Part III – also came to influence film theory and analysis via such literary theorists as Gerard Genette, and was later elaborated by David Bordwell and Kristin Thompson in their (generally non-semiotic) work. Also crucial to sub-sequent film semiotics was the Formalist view of the text as a kind of battleground between rival elements or codes. The Formalists came more and more to see artistic texts as dynamic systems in which textual moments are characterized by a **DOMINANT**, i.e. the process by which one element, for example rhythm or plot or character, comes to dominate an artistic text or system. Although first conceptualized by Tynianov, the concept is best known to us as developed by Jakobson in his essay "The Dominant," where it is defined as "the focusing component of a work of art: it rules, determines, and transforms the remaining components. It is the dominant which guarantees the integrity of the structure . . ."[1] As Jakobson develops it, the notion applies not only to the individual poetic work, but also to the poetic canon and even to the art of a given epoch when seen as a

11

totality. (In the Romantic period, for example, supreme value was assigned to music.)

Another aspect of Russian Formalist theory subsequently taken up by contemporary film theorists is the notion of **INNER SPEECH**. This concept, very much "in the air" in the Soviet Union of the late 1920s and early 1930s, was formulated with the greatest depth and precision by the psychologist Lev Vygotsky, in essays ultimately collected in the volume *Thought and Language*, first published in 1934. Influenced by Jean Piaget's investigations into the speech behavior of pre-school children, Vygotsky posited the existence of a modality of speech, having origins in childhood but continuing into adult life, which entailed a verbalized mode of intra-psychic signification, a flux of dialogue within the individual consciousness. Inner speech is characterized by a radically altered and abbreviated syntax, a tendency to syncretic imagery, and condensations and syntagmatic distortions. Boris Eikhenbaum posited inner speech as a kind of discursive glue which holds the meaning of films together in the spectator's mind. The director constructs the film in such a way as to elicit the appropriate inner speech in the consciousness of the spectator. Eikhenbaum also discusses film images which translate, as it were, the colloquialisms of natural language, where linguistic tropes provide an anchorage for meaning. (We will discuss the ways that these ideas were developed in the 1970s in Part II.)

THE BAKHTIN SCHOOL

During the later period of Russian Formalism, the so-called "Bakhtin Circle" or "Bakhtin School" developed a provocative critique of the Formalist method. (The authorship of several key works from the Bakhtin School is in dispute, and for purposes of simplicity we will treat even the co-authored works as by "Bakhtin.") The relevance of the work of the Bakhtin School to our discussion derives from its critique of two of the source-movements for film semiotics – Saussurean structural linguistics and Russian Formalism – as well as from its indirect influence on film semiotics through its translators and "promoters" in the 1960s, most notably Julia Kristeva and Tzvetan Todorov. Bakhtin's feat was to manage to "go beyond" structuralism even before the movement had fully constituted itself as a paradigm. *Marxism and the Philosophy of Language*, which first appeared under Volosinov's name in 1929, but which many commentators think to have been largely written by Bakhtin, constitutes a major intervention within the contemporary tradition of reflexion on language. The book must be seen against the backdrop not only of a generally expanding semiotic consciousness growing out of the native tradition of Russian linguists (Fortunatov, Chakmatov, Jan Baudouin de Courtenay), but also in the context of the dissemination, in the Soviet Union of the 1920s, of the ideas of Saussure. In *Marxism and the Philosophy of Language*, Bakhtin radically challenged the founding Saussurean dichotomies of diachronic/synchronic and *langue/parole*, reversing Saussure's priorities by emphasizing the diachronic and downplaying the language-system as abstract model and stressing instead *parole*, speech as lived and shared by human beings in social interaction.

The desire to see language as a static synchronic system, according to Bakhtin, was symptomatic of a kind of linguistic necrophilia, a nostalgia for deceased languages, whose systems could be fixed precisely *because* they were dead. The fundamental categories of Saussurean linguistics, which are phonetic (units of sound) and morphological (units of sense) ultimately derive, he argued, from the categories of Indo-European comparative linguistics, precisely those categories most appropriate to a dead or alien language. Saussure belongs to a tradition of reflexion on language which Bakhtin labels **ABSTRACT OBJECTIVISM**, i.e. a view of language which strives to reduce its constantly changing heterogeneities into a stable system of normative forms. As an heir to the tradition of Descartes, Leibniz and Condillac, Saussure emphasizes those phonetic, lexical and grammatical features which remain identical and therefore normative for all utterances, thus forming the ready-made "code" of a language. Within this system, individual and social variations of speech play little role; they are seen as random, "messy," too heterogeneous and multi-faceted for the linguist's theoretical grasp, and therefore irrelevant to the fundamental unity of language as system.

Although Bakhtin's thoughts on language permeate his work, it is in *Marxism and the Philosophy of Language* that he offers the most comprehensive account of **TRANSLINGUISTICS**, a theory of the role of signs in human life and thought. Translinguistics might be compared to Saussure's semiology were it not for the fact that it is precisely Saussure's notion of both sign and system that Bakhtin is attacking. For Saussure, the sign possesses a stability based on the orderly matching of signifier and signified which allows it to be placed within a code. Individual texts can disturb this stability through processes of polysemy and displacement, but the displacement is always premised on an initial stability. For Bakhtin, in contrast, the stability of the sign is a mystification advanced by "abstract objectivism," for multiplicity of meaning is the constitutive feature of language. For Bakhtin, a socially and historically generated dynamism animates the sign itself. The stability of the sign is a fiction, since "the constituent factor for the linguistic form, as for the sign, is not at all its self-identity as a signal but its specific variability. . . ." (Volosinov 1973: 69) The sign, within this view, is an object of struggle, as conflicting classes, groups and discourses strive to appropriate it and imbue it with their own meanings, whence what Bakhtin calls its **MULTI-ACCENTUALITY**, i.e. the capacity of the sign to elicit variable social tones and "evaluations" as it is deployed within specific social and historical conditions.

13

Of equal pertinence to any discussion of cine-semiology is the Bakhtinian critique of Formalism. In *The Formal Method in Literary Scholarship* (co-authored with Medvedev), Bakhtin develops a thoroughgoing critique of the underlying premises of first-phase Russian Formalism. It is important to note at the outset that Bakhtin's "sociological poetics" and its dialogical adversary, Formalist poetics, share a number of common features. Both schools refuse a romantic view of art as expressive of the artist's vision. Both resist as well a "vulgar Marxist" reduction of art to questions of class and economics, insisting instead on the self-purposeful specificity of art. Both see "literariness" not as inhering in texts *per se* but as a differential relation between texts, which the Formalists call defamiliarization and which Bakhtin subsumes under the more comprehensive rubric of dialogism. Both reject naively realist or referential views of art. A literary structure does not reflect reality, Bakhtin argues, but rather the "reflections and refractions of other ideological spheres." *The Formal Method*, furthermore, gives considerable credit to Formalism, praising its "productive role" in formulating the central problems of literary scholarship, and doing so "with such sharpness that they can no longer be avoided or ignored" (Bakhtin and Medvedev 1985: 174).

PRAGUE STRUCTURALISM

While the work of both the Russian Formalists and the Bakhtin Circle was being threatened by the advent of Stalinism in the Soviet Union, Czechoslovakia was becoming a vigorous nucleus of linguistic and literary study. Prague structuralism, sometimes called the Prague School or the Prague Linguistic Circle, can be seen both as a prolongation of and reassessment of Russian Formalism, one which saw the semiotic theory of literature as part of a larger social conjuncture. Indeed, Russian Formalism had already been moving in the same direction, towards "socio-formalism." The nine theses on "Problems of the Study of Literature and Language" formulated by Tynianov and Jakobson in 1928 can be seen as both summarizing the later phase of Formalism and containing in embryo some of the key ideas of Czech structuralism. Although most of the members of the Prague School were linguists, they saw the semiotics of art as central to their project, and did sophisticated work not only on literary history and form but also on theatre, the cinema, music and painting. The leading Czech literary theorist was Jan Mukarovsky, who described art as a self-referring **AUTONOMOUS SIGN**, i.e. as a self-purposeful discourse which need not denote real objects or situations. At the same time, Mukarovsky went beyond Formalist aestheticism by insisting that art was both autonomous and communicative. The same artistic object, Mukarovsky insisted, might have multiple functions, from the aesthetic to the social and epistemological. In his article "Art as a Semiotic Fact," Mukarovsky argued that "it

14

is the total context of so-called social phenomena – for example, philosophy, politics, religion and economics – that constitutes the reality which art must represent" (Mukarovsky in Matejka and Titunik 1976). Unlike the Formalists of the early period, then, Mukarovsky insisted on the social and institutional dimensions of art and its strong imbrication with the "historical series." Borrowing Tynianov's dynamic view of aesthetic structures, Mukarovsky emphasized the dynamic tension between literature and the social formation.

Prague structuralism, particularly Jakobson and Trubetskoy, effected the **PHONOLOGICAL REVOLUTION** by distinguishing between **PHONETICS**, i.e. the study of actual speech sounds, and **PHONOLOGY**, the investigation of those aspects of sound which function differentially to produce meaning. The job of the phonologist, for Jakobson and Trubetskoy, was to extract from the acoustic phenomena linked to language-use those elements which play a role in communication. Undergirding the protean variety of sounds in natural languages, Jakobson argued, was a small set of binary phonological oppositions or **DISTINCTIVE FEATURES**, i.e. the presence or absence of a distinctive trait: vocal cord vibration, lip-rounding, nasalization, and so forth. Jakobson classified all the distinctive oppositions operating in the world's languages into a series of twelve such oppositions. This methodological option allowed linguists to reduce the apparently chaotic heterogeneity of the speech sound continuum to a manageable network of binarily paired features. (Claude Lévi-Strauss' structural anthropology, as we shall see, was very much inspired by the work of Jakobson and Trubetskoy in phonology.)

JAKOBSON'S COMMUNICATIONS PARADIGM

Jakobson also turned his attention to the poetic function of language, a subject which he examined in turn as a Formalist, a linguist and a semiotician. In order to address the question of the specificity of poetic language, Jakobson expanded in "Linguistics and Poetics" (in Sebeok 1960) on a schema first formulated by K. Buhler, a model which would permit the developing theory of structural linguistics to deal with works of poetry and prose art. In order to facilitate this coordination of linguistics and poetics, Jakobson proposed a six-part **COMMUNICATIONS PARADIGM**, a kind of verbal loop or circuit which allows the analyst to distinguish the very different emphases of various language uses, and thus to isolate the poetic function from other, more prosaic functions of language. Jakobson begins by distinguishing six components in any speech event: *sender, receiver, message, code, contact* and *context*, themselves stemming from the basic trio of sender, receiver and message. Every message involves a **SENDER/ADDRESSER** and a **RECEIVER/ADDRESSEE**. The sender/addresser is the originating source of the message, while the receiver/addressee is the party to whom the message is directed. The **MESSAGE** is the utterance sent and received. Governing this exchange of the message are three additional elements. First, the sender and receiver must share a **CODE**, a kind of prescription or calculus which determines and correlates individual messages and which remains constant across a diversity of practices and messages. In the case of poetry or prose, the governing code is simply that of verbal language. Secondly, the message can be exchanged only if there is a contact. The **CONTACT** extends from the sense of an original face-to-face verbal exchange to more indirect forms of communication. The contact can also be understood as the **CHANNEL** of communication. While direct dialogue between individuals is the privileged form of contact in this communications paradigm, it is evident that more technology-intensive media do not entail such a relation between sender and receiver. Nevertheless, contact or a shared channel between sender and receiver is essential if the message is to be communicated. Many art-forms and media techniques actively promote a kind of simulacrum of intersubjective contact – for example the direct address of television news – which fosters the illusion of cohesion between sender and receiver.

Lastly, there is the **CONTEXT**, or the ambient systems of reference invoked in any communication to ensure that the message is understood. Frequently, the message will be oriented to the context, or the referent, as in a message about the world. The context usually refers to events in the world; the message, then, will be related to the context, which will either validate the message or refuse it. The interplay of these six elements can be summarized in this fashion: sender and receiver have a common code, and can send a message via a channel between them, about the context or world. Together, this ensemble of elements produces **MEANING**.

Linguistic communication and the message may stress any one of these six elements. The message can therefore be charted and analyzed according to the relative weight given each element within the ensemble of communication functions. The model for these six aspects of the message is patterned identically to the communications paradigm detailed above. The **EMOTIVE FUNCTION** corresponds to the position of the sender; the existential relation of the sender to the utterance betrays an attitude to the statement which originates with the sender, belonging neither to the code nor to the context nor to any of the other functions. The **CONATIVE FUNCTION** refers to the part of the message oriented to the receiver, as in commands or interdictions. The **PHATIC FUNCTION** corresponds to the contact or the channel; it is specifically geared to establishing an initial connection and ensuring a continuous and attentive reception. In short, it keeps the channels open. The phatic function can be discerned in ordinary language use in the sort of empty commonplaces and ritual interjections – "Well," "You know?" "You see?" – meant less to exchange information than to maintain communicative contact.

While the **REFERENTIAL FUNCTION** refers to the context, Jakobson isolates the **POETIC FUNCTION** as focussing on the message for its own sake; art is thus defined by its self-referentiality. The poetic function is not the sole function of verbal art but only its dominant, Jakobson argues, whereas in other verbal activities it is subordinate to other concerns. The poetic function foregrounds the self-referring palpability of signs. The poetic function concentrates on the texture of the message, its interweaving of symbolic and rhythmic qualities. Jakobson characterizes the operation of the poetic function as the projection of paradigmatic terms onto the syntagmatic axis. The verbal and syntactic patterns of poetic language concentrate attention on the operation of language itself, rather than on reference or context. (More socially oriented theories, such as those developed both by the Bakhtin Circle and by the Prague School, would obviously find such a formulation impoverished and reductionist.)

Jakobson also highlights what he calls the **METALINGUAL FUNCTION**, i.e. speech which focusses on the code. Language, even in its everyday usages, has the capacity to speak not only of objects and experience in the world, but also to reflect upon itself and describe its own operations. In literary and film studies, metalinguistic is often a synonym for reflexive, referring to all the ways in which an artistic discourse can, within its own texts, reflect on its own language and processes. A novel like Sterne's *Tristram Shandy* constitutes an archetypical example of literature reflecting on its own processes. In the cinema, by extension, the terms metalinguistic or metacinematic refer to those films or those aspects of films which reflect on cinematic language. The films of Jean-Luc Godard, like the films of the North American avant-garde (*A Movie, Wavelength*) can be seen as metalinguistic exercises, reflections on the particularities of film language or the film apparatus.

Jakobson's schema is broadly useful for classifying methodological approaches to artistic discourse. Romantic approaches might be said to emphasize the role of the sender and therefore the emotive function of art. Realist approaches, including some Marxist and early feminist approaches, emphasize the context and therefore the referential function of art. Formalism emphasizes the message and therefore the poetic function of art. Semiotic theory emphasizes the code and therefore the metalingual function of art, while textual analysis emphasizes the message and therefore the poetic as well as the phatic functions of artistic discourse. Reception theory and spectator-in-the-text theory as well as psychoanalytic approaches emphasizing the desiring spectator, finally, foreground the receiver and therefore the conative functions of art.

THE ADVENT OF STRUCTURALISM

As a kind of methodological success story, structural linguistics generated a rich proliferation of structuralisms, most of them premised on seminal Saussurean dichotomies such as diachrony/synchrony and *langue/parole*. Although Saussure never used the term "structuralism," his approach was premised on the idea that any serious study of linguistic phenomena had to be based on the view of *langue* as a structure, whose properties were structural properties; the structure itself creates the units and their mutual interrelations. Rather than an assemblage of pre-existing blocks, language exists only as a structural whole. It is important, at this point, to define structuralism and its relation to semiotics. Roland Barthes defined **STRUCTURALISM** as a "mode of analysis of cultural artifacts which originates in the methods of contemporary linguistics" (Barthes 1967a: 897). For Jean Piaget, structuralism is a method of inquiry based on the triple principles of totality, transformation and self-regulation (Piaget 1970: 5). For our purposes, we can define structuralism as a theoretical grid through which behavior, institutions and texts are seen as analyzable in terms of an underlying network of relationships, the crucial point being that the elements which constitute the network gain their meaning from the relations that hold between the elements. Hubert Dreyfus and Paul Rabinow (1982) distinguish between **HOLISTIC STRUCTURALISM**, i.e. one positing structures, deductively determined, which exceed empirical instantiations, and **ATOMISTIC STRUCTURALISM**, i.e. one positing structures determined by inductive generalization.

Common to most varieties of structuralism and semiotics was an emphasis on the underlying rules and conventions of language rather than on the surface configurations of speech exchange. In language, Saussure argued, there are only differences. Going against the tradition of linguistic thought which saw the core of language as consisting in an inventory of names designating things, persons and events already given to human understanding, Saussure argued that language is nothing more than a "series of phonetic differences matched with a series of conceptual differences. Concepts, therefore, are purely differential, defined not by their positive content, but rather by their relation with other terms of the system: Their most precise characteristic is in being what the other are not . . ." (Saussure 1966: 117–18).

Although structuralism developed out of Saussure's groundbreaking work on language, it was not until the 1960s that it became widely disseminated. The process by which structuralism came to form a dominant paradigm is now retrospectively clear. The scientific advance represented by Saussure's *Course*, as we have seen, was transferred to literary study by the Formalists and later by the Prague Linguistic Circle, which formally instituted the movement in Prague in 1929. The phonologists demonstrated the concrete

18

fruitfulness of looking at language from a Saussurean perspective and thus provided the paradigm for the rise of structuralism in the social sciences and the humanities. Lévi-Strauss used the Saussurean method with great intellectual audacity in anthropology and thereby founded structuralism as a movement. By seeing kinship relations as a "language" susceptible to the kinds of analysis applied by Trubetskoy and Jakobson to questions of phonology, Lévi-Strauss took the fundamental step which made it possible to extend the same structural-linguistic logic to all social, mental and artistic phenomena and structures.

When Lévi-Strauss delivered his inaugural lecture in 1961 at the Collège de France, he situated his structural anthropology within the broad field of "semiology." The true constituent units of a myth, Lévi-Strauss argued in *Structural Anthropology* (1967), are not the isolated elements involved but rather whole "bundles of relations." Lévi-Strauss extended this idea of universal binarism, as the organizing principle of phonemic systems, to human culture in general. The constituent elements of myth, like those of language, have no fixed meaning in themselves, but only acquire meaning in relation to other elements. A particular myth could only be comprehended in relation to a vast system of other myths, social practices and cultural codes, all of which could only be made comprehensible on the basis of structuring oppositions. The ultimate function of myth, for Lévi-Strauss, was to represent the apparent resolution of a social conflict. (Lévi-Strauss, as we shall see subsequently, also catalyzed development in narratology and in structuralism as a whole.)

The development of narrative semiotics or narratology was also directly fueled by the structuralist adaptation of the work of Saussure. The ambition of the structuralist approach to narrative, as formulated by Lévi-Strauss and Algirdas Greimas, was to disclose the generative matrix of narratives, the elementary articulations of the story form, which would in turn provide a model for a universal narrative grammar. First, however, structuralist theorists were obliged to address the dominant theory of narrative already in the field – the work of Vladimir Propp – which argued for a diachronic concept of story-structure, an approach which could not be accommodated within the synchronic methods of structuralist analysis. Propp's *Morphology of the Folk Tale*, first published in 1929, defined certain properties of narrative form and devised an initial set of methodological procedures. Propp analyzed the morphology, or generic structure of the Russian wondertale, by determining the elements which were constant and those which were variable. He found that virtually all of the tales considered within his analysis had identical structural features. The multiform events and characters of folk tales could be distilled into a table of thirty-one functions which were invariant, recurring in every tale in exactly the same order. The pageant of characters in the folk tale could be reduced to a set of six *dramatis personae*. A principle of regularity and systematicity was thus discerned within what had been seen as a heterogeneous assemblage of unrelated stories. Propp's basic story armature of thirty-one functions, such as "(a) Villainy," and "(b) Mediation: The Connective Incident," was conceived as the deep structure of the folk tale, and provides the point of departure for all subsequent developments in narratology (the focus of our Part III).

Although Propp carefully limited his model to the Russian wondertale, later theorists tried to transform his approach into a universal model of narrative structure. The structuralists aimed to provide a more supple and "scientific" approach to the study of narrative by dissolving the thirty-one functions into synchronic patterns of opposition which would not depend on the unfolding of a uniform sequence of events. Basing its definition of deep narrative structure on the linguistic structures of phonemic oppositions, structural narratology shed the cumbersome functional syntax of Propp's model, while retaining the basic idea of a kernel narrative structure, a kind of structural DNA. Lévi-Strauss and Greimas proposed a new model of narrative deep structure that was based on the key theses of Saussurean linguistics. Stories were structured, they maintained, in the same fashion as the linguistic sign. At the primary level (or the "second articulation" in linguistic terms), the elementary units of stories were non-referential and thus comparable to phonemes; no necessary connection linked apparent significance and actual meaning. Secondly, the meaning of the elementary units of narrative could be discovered in their patterns of opposition, which formed an invisible semantic core underpinning the visible text and providing the narrative with its essential significance. Myths, for example, rather than being read in terms of primary motifs or individual patterns of conflict and resolution, were seen as "systems of differences" or "bundles of relations" which could be interpreted only in terms of larger cultural paradigms.

In the wake of the work of Lévi-Strauss, a wide range of apparently non-linguistic domains came under the jurisdiction of structural linguistics. Figures such as Roland Barthes, Tzvetan Todorov, Umberto Eco and Gerard Genette became powerful advocates for literary structuralism. In *Elements of Semiology* (1964), Barthes argued that any culturally-shaped utterance – from the wearing of clothes to the choice of an entrée in a meal – presupposed a system (of fashion, cuisine or language) generating the possibilities of social meaning. Even economics came to be seen in its semiotic dimension, as a symbolic system comparable to the symbolic exchange of words in a language, while psychoanalysis, with Lacan, came to see the unconscious itself as "structured like a language." (Lacanian developments will be discussed in Part IV.)

The 1960s and early 1970s might be seen as the height of semiotic "imperialism," when the discipline annexed vast territories of cultural phenomena for exploration. In *A Theory of Semiotics*, Eco (1976) defined the field as including such diverse enterprises as *narratology* (the subject of Part III), **ZOOSEMIOTICS** (the communicative behavior of non-human communities), **KINESICS** and **PROXEMICS** (sociocultural codes having to do, respectively, with human movement and closeness), text theory, unknown alphabets, secret codes, musical codes, medical semiotics and olfactory signs. A good deal of semiotic analysis has been applied to areas previously considered either flagrantly non-linguistic – fashion, cuisine – or to areas traditionally deemed beneath the dignity of literary or cultural studies – comic strips, photo-romans, James Bond novels. Film semiotics emerged, in the early 1960s, as part of this structuralist euphoria, leading to short-lived dreams of a total scientificity, dreams which were to be undone by internal self-questioning, by the attraction of other methodological models, and by the political developments summed up in the phrase "May 1968."

The political orientation of much of contemporary film theory had its origins in the political and cultural upheaval of the 1960s. This upheaval had major consequences for intellectual film culture, marked in France by the leftward turn of *Cahiers du Cinéma* and the work of the Marxist film journal *Cinétique*. A key figure in these developments was the structuralist-Marxist Louis Althusser and especially his theory of ideology. Raymond Williams has argued that the term **IDEOLOGY** can be understood in three senses: (1) a system of beliefs characteristic of a particular class or group; (2) a system of illusory beliefs – false ideas or false consciousness – which can be contrasted with true or scientific knowledge; and (3) the general process of meanings and ideas (Williams 1983: 152–7). The notion of **BOURGEOIS IDEOLOGY** was an attempt by Marxism to explain the ways that capitalist social relations are reproduced by its subjects in ways that do not involve force or coercion. By what processes does the individual subject internalize social norms? As defined by traditional Marxism, ideology referred to a distortion of thought which both arises from and conceals social contradiction. As defined by Lenin, Althusser and Gramsci, the concept of bourgeois ideology refers to that ideology generated by class society through which the dominant class comes to provide the general conceptual framework for a society's members, thus furthering the economic and political interests of that class. Althusser's structuralist reread-ing of Marxist theory challenged the humanist "Hegelian" understanding of Marx's work inspired by the rediscovery of Marx's early writings. For Althusser, **IDEOLOGY** was a "system (possessing its own logic and rigor) of representation (images, myths, ideas or concepts as the case may be) existing and having a historical role within a given society" (Althusser 1970: 231). Ideology was, furthermore, as Althusser expressed it in a widely quoted definition in *For Marx*, "a representation of the imaginary relation of individuals to the real conditions of their existence" (Althusser 1970: 233). Ideology operates, for Althusser, through **INTERPELLATION**, i.e. through the social practices and structures which "hail" individuals, so as

21

to endow them with social identity constituting them as subjects who unthinkingly accept their role within the system of production relations. The novelty of Althusser's approach, then, was to see ideology not as a form of false consciousness deriving from the partial and distorted perspectives generated by distinct class positions, but rather, as Richard Allen puts it, as an "objective feature of the social order which structures experience itself."[2] (We will discuss some of the critiques of this view in Part V.)

The theoretical discourse concerning the cinema that developed in France in the 1960s was then taken up in the 1970s by the British journal *Screen* and subsequently migrated to the United States with the growth of cinema studies programs, many of them with a strong Parisian link. This political current tended to be critical of what it saw as the atemporal and ahistorical character of a structuralism which privileged the spatial and the synchronic. Semiotics, in any case, always had a left-wing and a centrist wing. The centrists tended to use semiotics as an apolitical scientific instrument, while the left wing deployed semiotics as a means of demystifying cinematic representation, exposing it as a constructed system of socially informed signs. This left-leaning semiotics performed a subversive work of **DENATURALIZATION**, i.e. the scrutinizing of social and artistic productions in order to discern the cultural and ideological codes operative in them. This critical semiotics challenged the conventional notions of history, society, signification and human subjectivity embodied in traditional film criticism. Contemporary film theory generally, in fact, developed a discourse to the left of many other more traditional disciplines, not only because of a strong "French connection" but also because of its simultaneous emergence, in the 1960s, alongside such counter-cultural disciplines as women's studies, ethnic studies and popular culture studies.

A scientistic structuralism semiotics was also undercut by the emergence of alternative models. One of these alternative models was psychoanalysis. Beginning in the mid–1970s, semiotic discussion came to be inflected by psychoanalytic notions such as scopophilia and voyeurism, and by Lacan's conception of the mirror stage, the imaginary and the symbolic. The focus of interest was no longer on the relation between filmic and image and "reality," but rather on the cinematic apparatus itself, not only in the sense of the instrumental base of camera, projector and screen, but also in the sense of the spectator as the desiring subject on which the cinematic institution depends as its object and accomplice. The interest shifts, in this phase, from questions such as "What is the nature of cinematic signs and the laws of their combination?" and "What is a textual system?" to questions such as "What do we want from the text?" and "What is our spectatorial investment in it?" By analyzing the effects of the cinema on the spectator, the psychoanalytic approach highlighted the "metapsychological" dimension of the cinema, its ways of both activating and regulating spectatorial desire. At the same time, the shift from first-phase (linguistic) semiology to second-phase (psychoanalytic) semiology is arguably part of a coherent trajectory toward what Metz called the "semio-psychoanalysis of the cinema," since linguistics and psychoanalysis are the two sciences that deal directly with signification as such. (The terminology generated by the psychoanalytic phase of cine-semiology will be the subject of Part IV).

POST-STRUCTURALISM: THE CRITIQUE OF THE SIGN

Beginning in the late 1960s, especially in France, the Saussurean model, and the structuralist semiotics derived from it, came under increasing attack from Derridean deconstruction, an attack associated with the name **POST-STRUCTURALISM**. This movement, less a theory than a mode of enquiry, saw the drive toward systematicity typical of structuralism as needing to be confronted by everything excluded and repressed by that systematicity. Indeed, many of the seminal texts of post-structuralism performed explicit critiques of the central figures and the cardinal concepts of structuralism. Derrida's paper at the 1966 conference at Johns Hopkins, for example, offered an incisive critique of the notion of "structure" in the structuralist anthropology of Lévi-Strauss. Derrida called for a "decentering" of structures, suggesting that "even today the notion of a structure lacking any center represents the unthinkable itself" (Derrida 1978: 279).

Post-structuralism has been variously described as a shift of interest from the signified to the signifier, from the utterance to enunciation, from the spatial to the temporal, and from structure to "structuration." The post-structuralist movement, which along with Derrida is thought to include such figures as Foucault, Lacan, Kristeva and the later Barthes, demonstrated a thoroughgoing distrust of any centered, totalizing theory, a radical skepticism about the possibility of constructing a metalanguage which might position, stabilize or explain all of the other discourses, since the signs of the metalanguage are themselves subject to slippage and indeterminacy. (The very positing of the impossibility of a metalanguage, some critics suggested, was itself metalinguistic.) Metalanguages, for Derrida, cannot resist the powers of linguistic and textual **DISSEMINATION**, i.e. the process of semantic slippage by which signs move ceaselessly outward into unpredictably novel contexts of meaning, resisting closure by a process of constant rewriting, thus losing their stability as "proper" names to become mere signifying terms within a spiralling proliferation of allusive references from text to text.

Broadly speaking, post-structuralism entails a critique of the concepts of the stable sign, of the unified subject, of identity and of truth. Derrida adopts key words in the Saussurean vocabulary – especially "difference," "signifier," and "signified" – but redeploys them within a transformed framework. Saussure's emphasis on binary contrasts as the source of meaning in language gives way to Derrida's view of language as a place of semiotic "play," an indeterminate field of infinite slippages and substitutions. Saussure's notion of the differential relation between signs is reinscribed by Derrida as a relation within signs. Signs differ not only from each other, but also from themselves in that their constitutive nature is one of a constant displacement or **TRACE** – the trace left by an infinite chain of unstable re-signification within a boundless context of **INTERTEXTUALITY**, a word which for Derrida evokes the dependence of any text on a host of prior figures, conventions, codes and other texts. Language for Derrida is thus always inscribed in a complex network of relays and differential "traces" beyond the grasp of the individual speaker. Derridean terms, for this reason, are even less susceptible than most to neat lexical pinning down, since they do not designate any simple concept or thing and therefore disallow any proper self-definition. Derridean concepts are therefore placed **SOUS RATURE** or "under erasure," a practice Derrida inherited from Heidegger by which a concept is at once invoked and questioned.

Derrida introduced his neologism **DIFFÉRANCE** – a word which in French exists in suspension between "to differ" and "to defer" and whose "misspelled" orthographic difference ("a" instead of the conventional "e" of "différence") is inaudible and therefore "visible" only in writing – to refer simultaneously to the relatively passive "spatial" Saussurean sense of difference as constitutive of signification, and to an active temporal process of producing difference through deferment in time. *Différance* designates the process by which an opposition is reproduced within constituent terms, thus installing an undecidable alternation between structure and what is repressed by it. In *Positions*, Derrida defines *différance* as

> the systematic play of differences, of traces of differences, of the spacing [espacement] by which elements relate to one another. This spacing is the production, simultaneously active and passive (the **a** of différance indicates this indecision as regards activity and passivity, that which cannot yet be governed and organized by that opposition), of intervals without which the "full" terms could not signify, could not function.
>
> (Derrida 1981a: 27)

Derrida sees Saussurean structuralism as bearing the vestiges of western **LOGOCENTRISM**, i.e. that tradition which assigns the origins of truth to the *logos* – whether the spoken self-present word, or the voice of rationality, or God – as reflective of an internally coherent and originary truth. Logocentrism assumes the existence of an ontological ground or stabilizing matrix out of which meaning is generated. It presumes the possibility of an unmediated access to truth or knowledge. For John M. Ellis, logocentrism designates any essentialist faith in an order of meaning existing independently of the structures furnished by language: it "is the illusion that the meaning of a word has its origin in the structure of reality itself and hence makes the truth about that structure seem directly present to the mind" (Ellis 1989: 36–7).

Saussure's notion of the sign, for Derrida, is also characterized by **PHONO-CENTRISM**, the belief that phonetic sounds can adequately represent meanings that are present in the consciousness of the speaker, while writing constitutes a second-degree mediation of self-present speech. Phonocentrism, according to Derrida, generates a matrix of axiological binarisms – voice/writing, sound/silence, being/non-being – in which the first term of each pair is invariably privileged. Derrida argues that Saussure's work, like the western tradition generally, systematically privileges spoken as opposed to written language, and thus participates in a dualism deeply rooted in a western metaphysical tradition which treats the voice as the spontaneous expression of interior mental states, and which therefore regards speech as more authentic than writing. Derrida cites a series of passages from Saussure which treat writing as a derivative form of linguistic notation, ultimately dependent on the primary reality of speech and the sense of a speaker's "presence" behind the words. Saussure's concept of the sign, for Derrida, is based on a distinction between the perceptible and the intelligible: the signifier exists only to provide access to a meaning or transcendental signified. Derrida does not suggest that the notion of "sign" should be rejected entirely, only that it be freed of its residual attachment to a western metaphysics of meaning. (The distinction of signifier/signified still has operational value, Derrida points out, since without it the word signifier itself would have no signified.)

The Saussurean privileging of the phonic over the graphic signifier is predicated on an implicit distinction between the "inside" of human thought, expressed in speech, and the "outside" of writing, seen as a derivative and secondary form. Derrida therefore "rewrites" the relationship between language, speech and writing, preferring to speak of **ARCHI-WRITING**, i.e. a vastly extended conceptualization of writing by which it becomes the model of all linguistic operations as practices of articulation and differentiation, a general potentiality which grounds the possibility of both spoken and written language. Without rejecting the semiotic project or denying its historical importance, Derrida proposes instead of the Saussurean linguistic project a **GRAMMATOLOGY**, which would study the science of writing and textuality in general.

Derridean post-structuralism has not been an overwhelming presence within film studies. Most "post-structuralist" film theory and analysis has been based less on Derridean deconstruction than on Lacan's "return to Freud." But in the late 1960s and 1970s, the French Marxists of *Cinétique* and *Cahiers du Cinéma* did give a distinct Brechtian slant to the Derridean notion of deconstruction, using it to expose the subliminal ideological underpinnings of the cinematic apparatus and of dominant cinema. At the same time, certain strands of **DECONSTRUCTIVE READING** – defined as a strategy of reading filmic or literary texts in such a way as to expose their fractures and tensions, of seeking out blind spots or moments of self-contradiction and liberating the suppressed "plural" and figurative energies of a text – can now be assumed to form part of the received methodological wisdom of film theory and analysis. Some of deconstruction's implications have been explored, moreover, by such analysts as Marie-Claire Ropars-Wuilleumier, Michael Ryan, Gregory Ulmer, Peter Brunette, David Wills and Stephen Heath (via Kristeva). Marie-Claire Ropars-Wuilleumier, in *Le Texte Divisé* (1981), has tried to extend into film analysis an expansive Derridean notion of *écriture* – understood as a "theoretical hypothesis" which replaces the notion of sign with that of "trace," referring processes of signification back to a differential movement whose terms are unassignable and unfixable. Ropars-Wuilleumier sees cinematic montage, especially that practiced by Eisenstein, as exemplifying the means by which the cinema, and other figurative arts, can transcend merely mimetic representation in order to create an abstract conceptual space. For Ropars-Wuilleumier, montage refers less to the specific gesture of splicing shots than to a general process of engendering significance. Extending the earlier work of Eisenstein and Metz on the analogies between cinematic writing and non-western, non-phonetic script (hieroglyphs, ideograms), Ropars-Wuilleumier sees the hieroglyph, as a superimposed set of signifying systems, as an apt figure for the "scriptural vocation of the cinema" as a kind of "writing machine." Rather than merely extrapolate linguistic models to the cinema, Ropars-Wuilleumier insists on the reversability of the process; reflexion on cinematic montage can induce us to revise our very conception of language.

Peter Brunette and David Wills, finally, in their *Screen/Play: Derrida and Film Theory* (1989), deploy Derridean categories in order to explore such issues as "Derrida and Contemporary Film Studies," "Film as Writing," and the implications for film theory of Derrida's observations concerning "the frame" and the "postal." The authors interrogate the various totalizing notions which they see as surreptitiously informing film theory and analysis – the notion of "narrative film," of immaculately pure genres, of Hollywood as a self-identical coherent system, of the primacy of the visual (seen as analogous to the primacy of speech over writing in the logocentric tradition). Shying away from any "glib borrowing of a ready-made theory," the authors call for a move beyond "totalizations," invoking the possibilities of an "anagrammatical" reading practice that sees cinema as writing, text, as "an interplay of presence and absence, of the seen and not seen, in relations not reducible either to totalization of transcendence" (Brunette and Wills 1989: 58). In a form of "split writing," the authors read (on facing pages) Truffaut's *The Bride Wore Black* and David Lynch's *Blue Velvet*, not in order to demonstrate a methodology, but rather to expose textual "undecidabilities" and "fissures," all as part of a kind of meditation on reading which problematizes the very self-constitution of the text's meaning.

Considerable debate has raged around the question of whether post-structuralism is an extension of structuralism or a rejection of it, a neo-structuralism or an anti-structuralism. For Jonathon Culler, Derridean post-structuralism constitutes a radicalization of the Saussurean project, a working out of the implications of the Saussurean principle that in the linguistic system there are only differences without positive terms. For others, such as Christopher Norris, Derridean deconstruction marks a radical repudiation of the structuralist project. In fact, as its name implies, post-structuralism exists in both continuity and rupture with structuralism. It shares the structuralist premise of the determining, constitutive role of language, and generally continues within the structuralist problematic, especially the assumption that signification is based on difference. At the same time, it rejects structuralism's "dream of scientificity," its hopes of stabilizing the play of difference within an all-encompassing master-system. (We will return to issues of Derridean post-structuralism and deconstruction in subsequent chapters, when we speak in more detail of textual analysis, *écriture* and intertextuality.)

NOTES

1 Roman Jakobson, "The Dominant," in Ladislav Matejka and Krystyna Pomor-ska (eds), *Readings in Russian Poetics: Formalist and Structuralist Views* (Cambridge, Mass. and London: MIT Press, 1971), pp. 105–10.
2 See Richard Allen, "Representation, Meaning, an Experience in the Cinema: a Critical Study of Contemporary Film Theory," Ph.D. Dissertation, University of California at Los Angeles, 1989.

II

CINE-SEMIOLOGY

In Part I we spoke of the rise of linguistics as a kind of master discipline for the contemporary era. The cinema, for its part, has hardly been immune to the magnetic attraction of the linguistic model. Indeed, the notion of **FILM LANGUAGE** was already a commonplace in the writings of some of the earliest theorists of the cinema, even those untouched by the theoretical movements and schools of which we have spoken. One finds the metaphor in the 1920s writings of Riccioto Canudo in Italy and Louis Delluc in France, both of whom saw the language-like character of the cinema as linked, paradoxically, to its non-verbal nature, its status as a "visual esperanto" transcending the barriers of national language.[1] One finds the metaphor in the writings of poet-critic Vachel Lindsay, who spoke of film as "hieroglyphic language," as well as in the work of Hungarian film theorist Bela Balazs, who repeatedly stressed the language-like nature of film in his work from the 1920s through to the late 1940s.[2]

It was the Russian Formalists, however, who developed the analogy between language and film in a somewhat more systematic way. In *Poetics of the Cinema* the Formalists downplayed the mimetic dimension of film in favor of its "poetic" and "linguistic" qualities. Tynianov spoke of the cinema as offering the visible world in the form of semantic signs engendered by cinematic procedures such as lighting and montage, while Eikhenbaum saw film in relation to "inner speech" and "image translations of linguistic tropes." The cinema, for Eikhenbaum, is a "particular system of figurative language," the stylistics of which would treat filmic "syntax," the linkage of shots into "phrases" and "sentences." Close shot-by-shot analysis would allow analysts to identify a typology of such phrases – a project taken up some four decades later by Christian Metz in his Grand Syntagmatique of narrative cinema. While Eikhenbaum did not develop a full-blown typology, he did mention certain principles of syntagmatic construction – such as contrast, comparison and coincidence – which resemble in embryo the conceptions later developed by Metz.

Subsequent to the work of the Russian Formalists, the notion of film language came to form the implicit topos grounding the many normative

"Grammars" of cinema – for example, Raymond Spottiswoode's *Grammar of Film* (1935) and Robert Bataille's *Grammaire Cinégraphique* (1947). In other pre-semiotic discussions, the film-language metaphor became intimately linked to the cognate tropes of the "camera pen" (Astruc) and "film writing." In post-war France, especially, this "graphological" figure, as we shall see in some detail in Part V, became a key structuring concept subtending film theory and criticism.

THE CINEMATIC SIGN

It was only with the advent of structuralism and semiotics in the 1960s, however, that the film-language concept was explored in depth by theorists like Umberto Eco, Pier Paolo Pasolini and Christian Metz. Much of the early discussion had to do with the nature of the filmic analogon. The initial tendency was to contrast the arbitrary signs of natural language with the motivated, iconic signs of the cinema. In his earliest work, Metz emphasized both the analogical nature of the filmic image as well as the causal photo-chemical connection between representation and prototype. But in a 1970 article, "Beyond Analogy, the Image," Metz nuanced his argument, pointing out that to see an image as simply analogical is to forget that it can be analogical and motivated in some respects and yet be arbitrary in other respects. Representational images, in sum, can themselves be coded (Metz 1972).

Another important figure in the theorization of the image was Roland Barthes. For Barthes, the image is characterized by **POLYSEMY** (literally, many "semes" or meanings), i.e. it shares with other signs, including linguistic signs, the property of being open to multiple significations. The accompanying captions of photographs, or written materials in a film, Barthes suggested in "Rhetoric of the Image," often function as **ANCHOR-AGE**, i.e. as a verbal device which "disciplines" polysemy by coaxing the observer's perception into a preferred "reading" of the image. The anchoring words "fix the floating chain of signifieds"; they guide the viewer among the different possible significations of a visual representation. Barthes gives the example of an advertisement showing fruits scattered around a ladder, an image that might connote "paucity of harvest," "damage due to high winds," or "freshness"; the caption "as if from your own garden" anchors the meaning of "freshness" (Barthes 1977). In *Camera Lucida* (1980) Barthes theorizes the specific pleasures provoked by the "force of silence and immobility" typical of still photography. He speaks of two ways of apprehending the same photograph: the **STUDIUM** deploys objective signs and coded information, while the **PUNCTUM** triggers the play of chance and subjective association, investing the photo with personal desire.

Other analysts also took up the Peircean trichotomy. Peter Wollen argued in *Signs and Meaning in the Cinema* (1969) that cinema deploys all three categories of sign: icon (through resembling images and sounds); index (through the photo-chemical registering of the "real"); and symbol (in the deployment of speech and writing). In their essay *"Quia Ego Nominor Leo,"* Ronald Levaco and Fred Glass perform an exemplary Peircean analysis of the logos of diverse Hollywood studios (Levaco/Glass in Bellour 1980). The classical MGM studio logo features the celebrated MGM lion circled by a film strip on which is written "Ars Gratia Artis," under which we see a garlanded mask, placed, in turn, above the words "Metro Goldwyn Mayer." The diverse planar surfaces of the logo put in play iconic and symbolic elements, thus foiling nature – the lion – and culture – language. But the symbolic is thoroughly intermeshed with the iconic. The word "Metro," for example, is inscribed in Roman characters, while "Mayer" is inscribed in neo-Gothic. The polysemy of the mask, meanwhile, plays a mediating role, evoking the classical masks of both tragedy and comedy (and thus the lofty dignity of classical art) and the racist portraiture of safari films (evoked by the mask's stereotypically African traits and thick lips). The mask's hybrid construction thus points on one side to the classy artsiness claimed by the *"Ars Gratia Artis"* and on the other to the primitive power of the lion. Taken together, the iconic and symbolic signs designate the broad orientations of MGM productions – primitive adventure, sentimental tragi-comedy and spectacular epics.

Many semiologists, in their analysis of pictorial representations, draw on the notion of codes. Originating in information theory, a **CODE** is defined as a system of differences and correspondences which remain constant across a series of messages. Exported into linguistics, the concept came to be synonymous with *langue* or "language system." Code usually refers, however, to any systematized set of conventions, any set of prescriptions for the selection and combination of units. The **MESSAGE** refers to the meaningful sequences generated by the coded processes of communicative utterances. The term code has extensive applications; in sociology, as Metz points out, it refers to transpersonal codes of behavior or collective representations; in administrative language, the term crops up in such phrases as the "highway code," the "zip code" and the "telephone code," all instances which conform to the original definition as examples of conventionalized systems which remain constant across numerous and various particular messages. (Within textual analysis, a code is always a construction of the analyst, and not something inherent in the text or found in nature.) Within film analysis, the notion of code postulated the existence within a film of relatively autonomous levels of signification organized as part of an overall system.

Umberto Eco drew on Peirce, and on the notion of "codes," in his analysis of the filmic analogon. In his essay "Semiology of Visual Messages" (*Communications* 15), Eco inventories the following codes operative within the iconic sign: (1) **PERCEPTIVE CODES** (the domain of the psychology of perception); (2) **CODES OF RECOGNITION** (culturally disseminated taxonomies); (3) **CODES OF TRANSMISSION** (the dots of a news photo, the scan lines of a televisual image); (4) **TONAL CODES** (connoted elements having to do with stylistic convention); (5) **ICONIC CODES** proper, subdividable into (a) figures, (b) signs, and (c) semes; (6) **ICONOGRAPHIC CODES**; (7) **CODES OF TASTE AND SENSIBILITY**; (8) **RHETORICAL CODES**, subdividable into (a) figures, (b) visual premises, and (c) visual arguments; (9) **STYLISTIC CODES**; and (10) **CODES OF THE UNCONSCIOUS**. (The inventory, while in some ways suggestive, is at times redundant. The distinction between (a) tonal codes, as larger units of stylistic convention, (b) codes of taste and sensibility, and (c) stylistic codes, for example, is far from crystalline.)

In *A Theory of Semiotics*, Eco returns to the question of the nature of the iconic sign. He criticizes the naïve notions that the iconic sign "has the same properties" as its referent. A portrait of the Queen of England, Eco points out, is not composed of skin and bones. The stimuli clearly differ, but they share a perceptual structure, a system of relations between parts, so that the queen herself and the portrait provoke similar perceptual responses. Eco also criticizes the notion that the iconic image is in fact *similar*. This similarity is highly coded; one recognizes an object and its representation as similar because our cultural training teaches us to select pertinent features. (The documentary film-maker Robert Flaherty claimed that the Eskimo Nanook had to learn to recognize himself in a photographic portrait.) The impression of similarity, then, is historically informed and culturally coded. Eco cites thirteenth-century painters who depicted lions according to the heraldic conventions of their time rather than in accord with their actual appearance. Artistic representation, in this sense, responds to other representations rather than to "real-life" referents. Eco also speaks of **PSEUDO-ICONIC PHENOMENA**, citing the example of a child who straddles a broom pretending it is a horse. The analogy in such a case is not iconic; the broom does not resemble a horse; the two entities share only the functional capacity of being straddled.

MINIMAL UNITS AND THEIR CINEMATIC ARTICULATION

The cine-semiologists of the 1960s were working within the Saussurean tradition at a more advanced stage of development, a tradition which now included the work of Saussure's heirs such as the Danish linguist Louis Hjelmslev and the French linguists André Martinet and Emile Benveniste. The pioneer film semioticians of the 1960s spent much of their energies looking for quite literal equivalences between linguistic and filmic units. Much of the discussion revolved around the related issues of double articulation and minimal units. A semiotic or **LINGUISTIC UNIT** is a class of entities constructed by the linguist as part of a descriptive metalanguage in order to reduce the confusing heterogeneity of language to a manageable matrix of generating principles. Linguists thus tried to establish **MINIMAL UNITS** on the basis of which language as a whole was constructed. In semiotics, **ARTICULATION** refers to any form of semiotic organization which engenders distinct combinable units. The notion of **DOUBLE ARTICU-LATION** develops, and gives precision to, Saussure's view of the linguistic system as a kind of "matching" of phonetic differences with conceptual differences. Especially developed by the French linguist André Martinet, the concept of double articulation refers to the two structural levels on which natural languages are organized. Speech can be analyzed into **MOR-PHEMES**, i.e. "significant units," or units of sense (or to use Martinet's preferred term **MONEMES**) which constitute the **FIRST ARTICULATION**. (The temptation to equate phoneme with "word" was resisted because single words can include a number of morphemes – "anti-dis-establish-ment-arian-ism" being an obvious example.) These units are further analy-zable into the "meaningless," that is the purely distinctive units of sound or **PHONEMES** which constitute the **SECOND ARTICULATION**. (The temp-tation to equate phoneme with "letter" was avoided because the actual sounds used to create differential contrasts in meaning are not always exactly congruent with letters, especially in languages such as English which are rich in phonetic inconsistencies and alternative spellings for identical phonemes.) These minimal units can then combine to form part of larger units; the phoneme can become part of a syllable, for example, and a morpheme can become part of a sentence, or a novel. It is the differential interplay of these two articulations that explains the remarkable economy with which language, on the basis of a score or more of phomenic units, generates its infinite semantic wealth.

Although the concept of articulation is frequently used in cine-semiotics – for example in analyses of the articulation of single "codes" such as color or lighting – Metz points out that the cinema *as such* has no equivalent of the double articulation of natural language. (Metz specifies the cinema "as such" because the cinema can include natural language in the form of dialogue or written materials.) Although Metz later came to argue that the individual codes forming part of cinema as a pluri-codic medium *can* be seen as having minimal units, the cinema *per se* has no minimal units which operate differentially to produce it as a language-system. Nothing in film is purely distinctive in the same sense as the phoneme, which depends entirely on combination to produce significant units. Cinematic shots and even individual frames already signify separately without depend-ing upon combination.

In "The Cinema of Poetry," Italian film-maker and theorist Pier Paolo Pasolini suggested that the cinema is a system of signs whose semiology corresponds to a possible semiology of the system of signs of reality itself. Unlike literature, Pasolini argued, film entails no symbolic or conventional filter between the film-maker and "reality." The smallest units in the cinema, the equivalent of phonemes, are unaltered by being reproduced on film. Nevertheless, the language of the cinema has its own version of double articulation. The **MINIMAL UNITS** of cinematic language, he argues, are the various real objects that occupy the frame. He designates these minimal units **CINEMES** by analogy with phonemes. The cinemes are then joined into a larger unit, the frame, which corresponds to the morpheme of natural language (Pasolini, in Nichols 1985, vol. I: 542–8).

Umberto Eco, in "Articulations of the Cinematic Code," criticizes Pasolini's argument for failing to acknowledge the culturally coded, ideological and systematic nature not only of film but also of human behavior and communication generally. The real objects whose image occupies the frame, he points out, are merely effects of a conventionalization by which an iconically codified signifier triggers our attribution of a signified. In any case, Eco argues, these minimal units are not equivalent to linguistic phonemes. Pasolini's "cinemes" retain their own unit meaning; they do not depend on the second articulation of the frame to differentially produce meaning. Eco, for his part, suggests a cinematic code of **TRIPLE ARTICU-LATIONS** of the image, consisting of a first articulation, called **SEMES**, i.e. initially recognizable meaningful units – for example "gangster wearing trench coat" – which can in turn be broken down into a second articulation of smaller iconic signs such as "cigarette dangling from lip," all finally analyzable into a third articulation having to do with conditions of perception (Eco, in Nichols 1985, vol. I: 590–607).

CINEMA: *LANGUE* OR *LANGAGE*?

The key figure among the filmo-linguistic pioneers was Christian Metz, whose purpose, as he himself defined it, was to "get to the bottom of the linguistic metaphor" by testing it against the most advanced concepts of contemporary linguistics. Metz took the linguistic metaphor seriously, but also skeptically, in order to discern its quantum of truthfulness. In the background of Metz' discussion was Saussure's founding methodological question regarding the "object" of linguistic study. Thus Metz looked for the counterpart, in film theory, to the conceptual role played by *langue* in the Saussurean schema. And much as Saussure concluded that the rightful purpose of linguistic investigation was to disengage the abstract signifying system of a language, Metz concluded that the object of cine-semiology was to disengage the cinema's signifying procedures, its combinatory rules, in order to see to what extent these rules resembled the doubly articulated diacritical systems of "natural languages."

Metz makes the distinction, borrowed from Gilbert Cohen-Seat's contrast of "cinema" and "film," between the "cinematic fact" and the "filmic fact." The **CINEMATIC FACT**, for Metz, refers to the cinematic institution taken in its broadest sense as a multi-dimensional sociocultural complex which includes pre-filmic events (the economic infrastructure, the studio system, technology), post-filmic events (distribution, exhibition, and the social or political impact of film) and a-filmic events (the décor of the theatre, the social ritual of movie-going). The **FILMIC FACT**, meanwhile, refers to a localizable discourse, a text; not to the physical film-object contained in a can but rather to the signifying text. Thus Metz closes in on the goal of semiotics: the study of discourses, of texts, rather than of the cinema as an institution, an entity much too multi-faceted to constitute the proper object of the filmo-linguistic science, much as *parole* was for Saussure too multiform to form the proper object of the linguistic science. (Metz never argued that the institutional context of the cinema should *not* be studied, only that such study does not form part of cine-semiotics.) At the same time, Metz points out, the cinematic institution also enters into the multi-dimensionality of films themselves as bounded discourses concentrating an intense charge of social, cultural and psychological meanings. (Metz developed this imbrication of film with the cinematic institution further in his *The Imaginary Signifier* (Metz 1982).) Metz thus reintroduces the distinction film/cinema *within* the category "film," now identifying cinematic specificity as the specific and proper object of the semiotic study of film. In this sense, "the cinematic" represents not the industry but rather the totality of films. As a "novel" is to "literature," or a statue to "sculpture," so is "film" to "cinema;" the former refers to the individual film text, while the latter refers to an ideal ensemble, the totality of films and their traits. Within the filmic, then, one encounters the cinematic.

The question which oriented Metz' early work was whether the cinema was **LANGUE** (language system) or **LANGAGE** (language) and his well-known conclusion to his own question was that the cinema was not a language system but that it was a language. Metz offers a number of reasons why film does not constitute a language system. First, he argues, *langue* is a system of signs intended for two-way communication, while the cinema allows only for *deferred* communication. Cinematic communication is doubly deferred, first through the lapse of time between a film's production and its reception, and second, through the lapse of time between its reception and the filmic response ensuant to that reception. This initial argument, however, is open to a number of objections. First, nothing precludes, in principle, the possibility of a future interactive cinema that would allow for instant two-way communication. Second, Metz' emphasis on two-way communication as norm seems to assume spoken speech as a model in a way that leaves him open to the same charges that Derrida levelled against Saussurean phonocentrism, i.e. that such a view privileges speech over writing, seen as the mere transcription or supplement of spoken speech. (In *Language and Cinema* Metz transcends this phonocentrism by highlighting cinema as a form of textual *écriture*.) The real analogy, in this sense, is between cinema and literary writing, which also allows only for deferred communication in the form of a dialogically "answering" poem, novel, or act of literary criticism. It could also be argued that spectators do "respond" to films, in the form of inner-speech reactions, or of verbal commentaries during or after the film. (The utterance, to be communicative, Bakhtin points out, does not require an *immediate* response.)

Metz' other reasons for rejecting cinema as *langue* are more substantial. Cinema is not a language-system, Metz argues, because it lacks the equivalent of the arbitrary linguistic sign. Produced through a process of mechanical reproduction, film installs a different relationship between signifier and signified. The perceptual similarity between the filmic image of a dog and the actual pro-filmic dog, or between the recorded sound of a dog's barking and the actual bark, suggests that the relation between signifier and signified is not arbitrary but motivated. (One encounters a slippage, in early Metz, from the broad notion of "motivation" to the much more restricted category of "analogy.") Under the pressure of criticism by Eco and others, Metz later shed the implicit Bazinianism of these positions by acknowledging that the filmic analogon is indeed coded. The analogy, Metz suggests in *Language and Cinema*, is less between filmic signifier and signified than in the parallel perceptual situation common to everyday experience and the cinematic experience.

In suggesting that cinema lacks the arbitrary sign of linguistics, Metz was not suggesting that the concept of sign, or of the signifier/signified as composing the sign, is irrelevant to the cinema; it is only the relation between signifier and signified that differs, being arbitrary in one case and motivated in the other. In his later psychoanalytically-inflected work in the 1970s, as we shall see in Part IV, Metz came to insist on the doubly imaginary nature of the cinematic signifier, imaginary in what it happens to represent and imaginary in its very constitution as presence–absence.

It is in this same context that Metz explores the notion, familiar from the earliest days of reflection concerning film, that the shot is like the word while the sequence is like the sentence. For Metz, important differences render such an analogy problematic: (1) shots are infinite in number, unlike words (since the lexicon is in principle finite) but like statements, an infinity of which can be constructed on the basis of a limited number of words. (2) Shots are the creations of the film-maker, unlike words (which pre-exist in lexicons) but again like statements. (3) The shot provides an inordinate amount of information – a fact which becomes obvious in any attempt, as in shot-by-shot analysis, to register in words the semantic wealth of even a single, relatively straightforward cinematic image. (4) The shot is an actualized unit, unlike the word which is a purely virtual lexical unit to be used as the speaker wishes. The word "dog" can be associated with any type of dog, and can be said with any pronunciation or intonation available to English-speakers. A filmic shot of a dog, in contrast, has already undergone any number of determinations and mediations. It tells us, at the very minimum, that here is a certain kind of dog of a certain size and appearance, shot from a specific angle with a specific kind of lens. While it is true that film-makers might "virtualize" the image of a dog through backlighting, soft-focus or decontextualization, Metz' more general point is that the cinematic shot more closely resembles an utterance or an assertion – "here is the backlit silhouetted image of what appears to be a large dog" – than a word. (5) Shots, unlike words, do not gain meaning by paradigmatic contrast with other shots that might have occurred in the same place on the syntagmatic chain. (Certain avant-garde films can, however, mimic the paradigmatic nature of language by drawing analogies between linguistic and cinematic paradigms; Frampton's *Zorn's Lemma* sets up a structural system by which images are made to substitute for letters of the alphabet.) In the cinema, shots form part of a paradigm so open as to be meaningless. In a typical sentence, one imagines a limited number of substitutions at each point on the syntagmatic chain, whereas images in film are opposed to a completely open list of possible alternatives. (Michael Snow's *Wavelength* demonstrates this openness, with its vast number of distinct shots strung along the trajectory of a 45-minute simulated zoom shot produced within the confines of a single Manhattan loft.)

To these disanalogies between shots and words, Metz adds a further disanalogy concerning the cinema in general, i.e. that it does not constitute a language widely available as a code. All speakers of English of a certain age have mastered the code of English – they are able to produce sentences – but the ability to produce filmic utterances depends on talent, training and access. To speak a language, in other words, is simply to use it, while to "speak" cinematic language is always to a certain extent to invent it. One might argue, of course, that this assymetry is itself culturally and socially determined; one can hypothesize a society in which all citizens would master the code of film-making. But in society as we know it, Metz' point must stand. There is, furthermore, a fundamental difference in the diachrony of natural as opposed to cinematic language. Cinematic language can be suddenly prodded in a new direction by innovatory aesthetic procedures – those introduced by a film such as *Citizen Kane*, for example, or those made possible by a new technology such as the zoom or the steadicam – while natural language shows a more powerful inertia and is less open to individual initiative and creativity. The analogy, here again, is less between cinema and natural language than between cinema and literature, which can be suddenly inflected by the revolutionary aesthetic procedures of, for example, a James Joyce or a Virginia Woolf.

Although film texts do not constitute a *langue* generated by an underlying language system – since the cinema lacks the arbitrary sign, minimal units and double articulation – they do nevertheless manifest a language-like systematicity. Metz posits three metaphorical tendencies or extrapolations within the word "language." First, systems are called languages if their formal structure resembles that of natural languages, as in the expression "the language of chess." Second, everything that signifies to human beings even without a formal system can be seen as reminiscent of language (here Metz comes close to the Peircean definition of a sign as "something which stands to somebody for something in some respect or capacity"). Thus semioticians study the language of fashion or cuisine. Third, Metz places the notion of language in a more specifically Hjelmslevian context. One might call "language," Metz argues, any unity defined in terms of its **MATTER OF EXPRESSION** – a Hjelmslevian term designed to designate the material in which signification manifests itself – or in terms of what Barthes in *Elements of Semiology* calls its "typical sign." Literary language, in this sense, is the set of messages whose matter of expression is writing; cinematic language is the set of messages whose matter of expression consists of **FIVE TRACKS** or channels: moving photographic image, recorded phonetic sound, recorded noises, recorded musical sound, and writing (credits, intertitles, written materials in the shot). Thus cinema is a language in the sense that it is a "technico-sensorial unity" graspable in perceptual experience. Cinema is a language, in sum, not only in a broadly metaphorical sense but also as a set of messages grounded in a given matter of expression, and as an artistic language, a discourse or signifying practice characterized by specific codifications and ordering procedures.

THE GRAND SYNTAGMATIQUE

Film became a discourse, Metz argued, by organizing itself as narrative and thus producing a body of signifying procedures: "It was precisely to the extent that the cinema confronted the problems of narration that . . . it came to produce a body of specific signifying procedures." While no image entirely resembles another image, most narrative films resemble one another in their principal syntagmatic figures, those units which organize spatial and temporal relations in various combinations. The true analogy between film and language, then, operates not at the level of basic units, but rather in their common syntagmatic nature. By moving from one image to two, film becomes language. Both language and film produce discourse through paradigmatic and syntagmatic operations. Language selects and combines phonemes and morphemes to form sentences; film selects and combines images and sounds to form syntagmas, i.e. units of narrative autonomy in which elements interact semantically.

The **GRAND SYNTAGMATIQUE**, Metz' attempt to isolate the principal syntagmatic figures of the narrative cinema, comes in response to the question: "How does film constitute itself as narrative discourse?" The Grand Syntagmatique was proposed against the backdrop of the notorious imprecision of film terminology concerning the sequential arrangements of fiction films. Much of the terminology was based on theatre rather than on the specifically cinematic signifiers of image and sound, shots and montage. Terms like "scene" and "sequence" were used more or less interchangeably, and classifications were based on the most heterogeneous criteria – a posited unity of depicted action ("the farewell scene") or of place ("the courtroom sequence") – with little attention to the exact temporal and spatial articulation of the filmic discourse.

Two concepts, one theoretical and the other methodological, undergird Metz' work in the Grand Syntagmatique. First, Metz draws on the notion, borrowed from the classical Greek tradition of literary commentary, of the "diegesis." In the *Poetics*, Aristotle uses **DIEGESIS** to refer to a mode of representation that involves "telling" rather than "showing." In 1953, Etienne Souriau revived the term to designate the "recounted story" of a film, after which it was elaborated by Gerard Genette in literary analysis, before Metz imported it into film theory. **DIEGESIS** (more or less synonymous with Genette's "story" (*histoire*)) refers to the posited events and characters of a narrative, i.e. the signified of narrative content, the characters and actions taken as it were "in themselves" without reference to their discursive mediation. The diegesis of the Nabokov novel *Lolita* and its filmic adaptation by Stanley Kubrick, for example, might be identical in many respects, yet the artistic and generic mediation in film and novel might be vastly different. The same "diegesis" can be "carried" by a wide variety of material signifiers or narrative media.

In the cinema, the word diegesis refers to the film's represented instance, the sum of the film's **DENOTATION**, i.e. the narration itself, plus the fictional space and time dimensions implied in and by the narrative (characters, landscapes, events, etc.), and even the story as it is received and felt by the spectator. The diegesis is thus an imaginary construction, the fictive space and time in which the film operates, the assumed universe in which the narrative takes place. The notion of diegesis, Metz insists, is only appropriate to a designation of a complete universe whose elements exist on the same level of reality (photographic reality in the case of the cinema, verbal in the case of the novel). In this sense, there can be no diegesis in the theatre, for fundamental to the notion of diegesis is the creation of a "homogeneous pseudo-world." Gerard Genette appeals to the notion of the diegetic in his analysis of levels of narration in literature, distinguishing between three levels: the **DIEGETIC** (arising from the primary narration), the **EXTRADIEGETIC** (narrative intrusion upon the diegesis) and the **METADIEGETIC** (pertaining to narration by a secondary narrator). Dominique Château in "Diégèse et Enonciation" (*Communications* 38) distinguishes between the diegesis as mental referent, and as a "world-producing activity." An element can be diegetic, she points out, without being iconic – for example, in the evoked off-screen presence of a monster in the direction of whom a frightened character looks but which we nevertheless do not see ourselves. Once familiar with a character, we represent that character to ourselves mentally, even when the character is no longer present on the screen. Thus the diegesis forms an implicit system, often becoming more implicit as the story progresses.

Daniel Percheron clarifies the notion of diegesis by placing it in differential opposition with certain related terms. *Diegesis/Film*: the time of the diegesis is not identical to the time of the film. Apart from rare exceptions such as Hitchcock's *Rope*, Varda's *Cleo from 5 to 7* and Louis Malles' *My Dinner with André* – and even they display momentary lapses – most films do not attempt to equate diegetic time with the time of the filmic discourse. At times the disparity is quite dramatic. The diegesis of Kubrick's *2001: A Space Odyssey*'s spans millennia, but its discourse is limited to a few hours. *Diegesis/Production*: in the classical fiction film, there is a frequent discordance between the posited world of the diegesis and the actual world of film production. Godard's *Made in USA* is diegetically set in the United States (Atlantic City) yet the images themselves (deliberately) make it transparent that the film was actually shot in France. Michael Curtiz' *Casablanca* is diegetically set in Morocco, but was actually made in a Hollywood studio. A close scrutiny of many period reconstruction films often reveals flaws in the diegetic representation – the television antenna on a picturesque "Victorian" rooftop, the automobile winding down a distant road in the far background of a Renaissance costume drama. The advantage of referring to a film's "diegesis" rather than simply to its "story" or its "plot" is that first, it helps focus attention on the constructed nature of the story, and second, it helps us separate the notion of story from its more dramatic and romanesque connotations of "exciting events." By shifting emphasis away from the events of the story, the term diegesis allows for a film in which little "happens," for example in certain avant-garde-inflected films (e.g. *Jeanne Dielman*) more or less lacking in dramatic incident in the conventional sense, but which retain a diegesis in the sense of a "posited world."

Metz' project also draws on the notion of **BINARY OPPOSITIONS** developed by phonologists such as Jakobson and Trubetskoy. Just as the phonologist extracts from the heterogeneous acoustic phenomena associated with language-use the key elements that play a role in communication, which serve in one way or another to transmit information, so Metz, in defining the syntagmas, works through a series of successive binary dichotomies: a syntagma consists of one shot or more than one shot; it is chronological or *a*chronological; if it is chronological, it can be either consecutive or simultaneous, linear or non-linear, continuous or discontinuous. The diverse kinds of syntagmas are susceptible to **COMMUTATION**

TESTS, i.e. **COMMUTABLE** – etymologically "change together" i.e. the sub-stitution of one for the other, on the plane of the signifier, produces a definite change on the plane of the signified. Using this method, Metz generated at first a total of six types (in the version published in *Communications* in 1966), and increased this to eight in 1968 (subsequently included in *Essais sur la Signification au Cinéma* as well as in *Film Language*).

THE EIGHT SYNTAGMATIC TYPES

The Grand Syntagmatique constitutes a typology of the diverse ways that time and space can be ordered through editing within the segments of the narrative film. For Metz, three criteria serve to identify, delimit and define autonomous segments: unity of action (diegetic continuity), the type of demarcation (i.e. the visible or invisible punctuating devices used to sepa-rate and articulate the major segments), and syntagmatic structure (the principles of pertinence which identify the syntagmatic type). The syntag-matic units combine with other codic systems to make up the internal unfolding of events represented in the filmic chain. Metz uses the word **SYNTAGMA** as the general term to designate the units of narrative auton-omy, the pattern according to which individual shots can be grouped, reserving both "sequence" and "scene" to designate specific types of syn-tagmas. Syntagmatic analysis enables the analyst to determine how images come together in a pattern which forms the overall narrative armature of the film-text. Once the syntagmatic arrangement has been discerned, the analyst is better equipped to generalize about the frequency, distribution or preponderance of certain syntagmatic types.

The eight syntagmas, then, are:

(1) the **AUTONOMOUS SHOT** – a syntagma consisting of one shot, in turn subdivided into (a) the **SINGLE-SHOT SEQUENCE**, and (b) four kinds of **INSERTS: NON-DIEGETIC INSERT** (a single shot which presents objects exterior to the fictional world of the action); the **DISPLACED DIEGETIC INSERT** ("real" diegetic images but temporally or spatially out of context); the **SUBJECTIVE INSERT** (memories, fears) and the **EXPLANATORY INSERT** (single shots which clarify events for the spectator);

(2) the **PARALLEL SYNTAGMA** – two alternating motifs without clear spatial or temporal relationship, such as rich and poor, town and country;

(3) the **BRACKET SYNTAGMA** – brief scenes given as typical examples of a certain order of reality but without temporal sequence, often organized around a "concept";

(4) the **DESCRIPTIVE SYNTAGMA** – objects shown successively suggesting spatial coexistence, used, for example, to situate the action;

(5) the **ALTERNATING SYNTAGMA** – narrative cross-cutting implying temporal simultaneity such as a chase alternating pursuer and pursued;

(6) the **SCENE** – spatio-temporal continuity felt as being without flaws

or breaks, in which the signified (the implied diegesis) is continuous, as in the theatrical scene, but where the signifier is fragmented into diverse shots;

(7) the **EPISODIC SEQUENCE** – a symbolic summary of stages in an implied chronological development, usually entailing a compression of time;

(8) the **ORDINARY SEQUENCE** – action treated elliptically so as to eliminate "unimportant" detail, with jumps in time and space masked by continuity editing.

Before proceeding to an overall evaluation, we might discuss the specific utility of the eight types of syntagma. The first syntagma, the **AUTONOMOUS SHOT**, consists of a single shot clearly separated and without close connection to neighboring shots. The only syntagma defined in terms of its signifier (i.e. that it consists of a single shot), it is by definition not a syntagma, but it is a syntagmatic type in that it is one of the types that occur within the global syntagmatic structure of narrative films. Metz subdivides the autonomous shot into two subtypes, the single-shot sequence and inserts, themselves divided into four subtypes – non-diegetic, subjective, displaced diegetic, and explanatory.

Examples of the **SINGLE-SHOT SEQUENCE** would include many of the first Lumière shorts such as *The Waterer Watered* in which complete episodes are handled in a single shot. The French New Wave, encouraged both by André Bazin's admiration for the spatial and temporal integrity he discerned in the work of such directors as Flaherty, Welles and Wyler, and by direct cinema's penchant for long takes, made the one-shot sequence an integral part of its aesthetic. That the prolonged one-shot sequences of Hitchcock's *Rope* would also qualify as autonomous shots points to a potential problem in applicability. Does the term cease to be useful when so much can "happen" within a single shot, when the equivalent of shot changes, usually performed through editing, can be simulated through camera movement, the disposition of actors within the frame, and interventions on the soundtrack? Any film, such as Fellini's *8½*, which develops complex single-shot sequences whose meaning unfolds slowly over time, will also fit only awkwardly into this category.

The four subtypes of **INSERT** – single shots which stand out from their context in particularly striking ways – are no less problematic. These inserts include: (1) the **NON-DIEGETIC INSERT**, for example, a single interpolated metaphoric shot such as the image associating Kerensky with a peacock in Eisenstein's *October*; (2) the **SUBJECTIVE INSERT**, an interpolated shot representing, within the diegesis, an image representing a memory, a dream, or hallucination clearly marked as subjective; (3) the **DISPLACED DIEGETIC INSERT**, i.e. a shot which is temporally or spatially displaced relative to the series of shots in which it is inserted, such as the shot of a loafing Michel in *Adieu Philippine*, offered by the film-maker to contradict that character's grandiose claims of importance; and (4) the **EXPLANATORY**

41

INSERT, in which material is abstracted from the fictional space and enlarged for didactic or explanatory purpose, for example closer shots of letters, newspaper headlines, maps and so forth.

While these subdivisions of the autonomous shot are useful, and while they do clarify certain procedures of filmic narration, they are problematic in so far as they are somewhat arbitrarily identified with the single shot. There is no reason, for example, why the subjectivity of a memory or fear must be represented or evoked within the confines of a single shot. A film like *Last Year at Marienbad* might be regarded as itself a lengthy subjective "insert" composed of hundreds of shots. The same objection holds true for the other subtypes. In *Singin' in the Rain*, certain early shots serve to contrast the squalid truth about matinée idol Don Lockwood's (Gene Kelly) past with his mendacious tale of his glorious rise to stardom, and are thus reminiscent of Metz' "displaced diegetic inserts," yet the ironic undercutting does not take the form of single shots. Explanatory material, similarly, often extends beyond a single-shot format, as in the police investigation sequences of Fritz Lang's *M*. In sum, all of these "inserts" might just as easily operate over much larger syntagmatic units such as the segment, the sequence or even an entire film.

The notion of the subjective shot, furthermore, has meaning only in relation to the signified of the diegesis; it cannot be so clearly separated from its narrative context. Subjectivization, in film, is in no way restricted to single-shot situations. Hitchcock's *Marnie*, for example, evokes the subjectivity of its female protagonist through a number of devices in a variety of registers: by Hitchcock's classical point-of-view editing structures, by interpolated red-filtered shots, by a *mise-en-scène* evoking the spatiality of dream, by subjective sound, and by selective focus. Only rarely does this subjectivization take place within the confines of the autonomous shot. By "ghettoizing" the subjective shot, furthermore, Metz elides the thorny problem of point-of-view, i.e. that subjectivity and point-of-view articulate films in their entirety. The subjective insert category, then, creates an awkward "bulge" in the system, for all subjectivity in film cannot be neatly assigned to a subset of the autonomous shot. Metz' approach seems to assume a conventional kind of realism – occasionally interrupted by interpolated subjective shots – which does not allow for the possibility of extended subjective realism (for example, *Red Desert*) and even less for a thoroughgoing reflexivity. For all these reasons, the autonomous shot category, while pointing to useful distinctions, is the weakest and most unwieldy feature of the Grand Syntagmatique.

The **PARALLEL SYNTAGMA** displays none of these problems. The parallel syntagma consists of more than one shot, is achronological and is based on alternation. It characteristically interweaves two motifs without positing any clear spatial or temporal relationship between them. Thus a series of two or more images are intercut to denote a symbolic or thematic parallel or contrast rather than to communicate a narrative development. D. W. Griffith was especially fond of the parallel syntagma, a trait correlatable, perhaps, with the dualistic, often Manichean thinking which typifies his work. *Corner in Wheat* develops a thematic counterpoint between images of wealth (rich men's banquets) and poverty (poor people's breadlines). *The Birth of a Nation* contrasts images of war and peace, without suggesting any clear sequential, spatial or temporal relation between the two sets of images. Many militant leftist films, such as *Hour of the Furnaces*, similarly exploit parallel syntagmas in order to highlight class differences or oppression, juxtaposing images of upper-class leisure (the bourgeoisie at the horse races) with images of lower-class squalor (the lumpenproletariat scavenging in garbage dumps).

The **BRACKET SYNTAGMA** consists of more than one shot, is achronological and, unlike the parallel syntagma, is not based on alternation. The bracket syntagma provides typical samples of a given order of reality without linking them chronologically. As in the parallel syntagma, the shots are related to each other thematically, with no spatial or temporal continuity, but this time there is no alternation between motifs. The audio-visual logos which open television sitcoms – for example the initial montage-segment showing the typical activities of a day in the life of Mary Richards on the *Mary Tyler Moore Show* – might be seen as bracket syntagmas. The fragmented shots of two lovers in bed that open Godard's *A Married Woman*, similarly, provide a typical sample of an order of reality known as "contemporary lovemaking"; indeed, the sequence's lack of teleology and climax form part of a Brechtian strategy of de-eroticization, a "bracketing" of eroticism. (Many of the films featuring significant numbers of bracket syntagmas can be characterized, not coincidentally, as "Brechtian," precisely because the bracket syntagma is especially well equipped for representing the socially "typical.")

Metz calls the opening segment of *Adieu Philippine* – a series of shots showing the film's protagonist working in a television studio – a bracket syntagma, a problematic classification in that it is contradicted by the music of the segment, which is diegetic, synchronous and uninterrupted. The temporality of the music, with its unfolding temporal continuity correlated with the visual continuity of the images of the performing musicians, differs from and contradicts the supposed atemporality of the image track. (In his later *Language and Cinema*, Metz opens up a theoretical space for a film text characterized by multiple temporalities.) But despite this misapplication in the case of *Adieu Philippine*, the category of the bracket syntagma remains broadly useful in characterizing the function of certain sequences in films. The bracket syntagma which comprises the opening of Resnais' *Muriel* sets the tone of unnameable mystery which lingers around that film. Godard's *Les Carabiniers* features a preponderance of bracket syntagmas which are none the less organized into the larger narrative structure of a

43

Brechtian fable about war. Here the bracket syntagma is mobilized as part of the film's deconstructive procedures – the systematic destruction from within of the dominant cinema's traditional narrative approach to dramatic conflict. The bracket syntagma's emphasis on the typical – here the behavioral typicalities of contemporary war – is eminently suited to the social and generalizing intentions of politicized directors.

The **DESCRIPTIVE SYNTAGMA** is chronological and consists of more than one shot. It involves the successive display of objects so as to suggest spatial coexistence. Metz cites the sequenced presentation of shots of a flock of sheep, of particular sheep, of shepherd and sheepdog. The descriptive syntagma, in Metz' view, is not necessarily restricted to inanimate or non-human objects or motionless human figures; human beings in the shot can be performing actions as long as the film does not emphasize the purposeful narrative development of these actions. But the distinction between the bracket syntagma and the ordinary sequence is sometimes hard to draw. In theory, spatial coexistence is absolutely necessary to the descriptive syntagma, while the bracket syntagma allows for a looser, more discontinuous form of organization. But in practice the two are often difficult to distinguish; it is at this point that more specific signifying criteria come into play. Is an opening segment of "establishing" shots of city landmarks to be seen as a "typical sample of a certain order of reality," and therefore as a bracket syntagma, or as a descriptive syntagma? What about cases such as the opening of Hitchcock's *Psycho*, with its precise marking of time and place – "Phoenix, Arizona, Friday, December the Eleventh, 2.43 p.m." – where the superimposed titles almost instantly mark the initial moment of the diegesis (a lunchtime tryst) – and where the airborne crane shots are marked by an overriding sense of teleology, prefiguring the film's obsession with avian imagery by literalizing the notion of a "bird's-eye-view" of a city named after a mythical bird. Such complex interweavings point up the difficulty in assigning a single syntagmatic category to such a segment.

The **ALTERNATING SYNTAGMA**, the least controversial of Metz' categories, refers to what was traditionally called narrative cross-cutting. It consists of more than one shot, and is chronological, consecutive and non-linear. Its quality of consecutiveness makes it a narrative syntagma; unlike the parallel syntagma, it is chronological rather than achronological. It involves spatial separation – for example, between pursuers and pursued, cops and robbers – but temporal simultaneity or quasi-simultaneity.

The **SCENE** consists of more than one shot and is chronological, consecutive and linear. The signifier is fragmented (into diverse shots) but the signified (the implied diegetic event) is continuous. The scene offers a spatio-temporal continuity experienced as if without flaws or breaks. Any sequence of continuous conversation in a classical Hollywood film would qualify as a scene in the Metzian sense in that such sequences imply a

44

complete coincidence of screen time and diegetic time. The signifier is fragmented – by a series of shot/counter structures for example – but the signified – the conversation – is felt to be continuous, whole and uninterrupted. The scene is the only syntagmatic type, if one excludes the one-shot sequence, that resembles the theatrical scene. Films which attempt to maintain a strict spatio-temporal continuity throughout, such as Agnes Varda's *Cleo from 5 to 7* or Louis Malles' *My Dinner with André*, might be regarded as virtuoso exercises in the extended scene. The signifier is fragmented – both films consist of hundreds of shots – but their signified is, generally speaking, continuous. The scene can be contrasted with syntagmas such as the episodic sequence or ordinary sequence where not only the signifier but also the signified is discontinuous.

The **EPISODIC SEQUENCE** is chronological, consecutive and linear, but not continuous and usually consists of more than one shot. The episodic sequence brings together a series of brief episodes – often separated by optical devices such as dissolves and sometimes unified by musical accompaniment – which succeed each other chronologically within the diegesis. The meaning of this succession of "scenelets" lies in the totality, that is in the overall progression and development, rather than in the scenelets themselves. Each scenelet constitutes a symbolic summary of a stage in a part of a larger development. In *Adieu Philippine*, for example, one episodic sequence showing three successive rendezvous between Michel, Liliane and Juliette is organized by the teleology of the threesome's growing friendliness. The celebrated "breakfast sequence" in *Citizen Kane* (part of Leland's flashback account of Kane's first marriage), meanwhile, demonstrates a kind of reverse teleology. The individual scenelets in themselves are of less consequence than the developing sense of estrangement as the couple passes from newly-wed passion to bored hostility. In the episodic sequence the signifier is discontinuous – since the sequence deploys itself over a number of shots – as is the signified – since there are implied temporal ellipses between the scenelets. (Although Metz does not himself do so, one might posit as a subcategory of the episodic sequence the "montage sequences" (named Vorkapich after their creator) of Hollywood films which summarize, for example, the meteoric rise to fame of a character in a musical or the precipitous fall of a politician through a highly condensed series of images of newspaper headlines, radio announcements, or movie marquees.)

The final syntagma, the **ORDINARY SEQUENCE**, is, like the episodic sequence, chronological, consecutive, linear and discontinuous. But whereas the episodic sequence involves a series of clearly separated scenelets linked by an overall trajectory of development, the ordinary sequence develops a more or less continuous action, but with temporal ellipses whereby "unimportant details" and "dead time" are excised so as not to bore the spectator. Almost any cinematic dinner in the classical fiction film – for example, the filmic reduction of a meal to a few characteristic gestures and a short exchange of dialogue – would qualify as "ordinary sequence." (The innovation of *My Dinner with André* was to expand one of those dinners into a feature-length "scene.") While the signifier in the ordinary sequence is discontinuous, the signified of the diegesis is often implied to be continuous. The spectator, that is, is not intended to be made conscious of the temporal fissures of the narrative. The ordinary sequence is frequent not only in the classical fiction film but also in many documentaries and even in filmed television news segments.

The Grand Syntagmatique, while fairly widely disseminated and while engendering a diverse progeny of syntagmatic analyses, also encountered considerable criticism, and Metz himself came to express reservations about it and ultimately redefined its status. Some critiques focussed on the general thrust of Metz' project as unduly privileging the mainstream narrative film. The definition of cinematic language as "first of all the literalness of a plot" apparently excluded both documentaries and avant-garde film. Metz granted the point subsequently in *Language and Cinema* by redefining the Grand Syntagmatique as merely one of many cinematic codes, and more specifically as a subcode of editing within a historically delimited body of films: the mainstream narrative tradition from the early 1930s (the consolidation of the sound film) through to the late 1950s, with the demise of the studio aesthetic and the challenge of the diverse "new waves."

Since the Grand Syntagmatique deals with the spatial and temporal articulation of the diegesis, it is most effective with those films which presuppose a narrative substratum, a pre-existing story or anecdotal nucleus from which the "high points" have been extracted. Problems with the model arise when it is applied to avant-garde films such as *Nostalgia* and *Wavelength* or even *Le Gai Savoir*. The Grand Syntagmatique can be useful even when it turns out to be inapplicable, in the sense that it reveals the degree to which a given film departs from classical narrative procedures. Apart from its privileging of narrative denotation, the Grand Syntagmatique was also faulted for the vestigial phenomenology of its theoretical underpinnings. This critique argued that Metz implicitly appeals to "common observation" and "general experience" as if these were unproblematic notions. Metz proceeds inductively as if he were searching for syntagmatic types in the films themselves rather than constructing a theoretical model which would both generate and account for the entire range of possible types. However, if the Grand Syntagmatique is seen as a general model for the textual actualization of the logic of narrative progression, it does provide a system which can account for the material unfolding of films. In this light, one might imagine a more inclusive model applicable not only to classical narrative films but also to documentaries and to "advanced" films such as *Numéro Deux* and ultimately to all possible time–space relations in the films of both the past and the future.

Some of the "bugs" in Metz' schema emerge in the syntagmatic analysis of *Adieu Philippine*. Apart from perceptual inaccuracies – a jump-cut edited series of twelve lateral tracking shots is treated as a single shot – there are other problems. The Grand Syntagmatique pretends to limit its attention to the image track, yet it has frequent recourse to information drawn from the soundtrack. The characterization of a shot of Michel loafing at the TV studio (contradicting his exaggerated claims of importance) as a "displaced diegetic insert" depends on our knowledge of Michel's boasting, knowledge provided by the dialogue rather than the image track. A less monolithic schema would allow for the possibility of multiple syntagmatic attributions depending on which track or which dimension of the sequence is being discussed. Thus one might speak of a certain film segment having both bracketing and descriptive "functions" or of having a diversity of syntagmatic "operations." (Such a move would parallel Eco's progression from speaking of "signs" to speaking of "sign functions," or Metz' own shift of interest, in "Metaphor/Metonymy" (in Metz 1981), from defining a given textual instance as essentially either metaphor or metonymy to speaking of simultaneous metaphorical and metonymic "operations" within the same instance.)

The Grand Syntagmatique also assumes that films develop a single temporality, when in fact even some Hollywood films develop multiple temporalities. An altered schema would allow for the possibility of distinct and even contradictory temporalities at the same textual point within the same film, depending on whether one is analyzing the image track, the dialogue track, the music track or even the written materials track. The permutations of these coordinates, systematically explored in a film like *Numéro Deux*, are anticipated in *Adieu Philippine*. The "episodic sequence" in which Michel accompanies Liliane and Juliette to three distinct locales (a train station, a country road, an airfield) combines flawless continuity on the dialogue track with clear spatial and temporal discontinuity on the image track.

Much of the hostility initially provoked by the Grand Syntagmatique was based on the misperception that it was intended to be definitive and exhaustive, as *the* master code of the cinema. After such an analysis is finished, critics pointed out, virtually everything important remains to be said. But Metz offered the Grand Syntagmatique in a more modest spirit than was often granted by his detractors, as a first step toward establishing the main types of image ordering. To the objection that "everything remains to be said" Metz would presumably answer that, first, it is in the nature of science to choose a principle of pertinence. To speak of the Grand Canyon in terms of geological strata, or of *Hamlet* in terms of syntactic functions, hardly exhausts the interest or signification of experi-

47

encing the Grand Canyon or reading *Hamlet*, yet that does not mean that geology and linguistics have nothing to offer. Secondly, the work of addressing all levels of signification in a film is the task of textual analysis, not of film theory or of the Grand Syntagmatique. The Grand Syntagmatique is merely one of the subcodes, functioning as an armature or support for the work of the codes comprising the film's textual system.

Although the Grand Syntagmatique belonged to a euphorically scientistic phase of the semiotic project, a phase subsequently both complemented by and relativized by psychoanalytic methods before being aggressively questioned by the proponents of deconstruction, it would be wrong to underestimate its importance or Metz' achievement. In contrast to the imprecision of previous models, Metz introduced a relative rigor by shifting attention away from the narrative signified onto the cinematic signifier. Metz' schema, if not infallible, at least addressed an important question: what are the diverse possibilities of temporal and spatial articulation within the fiction film? In practical terms, the Grand Syntagmatique can serve as an attention-focussing device, of interest even when only partially applicable. The syntagmatic types are also broadly useful in defining the spatio-temporal coordinates of specific genres, or the stylistic options of given directors, genres or films. John Ellis, in his analysis of Ealing Studios (*Screen*, Spring 1975), shows that two-thirds of *Passport to Pimlico* consists of syntagmas favoring spatio-temporal integrity (scenes, ordinary sequences and autonomous shots), a feature reflective of the illusion-istic thrust of the film. In "The Real Soap Operas," Sandy Flitterman-Lewis delineates the syntagmatic patterns typical of television commercials (in Kaplan 1983). It is easier, finally, to point out flaws in a model than to construct one. The Grand Syntagmatique, whatever its flaws, still offers the most precise model to date for dealing with the specific image-ordering procedures of the narrative film.

CODES AND SUBCODES

Although lacking a grammar or phonemic system, Metz argues in *Language and Cinema* (published in French in 1971 and translated into English in 1974),[3] film still constitutes a quasi-linguistic practice as a **PLURICODIC MEDIUM**. Like any artistic language, the cinema manifests a plurality of codes. In cinema, numerous codes remain constant across all or most films; unlike language, however, film has no "master code" shared by all films. Filmic texts, for Metz, form a structured network produced by the inter-weaving of **SPECIFIC CINEMATIC CODES**, i.e. codes that appear only in the cinema, and **NON-SPECIFIC CODES**, i.e. codes shared with languages other than the cinema. Metz describes the configuration of specific and non-specific codes as a set of concentric circles ranging on a spectrum from the very specific – the inner circle – for example, those codes linked to film's definition as deploying moving, multiple images (e.g. codes of camera movement and continuity editing), through codes shared with other arts (e.g. narrative codes, shared with the novel and the comic strip, or codes of visual analogy, shared with painting) to demonstrably non-specific codes which are widely disseminated in the culture (for example, the codes of gender roles). Rather than an absolute specificity or non-specificity, then, it is more accurate to speak of "degrees" of specificity. Examples of specifically cinematic codes would be camera movement (or lack of it), lighting, and montage; they are attributes of all films in that all films involve cameras, all films must be lit, and all films must be edited, even if the editing is minimal. (Avant-garde attempts to do away with even these basic traits, as in flicker films, reveal the covert dependency of Metz' model on classical cinema.) The distinction between specifically cinematic and non-cinematic codes is obviously often a tenuous and shifting one. While the phenomenon of color belongs to the arts generally, the particularities of 1950s technicolor belong specifically to film. While a recorded voice seems non-specific, a voice recorded in Dolby sound for a "concert film" approaches the specific. While gestures and mimicry are common to film, theatre, and everyday life, there also exist specifically cinematic forms of acting. Even non-specific elements, moreover, can be "cinematized" through their simultaneous coexistence with the other elements featured on other "tracks" at the same moment in the filmic-discursive chain.

Within each particular cinematic code, cinematic **SUBCODES** represent specific usages of the general code. Expressionist lighting forms a subcode of lighting, just as Eisensteinian montage forms a subcode of editing, contrastable in its typical usage with a Bazinian *mise-en-scène* that would minimize spatial and temporal fragmentation. According to Metz, codes do not compete, but subcodes do. While all films must be lit and edited, not all films need deploy Eisensteinian montage. Metz notes, however, that certain film-makers (such as Glauber Rocha) at times mingle contradictory subcodes in a "feverish anthological procedure" by which Eisensteinian montage, Bazinian *mise-en-scène* and cinema verité coexist in tension within the same sequence. The diverse codes can also be made to play against one another, for example, by using expressionist lighting in a musical, or a jazz score in a Western. The code, for Metz, is a logical calculus of possible permutations; the subcode is a specific and concrete use of these possibilities, which yet remains within a conventionalized system. **CINEMATIC LANGUAGE**, for Metz, is the totality of cinematic codes and subcodes in so far as the differences separating these various codes are provisionally set aside in order to treat the whole as a unitary system, thus allowing us to formulate general propositions. Cinematic language, Metz acknowledges, has neither the same cohesion nor the same precision as a *langue*; it is not pre-given, furthermore, but rather a system to be forged by the analyst.

49

A history of the cinema, for Metz, would trace the play of competition, incorporations and exclusions of the subcodes. A number of analysts have complained about the circularity of definition and argument in Metz' early work, and the lack of clear criteria, with regard to both code and subcode. In his essay "Textual Analysis etc.," (*Enclitic*) David Bordwell points out some of the problems. While Metz insists that codes are potentially "common to all films," Bordwell argues that no code is *actually* present in all films, while all codes are *potentially* present in all films, since anything could have been put in a film. Metz' characterization of the subcodes, Bordwell argues further, shows covert dependency on received ideas about film history and the "evolution of film language," ideas which provide the unstated grounding for the recognition of the subcodes. Bordwell therefore calls for the historicization of the study of cinematic subcodes. He appeals to Jan Mukarovsky's concept of **AESTHETIC NORMS**, i.e. the historically evolving sets of alternatives available to the film-maker, the set of more or less probable substitutions within a functional context. Thus a given mode of film practice at any historical moment ranks certain paradigmatic alternatives as more or less likely. The wipe, for example, is an unlikely alternative in a 1920s film but a highly likely one in the mid–1930s. These norms should be studied, furthermore, in terms of their relation to the forces and relations of film production. (Such is the project of Bordwell/ Thompson/Steiger's *The Classical Hollywood Cinema*.) Hollywood film-makers clung to certain schemata, Bordwell argues, because of already fixed patterns of capitalist film production. A style based on extensive cutting, for example, allowed the studios to plan scripts as ensembles of shots which could be routinely dispatched during the shooting.

TEXTUAL SYSTEM

It is also in *Language and Cinema* that Metz develops the notion of **TEXTUAL SYSTEM** – the undergirding organization of a film-text considered as a singular totality. Every film has a particular structure, a network of meaning around which it coheres – even if the system chosen is one of deliberate incoherence – a configuration arising from the diverse choices made among the diverse codes available to the film-maker. The textual system does not inhere in the text; it is constructed by the analyst. The concept of the textual system as a structured network of codes helps Metz define the task of the film analyst as opposed to that of the theorist, though the distinction is often far from clear. Just as cinematic language is the object of cine-semiological theory, so the text is the object of filmo-linguistic analysis. What the cine-semiologist studies is not the film-making milieu, or the lives of the stars, or the technological supports of the cinema, or their reception, but the text as a signifying system. (This New-Critical-style "ghettoizing" of the text was questioned subsequently, even by Metz himself.) Metz is not concerned, in *Language and Cinema*, with providing a "how to" book for textual analysis, but rather with determining its theoretical status, its "place." Metz repeatedly emphasizes the notion of constructing codes, or better, of doing textual analysis so as to expose codes not previously recognized as codes. Second, Metz suggests that no film is constructed uniquely out of cinematic codes; films always speak of something, even if they speak about nothing more than the apparatus itself, the film experience itself, or our conventional expectations concerning that experience.

At certain points in *Language and Cinema*, Metz' theorizations are inflected by post-structuralist literary currents, and particularly by the theoretical interventions of Barthes, Kristeva, and more generally, by the writers associated with the French journal *Tel Quel*, a group which had as its goal the promotion of a new kind of literary-textual practice. Kristeva saw in the avant-garde writings of Lautréamont, Mallarmé and Artaud the paradigm of a revolutionary *écriture*. These literary currents were absorbed to a certain extent by the film-theoretical milieu, especially in such film journals as *Cahiers du Cinéma* and especially *Cinétique*. Within film studies, *Tel Quel*ism urged a radical rejection of all conventional mainstream films, and even of aesthetically conventional left militant films, in favor of films like Jean Daniel Pollet's *Méditerranée* and the experimental films of the Dziga Vertov group (Jean-Luc Godard and Jean-Pierre Gorin) which provoked a dramatic rupture with conventional practices.

In *Language and Cinema* Metz tended to oscillate between a more neutral notion of **TEXT** as any finite, organized discourse intended to realize communication, and a more programmatic avant-garde deconstructionist sense of text. But unlike the *Tel Quel*ists, Metz does not generally use the word "text" to separate out radical avant-garde films; for him, all films are texts and have textual systems. There exists a clear tension in *Language and Cinema*, consequently, between a static, taxonomic, structuralist–Formalist view of textual systems, and a more dynamic post-structuralist Barthesian–Kristevan view of text as productivity, "displacement," and "*écriture*." Influenced by the Kristevan critique of the Saussurean paradigm (a critique indebted not only to the Derridean critique of the sign but also to Bakhtin's translinguistic critique of Saussure), Metz describes the moment of filmic *parole* as the dissolution of the very systematicity he has elsewhere emphasized.

The system of the text is the process which displaces codes, deforming each of them by the presence of the others, contaminating some by means of others, meanwhile replacing one by another, and finally – as a temporarily "arrested" result of this general displacement – placing each code in a particular position in regard to the overall

51

structure, a displacement which thus finishes by a positioning which is itself destined to be displaced by another text.

(Metz 1974: 103)

It is this latter, more dynamic view of the text as a "non-finalized" perpetual **DISPLACEMENT** that constitutes the more dynamic pole in *Language and Cinema*. A film's text, within this more dynamic conception, is not the "list" of its operative codes, but rather the labor of constant restructuration and displacement by which the film "writes" its text, modifies and combines its codes, playing some codes off against others, and thus constitutes its system. The textual system, then, is the instance which displaces the codes so that they come to inflect and substitute one another. What matters is the passage from code to code, the way in which signification is relayed from lighting, for example, to camera movement, from dialogue to music, or the way that music plays against dialogue, or lighting against music, or music against camera movement. Cinematic **ECRITURE** refers to the process by which the film works with and against the various codes in order to constitute itself as text. While film language can be seen as an ensemble of codes, *écriture* is an operation, the process which displaces the codes. This formulation has the corollary advantage of "socializing" the process of artistic creation. By foregrounding *écriture* as the re-elaboration of codes, Metz envisions film as a signifying practice not dependent on romantically connoted entities such as "inspiration" and "genius" but rather as a reworking of socially available discourses.

One film theorist who took very seriously the post-structuralist critique of first-phase semiology was Stephen Heath. Besides presenting Metz' work for an Anglo-American audience, Heath also criticized certain aspects of that work from a Lacanian–Kristevan perspective. Heath called for a shift in attention away from the text as an interweaving of codes toward a view of the text as "process" and "operation." Both Stephen Heath and Ben Brewster found Metz' notion of codes somewhat too restrictive, and out of keeping with the idea of the cinema as a *langage* without *langue*. Heath therefore redefined codes, in a somewhat looser way, as "systems of constraints" or "systems of possibilities" bearing on both paradigmatic and syntagmatic relations. Heath's redefinition was obviously influenced by *S/Z*, Barthes' prolonged analysis of the Balzac novel *Sarrasine*, where Barthes suggests that signifiers partially "escape" their codes during their passage through the text. (We will discuss *S/Z* in detail in Part V.) But Heath also builds on other aspects of Metz' writing which he finds congenial, notably the notion of filmic *écriture* as "displacement." Building on the Derridean–Kristevan critique of the sign, Heath suggests that the systems constructed by the analyst will always be inadequate, always leaving gaps, losses, producing "waste," or in Lancanian terms, **EXCESS**. Heath used the term excess to refer to manifestations of the imaginary within the symbolic which betray or point to the menacing plurality of the subject and more broadly to all aspects of the text not contained by its unifying forces. He also distinguishes between **HOMOGENEITY**, i.e. the unifying forces in the text – what Bakhtin would call the **CENTRIPETAL** forces – and **HETEROGENEITY**, i.e. the forces which disrupt and fragment unity (Bakhtin's "**CENTRIFUGAL** forces"). Mainstream cinema, for Heath, proliferates in examples of "excess": play with the frame line designating an off-screen space which escapes the perspectival organization of the frame, improbable virtuoso camera set-ups, unmotivated camera movements. (We will return to Heath's work in Parts IV and V.)

TEXTUAL ANALYSIS

The publication of *Language and Cinema* was followed by an international deluge of textual analyses of films. These analyses investigated the formal configurations making up textual systems, usually isolating a small number of codes and then tracing their interweavings across the film. Among the more ambitious semiotic textual analyses are Stephen Heath's of *Touch of Evil* (in Heath 1981), Pierre Baudry's of *Intolerance*, Thierry Kuntzel's of *M* (in *Communications* 19, 1972) *Cahier*'s of *Young Mr Lincoln* (in Nichols 1985), and the collective analyses of *Muriel* (see Bailble *et al.* 1974) and *October* (see Lagny *et al.* 1976). Although most of the analyses generated by this wave belonged, broadly speaking, to the general semiotic current, not all of them were based on Metzian categories or assumptions. Historian Pierre Sorlin's textual analyses formed part of a sociological project largely inspired by the work of Pierre Bourdieu and Jean-Claude Passeron. Marie-Claire Ropars-Wuilleumier's extremely intricate analyses of such films as *India Song* and *October* synthesized semiotic insights with a more personal project, partially inspired by Derridean grammatology, concerning filmic "writing." Many textual analyses betrayed the influence of literary critical models, such as Barthes' *S/Z*, while Kristin Thompson's book-length study of *Ivan the Terrible* demonstrates the possibilities of "neo-formalist analysis." Some textual analyses were inspired by Proppian narratological methods – Peter Wollen on *North by Northwest* – or by other theoretical currents. While some analyses sought to construct the system of a single text, others studied specific films as instances of a general code informing cinematic practice. Here, too, the distinction is not always clear, however; Raymond Bellour's analysis of *The Birds* offers both a microcosmic textual analysis of the Bodega Bay sequence of the Hitchcock film and an extrapolation to broader narrative codes shared by a larger body of films – to wit the constitution of the couple as the telos of Hollywood narrative.

TEXTUAL ANALYSIS finds its historical antecedents in biblical exegesis, in hermeneutics and philology, in the French pedagogical method of close reading (*explication de texte*) and in New-Critical "immanent" analysis. What was new, then, in the semiotic approach to textual analysis? First, the semiotic method demonstrated, in comparison with antecedent film criticism, a heightened sensitivity to specifically cinematic formal elements as opposed to elements of character and plot. Second, the analyses were methodologically self-aware; they were at once about their subject – the film in question – and about their own methodology. Each analysis thus became a demonstration model of a possible approach to be extrapolated for other films. Unlike journalistic critics, these analysts saw it as their obligation to cite their own critical and theoretical presuppositions and intertext. (Many analyses began with quasi-ritual invocations of the names of Metz, Barthes, Kristeva or Heath.) Third, these analyses presupposed a radically different approach to studying a film. The analyst had to abstract him/herself from the "regressive" conditions imposed by conventional movie-going. Rather than a single screening, the analyst was expected to analyse the film shot by shot, preferably on a flatbed editing table. (The existence of VCRs has to some extent democratized the practice of close analysis.) Analysts such as Marie-Claire Ropars-Wuilleumier and Michel Marie developed elaborate schemas for notation, registering such codes as angle, camera movement, movement in the shot, off-screen sound and so forth. Finally, these analyses rejected the traditional evaluative terms of film criticism in favor of a new vocabulary drawn from structural linguistics, narratology, psychoanalysis and literary semiotics.

Given the closeness of attention seen as *de rigueur* in such analyses, it became impossible to say everything about a film. As a result, many analyses focussed on isolated segments or fragments of films. Thus Thierry Kuntzel focussed long analyses on especially dense beginnings of films, for example, the opening shots of Fritz Lang's *M* or *King Kong*. Marie-Claire Ropars-Wuilleumier devotes forty pages to the first two minutes of *October*; Thierry Kuntzel devotes fifty-two pages to the first sixty-two shots of *The Most Dangerous Game*. These analyses are also characterized by a sense of relativism. In an intimation of the post-structuralist refusal of mastery, criticism begins to be written in the conditional "might have" mode. The analyst demonstrates awareness that the analysis "might have" been based on other theoretical references, "might have" dealt with a different corpus, "might have" discerned or constructed other "textual systems." The limits of the text, meanwhile, might be defined by the segment (Bellour on *The Birds*, Kuntzel on *King Kong*), by an entire film (Heath on *Touch of Evil*, Bellour on *North by Northwest*), or even by the entire *oeuvre* of a film-maker (René Gardies on Glauber Rocha).

Raymond Bellour combined many of these currents in an ongoing reflexion both on films themselves and on the methodology of their analysis, performing painstaking analyses of a number of Hollywood films. His analysis of *The Birds* explores the textual logic of what Bellour calls an "undetermined fragment" (i.e. one established by the analyst rather than based on a pre-existing code such as the Grand Syntagmatique), in terms of three pertinent codes – the absence or presence of camera movement, framing and point-of-view – in order to reveal the "desire of the film" and the fundamental mechanisms of repetition and variation characteristic of Hitchcockian cinema. Bellour's second analysis, of Howard Hawks' *The Big Sleep*, treats the textual logic of a determined fragment – i.e. one which the film itself isolates as a segment – which despite its apparent banality still serves to advance the text and the constitution of the couple. Bellour's third analysis, of Hitchcock's *North by Northwest*, relates smaller segments such as the "crop dusting sequence" to the scenario as a whole, all in terms of the Oedipal trajectory of the film's male protagonist. Bellour's analysis of *Gigi*, meanwhile, explores the textual logic of the film as a whole, foregrounding the elaborate mirror effects and symmetries operative in the film. The large narrative units, Bellour demonstrates, entertain between themselves highly organized relations of displacement, condensation, resolution, acting on a larger scale the way shots do within a segment. Bellour's analysis of *Marnie* concentrates on the first forty-four shots of that film in order to disengage (1) the "work of the film" in its opening segment, and (2) the inscription of the look in terms of identification in so far as it bears on sexual difference, constituting the woman as an object of the gaze while positing both Hitchcock the enunciator and the spectator as those who look.

Building on aspects of the work of Barthes and Metz, Bellour discerned in the classical film a complex system of repetitions and regulated differences. In "Segmenting/Analyzing," he calls attention to the **RHYMING EFFECTS** frequent in American classical cinema, i.e. the devices that "carry" narrative difference through an ordered network of resemblances, contrasts and unfolding symmetries and assymetries. Bellour called attention to the importance of **REPETITION** in creating what he called **TEXTUAL VOLUME**, the process of repetition and variation whereby the filmic discourse advances thanks to differential increments which repeat codical elements so as to generate both continuity (and thus comprehension) and discontinuity (and thus interest). Repetition, for Bellour, "saturates" narrative space, and operates at both micro and macro levels. Through systems of alternation (e.g. between shots, between syntagmatic units, *mise-en-abyme* constructions), smaller units become mobilized as part of the larger unit of the narrative achieving its resolution. Within the segment, the transition from shot to shot is governed by a process of alternation whereby each match results from the mutual interplay of cinematic codes such as point-of-view and camera angle (the specific subject of Bellour's analysis of *The Birds*). On a macro level, we find a similar play of difference and identity in terms of the interplay of entire segments (the focus of Bellour's analysis of *Gigi*).

Bellour further distinguishes between **EXTERNAL REPETITION (1)**, i.e.

those repetitions inherent in the production process, for example the rehearsal of actors or the multiple takes involved in getting a shot, and **EXTERNAL REPETITION (2)**, i.e. the repeatability or "obstinate textual identity" of the film/text itself, which is, ideally at least, repeated unchanged, but which in fact rarely occurs, due to the variability of screening conditions, or change of medium (films shown on television, for example). **INTERNAL REPETITION (1)** refers to the elementary repetition of the frame itself, usually masked by the projection, but which only becomes visible on an editing table or in certain avant-garde films which privilege the frame. **INTERNAL REPETITION (2)** refers to the alternation or structural opposition of two terms, which develops through the return of either one or both terms according to a process of more or less limited expansion: a/b/a/. a/b/a/b/ and so on. This principle of alternation can then be subdivided according to specific codifications such as point-of-view, framing, and opposition of stasis and movement. This principle, for Bellour, founds the narrative on an ordered return of its elements. **INTERNAL REPETITION (3)** refers to an all-encompassing textual repetition characterized by the fact that its level constantly changes, displaces itself, and is fed by elements drawn from all levels: a gesture, a sound, a frame, a color, a décor, an action, a camera movement, or any of these together. Bellour points to three determinants, the conjunction of which outlines a type of global apparatus by which the classical American cinema reveals itself as a scenography of repetition: micro-repetitions which structure the minor units, the macro-repetition which makes the film both progressive and circular, and positive and negative resolutions which advance or retard the narrative.

Bellour's work on filmic repetition and "rhymes" was obviously inflected by his background in close literary study. In "The **UNATTAINABLE TEXT**," Bellour addresses some of the difficulties in extending literary models to film. Whereas literary criticism emerges from millennia of reflexion, film commentary is of recent date. More important, the film-text, unlike the literary text, is not "quotable." Whereas literature and literary criticism share the same medium – words – film and film analysis do not. While the film medium entails five tracks – image, dialogue, noise, music, written materials – the analysis of the film consists of a single track – words. Critical language is therefore inadequate to its object; the film always escapes the language that attempts to constitute it. Bellour then compares film to other artistic texts in terms of their coefficient of "quotability." The pictorial text is quotable, and can be taken in at a glance. The theatrical text can be rendered as written text, but with a loss of "accent." Bellour then analyzes the relative susceptibility of the five matters of cinematic expression to verbal rendering. Dialogue can be quoted, for example, but with a loss in tone, intensity, timbre, and the simultaneity of bodily and facial expression. In the case of noise, a verbal account is always a translation, a distortion. The image, finally, cannot possibly be rendered in words. Individual frames can be reproduced and quoted, but in stopping the film one loses what is specific to it – movement itself. The text escapes at the very moment one tries to "seize" it. Given this obstacle, the analyst can only try, in "principled despair," to compete with the object he/she is attempting to understand.

FILMIC PUNCTUATION

Apart from grand theorizations, cine-semiology has also devoted itself to more "local" questions having to do with specific codes. In "Punctuation and Demarcation in the Diegetic Film," (in Metz 1971) Metz attempted to clear up some of the confusion concerning the nature of filmic **PUNCTU- ATION**, i.e. those demarcating effects – dissolves, fade-ins and fade-outs, direct cuts – used simultaneously to separate and connect filmic segments. Metz rejects the view that these devices are analogous to punctuation in written language. Since film is not a language-system, their structure is radically different from that of natural languages and therefore involves units of different nature, size and boundaries. The typographical model, on which the notion of filmic "punctuation" is based, is indirectly linked to the structure of natural languages, and as a result there is no equivalent to typographical punctuation in film. What is called punctuation in the diegetic film is in fact a kind of **MACRO-PUNCTUATION**, which intervenes not between shots – which might be seen as the minimal units of the syntagmatic chain of the editing code – but rather between whole syntagmas. These demarcating devices articulate the large segments which form the diegesis of the narrative film. Their special status derives from the fact that they are not analogical signs and therefore do not directly represent any object or set of objects. Yet the spectator accepts them "as if" they formed part of the diegetic "universe" and thus are indirectly linked to analogical representation. Devices such as the lap-dissolve foreground the essential unreality of filmic representation, since they represent nothing yet are transformed by the desiring spectator into the "imaginary" of the diegesis.

Since the cinema does have devices which function as macro-punctuation, the problem arises of differentiating between the diverse types, between those, for example, which connect two individual shots and those which articulate entire segments. Markedly visible punctuation effects, for Metz, are optional, since the film-maker can also choose the "straight cut" or "zero-degree" of enunciation. In *Rosemary's Baby*, the passage from one segment to another is frequently marked only by a shot dramatically closer in scale, one which provokes questions in the spectator's mind – What object is this? Where is it? Why is it being foregrounded here? In short, it is only the overall diegetic coherence that retroactively allows us to

57

recognize the sudden close-up as a variation on a punctuating effect. The straight cut, meanwhile, avoids all markers of transition from segment to segment. It stands in paradigmatic relation to the other visible optical effects, but is evidenced, paradoxically, only by the *refusal* of marks of punctuation.

Some optical effects, furthermore, do not function as macro-punctuation. Certain lap-dissolves function as the filmic equivalents of Genette's **ITERAT-IVE** – i.e. they denote duration of repeated actions, as in the cinematic evocation of a woman's fruitless search for employment in Marcel Hanoun's *Une Simple Histoire*, in which successive lap-dissolves suggest the frustration of repetition. In Hitchcock's *Vertigo*, repeated lap-dissolves denote a semi-oneiric state, and in Chris Marker's *La Jetée*, the lap-dissolves generate ersatz movement in a film consisting almost entirely of still photographs. In all these cases, the lap-dissolves do not demarcate distinct segements of the diegesis but operate strictly within one of them. Other "unorthodox" uses of optical devices would include the "jump-cut" lap-dissolves within Antoine's interview with the psychologist in Truffaut's *400 Blows*, or the fade-ins and fade-outs which intervene between the individual shots that compose the initial lovemaking sequence in Godard's *A Married Woman*. In such cases the optical devices mark a mini-autonomy within a larger segment while simultaneously rendering it more formally coherent and homogeneous.

Metz speaks of the punctuating "functions" of certain cinematic signifiers which themselves have no intrinsic signifieds apart from that given them by a specific text. When a lap-dissolve separates two segments, it functions as a punctuating device; when it smooths over distinct moments within a larger segment evoking duration, it functions differently. In the classical fiction film, the lap-dissolve generally marks a temporal ellipsis, but it can also vary in function, since its function is also determined by the structure of the filmic chain as well as by other diegetic factors. Although punctuating devices "carry" no intrinsic signified, then, we can speak of certain connotative tendencies in their signification. The dissolve tends to emphasize transition, while the fade-out emphasizes separation; the former carries us from one place and time to another, while the latter provides time for contemplation.

In the classical film, especially those of the silent period, iris-ins and iris-outs were used either to isolate a specific portion of the frame or as equivalents to fade-ins or fade-outs. With the advent of the French New Wave, iris-ins and iris-outs became a virtuoso stylistic effect connoting "archaic film style," as in Godard's *Breathless* and in Truffaut's *Two English-women*. Iris-ins and iris-outs, along with wipes, also form part of Tony Richardson's adaptation of Fielding's *Tom Jones*; here too they connote the archaic, as well as being a reflexive attempt to analogize the aesthetic procedures of the eighteenth-century "self-conscious" novel.

Metz returns to the subject of punctuation in his article "Metaphor/ Metonymy" (Metz 1981). Whereas Jakobson sees montage as metonymic and dissolves as metaphoric, Metz finds it more precise to see both as syntagmatic. Both lap-dissolves and superimpositions are syntagmatic, but with superimposition the syntagmatic is simultaneous while with lap-dissolve it is consecutive but with a moment of simultaneity. In a later passage, Metz returns to the question of the lap-dissolve, this time in the contexts of condensation/displacement and primary/secondary process. In the lap-dissolve, Metz suggests, the film exhibits, almost in a pure state, the process of its own textual advancement. The lap-dissolve foregrounds the passage from one image to another in such a way as to suggest a quasi-metalinguistic commentary on the very fact of this displacement. By hesitating on the threshold of a textual bifurcation – the passage from shot to shot – the lap-dissolve can be seen as offering an emblem of film's constant process of contiguous weaving of shots. Condensation, meanwhile, is present in the ephemeral co-presence of two images on the screen, in the brief moment in which they are mutually indiscernible. A lap-dissolve is not a "nascent figure" but a "dying figure," in which two images "run toward" each other and then "turn their back" to each other; condensation is begun, but through a process of progressive "extinction." (Metz' evocations of these operations are themselves highly metaphoric.)

THE SEMIOTICS OF FILMIC SOUND

Metz' definition of the cinema's matter of expression as consisting of five tracks – image, dialogue, noise, music, written materials – served to call attention to the soundtrack and thus to undercut the formulaic view of the cinema as an "essentially visual" medium which was "seen" (not heard) by "spectators" (not auditors). (Rick Altman [1980] traces this privileging to the assumption that a medium's earliest forms are also its most essential forms.) Many specifically cinematic analyses have focussed on the theorization and analysis of sound, a shift in interest reinforced by the technological evolution of the medium (Dolby, multi-track sound) and by sound experimentation by both avant-garde (Duras, Godard, Robbe-Grillet) and mainstream directors (Altman, Scorsese, Coppola). Explicitly indebted to semiotics, this work – by analysts such as Daniel Percheron, Michel Marie, John Belton, Mary Ann Doane, Alan Williams, Rick Altman, David Bordwell, Kaja Silverman, Elizabeth Weis, Claudia Gorbman, Maire-Claire Ropars-Wuilleumier, Francis Vanoye and Michel Chion – gave to the soundtrack the kind of precise attention previously only dedicated to the image track. Theorists such as Rick Altman, Tom Levin and others theorized the differences between the imagistic and the acoustic analogon in terms of the relation between "original" and "copy." The reproduction of sound, they pointed out, involves no dimensional loss – both original

59

and copy involve mechanical radiant energy transmitted by pressure waves in the air; thus we perceive sound as three-dimensional. For Mary Ann Doane, the cinematic situation deploys **THREE AUDITORY SPACES**: the space of the diegesis, the space of the screen, and the acoustical space of the theatre or auditorium. At the same time, these theorists point out, it is a mistake to see acoustic sound as unmediated, uncoded, non-conventional.

Feminist currents have also inflected the theorization of the sound. Many feminist analysts, such as Joan Copjec and Marie-Claire Ropars-Wuilleumier, have focussed on the films of Marguerite Duras as a film-maker who constantly foregrounds the voice. Feminist discourse often contrasts the voice as fluid and continuous expression with the rigidity and discontinuity of writing. The voice, in this sense, is seen as a free space to be reconquered. Kristeva especially speaks of a pre-languaged vocal freedom, close to the marvelous original language of the mother, a language which would be incarnated purely in the form of voice. Luce Irigaray claims that patriarchal culture has a heavier investment in seeing than in hearing. Mary Ann Doane, for her part, points out that the use of the voice in the cinema appeals to what Lacan calls the **INVOCATORY DRIVE** (*la pulsion invocatrice*), that is, the desire to hear. At the same time she warns against any feminist idealization of the voice, since the voice, in psychoanalysis, is also the instrument of interdiction, of the patriarchal order; the voice, therefore, can provide "no isolated haven within patriarchy."

The notion of the "diegesis" as the posited world of the film's fiction also facilitated a more sophisticated analysis of the diverse possible relationships between the soundtrack and the diegesis. In the case of verbal dialogue within film, for example, Metz distinguished between **FULLY DIEGETIC SPEECH** (that spoken by characters as voices in the fiction), **NON-DIEGETIC SPEECH** (commentary "off" by an anonymous speaker), and **SEMI-DIEGETIC SPEECH** (voice-over commentary by one of the characters of the action). Daniel Percheron distinguished between films with an **UNMARKED DIEGESIS**, i.e. films which dissemble the narrative activity, and those, such as *Jules and Jim*, with a **MARKED DIEGESIS,** i.e. films which foreground the act of narration. David Bordwell and Kristin Thompson distinguish between **SIMPLE DIEGETIC SOUND**, i.e. sound represented as emerging from a source within the story, and temporally simultaneous with the image it accompanies, **EXTERNAL DIEGETIC SOUND**, i.e. sound represented as coming from a physical source within the story space and which we assume the characters to be aware of, **INTERNAL DIEGETIC SOUND**, i.e. sound represented as emerging from the mind of a character within the story space of which we as spectators are aware but of which the other characters are presumably not aware, **DISPLACED DIEGETIC SOUND**, i.e. sound which originates in the represented space of the story but which evokes a time anterior or posterior to that of the images with which it is juxtaposed, and

NON-DIEGETIC SOUND, for example, mood music or the voice of a narrator represented as being outside the space of the narrative. The tripartite division of the soundtrack into phonetic sound (dialogue), music, and noise, drawn from the vocabulary of film-making practice, is hardly adequate to the analysis of the audio-visual logic of the represented world of the film. Music, for example, is open to any number of possible permutations, deployed along a wide spectrum from total diegetization to dediegetization. Totally diegetic music would involve instances where the music is diegetic, on-screen and sung in synch: for example Ronee Blakley, recorded direct, singing "Daddy" in *Nashville*. At the other end of the spectrum, music can be non-diegetic, i.e. purely commentative, as in the case of the orchestral music of "Try a Little Tenderness" superimposed on shots of B-52s in flight in Stanley Kubrick's *Doctor Strangelove*. At times a director can play with audience expectations, as when the diegetic status of a given piece of music is temporarily obscured for comic or reflexive effect. Thus Woody Allen, in *Bananas*, underlines his protagonist's happiness at receiving a presidential invitation by providing harp music, which we assume to be commentative until he opens the door of a closet and uncovers a harpist at work. **PROGRESSIVE DIEGETICIZATION** refers to the process by which music first presented as non-diegetic comes, by the end of the film, to function diegetically. The theme music from Grieg in Fritz Lang's *M*, for example, begins as non-diegetic – as accompaniment to the credits – but is diegetized when it is whistled in conjunction with the killer (Peter Lorre), then whistled again by the blind man who identifies the murderer.

Among the most acute analysts of filmic sound is Michel Chion, who has explored the subject in three volumes: *La Voix au Cinema, Le Son au Cinema*, and *La Toile Trouée*. Filmic sound, for Chion, is multi-track, and has diverse origins. The synchronous voice in the cinema, for Chion, can be traced back to the theater; film music derives from opera; and voice-over commentary goes back to commented-on projections such as magic lantern shows. For Chion, both film practice and film theory/criticism are characterized by **VOCOCENTRISM**, i.e. the tendency on the part of both film-makers and critics to privilege the voice *vis-à-vis* the other soundtracks (music and noise). The film-makers' practice of aiming the camera toward speaking personages is "echoed," as it were, by a parallel privileging of spoken dialogue on the part of film analysts. In the classical cinema, especially, all the phases of the sound production process are subordinated to the goal of showcasing the human voice and making it audible and comprehensible; other sounds (music, noise) are subordinated both to the dialogue and to the image.

Chion borrows from Pierre Schaeffer (1966) the word **ACOUSMATIC** to refer to those sounds which one hears without seeing their source, a situation Schaeffer sees as typical of a media-saturated environment where we constantly hear the sounds of radio, telephone, records, without seeing

61

the literal sources of the sounds. The term also evokes highly personal intra-familial associations. The voice of the mother for the child still within the womb is strangely acousmatic. (Kaja Silverman argues in *The Acoustic Mirror* that Chion's analysis is limited by its subservience to existing gender demarcations, placing the female subject on the side of spectacle, castration and synchronization, and her male counterpart on the side of the gaze, the phallus and what exceeds synchronization (Silverman 1988: 50).) Within the history of religion, the term had another meaning, referring to the voice belonging to a divine Entity which mere mortals were forbidden to see. The acousmatic voice, Chion suggests, provokes a certain fear because of four of its capacities: to be everywhere (ubiquity), to see everything (panopticism), to know everything (omniscience), and to do everything (omnipotence). Hal the Computer, in *2001: A Space Odyssey*, by being omnipresent in the spaceship, illustrates the capacity of the acousmatic voice to be everywhere. The voice of Mabuse in Lang's film *Dr Mabuse* illustrates its capacity to see everything, gradually accumulating all possible powers by passing itself off as the voice of another, by becoming the voice of a dead man, becoming a pre-recorded mechanical voice, etc. The confident voice-over narration of the canonical documentary illustrates its capacity to know everything. The voice of the Wizard in *The Wizard of Oz*, finally, evokes the voice as all-knowing and all-seeing, although the film also culminates in an ironic **DE-ACOUSMATICIZATION**, i.e. the process by which a bodiless voice is finally given a body, as the Grand Oz is discovered behind the curtain.

While analysts have spent considerable energy on the clarification of issues concerning point-of-view, they have paid little attention to what Chion calls **POINT-OF-HEARING** (*point d'écoute*), i.e. the positioning of sound both in terms of placement during the production, placement within the diegesis and in terms of the apprehension of that placement on the part of the spectator. Often there is no strict coincidence between aural and visual point-of-view/hearing, as in the countless cases where distant human figures are heard as if in close-up, or as in the musical, where visual scale and distance change, but where the recording maintains a constant (ideal) level of fidelity and proximity. Dialogue, in the classical film, is meant to be understood, even at the sacrifice of consistency in terms of point-of-view/point-of-hearing. Filmic telephone conversations often allow us to hear either one of the interlocutors – and thus remain restricted to that person's point-of-hearing – or both, making us an "observer" of both ends of the conversation. Chion also speaks of **AURAL MASKING EFFECTS**, analogous to visual masking effects, whereby a sudden noise – a storm, a wind, a passing train or airplane – strategically blocks out part of the soundtrack. Chion also cites examples of **AURAL POINT-OF-VIEW** as in Abel Gance's *Un Grand Amour de Beethoven*, where the director makes us empathize with the composer's growing deafness by depriving us of the sounds engendered by the visual objects and activities on the screen. Such effects always work in tandem with and not independently of the image; close-shots of the composer "anchor" our impression that the aural effects evoke the protagonist's handicap.

Film semioticians have also brought increased precision to the question of the emotional tonality of music in relation to the action and the diegesis. Prior analysts tended to distinguish only between **REDUNDANT MUSIC** – i.e. music which simply reinforces the emotional tone of the sequence – and **CONTRAPUNTAL MUSIC** – i.e. music which "goes against" the emotional dominant of the sequence. But Chion distinguishes between three possible attitudes on the part of the music track: **EMPATHETIC MUSIC**, which participates in and conveys the emotions of the characters; **A-EMPATHETIC MUSIC**, which displays an apparent indifference toward dramatically intense incidents, simply pursuing its rather mechanical course, providing a distanced perspective on the individual dramas of the diegesis; and **DIDACTIC CONTRAPUNTAL MUSIC**, which deploys music in a distanciated manner in order to elicit a precise, usually ironic, idea in the spectator's mind.

LANGUAGE IN THE CINEMA

The question of the relations between film and language was seen in a very partial and limited manner by the pioneer film semiologists. The discussion has tended to focus on one or two questions – Is film a language system? A language? Like a language? But in fact questions having to do with film and language, and the potential contribution of linguistically inflected methods, are infinitely more diverse. Does film syntax function in ways analogous to verbal language? Do we know the world through language, and if so, how does this fact inflect the cinematic experience? What is the link between the broad intertext of verbal recounting and the conventional modalities of filmic recounting? What role does language, in its diverse forms, play in film? How does language itself "enter" film? How does the fact of cinema's involvement with a variety of languages impinge on film as a discursive practice? (Those who dismiss all language-based discussion of the cinema tend to collapse all these questions.) Imagining this range of questions suggests that first-phase cine-semiology was both too linguistic – i.e. too constrained by the Saussurean model – and not linguistic enough. If we scrutinize the cinema as a multi-leveled discursive practice, and not just as a signifying language, we can see cinema and language as even more thoroughly imbricated than cine-semiology managed to suggest.

Take, for example, the issue of exactly where and how language "enters" the cinema. In *Language and Cinema*, Metz stresses the linguistic character of two of the five tracks – recorded phonetic sound and written materials within the image. In "The Perceived and the Named" (in Metz 1977),

Metz points to the linguistic presence even in the image track. The codes of **ICONIC RECOGNITION** – the codes by which we recognize objects – and of **ICONIC DESIGNATION** – the codes by which we name them – structure and inform spectatorial vision, thus bringing language, as it were, "to" the image. This infiltration of the iconic by the symbolic, to use Peircean terminology, takes many forms. Verbal discourse structures the very formation of images. Boris Eikhenbaum, as we have seen, viewed film metaphors as parasitic on verbal metaphor, speaking of "image translations of linguistic tropes," while Paul Willemen, elaborating on Eikhenbaum, speaks of **LITERALISMS**, i.e. filmic instances in which the visual impact of a shot derives from strict fidelity to a linguistic metaphor, for example, the way camera angle might literalize specific locutions such as "look up to" or "oversee" or "look down on" (*Screen* 15, Winter 1974–5). Hitchcock's films constantly highlight the interface of word and image, at times structuring sequences and even entire films "through" linguistic formulations. *The Wrong Man* (1957) is informed in its entirety by the quibbling sentence: "Manny plays the bass." He plays the bass, quite literally, in the Stork Club, but he also plays the role of the *base* when he is falsely accused and forced to mimic the actions of the real thief. The overture sequence of *Strangers on a Train* (1951), as a number of commentators have pointed out, orchestrates an elaborate verbal and visual play on the expressions "criss-cross" and "double-cross" (crossed railroad tracks, crossed legs, crossed tennis racquets, tennis doubles, double scotches, alternating montage as double, lap-dissolve as a criss-cross of images and so forth). Hitchcock's cameo appearance, significantly, shows him carrying a double bass, in a film featuring two *doppelgänger* characters each, in his way, "base."

Language, at least potentially, exerts pressure on *all* the filmic tracks. The music and noise tracks, for example, can embrace linguistic elements. Recorded music is often accompanied by lyrics, and even when not so accompanied, can evoke lyrics. The purely instrumental version of "Melancholy Baby" in Lang's *Scarlet Street* (1945) elicits in the spectator the mental presence of the words of that song. Even apart from lyrics, the allegedly abstract art of music is permeated with semantic values. Musicologist J. J. Nattiez (1975), for example, sees music as embedded in social discourses, including verbal discourses. Nor are recorded noises necessarily "innocent" of language. Setting aside the question of the cultural relativity of the boundaries separating noise from music from language – one culture's "noise" may be another culture's "language," as in the case of African talking drums – we discover the frequent imbrication of noise and language in countless films. The stylized murmur of conversing voices in classical Hollywood restaurant sequences renders human speech as background noise, while Jacques Tati films give voice to an international esperanto of aural effects – vacuum cleaners that wheeze and vinyl seats that go "pooof" – characteristic of the postmodernist environment.[4]

64

Even when verbal language is absent from both film and movie theater, semantic processes take place in the mind of the spectator through what the Russian Formalists called "**INNER SPEECH**," the pulse of thought implicated in language. Film viewing, according to Boris Eikhenbaum, is accompanied by a constant process of internal speech, whereby images and sounds are projected onto a kind of verbal screen which functions as a constant ground for meaning, and the "glue" between shots and sequences. In the 1970s and 1980s, the journal *Screen* published a series of essays both by and about Eikhenbaum's theories of inner speech. Paul Willemen (*Screen* 15, Winter 1974–5) saw the notion of inner speech as potentially filling a gap in Metz' theories by demonstrating the linguistic nature of meaning and consciousness, as well as the link to psychoanalysis, since the condensations and distortions of inner speech were closely akin to the mechanisms explored by psychoanalysis. Willemen went on to evoke the possibility of a specifically cinematic kind of inner speech essential to the construction and understanding of films. Since this inner speech is language-specific, the filmic images are often grounded in the tropes of specific languages. Much of the discussion in the 1970s centered on the meaning of inner speech for the filmic work and theory of Eisenstein. David Bordwell (*Screen* 15, Winter 1974–5 and *Screen* 16, Spring 1975) argued that Eisenstein's work in the mid–1930s was partially designed to engender a spectatorial inner speech conceived as sensuous and pre-logical and, ultimately, private. Eisenstein's view of inner speech, for Bordwell, involves a "non-verbal psychic associationism underlying all behavior, including language." Ben Brewster (*Screen* 15, Winter 1974–5), in response, argued that Eisenstein's vision of inner speech is neither private nor constitutively pre-verbal but rather involves a psychic process rooted in everyday social language.

BEYOND SAUSSURE

Our discussion so far has privileged certain current within the broader movement of semiotics – Russian Formalism, the Bakhtin Circle, Prague structuralism, Saussurean semiology and its prolongations and, to a lesser extent, the American Peircean semiotic tradition. We have neglected, for reasons of space, a number of other important traditions. First, the application of Peircean "pragmatist" semiotics to the cinema has not been limited to the explication and extrapolation of Peirce's trichotomy of icon, index and symbol. Peirce's ideas have been taken up with interest by Kaja Silverman, Teresa de Lauretis, Gilles Deleuze and Julia Kristeva. Gilles Deleuze in *Image/Movement*, especially, deploys Peirce, in conjunction with Bergson, in a defiantly non-linguistic manner, reproaching Metzian semiotics for displacing interest from the visual and auditory material to signs and syntagmas. Deleuze proposes instead to study the plenitude of a nonsignifying image and all the dispersed and moving figures of which the cinema is capable. Second, a strong semiotic movement has operated in the Soviet Union, one drawing strength from Russian Formalism, the Bakhtin School, and from Prague structuralism – a movement centered especially in Moscow and Tartu (Estonia). Soviet scholars, some direct heirs of the Formalist movement, have made strong contributions in the area of what they call "secondary modelling systems." In this perspective, natural language is a **PRIMARY MODELLING SYSTEM**, i.e. a grid which shapes our apprehension of the world, while artistic languages constitute **SECONDARY MODELLING SYSTEMS**, i.e. apparatuses, existing at a higher level of abstraction, through which the artist perceives the world and which model the world for the artist. The Tartu group treats language, myth and other cultural phenomena as closely interrelated models of meaning, and tries to draw up cultural typologies on the basis of norms, rules and typical signs. In *Semiotics of Cinema*, Jurij Lotman, the most active and representative of this school, discusses cinema both as language and as secondary modeling system, while trying to integrate the analysis of cinema into a broader cultural theory.

There have also been attempts to apply Noam Chomsky's transformational linguistic models to the cinema. Chomsky's **GENERATIVE GRAMMAR** is concerned with the speaker's capacity both to generate and to understand "new" sentences. Rather than restrict itself to **SURFACE STRUCTURES**, i.e. the syntactic organization of the sentence as it occurs in speech, it seeks the **DEEP STRUCTURES**, i.e. the fundamental mechanisms of language, the grammar or underlying logic, which make possible the engendering of an infinity of grammatical sentences. This grammar has a **SYNTACTIC DIMENSION** – the system of rules determining which sentences are allowable in a language, a **SEMANTIC** dimension, the rules defining the interpretation of the sentences generated, and a **PHONOLOGICAL/PHONETIC DIMENSION**, a system of rules organizing the sequence of sounds used to generate sentences. Extended to the study of the film-text, generative semiology studies the rules which guarantee the coherence and the progression of a film. It asks such questions as: What are the operative rules which render a series of shots "readable?" Is it possible to compare these rules to those of natural language? The major American proponent of a transformationalist approach to the cinema has been John M. Carroll. In "A Program for Film Theory" (1977) Carroll argues that cinema does indeed have a grammar, that its "deep structure" consists of events while its "surface structure" consists of actualized film sequences, felt by ordinary viewers to be "grammatical" or "ungrammatical." Carroll's reliance on Chomsky's early work, especially *Syntactic Structures* (1957), leads him to privilege, the syntactic over the semantic, an option which makes it difficult to account for the enormous differences of signification of syntactically similar sequences. Carroll's normative view has the effect, moreover, of

66

naturalizing and universalizing one historically bound set of film practices – those of dominant cinema.

Michel Colin's *Langue, Film, Discours: Prolégomènes à une Sémiologie Générative du Film* (1985) constitutes a much more subtle and ambitious attempt to think through the possibilities of transformationalist models for the cinema. Unlike Carroll, Colin builds on Chomsky's later work in order to compare its productivity to that of non-transformationalist approaches. Rather than look for exact equivalents between film and natural language, or for merely metaphorical analogies between film and transformational grammar, Colin emphasizes the concrete processes of transformation (for example addition, effacement) and the structures common to the filmic and the verbal utterance. He seeks, therefore, the deep structures undergirding both filmic and linguistic utterances. Colin's object, then, is less film itself than grammar, the set of rules which make possible both the production and the comprehension of filmic statements. Colin suggests that all statements, whether linguistic or filmic, entail both given knowledge and new knowledge. Colin distinguishes between **THEME**, as the nominal syntagma at the head of an utterance, and **RHEME**, the element at the tail of an utterance. The question of knowledge leads Colin to move from the level of individual utterance to the level of discursive context. Utterances form part of discourse as a succession of utterances generated and received by a sociocultural community accustomed to seeing films, i.e. equipped with cinematic **COMPETENCE**, the capacity to generate or understand linguistic/filmic utterances. Filmic and linguistic competence, for Colin, are homological, in that the spectator, to understand filmic configurations, deploys the mechanisms already internalized in relation to language. In an intricate argument impossible to summarize here, Colin uses theme/rheme distinctions in an attempt to demonstrate the superiority of a generative model for dealing with specific filmic figures such as the single-shot sequence and shot/reverse shot. He also attempts to synthesize transformational theory with Marxist-inflected theories (especially those of Michel Pêcheux) of the social production of meaning. Ultimately, Colin is less interested in developing a semiotics of the cinema than in imagining how the analysis of film might contribute to a general transformationalist theory of discourse.

NOTES

1 Language-related citations from Canudo and Delluc can be found in a number of classical anthologies: Marcel Lapierre, *Anthologie du Cinéma* (Paris: La Nouvelle Edition, 1946); Marcel L'Herbier, *Intelligence du Cinématographe* (Paris: Ed. Correa, 1946) and Pierre L'Herminier, *L'Art du Cinéma* (Paris: Seghers, 1960).

2 See, for example, Bela Balazs, *Theory of the Film: Character and Growth of a New Art* (New York: Arno Press, 1972).

3 See Christian Metz, *Language and Cinema* (Hague: Mouton, 1974). An egregiously

inept translation turned Metz' already difficult text into an unreadable monstrosity. Two of Metz' key terms – *langue* and *langage* – were more or less systematically mistranslated into their opposites, thus transforming much of the book into nonsense.

4 For more on language in the cinema, see Ella Shohat and Robert Stam, "The Cinema after Babel: Language, Difference, Power," *Screen*, 26 (3–4) (May-August 1985), and Robert Stam, *Subversive Pleasures: Bakhtin, Cultural Criticism and Film* (Baltimore: Johns Hopkins, 1989).

III

FILM-NARRATOLOGY

THE SEMIOTICS OF NARRATIVE

The narrative analysis of film is the most recent branch of semiotic inquiry to emerge from the critical initiatives which redefined film theory in the 1970s. Although it has developed its own terminology and modes of investigation, its roots clearly lie in the major semiotic movements of our time. Film narrative theory draws its basic concepts from the two primary sources of semiotic thought: structuralism and Russian Formalism. This dual influence is reflected in the questions film narrative theory asks of the text, including the attempt to designate the basic structures of story processes and to define the aesthetic languages unique to film narrative discourse. Like all semiotic inquiry, narrative analysis seeks to peel away the seemingly "motivated" and "natural" relationship between the signifier and the story-world in order to reveal the deeper system of cultural associations and relationships that are expressed through narrative form. Viewed through the prism of semiotic methodology, the conventional elements of narrative structure – characters, plot patterning, setting, point-of-view and temporality – can be regarded as systems of signs which are structured and organized according to different codes. Each of these signs communicates highly specific messages which relate to the story-world in diverse ways.

The question of what constitutes a narrative has been considered by a number of theorists. The following definition synthesizes the work of many writers: **NARRATIVE** can be understood as the recounting of two or more events (or a situation and an event) that are logically connected, occur over time, and are linked by a consistent subject into a whole. Different theorists emphasize different aspects of this definition. Gerald Prince, for one, focusses on the conjunction of events and on the fact that narrative involves a recounting (1987: 58); A. J. Greimas, on the other hand, emphasizes the orientation towards a goal, and therefore a sense of closure and wholeness, as a crucial determinant of narrative (Greimas 1965); while Shlomith Rimmon-Kenan stresses the temporal nature of narrative: "tem-

69

poral succession is sufficient as a minimal requirement for a group of events to form a story . . . causality can often (always?) be projected onto temporality" (Rimmon-Kenan 1983: 19). Prince makes the valuable point that narrative is a kind of knowledge: etymologically derived from the Latin *gnarus* or "knowing," narrative is a way of coming to grips with the meaning of events, of perceiving the transformative effects of an action, and of grasping the role of time in human affairs:

> It does not simply mirror what happens; it explores and devises what can happen. It does not merely recount changes of state, it constitutes and interprets them as signifying parts of signifying wholes. . . . Most crucially, perhaps . . . by discovering meaningful designs in temporal series . . . narrative deciphers time . . . and illuminates temporality and humans as temporal beings.
>
> (Prince 1987: 60)

The study of narrative structures and the activity of narrative comprehension is the subject of **NARRATIVE ANALYSIS**. Narrative analysis focusses on the interaction of the various strata of the narrative work, distinguishing such elements as story outline and plot structure, the spheres of action commanded by different characters, the way narrative information is channeled and controlled through point-of-view, and the relationship of the narrator to the inhabitants and events of the story-world. The canonical versions of narrative analysis deal with the structural characteristics or regularities that all narrative forms have in common, regardless of medium. Narrative analysis also specifies the ways in which actual narratives differ from one another. The term **NARRATOLOGY**, introduced by Tzvetan Todorov, has in recent years become the formal name for narrative analysis, although for some writers it has a more specific meaning, relating strictly to the structuralist study of narrative or to the subcategories of tense, mood and voice (defined later in Part III).

What follows is a summary of the existing state of knowledge in what might be called the tradition of formal analysis of narrative. Recently, theorists have developed ideological critiques of certain cultural features of narrative form, for example, its mechanisms of closure and its privileging of the male point-of-view and male patterns of agency. While this part discusses these ideas at specific points, the most significant criticisms of narrative from an ideological perspective have been developed in psychoanalytic approaches to film, and are discussed at greater length in Part IV.

FILM AS A NARRATIVE ART: FORMALIST APPROACHES

One of the founding principles of narrative analysis is the distinction introduced by the Russian Formalists between the fabula and the syuzhet.

In Victor Shklovsky's original formulation, the **FABULA**, sometimes translated as story, is understood as the "pattern of relationships between characters and the pattern of actions as they unfold in chronological order" (in Eagle 1981: 17). Later writers have expanded on this definition to emphasize the events of the fabula as a cause and effect chain occurring in time and space: "A fabula is a series of logically and chronologically related events that are caused or experienced by actors. . . . Events, actors, time and location together constitute the material of a fabula" (Bal 1985: 5, 7). It is usually understood as the raw material or basic outline of the story, prior to its artistic organization. Another way of understanding it is to view the fabula as an imaginary construct which the viewer or reader creates or abstracts from the various cues and evidence provided by the narrative: "Presented with two narrative events, we look for causal or spatial or temporal links. The imaginary construct we create, progressively and retroactively, was termed by Formalists the fabula" (Bordwell 1985: 49). Other writers, however, such as Rimmon-Kenan and Seymour Chatman, have stressed the structured nature of the fabula, focussing on the network of internal relations, the "immanent story structure" formed within it.

This immanent story structure or set of inferences is complicated and expanded in the **SYUZHET**, which can be understood as the artistic organization, or "deformation," of the causal-chronological order of events. The syuzhet is often translated as **PLOT**; in the syuzhet, the basic armature of fabula events is refashioned into an aesthetically satisfying form through the use of artistic devices such as *in medias res* construction, retardation, parallel plots, ellipsis, and others. Central to Shklovsky's concept of the syuzhet was the Formalist notion of defamiliarization. The basic, rudimentary pattern of the fabula was seen as the "familiar" order of occurrences, "each event coming in the order in which it would occur in real life and the events bound to each other in a cause and effect relationship" (Lemon and Reis 1965: 25). The elaborate, artistic pattern of the syuzhet, on the other hand, took shape through the foregrounding of artistic devices, which caused the defamiliarization or distortion of the fabula. There are many techniques for deforming the fabula, but all involve some kind of "disarrangement" of the chronological sequence of events, creating gaps, retarding the flow of information or conveying the same information several times over from a variety of different perspectives.

Although primarily concerned with literature, the Formalists applied these categories in their discussions of film narrative, which were assembled in a volume called *Poetica Kino* in 1927. Here, an intriguing problem concerning the category of the syuzhet in film presented itself from the outset. A central issue of two of the articles in this volume – the essay by Shklovsky, "Poetry and Prose in Cinematography," and the text by Juri Tynianov, "On The Foundations of Cinema" – was the relation between fabula, syuzhet and style in film. This debate took shape around the question of fundamental structures: is the fabula, understood as a linked sequence of actions, the irreducible core of narrative structure? Or is film narrative rather defined by stylistic manipulations of space and time? In other words, can a narrative proceed on the basis of stylistic variation rather than by way of story actions? At the center of this debate was the encompassing category of the syuzhet – the artistic organization of the story into a plot. The Formalists held two different conceptions of the syuzhet. Certain writers argued that the syuzhet was integrally related to the fabula, to the level of story actions, while the other approach maintained that the syuzhet was largely responsive to and controlled by style, the stylistic features unique to the medium. Boris Eikhenbaum, for one, felt that although film narrative proceeded through syntagmatic linkages, which were rendered through montage (a form of style), it was ultimately grounded in the narrative syntax of actions and events. Juri Tynianov, on the other hand, argued that style, the stylistic relationships between shots, could serve as the fundamental principle of linkage, operating, in some cases, as the "principal mover of the plot" (Eagle 1981: 97). In Jan Mukarovsky's supporting argument, style – the spatial and temporal structures of film – was held to supply a sufficient syntagmatic framework for the articulation of a narrative without a story, without characters and actions (Eagle 1981: 42).

Shklovsky's original definition of the fabula implied that the level of story actions comprises the raw material of the narrative work, functioning as a kind of pre-existing schema or core structure. It is this concept in Shklovsky that Tynianov sought to refine by insisting that the fabula is a construct, a projection by the spectator or reader who in "searching for the story" relies on the cues or indicators provided by the semantic or stylistic "basting" of the action. For Tynianov, the most advanced works almost wholly dispense with the fabula; a poetic cinema, according to Tynianov, unfolds on the basis of syuzhet patterning and formal variations – in F. W. Galan's paraphrase of Tynianov, "poetic film is story-less film" which does not rely upon the "theater," the register of dramatic actions and characters (Galan 1984: 99). Tynianov argued that film is closer to verse than to prose, and used verse forms as his principal analogies: he wrote, for example, that "the 'jumping' nature of cinema, the role of shot unity in it, the semantic transformation of everyday objects (words in verse, things in cinema) – all of these bring cinema and verse together" (in Eagle 1981: 94). Shots do not unfold in succession, Tynianov maintained, but rather replace one another – the distinction between shots could be compared to the separate lines in a poem. Shots infect one another, color one another on the purely formal level, he argued, a level not necessarily tied to story articulation. Films with a maximum of syuzhet patterning, or stylistic dominance, for Tynianov, were those that were least dependent on or related to story categories; films that had a minimum of syuzhet patterning were those that slavishly followed the fabula, and hence were least interesting.

Shklovsky, on the other hand, appeared to link film less to verse than to prose, and hence emphasized the strong link between the syuzhet and the level of story, or fabula. But where Tynianov's argument was very one-sided, Shklovsky seemed willing to countenance both sides of the question. He wrote that the emphasis in films on either formal resolutions or story actions could define the difference between film genres. Charlie Chaplin's *Woman of Paris*, for example, can be likened to a prose work, for its transactions, developments and resolution are based on story actions rather than on formal patterning. Dziga Vertov's *The Sixth Part of the Earth*, in contrast, unfolds entirely on the basis of formal oppositions, repetitions and parallelisms, and has a "verse-like resolution." This film was celebrated by the Formalists precisely for its freedom from "the convention of narrative linkage and the illusion of a linear progression of time" (in Eagle 1981: 146). The film *Mother*, by Vsevolod Pudovkin, incorporates elements of both, in Shklovsky's view, beginning with a prose-like exposition and development, but ending, by way of repetition of certain images, "as a purely formal poetry" (in Galan 1984: 99). In other passages of this short article, Shklovsky mentions that the analogy of film to verse is "curious" and "loose," perhaps, as Galan suggests, to correct the imbalance of Tynianov's preference for "story-less" films (Galan 1984: 99).

Eikhenbaum also believed that filmic construction followed the principles of narrative prose, and was tied to plot, action and character. Eikhenbaum focussed on the **FILM PHRASE** – the basic editing schemas that carved out the action in successive bits and pieces, as in the interaction of establishing shot, medium shot and close-up. He also stressed the role of style in complicating the story: film space and film time were explicitly related to the story, in Eikhenbaum's view, but were not subordinate to it. In many ways the Formalists' positions on this matter reflect their individual preferences for avant-garde or "classical" films, with Tynianov clearly supporting an experimental cinema, while Eikhenbaum favored a classical, Griffith-style narrative cinema.

CONTEMPORARY MODELS OF FORMAL STRUCTURE

Despite its suggestiveness, the position staked out by Tynianov was largely ignored in film studies until David Bordwell took up its central premises and developed them at length in *Narration in the Fiction Film* (1985). Bordwell first provides a detailed description of the way in which the syuzhet relates to the fabula. The primary role of the syuzhet is to present the fabula, or better, the fabula information that the spectator uses to construct the story. The function of the syuzhet is here spelled out as the elaboration – and complication – of narrative logic, narrative time and narrative space (Bordwell 1985: 51). Narrative logic in the syuzhet can be linear and proceed according to a distinctly causal development, presenting the fabula information in a direct and accessible way. Or it can be complex, blocking the relation of cause and effect with intervening materials, digressing from the linear order one imagines the fabula to assume. Narrative time, similarly, may be straightforward, and simply articulate consecutive moments in a neatly successive order. Or it may be complex, with the syuzhet employing the full battery of temporal relations between it and the fabula.

The concrete particularity of this description of syuzhet patterning is a valuable contribution to film analysis. But the more dramatic and adventurous aspect of *Narration in the Fiction Film* is the effort by Bordwell to undertake the type of analysis called for by Tynianov, emphasizing the role of style in syuzhet construction: "in classical narrative . . . film technique, though highly organized, is used principally to reinforce the causal, temporal and spatial arrangements of events in the syuzhet," and arguing that in some cases "the film's stylistic system creates patterns distinct from the syuzhet system. Film style may be organized and emphasized to a degree that makes it at least equal in importance to syuzhet patterns" (1985: 275). Bordwell would agree with Tynianov that in certain works, "style, the stylistic relationships between the pieces that are linked together, comes forward as the principal mover of the plot" (in Eagle 1981: 97). Moreover, in cases of "parametric narration," such as Robert Bresson's *Pickpocket* or R. W. Fassbinder's *Katzelmacher*, when the syuzhet does come forward, "it tends to do so on the style's own terms" (Bordwell 1985: 288). The overall effect of such strong stylistic patterning laid over the syuzhet is to "frustrate our fabula-constructing activity . . . [thwarting] the chief method of managing viewing time – constructing a linear fabula" (ibid.).

This is a promising approach, and the analysis of *Pickpocket* which demonstrates the method is highly illuminating. Some troubling questions remain, however, for Bordwell's theory favors the film-specific, stylistic "basting" of the syuzhet – which for Tynianov depended on the analogy of film to verse – over a concept of the syuzhet as primarily related to the fabula, to story actions and categories. Here the specifically narrative dimension of the text – the succession of logically and chronologically related events, caused or experienced by actors, unfolding in space and time, as the contemporary narratologist Mieke Bal describes it – is de-emphasized to the point that it all but disappears. To paraphrase Bal, one can use narrative theory to analyze poetic or verse texts which possess a narrative component, such as T. S. Eliot's *The Waste Land*; but the narrative dimension is of secondary importance in such works, so that narrative analysis is perhaps not the most salient approach (Bal 1985: 9).

Moreover, the inclusion of stylistic features makes it seemingly impossible to derive general patterns of composition which might be applied to a variety of narrative texts in different media. Instead, this type of analysis focusses on the specific, micro-textual functioning of individual films, working against the goal of narrative theory to provide a comprehensive account of the laws of narrative structure which operate across genres and across different media. Narrative analysis traditionally endeavors to disclose the deep structural patterning beneath the surface features of the artifact. It is the autonomy of the narrative structure from media-specific manifestations that permits narrative forms to be translated into any medium. A novel may be transformed into a film, for example, or into a ballet, and while wholly changing its surface texture, its narrative form retains a recognizable outline, an identifiable shape.

The exclusion of style for this reason by most narrative theorists is acknowledged by Bordwell, although his citation of Tynianov as a theorist who includes "stylistic linkage" in his definition of the syuzhet carries substantial weight. As Tynianov writes:

the style and laws of construction in cinema transform all the elements – all those elements which, it seemed, were indivisible, applicable in the same way to all art forms and to all their genres. Such is the situation of the question of story (fabula) and plot (syuzhet) in cinema. In resolving the question of story and plot it is always necessary to pay attention to the specific material and style of the art form.

(in Eagle 1981: 95)

The primary influence of Formalist thought on film narrative theory may therefore prove to by Tynianov's argument that stylistic and semantic processes determine story categories. Pavel calls this general approach **DISCOURSE-NARRATOLOGY**, and associates it with the most recent tendencies in narrative theory. Nevertheless, he maintains that the importance of plot analysis based on its relation to the fabula rather than to style should not be overlooked:

after a period of intensive research on the structure of plot, narratologists gradually turned their attention to the discursive aspects of narrative. While . . . narratology includes both the poetics of plot and its textual manifestations, some researchers . . . tend to restrict narratology to the textual study of narratives, thus eliminating . . . the abstract level of plot. . . . There are areas where an abstract narrative structure *independent of its discourse-manifestation* is indispensable for an adequate representation of our literary knowledge.

(Pavel 1985: 15, emphasis added)

THE STRUCTURALIST ANALYSIS OF NARRATIVE

While the first discussions of narrative structure in film were conducted by the Russian Formalists in the late 1920s, the two most important influences on the development of film narrative analysis in the 1970s were the structuralist theory of Claude Lévi-Strauss and the folklore studies of Vladimir Propp. Here, although the terminology is different, we find a debate that nearly replicates the Formalist discussion of the relative importance of fabula or style in syuzhet patterning. While Lévi-Strauss had an enormous impact on all branches of semiotic inquiry, his influence on early film narrative theory was especially pronounced, inspiring an approach which used the methodology of linguistics to provide wide-ranging cultural readings of certain film genres, notably the Western and the musical. The work of Propp, on the other hand, was influential primarily for its usefulness in analyzing the plot structure of individual films. By focussing on the formal structure of plot composition, sometimes by directly applying Propp's model for the Russian wondertale, writers on film began to illuminate the underlying dynamic principles governing the movement of narrative – the cause and effect logic linking one narrative event to another. These two influences led to two different schools of narrative inquiry, which are largely distinct even today; **SEMANTIC** – which deals with the relation of the signs and messages produced by narrative to the larger cultural system which gives it meaning; and **SYNTACTICAL** – the study of the syntagmatic ordering of plot events as a kind of armature of narrative progress and development.

Analyzing North and South American Indian myths in terms of the logical structure of binary oppositions, Lévi-Strauss proceeded by breaking up the lateral, cause and effect relations of the plot and setting the events, characters and settings into new paradigmatic groups. The syntagmatic relations of the narrative, the order of events occurring in succession, were seen as a kind of surface structure, which concealed the deeper logic of the myth. Greimas characterized the arrangement of the narrative elements of myth into binary oppositions as its "deep structure": while the ostensible signification of the myth resided in the unfolding sequence of events, its deep meaning was "paradigmatic and achronic." "We therefore decided to give the structure evolved by Lévi-Strauss the status of deep narrative structure, capable, in the process of syntagmatization, of generating a surface structure corresponding roughly to the syntagmatic chain of Propp" (Greimas 1971: 796; in Rimmon-Kenan 1983: 11). Although the binary oppositions may not in themselves be narrative, they are, in Greimas' words, "designed to account for the initial articulations of meaning within a semantic micro-universe" (Greimas 1970: 161; in Culler 1975: 92). In Lévi-Strauss' hands, the structure of myth was reduced to an achronic binary system, "A is to non-A as B is to non-B," a pattern which articulated the logical or social contradiction which formed the myth's fundamental subject. The details of the myth were held to be unimportant, and were excluded from the analysis.

One of the early approaches to film narrative directly influenced by Lévi-Strauss was the analysis of film genres as a form of mythic text, best exemplified in the work of Will Wright and Jim Kitses on the Western. In *Sixguns and Society*, Will Wright makes explicit comparisons between mythic discourse and the Western, arguing that the genre transmitted a clear set of messages and values to society that "reinforce rather than challenge social understanding" (Wright 1975: 23). These messages could be defined by analyzing the patterns of opposition which formed the semantic universe of the Western. Wright discovered that such binary oppositions as wilderness/civilization, inside/outside, strong/weak, etc. recurred throughout the generic corpus. Variety and change in the historical development of the Western was seen primarily in terms of changes in the patterns of the plot; the central semantic antinomies, however, remained the same, and constituted a kind of deep structure. Jim Kitses applied a similar antinomic approach in *Horizons West* (1969). Although he was not directly influenced by Lévi-Strauss, Kitses defined a number of structural oppositions characteristic of the Western genre. By composing a table of oppositions which flow from the central antinomy animating the Western – the dual conception of the American West as both a garden and a desert, an idea first set forth in the writings of Henry Nash Smith – Kitses provides a satisfying description of the semantic universe of the genre. Basic elements, such as wilderness vs. civilization, the individual vs. community, nature vs. culture, are supported by subsidiary oppositions, which have a wide range of variation. In Kitses' hands, these variations are used to distinguish the work of one auteur from another. Overall, Kitses offers a comprehensive and elegant treatment of the oppositional patterns defining the semantic register of the genre.

Even among the early adherents to Lévi-Strauss' method, there was some criticism of his outright rejection of plot. Wright, for example, argued that the semantic approach is insufficient for comprehending the meaning of narrative:

> His denial of significance to the story itself is simply untenable . . . each particular myth must be interpreted as in some sense an allegory of social action . . . interaction takes place in the story of a myth, not in the structure of oppositions . . . in order to understand the social meaning of a myth, it is necessary to analyze not only its binary structure but its narrative structure – the progression of events and the resolution of conflicts.
>
> (Wright 1975: 24)

Lévi-Strauss' influence was extremely widespread, however, and the methods of structural analysis were often adopted by writers who simply employed binary oppositions as a formal tool without being bound to the questionable analogy of films to myths. (For a thorough critique of this analogy, see Sheila Johnston's discussion of myth criticism in Cook 1985: 233, 234.) Raymond Bellour, for example, found that the formal level of the text – the level of shot sizes, framing and movement – could be analyzed in terms of binary oppositions, and that variation and repetition among the oppositions gave the narrative sequence its central thrust and impetus (Bellour 1979).

Bellour takes as his object of inquiry the classic American film, with the films of Hitchcock serving as a primary example. Unlike Kitses and Wright, who emphasize semantic oppositions at the level of the story, Bellour focusses on the formal permutations of editing and framing. Seeking to define the qualities of transparency, closure, and the impression of naturalness that characterizes the works of the classic American cinema, Bellour (1979) closely analyzes the shot patterning – the alternation and repetition of shots – as a vehicle for narrative advance in films such as *North by Northwest*, *The Birds*, *Gigi* and *The Big Sleep*. Bellour's approach, at this stage of its development, was quite close to the stylistic narrative analysis called for by Tynianov, and later championed by Bordwell.

Narrative progress and development in film, he argues, is built on a shot-by-shot basis. Rather than emphasizing story events, Bellour's work stresses the pattern of binary oppositions, including framing, point-of-view and movement, which link and disrupt a given series of shots. Narrative progress occurs almost as a by-product of these formal permutations and oppositions, he suggests. Describing the basic narrative dynamic of film as a structure of **SEGMENTATION** – an internally coherent shot series containing a number of oppositions – and **ALTERNATION** – the systematic distribution of oppositions from one shot to the next – Bellour sought to chart the trajectory of narrative development in terms of certain cinema-specific codes. His analysis of the Bodega Bay sequence in Hitchcock's *The Birds* is characteristic; it stresses the organization of oppositions within three codes: point-of-view (seeing/seen); framing (close/distant); and camera movement (still/moving). The dynamic movement of narrative through these oppositions is caused by a rupture or dissymmetry occurring at one level, which is then covered over by symmetry and repetitition at another level. In the Bodega Bay sequence, the seeing/seen opposition which dominates the first part of the scene, and which is repeated a number of times, is suddenly interrupted by a structure of seeing/seeing. The break in the pattern is naturalized, however, by displacing the overall quality of repetition to another code, that of camera movement. Camera movement carries the rhythm of the segment across these breaks; it displaces the break to another level.

Another early approach to narrative form in film can be found in the

'Grand Syntagmatique' of Christian Metz. Focussing on the various ways editing configures the temporal and spatial dimensions of the diegesis, the Grand Syntagmatique marks an explicit attempt to relate features of the discourse, or the textual style of film – especially the code of editing – to the level of the story, or fabula. Metz argued that the organization of images into a narrative was one of the most important ways that film was like a language. The Grand Syntagmatique sought to designate and classify the specifically narrative segments of film language, which Metz understood in terms of sequences of shots, called syntagmas. These eight syntagmas, which were distinguished primarily through editing, expressed the spatial, temporal and logical connections that form the universe of the fabula. True to structuralist methods, Metz broke the eight syntagmas down into sets of binary oppositions.

Although it was widely discussed and somewhat influential in film studies, the context in which the Grand Syntagmatique was circulated was not that of narrative theory but rather that of linguistics and the attempt to comprehend film as a language. From the perspective of narrative theory, the Grand Syntagmatique can be seen as an ambitious and highly suggestive attempt to model the relation between narrative discourse and the story-world, a concrete application of the type of analysis begun by Eikhenbaum of the film phrase – the basic editing schemas which carve out the action of the story, and create the spatial and temporal contiguities which produce the illusion of continuity in the story. Like Metz, Eikhenbaum emphasized the constructed nature of screen space and screen time, and focussed on the ways in which editing both articulates and complicates the story, interrupting scenes, retarding the process of the narrative and distorting the tempo. All of these techniques are specified in the Grand Syntagmatique. Metz' concern, however, was less with narrative structure than with the description of the language of film, which in this early work was comprehended as the syntagmatic unfolding of the image-track, varied, controlled and differentiated through editing.

PLOT ANALYSIS: THE PROPPIAN MODEL

At about the same time as Lévi-Strauss' influence was being felt in film theory, an alternative method to the structuralist approach was emerging among writers guided by the work of Vladimir Propp. Propp's *Morphology of the Folktale* was first published in 1928, but was not translated into English or widely disseminated until 1968, whereupon its importance was immediately recognized. Although he was a tangential member of the Russian Formalist school, the reception of his work was shaped primarily by questions of narrative form which arose within the structuralist debates of the 1970s. Emphasizing story events and temporal sequence, the Proppian method stressed the conjunctural logic of plot development in a

79

way that directly contradicted Lévi-Strauss' assertion that plot events merely formed a surface structure which concealed the deeper logic and meaning of the myth. Although film theorists did not stress the fundamental difference between the two approaches, the two principals, Propp and Lévi-Strauss, engaged in a heated polemic, with Propp writing in 1966 that "plot has no interest for Lévi-Strauss." For Propp, and for the writers influenced by him, the deep structure of narrative form consists precisely of the causal logic of events unfolding in time, and not the achronic, binary system of Lévi-Strauss.

> Carrying out his logical operations in a completely abstract way . . . [Lévi-Strauss] removes the functions from their temporal sequence . . . the function . . . takes place in time and cannot be removed from it . . . the forced removal of the functions from their temporal sequence destroys the delicate thread of the narrative, which, like a subtle and elegant web, falls apart at the slightest touch.
>
> (Propp 1976: 287)

Proppian analysis thus focusses on a very different level of the narrative artifact than did Lévi-Strauss', attempting to disclose the structural syntax of the narrative work rather than the semantic messages conveyed through patterns of contradiction and opposition. The method sought to reveal a universal pattern of organization underpinning all plot structures: in film, the model Propp developed to account for the structure of the Russian wondertale was applied to works as diverse as *North by Northwest*, *Sunset Boulevard* and *Kiss Me Deadly*, suggesting a pattern of plot events that all narratives have in common. While Propp himself restricted his findings to the Russian wondertale, writers in film and television felt that his model had much wider applications, and could illuminate popular forms such as Hollywood genre films and television programs.

There are several ingredients to the Proppian model, most of which have been adapted in whole or in part by later theorists. Of primary importance is the notion of the **FUNCTION**. In seeking to define the characteristics that a particular corpus of tales called the wondertale have in common, Propp discovered that the seemingly innumerable "actions" or "events" of the tales he studied could be distilled into a table of thirty-one functions, which were constant and recurred throughout the genre. Moreover, these invariant events, such as "An interdiction is addressed to the Hero," and "The Villain attempts to deceive his victim," occurred in exactly the same sequence in each tale, although some might be omitted: "The sequence of functions is always identical . . . an action cannot be defined apart from its place in the course of narration" (Propp 1968: 21, 22). Not only were the functions found to be constant, but the characters who triggered the events were also found to be consistent: "Function is understood as an act of character, defined from the point of view of its significance for the course of the action" (ibid.: 21). Propp condensed the myriad characters of the stories he studied into seven standard figures, called the *dramatis personae* or **TALE ROLES**: the villain, the donor, the helper, the princess and her father, the dispatcher, the hero and the false hero. Propp states that the princess and her father "cannot be exactly delineated from each other according to functions" (1968: 79). Various tale roles control various functions; for example, the villain controls the functions having to do with villainy, such as the struggle with the hero and the pursuit of the hero, while the helper performs the functions of transference of the hero, liquidation of misfortune, rescue from pursuit, and others. The functions and tale roles together constitute the **SPHERES OF ACTION**, with each of the seven tale roles commanding a specific sphere of action. Propp defined the tale roles as distinct from the actual characters in a story, showing that one character may perform several different tale roles; for example, the princess may also be the helper. On the other hand, several characters may fulfill one tale role, when, for example, more than one villain appears in a story. In addition, Propp divided the overall composition of the tale into a set of **MOVES**, consisting of several functions strung together which represent a distinct line of action, such as the line of action begun with the villainy function: "each new act of villainy, each new lack creates a new move" (1968: 93). Functions which terminate a move might be reward, liquidation of misfortune or an escape from pursuit. A tale may consist of only one move, or it may have several; one move may follow directly after the other, or they may be interwoven.

Extrapolating the thirty-one functions of the wondertale and applying them to diverse films, writers such as Peter Wollen, Patricia Erens, John Fell and, to some extent, Will Wright found a strong degree of correspondence between the plots of various films and Propp's morphology. While some of the functions of the wondertale proved to be specific to the genre Propp studied, the application of Propp's model met with enough success to persuade researchers that something like an abstract model of plot structure could be devised. The individual analyses were less important for the insights they provided into specific films than for the attention they gave to the structural organization of plot. Indeed, many of the individual treatments of films exhibit striking lapses, as has been pointed out recently by Bordwell:

> morphological analyses have failed through distortion, omission, unconstrained associations, and theoretical inadequacy. There is at present no sound reason to conclude that films share an underlying structure with folktales, or that film studies' version of Propp's method can reveal the structure underlying a narrative film.
>
> (Bordwell 1988: 16)

The larger point, however, is that Propp's method provided the context and the groundwork for research on plot grammar in film, just as it did for literature. Literary narratology has since made great strides in the area of plot analysis, particularly in the work of Bremond, Greimas, Barthes and Pavel; all of these approaches were derived in some fashion from Propp. Plot analysis in film has not yet developed as a research area, probably because of the pressing interest of other theoretical programs, but it remains one of the founding gestures of narratological inquiry. Writers working in feminist theory, such as Laura Mulvey and Teresa de Lauretis, have sometimes used Proppian categories as a way of defining gender codes in film, suggesting that plot analysis can inform some of the most difficult areas in contemporary theory.

SEMANTIC AND SYNTACTIC APPROACHES

Certain writers on film have attempted to unify the semantic and the syntactic approaches. A case in point is the work of Rick Altman on genre. Altman argues that a combined **SEMANTIC/SYNTACTIC** model of genre can account for the difficult problem of historical development and change in the generic corpus. While not strictly a theory of narrative, his approach has relevance to narrative analysis for it stresses the interplay of these two registers in ways which can be seen as characteristic of narrative in general. For example, Altman finds that the musical genre in film developed different semantic and syntactic conventions as it evolved over time. In the first musicals, a backstage or nightclub semantic universe was linked to a melodramatic plot syntax, which is structured around sorrow and death. Yet in 1930s musicals these same semantic elements were joined to a syntax emphasizing the couple, the community and the joys of entertainment. Here the genre is seen to grow out of the linking of a stable set of semantic elements to a changing syntax, similar to the approach Will Wright takes concerning the Western. An opposite but complementary process is found in the case of genres such as the war-time anti-German or Japanese films, which start with a syntax derived from the gangster films of the 1930s, and graft onto it a new set of semantic attributes. In a more general sense, Altman argues that the semantic codes provide the basic "linguistic" material, while the syntactic bonds create specific textual meanings:

> the semantic/syntactic distinction is fundamental to a theory of how meaning of one kind contributes to and eventually establishes meaning of another. . . . There is thus a constant circulation in both directions between the semantic and the syntactic, between the linguistic and the textual.

(Altman 1984: 16, 17)

The merging of syntactic and semantic approaches to film narrative

82

structure is characteristic of a later phase of development in narrative theory, which can be generally associated with the work of Roland Barthes in literature. In the mid–1970s the work of Barthes exerted an increasing influence on film analysis, particularly the study "Myth Today" (in Barthes 1972), the magisterial work *S/Z*, and the important summary of French narratology, "Introduction to the Structural Analysis of Narratives" (in Barthes 1977). It is in *S/Z* that we find the most important model for film analysis. Barthes argues that what he calls the classical "readerly text" consists of the orchestration of five different codes: the hermeneutic, proairetic, the symbolic, the semic and the referential. (See Part V for a complete exposition of these terms.) While the symbolic, semic and referential codes can be described as semantic – in so far as they deal with the general system of cultural beliefs, standard symbology, or connotative meanings associated with a particular milieu – two of the codes are directly tied to the syntactic unfolding of the plot. These are the proairetic, or the code of actions, which serves to vectorize the narrative, to ensure its logical and coherent progression, and which could be said to correspond generally to the level of Proppian functions; and the hermeneutic, which deals with the enigma or question posed by the text, together with the various detours and deviations by which the text keeps the resolution of the enigma hidden until the end of the narrative.

The model Barthes constructs in *S/Z* is an elegant fusion of semantic and syntactical approaches, for it demonstrates how the two message-generating registers of narrative form – the general semantic system of cultural meanings and the causal logic governing the plot – interact and support one another. But although *S/Z* was widely read and discussed, its program of analysis, the breaking down of the text into five codes, was not directly employed in film studies, with only two or three analyses based on *S/Z* appearing in the film literature. Nevertheless, Barthes' work had a decisive impact, if not a direct influence on film studies, for it energized the practice of close textual analysis.

THE PROBLEM OF POINT-OF-VIEW

By the late 1970s film narrative theory was still enmeshed in the larger semiotic enterprise generally known as textual analysis, although it had begun to develop into a recognizable field in its own right. The issue that led to a more specific and defined field of endeavor for film narrative theory was the question of **POINT-OF-VIEW** – usually understood as the optical perspective of a character whose gaze or look dominates a sequence, or, in its broader meaning, the overall perspective of the narrator toward the characters and the events of the fictional world. The **NARRATOR** can be defined as the agent, inscribed in the text, who relates or recounts the events of the fictional world. The narrator should be distinguished from the real author and from the characters who inhabit the fictional world, although at times a character may take on the role of narrator to a limited degree. The issue of point-of-view brought several theoretical strands together, including psychoanalytic-feminist criticism, which was based in large part on the theory of the gaze, and ideological criticism, as seen in the writings of Daniel Dayan and Jean-Pierre Oudart. Narrative analysis provided a kind of mantle under which different approaches to the question of point-of-view could be assembled, for both psychoanalytic and ideological approaches stressed the crucial importance of point-of-view to the overall narrative structuration of the work, a structure which was heavily criticized as mystifying and biased towards male characters and spectators. Narrative theory, in its turn, began to address the specificity of **NARRATIVE DISCOURSE** – the signifying techniques and formal strategies by which a narrative is related to a reader or spectator – and the different roles and levels involved in transmitting narrative messages by carefully studying the problem of point-of-view.

The category of point-of-view is one of the most important means of structuring narrative discourse and one of the most powerful mechanisms for audience manipulation. The manipulation of point-of-view allows the text to vary or deform the material of the fabula, presenting it from different points-of-view, restricting it to one incomplete point-of-view, or privileging a single point-of-view as hierarchically superior to others. It is also one of the areas of greatest difficulty and confusion in film analysis. It has been used to signify a vast range of functions, from the technical sense of the point-of-view shot, to the general sense of orienting the work through a certain character's perspective, to the "attitude" of the narrator, to the world-view of the author, to the affective response and epistemic range of the spectator. As Edward Branigan (1984) writes, the author, narrator, character and spectator can all be said to possess a point-of-view.

One of the first essays to come to grips with the plethora of activities signified by this term was Nick Browne's "The Spectator in the Text: The Rhetoric of *Stagecoach*" (1982). Using a methodology explicitly related to studies of narration in literature, Browne showed how **NARRATION** in film – which can be defined as the act of communicating a story to a spectator through images, editing, verbal commentary and point-of-view, as distinct from the narrative world itself in which the characters perform – consists of several activities ranged in a hierarchical order. The critical problem formulated here revolves around the relative importance of the literal, optical point-of-view. The question posed by Browne can be paraphrased quite simply: who or what system provides the attitudinal orientation guiding the spectator's reading of an individual sequence? In analyzing the well-known dinner scene in *Stagecoach*, Browne considers the fundamental problem of the hierarchy of narrative roles, an issue which in film has centered on the problem of point-of-view.

In the dinner scene in *Stagecoach*, Dallas, a woman of "easy virtue," is seated next to Lucy, a woman of aristocratic background. Lucy administers a haughty look of disapproval, rendered in a point-of-view shot which seems to establish her as the authoritative and narrative center of the scene. Nevertheless, Browne argues, the spectator reads the scene as an injustice committed against Dallas, despite the ostensible narrative privilege conferred on Lucy through her empowerment via the point-of-view shot. A higher narratorial "rhetoric," consisting of a range of effects including sequencing, framing, control of temporal processes, and the shifting of identifications, allows the spectator to distinguish between the glance and the power it conveys and the overall moral order of the film. Point-of-view, in this model, refers less to the character's optical facility than to the narratorial process of constructing the spectator's attitudes in the film.

In earlier treatments of the problem, narrative authority was held to reside with the character who commands the optical point-of-view; here a more powerful agency is shown to control the messages which flow from the scene, enabling the spectator to assess the validity of the represented point-of-view as simply one perspective among others. This argument takes shape in explicit opposition to the theory of suture which had entered narrative analysis by way of the psychoanalytic study of the cinema. Browne argues that a combination of narrative authority and spectatorial identification produces a perspective which overrides the represented, optical point-of-view: "A spectator is several places at once – with the fictional viewer, with the viewed, and at the same time in a position to evaluate and respond to the claims of each" (Browne 1982: 12). Controlling these multiple investments is another agent: "the film is directed in all its structures of presentation towards the narrator's construction of a commentary on the story and toward placing the spectator at a certain 'angle' to it" (ibid.: 13).

This approach to point-of-view emphasizes the narrator's techniques for rendering the subjectivity of the character – his or her emotional and cognitive state – as well as the techniques for evaluating, ironizing, confirming or disconfirming the character's thoughts, perceptions and attitudes. The relationship of the narrator to the character is posed in terms of consciousness and authority: point-of-view is understood in terms of the narrator's overarching or limited viewpoint on the agents and events of the fictional world. The essay thus advances a concept of point-of-view which opens onto the layered structure of fictional form: "It shows the importance of distinguishing between a glance, the view of a character, the location of the camera, and the point of view of the film" (Browne 1982: 15).

Browne's essay, despite its rejection of the priority of optical perspective, retained the term point-of-view in all of its myriad senses. It is a particularly misleading term when used to describe either the narrator's attitude or the spectator's process of reading, or both. For one, the narrator does not "see" the events of the fictional world, but recounts them; he or she does not observe from a post within the fictional world, but recalls events from a position outside the fictional universe.

As for the usefulness of the term to describe spectatorial engagement, Browne's introduction to the special issue on point-of-view in *Film Reader 4* (Browne 1979) indicates the problems associated with the notion that film promotes an identification between the point-of-view inscribed in the text and the point-of-view of the spectator. According to this approach, the control of point-of-view is the most powerful means of inducing a kind of imaginary response on the part of the spectator, "positioning" the spectator by addressing the viewer through visual devices such as the point-of-view shot and shot/reverse-shot cutting in order to fashion a very tight bond between spectator and text. In this way, the text may be said to "interpellate" the spectator into the fictional world so that its values, and its ideology, become one with the viewing subject. As Browne argues, however, this direct assimilation of the specific point-of-view inscribed within the text with the extremely general and universal notion of "subject positions" fails to take into account the concrete particularity of individual spectators. The focus of much feminist criticism, for example, has been to emphasize gender difference in the reception of films, arguing that the text has different receptor sites for men and women. Beyond these very important distinctions between male and female spectatorial investments and responses, issues of race, class and historical context are also involved in analyzing the issue of point-of-view from the perspective of the spectator. These issues have increasingly come to the forefront, as the analytic category of the audience, with its concrete historical and contextual dimensions, has in large part replaced the psychoanalytic category of the spectator in current theory.

Another influential and scrupulously observed work on point-of-view, "Formal Permutations of the Point of View Shot," by Edward Branigan (1975), appeared roughly contemporaneously with the essay by Browne, providing the two principal sources for most of the subsequent work on narrative form and point-of-view in film. Branigan has since extended this work to a consideration of the role of point-of-view in the overall architecture of film narrative form. In the later, book-length work, *Point of View in the Cinema* (1984), Branigan points out the vast range of functions covered by this term. Although he examines the full range of categories and problems stemming from the conflation of several different narrative functions in a single term, somewhat surprisingly he does not provide an alternative model, or an alternative terminolcgy.

Point of View in the Cinema argues forcefully for the subjective ingredient in all point-of-view structures, including the subjectivity of author, narrator, character and reader: "Subjectivity, then, is the process of knowing a story – telling it and perceiving it" (Branigan 1984: 1). But this all-encompassing term is prudently limited in his actual exposition to the narrow sense of character perception and narration: "Subjectivity may be conceived as a specific instance or level of narration where the telling is *attributed* to a character in the narrative and received by us *as if* we were in the situation of a character [such as the point-of-view shot]" (ibid.: 73). "Whenever a character glances – fastens upon an object – and we see the object of that glance, there exists an *inevitable subjectivization of film space*" (ibid.: 130).

Branigan's imbrication of point-of-view and subjectivity evokes perception, psychology and ideology, but the specific thrust of the argument is to locate the spectator as the fundamental organizing agency, the subject who makes use of the restrictions, the cues and the shifts among the various levels of narrative form to make sense of the fictional world. In the context of narrative theory, the most provocative aspect of Branigan's text is in his implicit argument that the category of point-of-view is the most significant aspect of narrative structure. Point-of-view, in this treatment, links the discourse, or the textual mechanisms of shot/reverse-shot, eyeline matches, camera movements, etc., to the story-world – the world of events, characters, fictional space and time. This linkage, in turn, provides a privileged set of highly significant cues to the spectator, producing an especially rich set of textual indicators: "I consider point of view to be a textual system which controls (expands, restricts, changes) the viewer's access to meaning. . . . Point of view basically answers the question: what work (by 'whom') has transformed matter into meaning?" (Branigan 1984: 212).

FOCALIZATION AND FILTRATION

Branigan's method, like Browne's does not distinguish the separate functions of narrative discourse with separate terminology. Because of the range of functions communicated by the term point-of-view, recent narrative theory has attempted to classify the different functions it signifies by using specific vocabulary for each of these levels. The term **FOCALIZATION** was introduced by Gerard Genette to distinguish the activity of the narrator recounting the events of the fictional world from the activity of the character from whose perspective events are perceived, or **FOCALIZED**. The distinction between the narrator and the **FOCALIZER** is commonly described in literary theory as a distinction between the agent "who speaks" and the agent "who sees."

The importance of distinguishing the different levels and techniques of narrative discourse is the subject of Genette's book, *Figure III*, translated into English as *Narrative Discourse: An Essay in Method* (1980). This study in literary narratology – a term suggested by Todorov to denote the structuralist analysis of narrative – had a very pronounced impact on film narrative theory, for it provided a precise delineation of the multiple processes involved in the representation of the fictional world.

One of the most important refinements Genette introduced – other contributions will be discussed later in this Part – was the division between the viewpoint established within the fictional world, the angle of vision "from which the life or the action is looked at," and the narrator's recounting or presenting of the narrative world from a perspective temporally removed from the immediacy of the represented events.

Narrative information in film will often be channeled through a particular character or group of characters, restricting our knowledge of the fictional world to their perceptions, knowledge or subjectivity. In an older terminology, this would be called point-of-view. By recasting point-of-view in terms of focalization, Genette restricts the term to the diegetic level of the text, to the level of characters and actions: it returns the question of point-of-view to the basic problem of "who sees." But even where a literal point-of-view shot is not present, narrative films may utilize specific characters as centers of consciousness, reflectors, or as "bottlenecks" which convey narrative information, activities which also come under the heading of focalization. Genette redraws the conceptual map of narrative with this refinement, situating the category of point-of-view, or focalization, on the side of the diegesis rather than on the side of narration.

Focalization has been subdivided by Genette into different types: **INTERNAL FOCALIZATION** occurs when a narrative is presented entirely from a given character's perspective, with the limitations and restrictions this implies. An example would be Robert Montgomery's *Lady in the Lake*, wherein the camera serves as the "eyes" of the character, with narrative information rendered from a single, optical point-of-view. This has traditionally been described as **FIRST-PERSON NARRATION** in film; the description, however, is misleading, for narration by definition involves an agency situated outside the story-world, presenting, quoting, recounting or commenting on the story events after they have occurred. Here, the character-camera "sees" the events simultaneously with their occurrence. Nor is the phrase "first-person point-of-view" desirable, for it relies on a metaphoric use of linguistic categories which do not exist in the image-track of film; moreover, a term like "first-person" implies a second- and third-person point-of-view, which multiples the quality of imprecision. Genette's improvement on this terminology is made clear by contrast: one can describe the technique in *Lady in the Lake* simply as an example of internal focalization, thus adhering to the strict sense of Genette's original definition of focalization as the "angle of vision, from which the life or the action is looked at," and conforming to the specific meaning of internal focalization as a viewpoint limited to a single character.

In film, however, the strict optical sense of focalization has a very limited usefulness. To insist on the "angle of vision" ingredient in filmic discourse would simply be redundant, for film criticism already contains many descriptive terms for analyzing the position of the camera in a scene, including the point-of-view shot. But when the term focalization is broadened to include a select character's general perspective, orientation or "take" on a scene, the concept acquires a high degree of usefulness for film analysis.

Although in Genette and Bal the term focalization has a strictly optical meaning – the position or angle of vision from which events are viewed – Rimmon-Kenan has expanded the definition to include what she calls the **FACETS OF FOCALIZATION**. In addition to the **PERCEPTUAL FACET**, which concerns the sensory range of the character, these include the **PSYCHOLOGICAL FACET**, where the cognitive and emotional focus of the text resides with a particular character, and the **IDEOLOGICAL FACET**, which concerns the character whose perspective could be said to express the general system of values, or the "norms of the text." As Rimmon-Kenan writes: "[Focalization's] purely visual sense has to be broadened to include cognitive, emotive and ideological orientation" (1983: 71).

An example of the cognitive and emotional components of the psychological facet working together with the perceptual facet of focalization can be found in *The Godfather*. Several scenes in this film are restricted to the perspective of Michael Corleone, thus corresponding to Genette's internal focalization, but these scenes are not presented entirely from his optical viewpoint. An example is the sequence at the hospital, when he discovers that his father has been left unprotected and is about to be attacked by rival gunmen. Clearly functioning as the central focus of the scene, Michael does command several optical point-of-view shots, and the acoustic material in the scene is also presented as the character would hear it. Much more important, however, is the way the character serves as the psychological and emotional center of interest: his quick reactions, his intelligence and his courage are emphasized throughout. Although the majority of the shots in the sequence deviate from his strict optical perspective, the psychological and cognitive focus is consistently oriented to him. Genette's narrow sense of optical focalization is insufficient to account for the decisive revelation of Michael's character expressed in this scene; in film the psychological facet of focalization often expresses the overall meaning of an individual sequence.

The perceptual facet of focalization, moreover, sometimes works in opposition to the emotional and cognitive component. We have already seen an example of this in Browne's reading of *Stagecoach*, which could be described as a split between the perceptual facet and the psychological facet, with Dallas serving as the emotional center of the scene while Lucy controls only the perceptual facet of focalization. A similar split occurs in

Stella Dallas: while the scenes which feature Stella alone or with her friends are focalized in every sense through her, as soon as her husband, Steven, or other representatives of the ruling class come into the scene, the perceptual facet shifts to these characters. Stella is invariably caught in what looks like a compromising situation to the outsiders, but which the spectator and Stella know is entirely innocent. Here the psychological facet of focalization remains with Stella, but the perceptual facet shifts to an outside character, whose reaction is invariably censorious. This creates a sharp division in the film between the emotional meaning of many scenes and the optical point-of-view "from which the life or the action is looked at."

Internal focalization can be **FIXED** – limited to a single character; **VARIABLE** – which occurs when the focalization shifts within a scene or a film from one character or another: or **MULTIPLE** – in which one event is viewed from several different perspectives, as in Akira Kurosawa's *Rashomon*, or Bernardo Bertolucci's *The Grim Reaper*. An example of variable focalization can be found in *The Godfather* in the opening wedding sequence. Here the focalization shifts rapidly and frequently from one character to another, first focussing on the group in Don Corleone's office, then on the wedding guests outside, then on the FBI agents in the driveway. Throughout the scene the focalization shifts freely among several different characters. The perceptual facet, as well as the psychological facet, switches from one group of characters to another, with no discernible hierarchy established. With this type of variable focalization, we arrive at a kind of composite portrait of the whole of the Mafia society; rather than a sense of individual psychology, this technique emphasizes the interactions and the general character of an entire social group.

Another type of focalization described by Genette is **EXTERNAL FOCALIZATION**. This refers to narratives in which our knowledge of the characters is restricted simply to their external actions and words, without the "subjectivity" of the characters, their thoughts and feelings, being invoked. This is a somewhat questionable category, which has been criticized from a number of quarters. The most common example given in literature is the Ernest Hemingway story "Hills Like White Elephants," where the characters are rigorously described from an external perspective. Yet in film, it is difficult to imagine any presentation of characters that would not include indications about their feelings, thoughts and emotions, qualities which would necessarily involve internal focalization.

Genette also distinguishes what he calls **NON-FOCALIZED** or **ZERO FOCALIZATION** from external and internal focalization. Zero focalization concerns narratives in which no character or group of characters is privileged in terms of emotional, perceptual or cognitive perspective. Genette compares zero focalization to "classic" narrative style, or to "omniscient narration." Here again, this category seems to have very limted use for film analysis, for with its link to the dramatic arts, film almost invariably employs characters as channels of narrative information, and makes especially heavy use of internal focalization as a means of displacing narrative agency to the characters.

Focalization in film does not comprise the ultimate horizon of its narrative discourse, despite its wide and powerful role. It should be remembered that Genette introduced the term to underline the distinction between narration and focalization, or between the agent who recounts or presents the fictional world to the spectator and the agent within the diegesis who serves as a kind of lens or medium through which the events and the other characters are perceived.

The value of distinguishing focalizaton from narration in film comes to the forefront when we consider texts that take an ironic stance towards the focalizing agent, or that manifest a critical attitude toward the focalizer. In Bertolucci's *The Conformist*, the character of Marcello is the subjective center of the film. He controls not only the optical and acoustic perspective, but also the memorial perspective, as much of the film is rendered through his subjective flashbacks. Nevertheless, this **CHARACTER-FOCALIZER** is treated both ironically and critically within the discourse of the film, as the narrator inscribes a level of critical commentary in the visual and acoustic texture of several sequences. In one scene, for example, Marcello is seen walking through Rome to the villa of his mother. During this walk, the camera is canted first to the left, then to the right, while rather comically bombastic music is heard on the soundtrack. When Marcello arrives at the villa, which is clearly in decay, he begins closing the gate. Just at this point, the man who will serve as Marcello's Fascist mentor arrives. As soon as he introduces himself to Marcello, the canted image rights itself, communicating a sense of stability and order, a corrective to the "decadent" family past he is about to revisit. The irony here is found in Marcello's sense of high purpose, communicated through his forceful stride and authoritative manner, and the narrator's almost comic undercutting of his motivation and his personality. In a later scene a more common type of disparity or distance is established between the focalization and the narration. As Marcello is finally about to make love to the beautiful wife of Professor Quadri, a woman he has sought to seduce from their first meeting, the lighting suddenly shifts from warm oranges and reds to a bluish-green tonality. Here the lighting "predicts" Marcello's impotence, and expresses the falseness of his seeming sexual obsession.

In short, it is difficult to imagine how this "higher" evaluation of the focalizer could be registered without a concept of the split between narration and focalization. As the "center of consciousness," Marcello commands the "point-of-view" in several senses – optical, emotional, memorial and cognitive. But he is still subject to the higher authority of the narration, which comments on and evaluates the agent "who sees."

An approach that attempts to deal with the possible confusion between focalization and narration is that of François Jost. Jost begins his article, "Narration(s): On This Side of and Beyond" (Jost 1984), by posing two questions – "How does the image signify?" and "How does the image tell (or narrate)?" – in order to establish a distinction between these two functions. Comparing literary with film studies, Jost emphasizes the essentially different tasks facing the two disciplines, since a literary narrative always contains a series of indicators (pronouns, "shifters," punctuation, etc.) which can be recognized immediately by a reader as characteristic of a narrative and its narrator. Written language will appear clearly as either **DISCOURSE** or **STORY** and force an author into narrative choices which a reader can easily identify. The problems of cinematic narration are more complex because of reasons that have to do with both the nature of cinematic narrative and its language. The first of these problems is that it is no longer possible to consider a cinematic narrative as *one* unique story. Divided as it is between the visual and the verbal, a film always risks being torn in contradictory directions, even if its strategies are organized towards the achievement of a global signified. The second problem concerns the identification of a cinematic narrator: we can be certain that a series of images is capable of telling a story and that the visual tale exists, yet we are not always able to say who is doing the telling. This difficulty in designating the degree of **DEIXIS** of a shot has as its narratological consequence the possible confusion between focalization and narration. (Deixis is a term used by linguists to indicate words whose reference can only be determined with respect to the situation of address, or to the context of the utterance. They are indicators of person or time that can be identified only by the instance of discourse that contains them; they have no value except in the instance in which they are produced. Jakobson calls them **SHIFTERS**. Pronouns, such as I and you, have no reference other than to designate the person speaking and the person spoken to. Aside from pronouns, other shifters can include demonstratives such as this and that, and indicators of time such as here and now.) Jost writes:

> In order to define the concept of narration, one must establish a border between *telling* and *seeing*. Methodologically speaking, it is not possible to assimilate, purely and simply, the question of *who sees?* to that which is known in literary theory as focalization. In fact, we have not sufficiently noted that this concept includes two distinct narrative realities: on the one hand, the *knowledge* of the narrator with regard to his characters (does he know more, less or as much as them?); on the other hand, his *position* (*localization*) with respect to the events that he narrates.
>
> (Jost 1984: 195)

Film works in two registers: it can *show* what a character sees and *say* what he thinks. If we don't want to restrict film analysis to the study of the image, we must differentiate the narrative "attitude" with respect to the character/hero in terms of both visual and verbal information.

Jost introduces the concept of **OCULARIZATION** in contrast or in addition to that of focalization. Focalization refers to that which a character knows; ocularization indicates the relation between what the camera shows and what a character *sees*. **INTERNAL OCULARIZATION** would refer to those shots where the camera appears to take the place of the character's eye. **EXTERNAL OCULARIZATION** (or **ZERO OCULARIZATION**) would indicate those shots where the field of vision is located outside a character's own.

Ocularization appears to be fundamentally different from focalization as it occurs in literature: since the latter participates in the verbal transformation of an event it always belongs to the narrative order, in other words to that which is related or recounted; ocularization, however, can leave the domain of narration in order to reproduce visual perception *per se*. Because of this direct connection with the seen, ocularization can be considered on the diegetic side of narrative.

The need to distinguish between the perceptual facet of focalization, or ocularization, and the psychological facet, or focalization, in Jost's terms, has also been addressed by Seymour Chatman. Although Chatman offers different terminology, the thrust of his argument is that the concept of focalization has not really remedied the confusion caused by the term point-of-view. Here, too, a single term has been used to signify several different concepts. He begins with the observation that the term focalization has suffered a fate similar to that of point-of-view – both have been used indiscriminately to signify the activity of both character and narrator. This is especially the case with Genette's category of external focalization which, Genette maintains, situates the focalizer in the diegesis but outside any of the characters, and the category of zero focalization, which Prince summarizes as "the narrated presented in terms of a nonlocatable, indeterminate perceptual or conceptual position," such as "omniscient" narration (Prince 1987: 103). Also symptomatic of this inflation of the term is Bal's "narrator-focalizer."

While the term was originally introduced by Genette to underline the distinction between these two functions – narration and perception – writers such as Bal and Rimmon-Kenan assume that all texts are always focalized, always perceived from a particular "angle." Consequently, if a character does not focalize the action, then the narrator must: the narrator, understood as the agent who relates the story, or who in literary narratives "puts the story into words," is then also assigned the power of focalization, becoming, in Bal's words, a **NARRATOR-FOCALIZER**. This results in a confusion of the basic distinction between "who speaks" and "who sees."

Chatman argues that such a confusion violates the distinction between **STORY** – the content plane of the narrative, the diegesis; and **DISCOURSE**

– the expression plane, the formal mechanisms which the narrator uses to recount the story. Such terms as narrator-focalizer, or external focalizer, collapse the crucial difference between the two categories:

> Only characters reside in the constructed diegetic world, so only they can be said to "see," that is, to have a diegetic consciousness which literally perceives and thinks about things from a position within that world. . . . The narrator cannot perceive or conceive things *in* that world, only *about* that world, since for him the story-world is always "past" and "elsewhere." He can report them, comment upon them, and even (figuratively) visualize them, but always and only from outside . . . the logic of narrative prevents him/her from literally seeing or thinking them from within the confines of the story-world.
>
> (Chatman 1986b: 196, 197)

Another problem with the term focalization is that it tends to denote an optical activity, even if the different facets of focalization are kept in mind. In film criticism, especially, there is an overwhelming tendency to assign hierarchical privilege to the agent controlling the optical point-of-view. This agent will be identified in most cases as the perceptual, psychological and ideological medium through whom events are perceived. The significance conventionally attributed to the control of the optical register is captured in a statement by Bal: "If the focalizer coincides with the character, that character will have a technical advantage over other characters. The reader watches with the character's eyes and will, in principle, be inclined to accept the vision presented by that character" (Bal 1985: 104).

Although Chatman acknowledges Rimmon-Kenan's effort to balance the optical activity with the psychological and ideological facets, he argues that her expansion of the term focalization changes its original meaning so drastically that it no longer corresponds to Genette's definition, especially in her questionable category of the "ideological facet." Instead, Chatman proposes new terminology for the function of focalization.

The character or characters who observe from a post within the fictional world may assume a special role as screen, reflector or **FILTER** of the fictional events and other characters. The narrator may elect to relate all or part of the story from or through a particular character's consciousness or perceptions. Chatman's use of the term filter provides advantages over the term focalizer, for it expresses well the sense of narrative information flowing through the psychological or emotional channel provided by a character, without insisting upon an actual visual outpost. With this refinement, the emotional filter of a particular scene and the concrete viewing position – the "screen" or "reflector" of events and the literal point-of-view – may be separated. Although Rimmon-Kenan argues for a similar separation, it is somewhat awkward to express this division in terms of the facets of focalization, for the primary meaning of focalization

remains that of a visual outpost: to speak of the primacy of the psychological facet over the visual violates the original sense of the term.

One area in which the concept of filtration should have immediate and
concrete advantages over the term point-of-view or the term focalization –
with its inevitable optical emphasis – is in feminist work in film. In so far
as the optical point-of-view in mainstream films is often controlled by male
characters, with the female character serving chiefly as the object of the
gaze, many films seem to reiterate in their visual structures a patriarchal
logic of power and domination. This pattern has been examined in depth in
feminist film criticism, resulting in a comprehensive if somewhat monolithic
modeling of gender-specific codes of looking in the classical cinema. The
concept of filtration may disclose a different hierarchy, however, wherein
the optical point-of-view can be shown to be subordinate to the role of the
psychological filter. The character functioning as the filter may not command a literal point-of-view shot, but can nevertheless serve as the delegate
of the narrator, the principal screen or medium through whom events are
channeled.

NARRATION IN FILM

CINEMATIC NARRATION can be understood as the discursive activity
responsible for representing or recounting the events or situations of the
story. The study of cinematic narration has been considered under several
different rubrics in different periods of film theory. The earliest treatments
of the problem were shaped by questions of realism and authorship. More
recently, it has been approached from the perspective of **ENUNCIATION**, a
linguistic borrowing which in film theory indicates the discursive markers
or stylistic traces in a film signaling the presence of an author or a narrator.
With the wide dissemination of Genette's *Narrative Discourse*, the elements
of cinematic narration began to be addressed in a rigorous and systematic
fashion.

As Genette points out, the term "narrative" has been used to cover
three quite distinct notions. While the distinction between fabula and
syuzhet in the work of the Russian Formalists discriminates between two
distinct levels of narrative communication, Genette found it necessary to
adopt a tripartite model, consisting of the *récit*, usually translated as "narrative"; the **HISTOIRE**, or "story"; and **NARRATION**, or "narrating." The
RECIT is the signifier, statement, discourse or narrative text itself, i.e. the
verbal or cinematic discourse that conveys the story-world to the spectator,
for example, the actual shot patterning in a film. The *récit* has both a
material substance and a form. *Histoire* by contrast, is the signified or
narrative content of the *récit*, i.e. the story-world or fabula. *Narration* refers
not to the events recounted, nor to the text itself, but to the act of
recounting, i.e. the act of utterance or presentation "producing narrative

action, and by extension, the whole real or fictional situation in which the act takes place" (Genette 1980: 27). *Narration* refers to the techniques, strategies and signals by which the presence of a narrator can be inferred, which in literature takes the form of certain pronouns and verb tenses. In film, however, the category of *narration* is associated with both voice-over or character-narration, and with the more elusive concept of general cinematic narration involving all of the codes of the cinema.

In both literature and film, it is only the narrative discourse or *récit* that is directly available for analysis. The *histoire*, also known as the story or fabula, must be inferred by the reader or viewer, for rather than having a substantive form it is the imaginary content of the narrative discourse; it does not have a material, signifying dimension, although it does have a logical structure. Similarly, *narration* is also only available to the reader or viewer by inference, for the act of narration is made manifest only through the unfolding of the *récit*.

Genette's study, *Narrative Discourse*, focusses on the *récit* itself, or the ribbon of signifiers that constitute the manifest narrative text, and its relation to the story on the one hand, and to the narration on the other. The *récit*, or narrative, is subdivided in Genette's method into three categories: **TENSE** – the temporal relations between narrative and story; **MOOD** – the study of focalization in terms of perspective and distance; and **VOICE** – "the narrating instance," the marks of *narration* in the *récit*.

While Genette's model is designed for literaray analysis, writers on film have frequently used his categories to clarify and systematize their approaches to film narrative form. An important article which specifies the correspondence and the distinctions between Genette's model for literary narratives and filmic modes of narrative expression is Brian Henderson's "Tense, Mood, and Voice in Film." Henderson found a high degree of correspondence between the two media, although he also discovered certain areas of difficulty. The greatest difference between the literary and filmic *récit*s, he found, was in the category of voice, which does not have a proper analogue, in his view, in film. Henderson understood voice in a very literal manner, interpreting it as vocalization by an overt voice-over or character-narrator in film. While the issue of narrative voice in film, or its non-verbal equivalents, is an extremely difficult problem which is still being debated, the lack of agreement on the category of voice does not diminish the value of Genette's approach for film, for it has allowed film theory to describe the various narrative agents and levels in film in a very precise manner.

TYPES OF FILMIC NARRATOR

There are two basic sites or zones in which a narrator operates in the film-text. The first zone is the personified **CHARACTER-NARRATOR,** who tells a story from within the frame of the fictional world. In Genette's terms, this is called an **INTRADIEGETIC NARRATOR**. If the character-narrator appears as an actor in his or her own story, he or she is called a **HOMODIEGETIC NARRATOR**; for example, the narrators in *Citizen Kane* appear as characters in their own accounts of Kane's life, making them homodiegetic. If the character-narrator does not appear in the story he or she recounts, they are called a **HETERODIEGETIC NARRATOR**. The second zone in which a narrator functions in film is in the overall control of the visual and sonic registers. This external, impersonal narrator is called an **EXTRADIEGETIC NARRATOR**: "external to (not part of) any diegesis" (Prince 1987: 29). In film, this type of narrator manifests itself not through verbal discourse but through a range of cinematic codes and channels of expression.

One area of ambiguity which is unique to film and does not seem to be covered by any of Genette's categories is the voice-over narrator who is not a character in the story, typically found in documentaries and in war films of the 1940s. Because this type of narrator is not really a character-narrator, he or she is not exactly a heterodiegetic narrator. Some commentators refer to this type as extradiegetic, because it appears at a "higher" level than the characters in the narrative, while others believe it to be a case of intradiegetic narration. David Alan Black has argued convincingly that it should be considered intradiegetic, for such voices are "contingent on the prior narrating act of the actual filmic text itself . . . the persistence of the text does not hinge on their activity. They do not instigate or cause the film" (Black 1986: 21).

CHARACTER NARRATION

This first zone of narrational activity – that of character-narration – can be illustrated without running into theoretical difficulties. The character-narrator, who is always situated at the intradiegetic level, may be an active participant in the story he or she relates, or may be a witness to it. Such narrators are homodiegetic, for the narrator relates his or her own experiences or perceptions, and functions in his or her own story as an actor. An example of this type is Captain Willard in *Apocalypse Now*, who is an active performer within the story he narrates, or Nick in *The Great Gatsby*, who acts primarily as a witness to the story he tells. Another type of intradiegetic narrator is the character of Molina in *Kiss of the Spider Woman*. Molina does not literally perform in the fictional work he recounts to his cell-mate Valentine; instead, he relates the plot of a movie he has seen. As narrator, he remains outside the frame of the story he narrates, thus functioning as a heterodiegetic narrator. In some cases the character-narrator's discourse will include another, embedded narration. This is found, for example, in *The Cabinet of Dr Caligari*, when Francis, the homodiegetic narrator, discovers the notebook of Caligari. The written account in the notebook becomes a visualized episode, depicting Caligari's initial encounter with Cesare, the somnambulist. Another example is Pasolini's *The Arabian Nights*, which consists entirely of embedded narrations. Typically, a character will start to narrate his or her story; before long, another character within the frame of the first story will begin telling their story, and so on, leading to a sense of infinite regress. This type of embedded narration is called **METADIEGETIC**.

A second consideration is whether the internal character-narrator tells the whole of the story, or whether the story is embedded within a larger narration, and if so, how much of the story is told from the limited perspective of the character-narrator. In literature, a character-narrator's discourse may comprise the whole of the story. But in film, the character-narrator always has his or her story embedded within the larger narration produced by the ensemble of cinematic codes, the overarching discourse of the external, impersonal cinematic narrator, who renders the text in a non-verbal form. This external, cinematic narrator has been called by various names: Sarah Kozloff uses the term **CAMERA-NARRATOR**, or **IMAGE-MAKER**; Black has labeled this the **INTRINSIC NARRATOR**, while André Gaudreault uses the term **FUNDAMENTAL NARRATOR** or **PRIMARY NARRATOR**. In many films the embedded character-narrations comprise a fairly small part of the overall film, such as in *Kiss of the Spider Woman*. But even in films such as *Apocalypse Now*, in which Willard's character-narration appears to be all-inclusive and seems to be responsible for the entire story, there always exists an overarching level of extradiegetic narration. Willard's narration is enclosed or embedded within the discourse of the external cinematic narrator, who inscribes another level of "commentary" in the film in the form of cross-cutting, rhyming images, superimpositions, manipulation of point-of-view, and expressive interpolations, such as the fade to black that follows the murder of the boat people. In film, the discourse of the character-narrator is always enveloped within a larger **PRIMARY NARRATIVE**, or first-level narrative, controlled by an extradiegetic narrator.

An interesting treatment of this problem of embedded character-narration in film is found in Black's article, "Genette and Film: Narrative Level in the Fiction Cinema" (1986). Black focusses on the capacity of a character-narrator to "invoke" a set of visual images as an accompaniment or illustration of his or her verbal narration. **INVOKING NARRATORS**, however, produce images which may or may not correspond directly to the verbal account they give. Often the images simply overrun or exceed the knowledge or capacity of the verbal character-narrator. But at other times there may be striking differences in tone, in content and in authority when two "versions" – one verbal, the other visual – are presented and juxtaposed. An example is Holly's voice-over narration in *Badlands;* at

98

times the tone and the content of her verbal narration is strikingly at odds with the images we see. Such is also the case with a film like *Last Year at Marienbad*, where the image-track frequently overtly contradicts the character's verbal account. Even in cases where the images closely correspond to the verbal narration, the character-narrator may be wholly unrealiable, despite the fact that he or she "produces" images that almost automatically convey a high degree of "truth-value." This is the case with the verbal-visual "lying" narration of Jonathon in *Stage Fright*, probably the most famous example of unrealiable character-narration in film. It is also seen in the character-narrators of *Rashomon*, whose contradictory versions of the central event place the veracity of all the narrators in doubt, even the spirit-narrator who speaks "from beyond the grave."

Kozloff provides several interesting examples and cases in her study of voice-over narration, *Invisible Storytellers* (1988). Wishing to avoid the awkwardness of Genette's terminology, Kozloff describes homodiegetic voice-over narration as first-person narration, and heterodiegetic voice-over narration as **THIRD-PERSON NARRATION**.

Under first-person narrators, Kozloff draws a distinction between **FRAME NARRATORS**, character-narrators who begin their narrations with the first images of a film, but whose actual act of narrating is not visualized, such as Alex in *A Clockwork Orange;* and **EMBEDDED NARRATORS**, who begin narrating after the story has begun, and who are visualized in the act of narration, as in *Mildred Pierce*. Kozloff claims that frame narrators possess a greater degree of believability, or what Lubomir Dolezel calls **AUTHENTI-CATION AUTHORITY** – the ability to establish and verify the facts of the fictional world – than do embedded narrators, who are more likely to be perceived as **UNRELIABLE NARRATORS**, and who must "earn" their authentication authority.

Frame narrators in some cases might even appear to "authorize" the images, as in *All About Eve*, so that the character's voice-over seems to create and control the images, with the image-track responding to cues from the verbal narration. This device is quite limited, however, and is never sustained throughout an entire film. Much more common is the opposite case, where a film or a sequence begins with the limited perspective of a character-narrator, only to give way to the unlimited powers of the extradiegetic, "image-maker" narrator, who presents information and an overall perspective which exceeds the knowledge and capacity of the character-narrator. Black has compared this operation to Genette's **PSEUDO-DIEGESIS**: "the process of transference of narratorial status from invoking narrator to intrinsic [extradiegetic or cinematic] narrator." He stresses the "dual agency" involved in such films as *Double Indemnity* and *Rancho Notorious*, in which the intrinsic narrator – "that which narrates the entire film," the agency that "is congruent with the discursive activity of the medium itself" – shares narratorial duties with the character-narrator

(Black 1986: 22). The limited authority and power of the character-narrator is underscored by André Gaudreault, who argues that even in *first-person films*, it is theoretically necessary to posit what he calls a fundamental narrator – a narrator who controls the ensemble of cinematic techniques, including voice-over (Gaudreault 1989).

Kozloff's treatment of third-person voice-over narrators, which in Genette's system would probably be labeled heterodiegetic, deals primarily with the quality of omniscience conveyed by these voices. As she writes: "When a narrator is not a character, not a participant in the story he or she relates, that narrator is not bound by the rules of plausibility that govern the characters; the narrator is superior to them, the shaper of their destinies" (Kozloff 1988: 97). Such heterodiegetic narrators "mimic" the authority and power of the extradiegetic cinematic narrator, while being restricted to the verbal register. The heterodiegetic voice-over narrator is usually a frame narrator – one whose act of narrating is not visualized, but is given a kind of free-floating, bodiless status, "a voice from on-high" – although some films employ an embedded heterodiegetic narrator, such as Peter Ustinov in Max Ophuls' *Le Plaisir*.

GENDER IN VOICE-OVER NARRATION

Within the general category of character-narration, there is a tendency to assign different subtypes on the basis of gender. As Kaja Silverman points out in "A Voice to Match: The Female Voice in Classical Cinema" (1985), the disembodied voice-over, or frame narrator, occurs relatively infrequently in the classical cinema. It seems to be separated from the main diegesis by an absolute partition, and to invert the usual sound–image hierarchy: it seems to control the images, and to dictate their order from a superior position of knowledge. As Pascal Bonitzer (1976: 33) suggests, it is not easily integrated into the rest of the film, for it proclaims its independence and its superior knowledge too aggressively. If the disembodied male voice-over is unusual, however, and limited to 1940s and early 1950s films, the disembodied female voice-over or frame narrator is all but non-existent. Silverman cites Joseph Mankiewicz's *Letter to Three Wives* as the only example known to her. In sum, it appears that while female first-person frame narrators, as in Hanoun's *Une Simple Histoire*, and Holly in *Badlands*, can be readily found, and female embedded or invoking narrators, such as *Mildred Pierce*, may be just as common as male, the third-person frame narrator seems to have been assigned strictly to male voices in narrative film up till now.

UNRELIABILITY

One of the features of character-narrators is that they can lie, make mistakes, or distort the facts of the fictional world. Unlike the extradiegetic, impersonal narrator, character-narrators do not possess an automatic authentication authority: what they say must be tested, compared to other versions of events, and judged according to the general characteristics of the milieu in which they reside. Their statements do not directly convey the facts of the **NARRATIVE WORLD** – defined by the literary narratologist Dolezel (1980) as the authenticated motifs of the narrative – but rather convey a version of the facts, which may be subject to the human biases and limitations of the character-narrator. The character-narrator simply reports on a world, he does not create or invent that world. The creation of a fictional world is the sole province of the extradiegetic, impersonal narrator, a difference in capacity which we will discuss in the next section of this part.

In film, *unreliability* is usually associated with an intradiegetic character-narrator. Although some works like *Last Year in Marienbad* and *La guerre est finie* by Resnais feature an unreliable, extradiegetic narrator, such experiments are rare. Unreliable character-narrators are also rare in film. *Breaker Morant, Rashomon* and *Stage Fright* are some of the more famous examples.

The classic example of unreliable character-narration in film is Hitchcock's *Stage Fright*. Several writers, including Chatman, Kozloff, Franceso Casetti and Kristin Thompson have proposed various explanations for the agency behind the "lying flashback" and the method the viewer uses to sort out the authentic from the authentic version of events. Thompson, for one, feels that Hitchcock violated one of the tenets of extradiegetic narration by illustrating and even embellishing Jonathon's verbal lie with what are taken to be inherently truthful images, thus colluding with Jonathon's deception (1988: 148). Kozloff, on the other hand, recognizes that the ostensible reliability of the image is not intrinsic, but merely a convention (1988: 115). Chatman, for his part, appeals to the higher narrative authority of the **IMPLIED AUTHOR** – an agent who stands between the real author and the narrator as the means by which we evaluate the truthful and the untruthful versions of the story (1986: 141). The implied author has been defined by Wayne Booth (1983) as the persona, or implicit image of an author in the text, standing behind the scenes and responsible for its design, its values and its cultural norms. The implied author should be distinguished from the real author, and from the narrator. Unlike the narrator, the implied author does not present or recount events, but is held to be responsible for the overall choices made in the text. Unlike the real author, the implied author varies with each text produced by the real author. In Chatman's view, the implied author sets the lying narration of *Stage Fright* in a context that allows the viewer to decide the issue.

101

Casetti provides yet another solution, albeit a very unorthodox one, by proposing that the "false" images actually correspond to what Eve, Jonathon's auditor, imagines as he tells her the lie. Thus the images are produced by the subjectivity of the character Eve, listening to Jonathon; Eve could be said to work in tandem with him to create this false homodiegetic narration: one character supplies the verbal discourse, the other the images. The extradiegetic narrator is thus relieved of his culpability of "duplicity" in illustrating the lie (Casetti 1986b).

Despite the apparent difficulty in accounting for this effect, lying character-narrators in general can be understood simply as invoking narrators who happen to be duplicitous. The character-narrator is under no compulsion to "narrate the truth", either in words or images; in so far as they merely "report" on the fictional world rather than "create" it, they can distort the facts of that world without calling the world itself into question. The fictional world still retains its authenticity, established by the extradiegetic narrator, despite the inaccuracy of a character-narrator's report. Although the images may appear to "overrun" the invoking narrator's knowledge or capacity, as they do in *Stage Fright*, they retain their status as character-narration despite the "assistance" of the extradiegetic narrator. The sequence in *Stage Fright* clearly unfolds as character-narration, returning to the character-narrator as he ends his story: the images that illustrate and embellish it simply do not carry the authentication authority of extradiegetic narration.

More common than duplicitous invoking narrators are cases where the voice-over narration and the images diverge creating discrepancies that are usually read as a qualification, an undermining, or explicit rejection of the character-narrator's verbal report. Kozloff cites several examples of this type, ranging from *Cat Ballou* to *The Marrying Kind*. A more recent example can be found in Robert Altman's *Fool For Love*. As the character May listens to her father narrate a story about her childhood, and the night the father and daughter found themselves in the middle of a herd of cows, the images accompanying the narration begin to diverge from the oral report in many of the details. While the father describes the little girl as crying incessantly on their car trip, the images depict her as silent. As he describes his efforts to calm her down, the images reveal him to be caught up in amorous activity with her mother in the front seat. The images undermine the veracity of the father's report, not in its broad outline, but in its details, suggesting an unreliability on the part of the character-narrator that is simultaneously "corrected" by the extradiegetic image-maker. The spectator assigns a higher authenticity value to the images than to the verbal character-narration. Guido Fink, writing on 1940s films such as *Laura* and *Mildred Pierce*, makes this point explicitly:

a silently accepted convention seems to state that images and visualized actions . . . may omit something but never distort the truth. . . . A curious balance or compensation rules that oral narration – conscious, subjective, deliberate – helps us to understand and rationalize events, but may be lying; narrated stories – that is, represented, shown events – may be partial, disturbing, incomplete, but never false.

(Fink 1982: 24)

An interesting exception to this general rule, aside from *Stage Fright*, is Buñuel's *That Obscure Object of Desire*. Here the invoking narrator Mathieu relates the story of his relationship with a beautiful woman to a group of avid auditors on a train. The story consists of the history of his frustrating encounters with Conchita, a woman who, according to him, has persecuted him with unkept promises of sexual fulfillment. The visualized story seems to correspond, initially, to his description. But at several points one beautiful woman is substituted for another: two different actresses play the role of Conchita, sometimes switching in the middle of a scene. The spectator cannot fail to notice this substitution, but the character-narrator Mathieu, who seems at first to authorize and control the narration, is utterly oblivious. The extradiegetic narrator has undermined Mathieu's version of events by substituting one actress for another, leading to a highly comic effect. But the extradiegetic narrator could not be said to communicate the "truth" of Mathieu's situation, the actual and legitimate version of events, over and above his personal, distorted account: one does not conclude that Mathieu has two girlfriends named Conchita. Instead, the dual messages illustrate the workings of the dialogical and ironic possibilities when voice and image are set against one another.

THE CINEMATIC NARRATOR

The question of **EXTRADIEGETIC NARRATION** in film is a considerably more ambiguous area of enquiry than that of character-narration. Extradiegetic narration in film can be defined as the primary narratorial or discursive activity flowing from the medium of cinema itself; it is "that which narrates the entire film," in Black's phrase, and it involves all the codes of the cinema. Various names have been proposed for this agency, including Kozloff's "image-maker," Metz' "grande imagier," Black's "intrinsic narrator," and Gaudreault's "fundamental narrator." Because extradiegetic narration is the primary agency responsible for relating events, it is always exterior and logically prior to the fictional world itself, which it encloses. For this reason, we will occasionally refer to this primary agency as the **EXTERNAL NARRATOR** or the **CINEMATIC NARRATOR**. In so far as film is a mixed medium, narration in film can be simultaneously discursive, providing story information through a variety of channels and

103

an ensemble of codes. Extradiegetic narration, therefore, should not be assimilated to any particular code or technique, such as the camera-narrator. Nor should it be confused with the author or the implied author, who are outside the discursive framework of narration. The implied author and the real author have no voice of their own in the fictional situation; they communicate only through their delegate, the extradiegetic or intradiegetic narrator.

The central debate concerning extradiegetic narration in film revolves around the question of whether film possesses the equivalent of the narrator of literature – understood as the illocutionary or expressive source of the discourse – or whether this function is actually a convention of reading whereby the spectator simply assigns the label of narrator, after the fact, to certain specific textual effects. A secondary question is whether extra-diegetical narration in film leaves its marks or its traces in the manifest text of the filmic *récit*, allowing the analyst to specify certain techniques, codes or inscriptions as signifiers of a narratorial presence, or mode of enunciation, or, on the other hand, whether narration in film should be understood globally, as a kind of message without a sender. For Genette, literary narratives manifest the traces of a narratorial presence through certain pronouns and verb tenses, through the register that he calls narrative voice; but the narration itself remains an abstraction, an inference on the part of the reader, whose tangible experience of the text is limited to the *récit*. In film, a vigorous debate has unfolded around the issues of narrative voice and discursive source, but only recently have these questions been formulated within the specialized discourse of narrative theory.

Prior to the emergence of the narrative theory of film as a distinct field of study, the issues surrounding narrative structure, particularly the complex issue of narration, were articulated within other theoretical paradigms and on the basis of different analogies. Bordwell has classified the earlier approaches to narration into mimetic and diegetic theories. **MIMETIC NAR-RATIVE** is defined by Plato as "narrative via imitation," in which the poet speaks through the characters, "as if he were someone else" (Plato 1963: 638, in Bordwell 1985: 16). It is usually characterized as the direct enactment or imitation of an action, as in the theater, without the mediation and retrospection of a narrator's act of recounting. More generally, mimetic approaches to film refer to the imitation of reality or of human perception in photographic processes. **DIEGETIC NARRATIVE**, on the other hand, is defined by Plato as "simple narrative," in which "the poet himself is the speaker" (ibid.). Diegetic approaches to filmic narration emphasize the discursive aspects of film, and analogize film to a type of rhetoric, discourse, or a quasi-linguistic form of enunciation. Proceeding from a concept of film as a form of "telling," shot composition, editing, lighting and so on are analogized to linguistic activities.

ENUNCIATION AND CINEMATIC NARRATION

This concept of filmic narration emerged in the early 1970s under the influence of structural linguistics. Initially, it was characterized by a special concern for the specific codes, the work of denotation, and the properties of connotation which characterize the fiction film, an approach best exemplified in the early work of Metz. Later, diegetic theories of narration shifted their emphasis to enunciation – defined by Prince in literary narratology as "The traces in a discourse of the act generating that discourse," such as the words "I" and "now" (Prince 1987: 27). In film theory, enunciation has also come to signify the constitution of subjectivity in language, and secondarily, the production and control of subject relations through the imaginary link established between the narrator and the spectator by way of their mutual investment in the discourse of the film.

The categories devised by Emile Benveniste in linguistics were particularly influential in film studies during this phase, especially the oppositions of **ENONCE** and **ENONCIATION, HISTOIRE** and **DISCOURS**. Briefly, Benveniste distinguished the *énoncé*, or the utterance itself, from the *énonciation*, or the act of uttering. Studies of enunciation focussed on the ways in which the speaker or narrator inscribes him or herself in the message, mainly through pronouns, such as "I" or "me," temporal indicators, such as "now" or "then," spatial references, etc., thus offering a certain **MODE OF ADDRESS** to the spectator. The messages that bear the explicit trace or mark of the speaker, in which the speaker is unambiguously inscribed as the source of the message, are characterized as instances of *discours*. Messages which do not bear the personalized stamp of a speaker are, in contrast, characterized as *histoire* – "No one speaks here; the events seem to narrate themselves" (Benveniste 1971: 208). Historical writing, and prose fiction in general, are, for Benveniste, examples of a message wherein the marks of enunciation are effaced: "the historical utterance characterizes the narration of past events. . . . Events that took place at a certain moment of time are presented without any intervention of the speaker in the narration" (ibid.: 206).

In film theory, the mode of *histoire* was said to characterize the classic narrative film. In a short essay that had an enormous influence on film theory, "Story/Discourse: A Note on Two Voyeurisms" (1976), Metz argued that the classic film effaces the marks of enunciation; in this type of film there are no explicit indicators of a speaker or a narrator in the message; the film seems to "tell itself." But concealed within this ostensibly transparent form of *histoire* is a covert, invisible discursive agency – the camera. The film in effect "masquerades" as *histoire*, although it is in fact a mode of *discours*, with a definite intentional quality whose purpose is to affect an audience. In this way it corresponds to Benveniste's description of *discours:* "every enunciation assuming a speaker and a hearer, and in the speaker the intention of influencing the hearer in some way" (Benveniste 1971: 242). By suppressing the marks of enunciation – the masking of the insignia of a "sender," or a "speaker" – the film facilitates an imaginary exchange whereby the spectator supplies his or her own links to the utterance, seeming to authorize and control the unfolding spectacle of the film as if it were the product of his or her own powers of enunciation. The film seems to be narrated by the spectator himself, who becomes, in imagination, its discursive source.

Other critics built on this characterization of the fiction film as *discours* masquerading as *histoire* to argue that the fiction film contains specific indications of enunciation in the most literal sense, that the *discours* of the film-text can be specified in ways that are similar to the pronouns, tenses and modes of language. One example of this literal application of Benveniste's categories is Mark Nash's (1976) treatment of Dreyer's *Vampyr*. Although Nash does not find examples of tense markers in film, he does attempt to analyze different shots, such as point-of-view shots and descriptive shots, as analogous to first-person and third-person types of utterance. Shots that simply render a character's perception, or the story-world itself, are considered examples of first-person or third-person *histoire;* shots that bear the inflection or marks of an author are said to be examples of *discours*. One of the problems with Nash's analysis is the absence of any equivalent to the "second person" in film. As Bordwell writes, "The second-person pronoun is a necessary component of Benveniste's conception of discours: it brings out the presence of the hearer" (Bordwell 1985: 23).

More frequently, critics utilized **ENUNCIATION THEORY** in a more metaphoric fashion to highlight the covert presence of *discours*, the marks of enunciation, concealed within the overall *histoire* of the text. One of the most important critics to accent the discursive marks of a narrator within a classic cinematic text is Bellour, who, in a series of articles on Hitchcock (Bellour 1979), finds the marks of "Hitchcock, the enunciator" in certain camera movements and positions, in certain repetitions of framing and imagery, in the direct glance by the character into the camera, and in Hitchcock's authographical insertion into the fictional space of his films. In these moments, Bellour argues, Hitchcock marks his presence as creator/narrator explicitly, revealing these films to be a mode of *discours*.

Stephen Heath arrived at a similar characterization of the classic film in an essay called "Narrative Space" (Heath 1981). Here the discussion of enunciation or mode of address links the categories of cinematic technique, narratorial discourse and the perceptions of the spectator. These registers are brought together by way of a structure or metaphor they hold in common – the notion of "position." Heath discerns four senses in which the concept of "position" could be said to structure the fictional experience in film: the perspective organization of the individual shot, the general spatial organization of the film – taken as supplying a kind of "ideal view" – the narrator's position, attitude or point-of-view, and the "subject positions" made available to the spectator through the other operations. His argument is that the eruption of a visible *discours*, through a violation of perspective, a break-up of overall spatial organization or a contradictory narrative point-of-view, will fracture the unified subject position of the spectator, leading to a fragmentation of identity and self-coherence.

The focus of these critics on narration as a mode of *discours* standing out from a general background of *histoire* is very much a product of the linguistic models which so influenced film analysis in the 1970s. Although used here to describe types of narration, the linguistic categories of *histoire* and *discours* should not be confused with the narratological categories of story and discourse, or fabula and syuzhet. Despite the similiarity of terms, and despite the fact that Genette uses the term *histoire* as a synonym for fabula, it should be remembered that the *histoire* and *discours* of enunciation theory and the story and discourse of narratology have entirely different meanings. *Histoire* and *discours* are each a type of *énonce*, two types of utterance which belong to the same "level" and which are, strictly speaking, mutually exclusive, despite the tendency in film criticism to find covert instances of one within the other. Story and discourse, on the other hand, refer to two very different "levels" – not different types – of narrative fiction. Rather than being mutually exclusive, they presuppose and necessitate one another. Story, in most narrative theories, is equivalent to the Formalists' fabula; it is the abstract content of the fiction, the basic level of story events, actors and places prior to their artistic ordering and presentation. It is a purely virtual construct, which, depending on one's perspective, either pre-exists or is projected from the *récit*. Discourse, equivalent to the syuzhet, is the actual narrative presentation, the words, images or gestures which we perceive, which are sensible and material. Unlike the linguistic terms *histoire* and *discours*, the narratological categories of story and discourse are not competing, different ways of rendering the message or utterance: both are involved in every fictional narrative.

COGNITIVE APPROACHES TO NARRATION

Recent work on the question of narration in film has progressed in two different directions: one is the cognitive approach advanced by Bordwell and Branigan, which focusses primarily on the reading process; the other approach is influenced by literary narratology and is principally concerned with modeling the hierarchy of narrative "voices" in film, a topic which has recently centered on the narratorial "source" or "instance of emission" of film narrative discourse. Both of these approaches have attempted to systematize the attributes of narration.

Several theorists have found the concept of the extradiegetic cinematic narrator to be questionable in its most basic premises. Writers such as

Bordwell, Branigan and George Wilson, for example, believe that the importance of designating an instance of emission or discursive source in film is minimal. Arguing that the verbal model which subtends the concept of the narrator is inappropriate in film, these writers adopt a version of the "non-narrator" theory of narrative fiction in literature. Because nothing akin to a human presence or a speaking subject can be discerned as the source of certain narratives, it is easier to assume, in Benveniste's phrasing, that "nobody speaks," or that the events simply "tell themselves" (1971: 206–8). Branigan endorses this view, which he describes as an empirical theory of narration, and places stress accordingly on the reading process:

> I want to emphasize, however, that in my view of narration there is no consciousness of a narrator to produce (originate) sentences which then control meaning for a reader but exactly the reverse: the systematic restrictions perceived by the reader within a text are simply labeled as narration in order to be located when needed in the logical process of reading.
>
> (Branigan 1984: 59)

Bordwell's view of narration in film is very similar:

> But in watching films, we are seldom aware of being told something by an entity resembling a human being. . . . Most films do not provide anything like such a definable narrator, and there is no reason to expect they will . . . Far better, I think, to give the narrational process the power to signal under certain circumstances that the spectator should construct a narrator . . . We need not build the narrator in on the ground floor of our theory.
>
> (1985: 62)

Bordwell presents a detailed rationale for his rejection of the concept of the cinematic narrator, offering in place of this a more global process he calls, simply, narration. Stressing the cognitive and perceptual processes involved in comprehending narrative, he argues that the notion that the narrative discourse emanates from a definable source or point of origin is simply a convention supplied by the viewer, and is not a privileged factor in narrative comprehension. What is important is the film's particular method of cueing the specator to make certain hypotheses and inferences, which will then be tested and refined as the film progresses: "In the fiction film, narration is the process whereby the film's syuzhet and style interact in the course of cueing and channeling the spectator's construction of the fabula" (Bordwell 1985: 53).

In some cases, disparity between style and syuzhet processes can be isolated as a generic characteristic, as in the European art cinema. Bordwell analyzes several genres and "historical modes of narration" from this basis, defining several types, such as "parametric narration," exemplified by

Robert Bresson's *Pickpocket*, "historical materialist narration," as found in Eisenstein, and "classical narration," characterized by the Hollywood style. These analyses fill something of a gap in approaches to filmic narration, for they illuminate particular films by combining close textual analysis with a theoretical perspective that demonstrates the usefulness of the method. The value of the approach is particularly well demonstrated in the analysis of Bresson's *Pickpocket*.

Although Bordwell's focus on narrative comprehension necessitates the analysis of stylistic processes, it should be noted that this situates his overall theory in the framework of what Pavel calls Discourse-Narratology. Traditionally, narrative analysis sought to define the elements that all narrative artifacts have in common, independent of media-specific manifestations such as "style." While Tynianov, a writer frequently cited by Bordwell, also argued for the inclusion of style as an element of narrative structure, the thrust of his approach was to discount the importance of the specifically narrative components of film in favor of "verse-like" or "poetic" film forms (in Eagle 1981: 94). The focus on style as an aspect of narrative comprehension in Bordwell's work inclines it toward cognitive and perceptual theory, but it can also be seen in the context of a partition in narrative theory proper. In his recent work, Genette has also argued against the idea of an abstract level of narrative events, maintaining that the distinction between fabula and syuzhet is open to question. Events, he argues, do not exist independently of their representation. The focus on representation, as opposed to story structure, has led several narratologists to emphasize textual manifestations, including style, rather than the story elements that all narratives have in common.

RECENT THEORIES OF THE CINEMATIC NARRATOR

Film narrative theory has also developed in another direction, with several writers focussing not on conceptual processes but on the architecture of narrative form. One of the central issues linking the work of different theorists is the question of the cinematic narrator. Theorists such as Seymour Chatman, André Gaudreault, Francesco Casetti and Tom Gunning have defended the concept of the cinematic narrator as essential to understanding the process and structure of film narrative communication. According to these writers, the presence of an extradiegetic narrator, whether manifest or implicit, is a logical necessity, providing the governing principles by which we understand the hierarchy of narrative roles, determine the quality of truth and authenticity in the fictional world, and comprehend the enacted events of film as a type of "message."

The general argument favoring a narrator in film is congruent with the view of many theorists of literature who believe the concept of the narrator is logically necessary of all fictions. Rimmon-Kenan, for one, argues that

even when a narrative text presents passages of pure dialogue, manuscript found in a bottle, or forgotten letters and diaries, there is in
addition to the speakers or writers of this discourse a "higher" narratorial authority responsible for "quoting" the dialogue or "tran-
scribing" the written records.

(Rimmon-Kenan 1983: 88)

Other literary critics, such as Dolezel and Marie-Laure Ryan, maintain
that the concepts of truth and authenticity in fiction are dependent on the
concept of the narrator: the category of the narrator provides the fundamental component of the basic fictional contract that narrative establishes
with the spectator or reader. The importance of the narrator to the overall
fictional contract resides in the fact that only the narrator can produce
truth-functional discourse within what is manifestly a fictional construct.
In other words, within the overall narrative contract in which a fiction is
related to an addressee, there is another level in which a narrator "tells
the truth" about the fictional world. As Ryan writes:

[The narrative] concerns what is, from the point of view of author
and reader, an alternate possible world, but on the level of the
embedded contract, speaker and hearer communicate about what is
for them the real world. Every narrative text whose narrator is not
hallucinating presupposes a level where a speaker tells a story as true
fact and not as invention.

(Ryan 1981: 524)

Casetti provides a demonstration of the importance of this particular
narratorial role in film in analyses of *Cronaca di un amore* by Michelangelo
Antonioni and *Stage Fright* by Alfred Hitchcock. He focusses on the function
of the **ENUNCIATOR** – a kind of hybrid of the extradiegetic narrator and
the implied author – in validating or sanctioning one character's version
of events over another's in these two films. The enunciator's role is defined
here in terms of four functions or manifestations of authority: **COMPETENCE**
– the knowledge required to relate the story; **PERFORMANCE** – the ability
to relate the story; **MANDATE** – designation as the agent responsible for
relating the tale; and **SANCTION** – the authentication authority to establish
the facts of the fictional world, over and above any false reports about the
fictional world or its inhabitants. When the enunciator transfers this role
to an internal character-narrator, all of these qualities must be present for
the discourse of the character-narrator to be taken as authentic. By detail-
ing just which of these powers is assigned to the internal narrators and
narratees of both stories, he discovers that the attribute of sanction is
withheld from the characters of *Cronaca*, and also withheld from Jonathon,
the "lying" character-narrator of *Stage Fright*. While these diegetic characters initially seem to possess all that is required to assume the duties of

the enunciator – to have a mandate, a competence, and an ability to perform (convey) the story – the crucial quality of being able to predicate, to sanction the story, is missing:

> The detective, Paolo, and Guido [in *Cronaca*] need something extra to ratify what they have been observing. They need a sanction . . . a sort of control coupon as a seal of guarantee; it would legitimize the presence and performance of the characters . . . But like the mandate, the sanction too cannot reach the interested parties unless someone weighs their actions from the outside . . . besides a receiver who is evaluated, a subject who evaluates . . .
>
> (Casetti 1986: 76)

Casetti's argument concerning *Stage Fright* details the process whereby predication authority is withheld from Jonathon as a character-narrator, leading to the disauthentication of his version of events – rendered in the famous "lying flashback" near the beginning of the film. Although the "lying flashback" appears to be an authentic report of the facts, the character-narrator or invoking narrator does not possess the authentication authority that the extradiegetic narrator commands as a matter of course. In order for Jonathon's discourse to be taken as true, the enunciator must confirm the character-narration in some fashion. In Casetti's model, the extradiegetic narrator may delegate to a character-narrator certain of the four narratorial functions, such as performance and competence, and may allow the mandate to be supplied by another character, such as Eve, who overtly requests the report from Jonathon, but the crucial ability to be able to sanction the report of the character-narrator can only reside with an extradiegetic narrator who alone controls the authentication function. While everything the extradiegetic narrator fashions yields a fact for the fictional world, the character-narrator, by contrast, has to "earn his authentication authority" (Dolezel 1980: 18).

A comprehensive and synthetic view of filmic narration is offered by Tom Gunning in *D. W. Griffith and the Origins of the American Narrative Film* (1991). Gunning begins by discussing the apparent difficulty of perceiving film as a narrative form, given its overtly mimetic character. How can film be understood to "tell" a story, when it primarily "shows" a fictional world, in a seemingly neutral way, without narratorial inflection or commentary? His solution is to argue that it is precisely the channeling and organizing of the mimetic dimension of the film-text that defines the role of cinematic narration.

> The primary task of the filmic narrator must be to overcome the initial resistance of the photographic material to telling by creating a hierarchy of narratively important elements within a mass of contingent details. Through filmic discourse, these images of the world

111

become addressed to the spectator, moving from natural phenomena to human products, meanings arranged for a spectator. It is through a shaping and defining of visual meanings that the filmic narrator functions.

(Gunning 1991: 17)

This is accomplished through a process Gunning calls narrativization, a concept derived from Stephen Heath, which refers to the binding of a film's wealth of mimetic details in the direction of narrative coherence: "the concept of narrativization focusses the transformation of showing into telling, film's bending of its excessive realism to narrative purposes" (Gunning 1991: 18).

Gunning focusses on the narrative discourse of film, the plane of expression as opposed to the plane of content, the level Genette calls the *récit*. In film, narrative discourse is especially complex in that it functions at three distinct levels simultaneously. These three levels, which Gunning describes as the **PRO-FILMIC** – the physical material of the scene prior to the act of filming – the enframed image, and the process of editing, each communicate narrative information, but it is through their combination, their working in concert, that storytelling in film is accomplished. Through the process of narrativization, these three levels are linked to one another, constituting the overall system of narration in film. The pro-filmic concerns the elements placed in front of the camera to be filmed: actors, lighting, set design, etc. These elements, rather than being seen simply as raw material, can be understood as narrative discourse by the fact that they have been chosen and selected to communicate narrative meanings. Recognizing the tension between the mimetic and the narrational aspects of film, Gunning remarks that "as narrative discourse the profilmic embodies a series of choices and reveals a narrative intention behind the choices."

The second level of filmic discourse is the enframed image. This entails composition and spatial relations. The construction of the image establishes a particular point-of-view on the action, involving perspective, selection of camera distance and angle, and the movement within the frame. Gunning includes camera movement and optical devices such as split screens, superimpositions, and matte shots in this category.

The third level of narrative inscription consists of editing. Editing creates various narrative syntagmas which allow a wide range of spatial and temporal articulations between the shots. Relations of tense, for example, are registered and manipulated primarily through editing.

The three levels, working in concert, are seen as the means by which films "tell" stories, and thus are said to constitute the cinematic narrator. "The narrator embodies the design organizing narrative discourse, the intentions which unify its effects" (Gunning 1991: 24). In the case of D. W. Griffith, a particular way of synthesizing these levels can be discovered, an approach to storytelling that Griffith developed while at the Biograph film studio. This particular organization of the three levels in Griffith, his systematic approach to narrative form, is called the **NARRATOR-SYSTEM** by Gunning. Other film-makers employ different narrative systems, which can be characterized by different choices within and between the three levels of filmic discourse. This allows one to specify a range of cinematic narrators, ranging from the "invisible" narrational style of the classic Hollywood cinema to the highly idiosyncratic narrative discourse of, for example, Jean-Luc Godard.

The narrator-system utilizes the three different levels of filmic discourse in order to convey messages about the story-world, or the fabula, and about the relation of the narrator to the discourse itself. Gunning adopts Genette's model of these relations, and shows how the categories of tense, mood and voice operate in film narrative discourse, specifically in relation to the three registers of the pro-filmic, enframed and edited images of Griffith's Biograph films.

This model offers many advantages over earlier approaches to filmic narrative, chiefly because the hierarchy of narrative functions Gunning discerns promotes a comprehensive view of filmic narration, while also permitting a great deal of specificity and nuance in the designation of the separate attributes of narration. The message fashioned through the pro-filmic event, for example, can be distinguished from the narrative message communicated by camera angle, although both messages are still considered as functions of cinematic narration. The conceptual unity which flows from this view of filmic narration does not override important distinctions of level and substance in film narrative discourse.

A different argument for the existence of an extradiegetic narrator in film is set forth by Chatman. Basing his theory on the communication model of narrative transmission, Chatman maintains that the notion of a narrative "message" presupposes the concept of a "sender:" " 'Sender' is logically implicated by 'message;' a sender is by definition built-in: inscribed or immanent in every message" (Chatman 1986a: 140).

The narrative message, however, need not be "told," that is, it need not be presented in verbal form. There is no reason to reject the concept of the cinematic narrator, in his view, simply because there is nothing akin to a speaking voice or an agent "resembling a human being" that emits sentences directed toward a viewer. The concept of narrative voice, after all, even in verbal fictions, is usually a metaphor: rather than "vocalization," Chatman points out, narrative voice refers to a kind of encoding that denotes a source or sender of the signifying material. The story can in fact be shown, rather than told, presented iconically rather than linguistically. Chatman's theory of the narrator as a constitutive element of narrative communication extends, as does Gunning's, even to the scenic presentation – the spatial organization of the shot, and seemingly, although this is not stated, to the pro-filmic organization of materials as well – elements that are often referred to as the mimetic aspects of the film-text: "films, in my view, are always presented – mostly and often exclusively shown, but sometimes partially told – by a narrator or narrators" (Chatman 1990: 133). In this sense, Chatman's narrator is very similar to Rimmon-Kenan's who, at the very least, "quotes" or "transcribes" the dialogue or the gestures of the characters.

In the cinema, this narratorial encoding is complex and utilizes both visual and audio channels: lighting, editing, camera angle and movement, color, *mise-en-scène*, can all be attributed to the visual articulations of the narrator. Music and voice-over or voice-off can be understood as its audio manifestations. For Chatman, the film-text is narrated in all its details; the activity of a narrator pervades every aspect of the text.

The stark opposition of Chatman and Gunning's positions and that of the non-narrator theorists illustrates the difficulty of specifying the role of the external narrator in film. Both arguments represent vigorous attempts to place film in the broad class of narrative forms, describing features of the film-text that compare to the dominant characteristics of literary narrative. But these theories seem to ignore the basic differences of the film-text from literary narratives, namely the overwhelming importance of what the literary narratologist Martinez-Bonati calls the **MIMETIC STRATUM** – the "real world of the fictional universe," the "factual domain" which the viewer imagines he or she perceives directly, rather than through representation:

> the "mimetic stratum" of the work is not experienced as language but directly as world: the reader does not simply conclude "the narrator says P" from the narrator's mimetic statements, he also derives "P is the case" and regards P as an unmediated fact of the real world of the fictional universe.
>
> (in Ryan 1984: 131)

In film, this would correspond to the distinction between the scenic presentation and what might be called the discursive aspects of the text, the distinction between the fictional world itself and the type of expressive interpolations which might be analogized to Genette's narrative voice.

Many of the textual elements that Chatman, for example, would assimilate to the agency of a narrator are perceived by the spectator directly as elements of the fictional world, rather than as elements of a narrator's discourse. Material such as the actor's appearance, the location or setting, the *mise-en-scène* – the entire mimetic stratum which Chatman ascribes to the presentational activity of a narrator – are perceived primarily as the fictional world itself, and only secondarily as a narrator's discourse. While his argument that the cinematic narrator quotes or "presents" the entire range of events in the fictional world does serve to keep the agency of the

114

narrator in the forefront of the model, it creates an equally difficult problem. How are we to distinguish the narrator's "mimetic statements," the
elements of the film-text that form the "unmediated fact(s) of the real world
of the fictional universe" from the narrator's expressive interpolations, the
filmic equivalent of a narrator's judgments, commentary, interpretation and
critique? In Chatman's model there is no way of distinguishing between
the narrator's "presentation" of the fictional world and the narrator's
"commentary" on the fictional world. Gunning, on the other hand, distinguishes the different activities of the narrator, but does not take into
account the pragmatic distinction between the mimetic stratum of the film-
text and the shaping activity of narration.

The narrative theory of film has long recognized the distinction between
"commentary" and "presentation," although the problem has been stated
in a variety of ways, and has yet to be satisfactorily resolved. In the
debates of the Russian Formalists this question took the form of arguments
over the relative dominance of "style" or "story" in film narrative construction. Story was held to be a mimetic category, evidenced by the Formalists'
comparison of story films to "theater"; style, on the other hand, was
related to the process and method of rendering the story, what might be
called the narratorial stance towards the story. In enunciation theory, the
issue was couched in terms of *histoire* and *discours*, with one or the other
form dominating in any given scene. More recently, film narrative theory
has dealt with the dualistic structure of film narrative directly, and has
set about constructing models which can account for two types of narration
– commentary and presentation – operating simultaneously.

André Gaudreault has advanced an original position on filmic narration
in the recent book *Du littéraire au filmique: système du récit*. He argues that
narrative film consists of a superimposition of a mimetic and a non-mimetic
form of diegesis, a lamination of *monstration* and narration. **MONSTRATION**,
in general, is the act of "showing forth," of presenting events in present
time, a kind of "rigorously synchronous simultaneous narration" (Gaudreault 1987: 32). In most instances, *monstration* is bound to a single temporality – the present – and can only "show" or "present" events as they
occur. While the purest mode of *monstration* is found in the theater, with
its unwavering present tense, *monstration* also occurs in film in terms of the
direct presentation of events as if they were occurring in present-tense
immediacy. In Gaudreault's theory, the camera is the chief device of the
monstrator.

The narrative film both presents the event mimetically, through *monstration*, and refigures the event, at a second level, according to the guiding
viewpoint of a narrator. The chief distinction marking the two modes,
according to Gaudreault, is the introduction of a complex temporality
characteristic of narration – the insertion of a "true narrative past" into
a seemingly mimetic event, a "time of reflection" between the moment at

115

which an event occurred and the moment at which it is received. The "unipunctual time" of *monstration* can be refashioned into a signifying pattern only through a second narrative inscription. It is only through narration that the temporal flow of the film can be restructured according to a specific logic and intent, and only through narration that a gap can be introduced between the occurrence and its recounting. As he writes:

> the "unipunctuality" to which the monstrator is bound prevents it irreducibly from modulating the temporal flow of the narrative . . .
> It is because the monstrator, any monstrator, clings so closely to the immediacy of the "representation" that it is incapable of opening up this gap in the temporal continuum. . . . Only the narrator can sweep us along on its flying carpet through time.
>
> (Gaudreault 1987: 33, 32)

The chief code through which the cinematic narrator expresses itself is editing: it is editing, Gaudreault argues, that comprises the "activity of the filmic narrator which allows for the inscription of a true narrative past" (ibid.: 32). Editing allows for the introduction of a time of reflection between the moment when events have occurred, rendered in the form of *monstration*, and the moment that they are received by a narratee, allowing the event to be replaced before the eyes of the spectator in whatever order the narrator desires, producing a "guided reading." The mastery of time is the privileged form by which the narrator manifests itself, taking the events recorded by the *monstrator*-camera and restructuring them according to a guiding temporal logic: "Only the narrator (= the editor) can inscribe between two shots (by means of cuts and articulation) the mark of its viewpoint, can introduce a guided reading and thereby transcend the temporal oneness which unavoidably constrains the discourse of narration" (ibid.: 33).

Gaudreault argues that filmic narration consists of a unique merging of these two modes of communication, a combination of narration and *monstration*; in essence, two types of narration: the *monstration* expressed at the level of the individual shot, and the narration made possible by editing and its power over the temporal dimension.

Although this approach is theoretically promising, the concrete application of the model requires that the film-text be programmatically divided according to technique rather than narratorial intention. His distinction between *monstration* and narration depends on the rigid separation of camera-work and editing. Aside from reprising one of the oldest oppositions in film theory – which, as he points out, has informed the theories of Eisenstein, Balasz and Bazin – this separation leads to an unfortunate atomization of the film-text. Clearly, camera-work can function as narration, in so far as camera angle, movement and shot size can provide the equivalent of a "guided reading." Indeed, the entire complex of cinematic representation, including lighting, image texture, color, sound, music, voice-over – in short, all the codes that Chatman associates with the narratorial presentation of the fictional world – can also be employed to convey the cinematic analogue of commentary, evaluation and emphasis that Gaudreault wishes to reserve only for editing.

An approach which holds promise for resolving these difficulties is the theory of **IMPERSONAL NARRATION**. The premises of this theory have been set out by Ryan in literary narratology, and have been adapted for film by the present author. The core concept of the theory of impersonal narration is that impersonal narrative discourse involves two activities: it both creates or constructs the fictional world while at the same time referring to it as if it had an autonomous existence, as if it pre-existed the illocutionary act. By contrast, **PERSONAL NARRATION** – for example, the narration of a character-narrator – does not create the fictional world, but simply reports on it, in the manner of a witness or participant. The paradoxical situation of impersonal narration – narrative discourse as world-creating as well as world-reflecting – allows us to conceive the narrator as both the illocutionary source of the fictional world and as the agent who comments on, evaluates, qualifies and embellishes the facts of the fictional world.

In creating the fictional world, the impersonal narrator produces a type of discourse that is read directly as the facts of the "real world" of the fictional universe. The impersonal narrator's lack of human personality allows the viewer to imagine that he or she is confronting the fictional universe directly, putting aside any reflection on the form of the narrative discourse. What Martinez-Bonati calls the mimetic stratum of the work is not experienced as discourse, but rather directly as world (in Ryan 1984: 131). This is even more apparent in film than in literature where the narrational discourse, consisting of a range of visual and acoustic signals, is read primarily as the facts of the fictional world, and only secondarily as a formal pattern of images and sounds.

The personal character-narrator, on the other hand, does not create a world, but simply reports on it. Thus he or she can distort the facts of the fictional world, which still remain intact despite the false report. Contrary to the opinion of many writers, however, the unreliable character-narrator can utilize images as well as words, as seen in *Stage Fright*. Although some writers, such as Kozloff, argue that it is the convention of realism that prevents the image-track from distorting the truth (Kozloff 1988: 115), and others, such as Bordwell, that the lying narration in *Stage Fright* does not simply report what the liar said but shows it as if it were indeed objectively true (Bordwell 1985: 61), the reliability of the image depends entirely on whether it is produced by the discourse of a personal narrator or invoking narrator as opposed to the impersonal narrator. As Ryan says, "everything the impersonal narrator says yields a fact for the

117

fictional world" (1981: 534), while the personal narrator, by contrast, "has to earn his authentication authority" (Dolezel 1980: 18).

The model described here has many elements in common with Gaudreault's two-tiered approach. The superimposition of *monstration* and narration in Gaudreault can be compared to the world-creating and world-reflecting activities characteristic of impersonal narration.

Secondly, Gaudreault's rightful insistence that the defining characteristic of narration is the temporal gap between the time of the event and the time of the telling can be understood in terms of the distinction set out above between the narrator's construction of the fictional world and the activity of referring to it as if it were a pre-existent entity. By recasting the problem of dual temporalities in terms of the more fundamental distinction between world-creating and world-reflecting activities of narration, we can avoid the problem of assigning narratorial capacities only to those codes or figures that have conventionally been used to overtly manipulate temporal relations, such as editing. The temporal gap Gaudreault rightly demands of a theory of cinematic narration can be found in the capacity of the impersonal narrator to comment on the fictional world as if it had an autonomous existence, independent of and pre-existing the narrator's illocutionary act.

TENSE

The relations of tense constitute one of the most important elements of narrative structure, providing a powerful artistic technique for rendering the story-world in a varied and aesthetically interesting manner. The category of tense refers to the temporal relations between the story and the *récit*, or the story and the discourse. At the level of story, events are conceived as occurring in strict chronological sequence, in a straightforward and linear order. At the level of the discourse, however, events may be presented in an order which deviates from straight chronology, in which the devices of flashback, parallelism and flashforward complicate the progression of the narrative. Moreover, the simple events of the story may be rendered in a complex pattern which involves repetition, ellipsis and the acceleration or freezing of time.

Although many narratologists have discussed the subject of tense, the most widely accepted survey of the category is provided by Genette in *Narrative Discourse*. Tense, along with mood and voice, comprise the *récit*, in Genette's system. He further separates the relations of tense into three major subdivisions: order, duration and frequency. **ORDER** refers to the relation between the sequence in which events occur in the story and the order in which they are recounted. Straight chronology is one type of order, while events presented out of sequence are called **ANACHRONIES**. Anachronies are of two types: **ANALEPSES**, or flashbacks, and **PROLEPSES**, or flashforwards. Analepses can be **EXTERNAL**, if they cover a period of time prior to the events of the primary narrative, for example when a narrative provides background information; or they can be **INTERNAL**, if they fill in a gap in the primary narrative.

In film, straight chronology is most frequently employed. As Brian Henderson writes: "It seems that the majority of films of every era have been told in straight chronological order whereas, according to Genette, such order is the exception among novels" (1983: 5). Deviations from straight chronology are especially rare in the first twenty years of film history, according to Henderson, although an internal analepsis can be found in *Birth of a Nation* when "the Little Colonel" tells his fellow Southerners of the bitter events that have occurred under Reconstruction. While analepses are somewhat more common in genres such as *film noir*, prolepses remain very unusual in film. Henderson cites Nicolas Roeg and Alain Resnais as film-makers who use prolepses in a highly purposeful way, but they remain the exception.

Because cinema has no built-in tense system, Henderson points out, any deviation from straight chronology must be abundantly signaled: voice-over, musical effects, changes in costume or locale, blurring or stippling of the image, as well as such devices as whirling leaves or turning calendar pages, guide the viewer whenever a change in order is introduced: "Classical cinema reacts to a tense shift as though to a cataclysm; the viewer must be warned at every level of cinematic expression, in sounds, in images, and in written language, lest he/she be disoriented" (Henderson 1983: 6).

The second of Genette's categories of tense is **DURATION**. The figures of scene, **DESCRIPTIVE PAUSE**, summary and ellipsis are the major forms of duration, which has to do with variations of speed or rhythm between the constant pace of the story and the variable tempos of the discourse. Descriptive pause occurs when time stands still in the story while the description is carried on at length. An example in film might be the opening shots of a sequence which introduces the viewer to a setting or a locale. Both Henderson and Chatman find descriptive pause to be a problematic category for film, for even simple descriptive shots of a landscape often covertly serve to advance the narrative. As Henderson writes:

> Even if no action occurs in this shot or in this setting, the time devoted to them builds expectations for action to come; they too are ticks on the dramatic clock. Indeed, few things build more expectancy than silent shots of objects in a narrative film.
>
> (1983: 10)

The opposite relationship between discourse-time and story-time occurs in **ELLIPSIS**. Here, time passes in the story while no time elapses in the discourse. Ellipsis allows film-makers to edit out unimportant events, to dramatically telescope cause and effect occurrences, and to cover vast stretches of story-time economically. While ellipsis is typically used for the purposes of narrative compression, certain film-makers use ellipsis in a highly expressive and symbolic fashion, among them Roberto Rossellini and Bernardo Bertolucci, in whose films temporal discontinuity is used to articulate a logical argument. In Bertolucci's *1900*, for example, ellipsis serves as one of the principal instruments of historical analysis and inter-pretation, linking separate moments of the historical past in such a way that a discursive relationship emerges. Similarly, in the films of Rossellini, as Henderson writes, "ellipses trace the movement of an argument uncon-cerned with conventional diegesis . . ." (1983: 10). Perhaps the most exemplary use of ellipsis can be found in the films of Robert Bresson, in which the technique expresses important themes. Often in Bresson, the principal events of the plot will be completely elided: the event will be represented only in its absence. The accumulation of such elided events suggests a realm in which phenomenal reality has less significance than things that cannot be figured directly, such as spirituality and grace. Thomas Elsaesser (1983) has noted that ellipsis is a strong mark of enunci-ation, but, unlike other enunciative systems such as montage, it usually hides the mark of enunciation, and lets the reader feel he or she is making the connections. In the language of enunciation theory, it is a classic case of *discours* masquerading as *histoire*. In the films of Godard, however, ellipsis is used in a directly authorial manner, dividing and disjoining the discourse of the film from the story-world in such a way that crucial events are elided, spatial and temporal continuities are disassembled, and even indi-vidual shots have sections deleted from them, as in the famous "jump-cuts."

SCENE is another category of duration, occurring when the discourse-time and the story-time are equal. In the scene, the event is recorded without temporal manipulation. The most common instances of scenes in film are long-take sequences, in which the event gains dramatic power through its durational emphasis. Certain film-makers, such as Renoir and Welles, are well known for their long-take scenes, which dramatically underline the most significant events in their films. Other film-makers make use of **ISOCHRONY** – the matching of discourse-time and story-time – to challenge the conventional sense of pace in film, and to call attention to the viewer's habitual rhythms of reception. Works such as *Jeanne Dielman*, by Chantal Ackerman, *Wavelength* by Michael Snow, *The Chronicle of Anna Magdalena Bach* by Straub and Huillet, and *Sleep* by Andy Warhol consist almost entirely of scenes which unfold with all the deliberateness and leisureliness of actual events.

The fourth category of duration is **SUMMARY**, in which a long stretch of story-time is condensed, or abridged, in a brief passage of discourse. Typically, summary is used to render a series of events, spread out over

120

time, in a succinct fashion, such as the montage of train tracks, wheels and stations that might be used to summarize a cross-country trip, or the montage of newspaper headlines rendering in condensed form a politician's or an actress's "rise to the top." A particularly noteworthy use of summary can be found in the famous "Breakfast Table" sequence in *Citizen Kane*, in which the disintegration of the Kanes' marriage over the course of several years is adumbrated in a series of breakfast table encounters.

Additionally, there is a category of duration not mentioned by Genette but quite evident in film, namely, what Bal calls **SLOW-DOWN**. This category stands in direct contrast to summary, and can be defined as the discourse swelling the time of an event that occupies a considerably shorter time in the story. In film, slow-motion scenes are primary examples of slow-down, as are events reiterated from a variety of different camera angles, such as the plate-smashing scene in *Potemkin* or the drowning scene in *Don't Look Now*. Another example can be found in the bike-riding sequence in Godard's *Sauve qui peute*, in which the stuttering, staggered images of the woman riding the bicycle effectively decompose the movement of the character into Muybridge-like fragments. Slow-down invariably heightens the dramatic effect of sequences. In some films it is associated with the subjective responses of characters, such as the scene in Martin Scorsese's *Taxi Driver* when Travis Bickle first sees Betsy on the street, or when Jake La Motta in *Raging Bull* experiences his out-of-body epiphanies in the prize ring.

Because film is simultaneously discursive in its different channels of signification, duration can be differently represented on different tracks. In *Badlands*, for example, the voice-over by Holly summarizes several years of events, while the image remains in the present. Films that utilize voice-over may set two different durational schemas alongside one another in this fashion.

The third large category Genette discusses under tense is **FREQUENCY**, which concerns the relation between the number of times something occurs in the story and the number of times it is represented in the discourse. These relations can be distilled into three types: repeated descriptions of unique events; single descriptions of repeated events; or a one-to-one relation of event to description. In film, the **REPEATING FORM** is rarely used, and thus clearly stands out. While *Rashomon* is the most famous example, with its repeated and divergent accounts of the rape and murder in the forest, other instances can be found, such as *Breaker Morant*, Bertolucci's *The Grim Reaper*, and to some extent, Errol Morris' *The Thin Blue Line*. All of these films center on the process of an investigation, with different characters supplying different narrations of the events. It would appear that the repeating form must be diegetically motivated in film, justified by the requirements of the story and the presence of more than one intradiegetic narrator.

The opposite type is the single description standing in for multiple occurrences, known as the **ITERATIVE** or the **FREQUENTIVE** mode. It is sometimes difficult in film to distinguish the iterative from events that are meant to be seen as singular occurrences. For example, a scene representing a typical daily dinner, which is meant to represent a series of such dinners, might suddenly prove to be the occasion of a unique occurrence. Genette acknowledges this indeterminacy by devising different classes of the iterative, including the **PSEUDO-ITERATIVE**, in which certain events will clearly mark the seemingly commonplace moment as out of the ordinary, unable to be duplicated.

The question of the iterative in film in general is complicated by the vividness of detail characteristic of the medium, its concrete expression of the unique texture of every moment, which makes it difficult for the cinema to achieve the quality of generalization which is necessary to the iterative. It might even be claimed that the iterative is impossible in film. Nevertheless, as Henderson says in a paraphrase of Metz, the important point is that films are understood, and the iterative is no exception (1983: 36).

The **SINGULATIVE** form of frequency can be described as a single description of a unique event. It is by far the most common form in film, and is the standard against which all deviations are measured. Genette also proposes another type of frequency, in which events that occur x number of times in the story are rendered x number of times in the discourse.

In sum, the relations of tense provide one of the principal means by which a film's discourse can vary, retard, elaborate or highlight the chronological relations of the story. The various artistic devices explored by the Formalists in literature have an analogue in film in the relations of tense. To date, very little work has been done in this area in film. Works by Bordwell, Gaudreault, Burgoyne, Gunning, Henderson and Marsha Kinder deal with this subject, but on the whole, the study of tense in film is one of the greatest unexplored areas of film theory.

IV

PSYCHOANALYSIS

Psychoanalytic film theory represents a development of – rather than a departure from – cine-semiotics, for, as Christian Metz points out, "both linguistic studies and psychoanalytic studies are sciences of the very fact of meaning, of signification" (Metz 1979: 9). Some film theorists saw a relation between the way that the human psyche (in general) and cinematic representation (in particular) function, and felt that Freud's theory of human subjectivity and unconscious production could shed new light on the textual processes involved in film-making and viewing. One of the aims, therefore, of psychoanalytic film theory is a systematic comparison of the cinema as a specific kind of spectacle and the structure of the socially and psychically constituted individual. This approach views psychoanalysis as a general field of investigation, a structuring matrix in which the various terms and concepts interconnect to provide a framework for elaborating this relation. For this reason, the discussion of film-specific terms will be preceded by a brief outline of psychoanalysis.

PSYCHOANALYTIC THEORY

Film theory's use of psychoanalysis is based primarily on French psycho-analyst Jacques Lacan's reformulation of Freudian theory, most notably his emphasis on the relations of desire and subjectivity in discourse (and it is this emphasis that allows psychoanalysis to be understood as a social theory). As Rosalind Coward puts it, "The unconscious originates in the same process by which the individual enters the symbolic universe" (Coward 1976: 8). This means, first, that unconscious processes are essentially discursive in nature, and second that psychic life is both individual (private) and collective (social) at the same time. For film theory, consider-ing the unconscious meant replacing the cinema as an "object" with the cinema as a "process," seeing semiotic and narrative film studies in the light of a general theory of **SUBJECT**-formation. The term subject refers to a critical concept related to – but not equivalent with – the individual, and suggests a whole range of determinations (social, political, linguistic,

123

ideological, psychological) that intersect to define it. Refusing the notion of self as a stable entity, the subject implies a process of construction by signifying practices that are both unconscious and culturally specific.

The emphasis on unconscious processes in film studies is what is known as the **METAPSYCHOLOGICAL** approach, because it deals with the psycho-analytic construction of the cinema-viewing subject. The term metapsychology was invented by Freud to refer to the most theoretical dimension of his study of psychology, the theorization of the unconscious. It involves the construction of a conceptual model (one that defies empirical verification) for the functioning of the psychical apparatus and is divided into three approaches: the dynamic (psychical phenomena are the result of the conflict of instinctual forces); the economic (psychical processes consist in the circulation and distribution of instinctual energy); and the topographical (psychical space is divided in terms of systems – unconscious, preconscious, and conscious – and agencies – id, ego, superego).

As a consequence of the shift from "object" to "process," the focus of analysis was turned from the systems of meaning within individual films to the "production of subjectivity" in the film-viewing situation; questions about film spectatorship began to be posed from the standpoint of psycho-analytic theory. If psychoanalysis examines the relations of the subject in discourse, then psychoanalytic film theory meant integrating questions of subjectivity into notions of meaning-production. Moreover, it meant that film-viewing and subject-formation were reciprocal processes: something about our unconscious identity as subjects is reinforced in film viewing, and film viewing is effective because of our unconscious participation. Moving from the interpretation of individual films to a systematic comprehension of the cinematic institution itself, some film theorists saw psycho-analysis as a way of accounting for the cinema's immediate and pervasive social power. For them the cinema "reinscribes" those very deep and globally structuring processes which form the human psyche, and it does so in such a way that we continually yearn to repeat (or re-enact) the experience.

PSYCHOANALYSIS is a discipline, founded by Freud, whose object of study is the unconscious in all of its manifestations. As a method of investigation, it consists in bringing repressed mental material to consciousness. As a method of therapy, it interprets human behaviour in terms of (1) **RESISTANCE** – the obstruction of access to the unconscious; (2) **TRANSFERENCE** – the actualization of unconscious wishes, typically in the analytic situation, by according a kind of value to the analyst which enables the repetition of early conflicts; and (3) **DESIRE** – the symbolic circulation of unconscious wishes through signs bound to our earliest forms of infantile satisfaction. As a theory of human subjectivity, psychoanalysis describes the way in which the small human being comes to establish a specific "self" and sexual identity within the network of social relations that constitute culture. It takes as its object the mechanisms of the unconscious – resistance, repression, infantile sexuality, and the Oedipal complex – and seeks to analyze the fundamental structures of desire that underlie all human activity.

For Freud, who discovered and theorized the unconscious, human life is dominated by the need to repress our tendencies toward gratification (the "pleasure principle") in the name of conscious activity (the "reality principle").[1] We come to be who we are as adults by way of a massive and intricate repression of those very early, very intense expressions of libidinal (sexual) energy. (As a concept, **LIBIDO** is fairly difficult to define, first because it continually evolved in Freud's thinking as he refined his theory of the drives, and second because a clear-cut definition does not exist in the literature. Still, several consistent features permit the provisional suggestion that libido is psychic and emotional energy associated with the transformation of the sexual instinct in relation to its objects, or more precisely, the dynamic manifestation of the sexual drive.) For Lacan, this process is also linguistic; the subject comes into being in and through language. He designates as "the **OTHER**" that unconscious site of speech, discourse, signification and desire that forms the matrix of this process. In Terry Eagleton's words,

> [The "Other"] is that which like language is always anterior to us and will always escape us, that which brought us into being as subjects in the first place but which always outruns our grasp. . . . We desire what others – our parents, for instance – unconsciously desire for us; and desire can only happen because we are caught up in linguistic, sexual and social relations – the whole field of the "Other" – which generate it.
>
> (Eagleton 1983: 174)

For obvious reasons, then, the **UNCONSCIOUS** is central to both Freud and Lacan. In very general terms, the unconscious refers to the division of the psyche not subject to direct observation but inferred from its effects on conscious processes and behavior. The "unconscious" is what Freud designates as that place to which unfulfilled desires are relegated in the process of repression which forms it. As such, it is conceived as that "other scene/stage" where the drama of the psyche (or in Lacanian terms, of "subject-construction") is played out. In other words, beneath our conscious, daily social interactions there exists a dynamic, active play of forces of desire that is inaccessible to our rational and logical selves (though this division is not as simple as it sounds – there is constant, transforming reciprocity between conscious and unconscious levels of activity).

The unconscious, however, is not simply a ready and waiting place for repressed desire – it is produced in the very act of **REPRESSION** – the unconscious exclusion of painful impulses, desires or fears from the conscious mind, and something which Freud considered a universal mental process because of its centrality in constituting the unconscious as a domain separate from the rest of the psyche. And its "contents" (representations of libidinal energy) are only known to us by the distorted, transformed and censored effects which are evidence of its work – dreams, neuroses (the result of an internal conflict between a defensive ego and unconscious desire), symptoms, jokes, puns and slips of the tongue. For Lacan, this unconscious is both produced and made available to us in language: the moment of linguistic capability (and the perception of a speaking self) is the moment of one's insertion into a social realm (and one's recognition of difference, one's mediation by others, and one's being taken up in a system of verbal exchange). The term "**SPLIT SUBJECT**" refers to this psychic division: the human subject is irremediably split between conscious and unconscious and is, in fact, *produced* in a series of splittings.

In describing the process by which the unconscious is formed, Freud takes the hypothetical life of the infant as it develops from an entity entirely under the sway of libidinal gratifications to an individual capable of establishing a position in a social world of men and women. This same process is formulated in Lacanian terms in this way: the subject is born in division and marked by **LACK**, a series of losses defining the constitution of self. These losses are activated in a number of **PSYCHIC SCENARIOS** – determining moments in which our identity is formed as the result of our engagement, at a very early age, with a network of family relations. "Who we are" as individuals is thus bound up with processes of desire, fantasy and sexuality.

Both Freud's and Lacan's descriptions present a theory of the human mind which is not simply a parable of individual development, but a general model for the way human culture is structured and organized in terms of the circulation of desire. This desiring process begins in the earliest moments of our existence. In Freud, this is seen in one of his most radical contributions to the theory of human personality, the discovery of **INFANTILE SEXUALITY** – eroticism exists in our earliest childhood experiences.

Even before the infant establishes a centered self (an ego, an identity), or is able to distinguish between itself and the outer world, the child is already a field across which the libidinal energy of the drives plays. Lacan reinterprets this, in the light of his linguistic emphasis, as the simultaneous birth of signification and desire – in "communicating," the infant becomes a desiring being. It is important to note that none of these formative "experiences" can be remembered in the usual sense, for it is precisely because of repression that they become part of our unconscious psychic make-up. Rather, in outlining these psychic scenarios both Freud and Lacan are concerned with demonstrating the work of the unconscious, the production of fantasy, and the erotic component of desire underlying even our most banal (and apparently neutral) activities; they are not concerned with the development of the individual *per se*.

The first moment of loss in the formation of the "subject" is associated with the breast, the absence of which – in both Freudian and Lacanian accounts – initiates the ceaseless movement of desire, that unconscious force, born of lack and evoking the impossibility of satisfaction, whose perpetual displacements are impelled by an engendering loss. The Freudian scenario can be summarized as follows: from the very first moment in an infant's life, the small organism strives for satisfaction of those biological needs (food, warmth, and so on) that can be designated as instincts for self-preservation. Yet at the same time, this biological activity also produces experiences of intense pleasure (sensuous sucking at the breast, a complex of satisfying feelings associated with warmth and holding, and the like). For Freud, this distinction indicates the emergence of sexuality; desire is born in the first separation of the biological instinct from the sexual drive. Importantly, the element of fantasy is already present, for all future yearnings for milk by the infant will be marked by a need to recover that *totality* of sensations that goes beyond the mere satisfaction of hunger. In other words, there is a process of hallucinating – a **FANTASMATIC PROCESS** – going on; each time the child cries for milk, we can say that the child is actually crying for "milk" (milk-in-quotes) – that representation or hallucinated image of the bonus of satisfaction that came when the need of hunger was fulfilled.[2]

Lacan discusses this moment in terms of the triad **NEED/DEMAND/DESIRE** in order to show how fantasy, desire and language mark the infant even in the originary loss that engenders subjectivity, the primal separation from the breast. At first there is simply a physical need for food, which the baby expresses by crying. Once the need is abolished by the mother's action of bringing milk, the infant connects crying to the satisfaction received, thereby making the simple signal (crying) into a demand conveyed to an "other," someone outside and distinct from the self. The cry thus becomes a sign, existing in a chain of meaning which also includes not-crying: the cry *signifies*. But, as noted above, once this signifying chain is started, there will always be something in excess of the mere satisfaction of need; the memory of experienced pleasure will forever be associated with a loss, with something not under the subject's control, and this impossibility becomes desire. Lacan calls what arises in this discrepancy between the satisfaction of need and the unsatisfied demand for love, **OBJECT SMALL A** (*objet petit a*), the object of desire caught up in the unfulfillable search for an eternally "lost" pleasure. What this means in the simplest terms is that desire will always exist in the register of fantasy, of memory, and of impossibility. The Lacanian subject (of desire) attempts, throughout its life, to recapture the fantasy of totality, wholeness and unity that is associated with the primordial experience of the breast. The original

127

object of desire is thus created *as fantasy* in the difference between the need for food and the demand for love, the difference between the satisfaction of instinctual need and the elaborated memory of that satisfaction. It is never, therefore, a relation to a real object independent of subject, but a relation to fantasy. And this "fantasmatic" creation is continually repeated throughout the life of the subject as various objects "stand in" for what can never be fully achieved. Thus Lacanians describe desire as "circulating endlessly from representation to representation."

A related concept is that of the **DRIVE**, or instinctual energy, defined as a dynamic process which directs the organism towards an aim. According to Freud, an instinct has its *source* in a bodily stimulus; its *aim* is to eliminate the state of tension deriving from the source; and it is in the *object*, or thanks to it, that the instinct may achieve its aim.[3] In "Instincts and their Vicissitudes," Freud points out that "an instinct may undergo the following vicissitudes: reversal into its opposite, turning around upon the subject, repression, sublimation" (Freud 1963c: 91). What is important to note about Freud's approach is that it distinguishes the drive from the biological instinct. The theory of component drives accounts for both the bisexual disposition of the child and the variability which will determine, through an individual's life, the kind of representation that will be associated with the drive.

In the Freudian account, as the child grows, there is a gradual organization of the libidinal drives (which had at first circulated **POLYMORPHOUSLY**, unattached to a specific object and not motivated in any single direction). This organization, while still centered on the child's own body, now channels sexuality toward various objects and aims. The first phase of sexual life is associated with the drive to incorporate objects (the oral stage); in the second, the anus becomes the erotogenic zone (the anal stage); and in the third, the child's libido is focussed on the genitals (the phallic stage).

Our discussion of Freud and Lacan is necessarily provisional, simplified for the sake of explanation. Given this qualification, a loose connection can be made between Freud's oral phase and Lacan's **MIRROR PHASE**. The second of the moments of loss which structure the life of the child in the Lacanian formulation involves the first acquisition of "self," that is, the way that the subject begins to establish *an identity* within a universe of meaning through a series of imaginary identifications, provoked by an initial sense of separation, or difference. Lacan considers this development of the self and the formation of the psyche in terms of **PSYCHOANALYTIC REGISTERS** that are roughly equivalent to Freud's pre-Oedipal and Oedipal phases in the child's life.

In what Lacan calls the **IMAGINARY** realm (imaginary in that, governed by visual processes, it is a repertoire of images), the child's first development of an ego – an integrated self-image – begins to take place. It is here in the mirror phase, Lacan says, that this ego comes into being through the infant's identification with an image of its own body. Between the ages of six and eighteen months, the human infant is physically uncoordinated; it perceives itself as a mass of disconnected, fragmentary movements. It has no sense that the fist which moves is connected to the arm and body, and so forth. When the child sees its image (for example, in a mirror – but this can also be the mother's face, or any "other" perceived as whole), it mistakes this unified, coherent shape for a superior self. The child identifies with this image (as both reflecting the self, and as something other), and finds in it a satisfying unity that it cannot experience in its own body. The infant internalizes this image as an **IDEAL EGO** – an ideal of narcissistic omnipotence constructed on the model of infantile narcissism (or investment of energy in the self) and distinct from the **EGO IDEAL**, which is formed in relation to the parental figures in the Oedipal situation and combines with the superego as a punitive agency of prohibition and conscience. This process forms the basis for all later identifications, which are imaginary in principle. Lacan is specific about the fictive nature of this very early sense of self: "[T]he important point is that this form situates the agency of the ego, before its social determination, in a fictional direction" (Lacan 1977: 2).[4] Thus the Imaginary, as one of the three psychic registers regulating human experience (together with the Symbolic and the Real), involves a narcissistic structure in which images of otherness are transformed into reflections of the self. It cannot simply be pinpointed as a phase, because its influences constantly return in adult life, particularly in love relations.

Simply put, in order for communication to occur at all, we must at some level be able to say to each other, "I know how you feel." The ability to temporarily – and imaginatively – *become* someone else is begun by this original moment in the formation of the self. There is thus **NARCISSISM**, **MISRECOGNITION**, and **ALIENATION** in the moment of the Mirror. The narcissistic subject sees itself in others, or, conversely, takes an "other" for itself. (Psychoanalysis takes the myth of Narcissus, who fell in love with his own reflection, as a paradigm for both the inevitable failure to possess the object of desire and for the love of self which precedes loving others.) It misrecognizes the imagined unity as perfect, as superior to itself, and so idealizes what it sees; or, conversely, it misrecognizes this image of the self as something other. This process can only occur if the subject is alienated, placed at a distance from this "perfect" image. Or, put another way, "The child is divided from the moment it forms a self-conception. . . . In saying 'That's me,' it is saying 'I am another' " (Lapsley and Westlake 1988: 69, 68).

Another moment of overcoming absence in the life of the subject involves the acquisition of language – and thus the ability to symbolize – described by Freud (and expanded on by Lacan) through the example of the child's

FORT/DA game. In 1915 Freud theorized his toddler grandson's game with a spool of thread as the child's manipulation of a meaningful "symbol" in an effort to control the experience of loss. The game involved the child's throwing the reel over the side of his cot and retrieving it, accompanied by "o-o-o-o" ("fort"/gone) and "da" (there). Hypothesizing that the child had made the spool into a symbol for his mother, Freud noted that the child's pleasure derived from "himself staging the disappearance and return of the objects within his reach" (Freud 1959: 34).

Lacan places the emphasis not on mastery but on the capacity to understand language as a system of differences in the Saussurean sense, in which meaning comes from the relations between words rather than from their intrinsic properties. Once the child has made the spool into a "sign" for the mother, he can also only interpret this sign in terms of what it is not: it is present because it is not absent, and vice versa. Lacan connects this activity of symbolizing to the fundamental absence at the heart of all signifying systems, relating this situation (in which the word is never adequate to the thing) to the primary gap which engenders desire:

> [T]he game of the cotton-reel is the subject's answer to what the mother's absence has created on the frontier of his domain – the edge of his cradle – namely, a *ditch*, around which one can only play at jumping. . . . [I]t is in the object to which the opposition is applied in act, the reel . . . to [which] we will later give the name it bears in the Lacanian algebra – the *petit a*. . . . The activity as a whole symbolizes repetition . . . it is the repetition of the mother's departure as cause of a *Spaltung* [splitting] in the subject – overcome by the alternating game, *fort-da*. . . . It is aimed at what, essentially, is not there.
>
> (Lacan 1977: 62–3)

This quote is of primary importance to psychoanalytic film theory because it contains three cornerstone concepts – splitting, *fort/da*, and object small a – which, while rarely mentioned explicitly in film analyses (a disappearing character may be described as "representing" the object small a, for example), form the basic matrix from which all psychoanalytic-semiotic discussions of film derive. The split subject of psychoanalysis is the spectator of psychoanalytic film theory; the presence and absence of the fort/da game is its central signifying mechanism; and the crucial concept of the gaze is nothing other than the object small a in the visual field.

The most significant loss that structures the psyche is that symbolized by **CASTRATION**, and in fact Lacan sees the **OEDIPAL COMPLEX** as the central moment in the formation of the unconscious, a moment so crucial that it functions to reinterpret all previous structures in terms of its main organizing principle: the recognition of sexual difference. Technically, the Oedipal complex refers to the organized body of loving and hostile wishes that the child experiences toward its parents. It gets its name from the Greek tragedy by Sophocles which, for Freud, dramatized the rivalry (and wish for death) with the parent of the same sex and sexual desire for the parent of the opposite sex that he found to be a truth of psychic life. The word **COMPLEX**, which refers to a group of interconnected unconscious ideas and feelings that exert a dynamic effect on the behavior of the individual, emphasizes the intersection of relationships rather than the (commonsense) idea of a personality disorder. In Freud, who called the Oedipal situation "the nuclear complex of the neuroses" (Freud 1963b: 66), this is a decisive point in the structuring of personality and the orientation of human desire, for it defines the individual's emergence into sexed selfhood. The infantile theory of castration is the result of the child's perplexity over the anatomical difference between the sexes; the child considers this difference attributable to the fact that the girl's genital has been cut off.

In the pre-Oedipal stages, both male and female child are in a dyadic relation with the mother and equally share masculine and feminine impulses. With the Oedipal moment, this two-term relation becomes three, and a triangle which is sexually defined is formed by the child and both parents. The parent of the same sex becomes a rival in the child's desire for the parent of the opposite sex. The boy gives up his incestuous desire for the mother because of the threat of punishment by castration perceived to come from the father; in so doing, he identifies with his father (symbolically becomes him) and prepares to take his position of a masculine role in society. The forbidden desire for the mother is driven into the unconscious, and the boy will accept substitutes for the mother/desired object in his future as an adult male. For the female, the Oedipal moment is not one of threat, but of realization – she recognizes that she has already been castrated, and, disillusioned in the desire for the father, reluctantly identifies with the mother. In addition, the Oedipal complex is far more complicated for the girl, who must change her love object from mother (the first object for both sexes) to father, whereas the boy can simply continue loving the mother.

The Oedipal complex signals the transition from the pleasure principle to the reality principle, from the familial order to society at large. The threat of castration and the Oedipal complex are the symbolic imposition of a culture's rules – they represent the law, morality, conscience, authority, etc. Freud uses this schema to describe the processes by which the child develops a unified sense of self (an **EGO**) and takes up a particular place in the cultural networks of social, sexual and familial relations.

Mary Ann Doane describes this process in Lacanian terms:

It is with the Oedipal complex, the intervention of a third term (the father) in the mother–child relation and the resulting series of

131

displacements which reformulate the relation to the mother as a desire for a perpetually lost object, that the subject accedes to the active use of the signifier.

(Doane 1987: 11)

The term "signifier" confirms Lacan's linguistic emphasis, in which the Oedipal situation becomes a conflict between desire and the Law, played out in what he calls the **SYMBOLIC** register of the psyche. In the broadest sense, this means that the Oedipal moment involves symbolic structures, representations which are significant to the subject, rather than actual individuals. And the drama is played out in the unconscious, thereby involving a web of signification radically distinct from our daily lives.

Because of his linguistic emphasis, Lacan rereads the Oedipal complex along these lines: the child moves out of the pre-Oedipal unity with the mother not only through fear of castration, but through the acquisition of language as well. Thus the moment of linguistic capability (the ability to speak, to distinguish a speaking self) is also the moment of one's insertion into a social realm (a world of adults and verbal exchange). Lacan emphasizes the connection between the linguistic and the social by subsuming the acquisition of language and the prohibition of incest under the general law of culture, designated as the **NAME OF THE FATHER**; it is the agency (not to be confused with the "real" father) who institutes and maintains the law and imposes a sexual identity on the subject.

Lacan sees two symbolic laws which characterize the human species – the capacity for language and the **INCEST TABOO** – as governing the formation of the unconscious itself. The incest taboo is the prohibition of sexual relations between blood relatives, seen in cultural terms as the proscriptive agency (or universal law of kinship structures) which establishes the minimal condition for the definition of a culture. As Lacan maintains,

The primordial Law is therefore that which in regulating marriage ties superimposes the kingdom of culture on that of a nature abandoned to the law of mating. The prohibition of incest is merely its subjective pivot. . . . This law, then, is revealed enough as identical with an order of language.

(Lacan 1977: 66)

Because a connection is made between language, a general structuring principle of culture, and the origins of the unconscious, it can be said that the unconscious is present in all of us who have learned to speak, to use language. We learn to speak in the language and customs of our particular culture; Lacan inverts this to say that we are in fact *spoken* by the culture itself. Our sense of self is formed through the perceptions and language of others, even at the deepest levels of the unconscious. This is another way of illustrating the symbolic function of the unconscious, in its intersection with an equally determining social function.

Thus Lacan's work hinges on an alliance between language, the unconscious, parents, the symbolic order and cultural relations. Language is what internally divides us (between conscious and unconscious), but it is also that which externally joins us (to others in culture). By reinterpreting Freud in linguistic terms, Lacan emphasizes the relations between the unconscious and human society. We are all bound to culture by relations of desire; language is both that which speaks from deep within us (in patterns and systems that pre-exist our birth), and that which we speak in our continual interplay of relations with others.

As an order of pre-established social structures (such as the incest taboo which regulates relations of marriage and exchange), the Symbolic introduces the recognition of cultural "others." Where the Imaginary was characterized by the harmonious and dual relation of mother and child, the Symbolic is marked by the intervention of a disruptive third term. Thus the figure of the father represents the fact that a wider familial and social network exists, and by implication, that the child must seek a position in that context. The child must go beyond the imaginary identifications of the dual realm in which the distinction between "me/you" is always blurred, to take a position as somone who can designate himself as an "I" in a world of sexually differentiated adult thirds ("he," "she," and "it"). The appearance of the father thus prohibits the child's total unity with the mother, and causes desire to be repressed in the unconscious. Because the Symbolic register connotes the realm of all discourse and cultural exchange, when we enter the **SYMBOLIC ORDER** we enter language/ culture itself. There is thus a shared social dimension to the unconscious; meaning is no longer simply a consequence of social development, it is the very wellspring from which social being derives.

Lacan opposes the Symbolic to the Imaginary (although they are in a complicated, imbricated relation) because it is the order of language-using social subjects. This opposition derives from three main points. First, because it refers to the organization of society in terms of paternal authority, the Symbolic is regulated by the law of the father while the Imaginary's dyadic relations can be seen to be dominated by the mother. Second, as the order of language and structured signification, the Symbolic is organized in terms of the speaking subject, while the Imaginary is largely pre-linguistic. And third, because accession to the Symbolic is predicated on the renunciation of incestuous feelings for the mother, it is seen as an order of law and language founded on the repression of the Imaginary.

For Lacan, the signifier of castration is the **PHALLUS**, and the Lacanian formulation of the Oedipal scenario is framed in terms of its possession. In classical antiquity the phallus was the figurative representation of the male organ; in psychoanalysis the term denotes the symbolic function of this organ as the possible object of castration in the Oedipal relation. In its function as signifier, and hence its difference from the actual male genital, the phallus is not the symbol of a thing; rather it represents the very fact of symbolization itself. Thus *both* sexes define themselves in relation to the phallus, as signifier of lack, and it is this representation of absence that symbolizes all prior separations. The moment of castration divides the world between those who possess the means to represent this lack and those who do not.

This is because in the Lacanian framework both sexes are presumed to *be* the phallus during the pre-Oedipal phase. The small child imagines itself to be what the (M)other desires, the object that will satisfy her desire for completion stemming from her sense of lack. The scenario of castration that the phallus represents marks the transition from being to having and thus creates the division between masculine and feminine that possession of the phallus signifies. But this is not the same thing as the biological or anatomical distinction between the penis and the vagina. Rather, the phallus has a symbolic value whose status as a transformable and detachable object makes it the single factor in relation to which both males and females take up a position, these positions being defined in terms of presence and absence, having and not having. The phallus can be seen to have two interrelated meanings, corresponding to the pre-Oedipal and Oedipal phases. First, as an imaginary and detachable organ – the penis that the child believes the mother to possess – it is an effect of a fantasy of unity and completion. Second, as a result of the recognition of castration, the phallus comes to signify the law of the father and entry into the Symbolic. As such, it is a presence representing an absence, a signifier of loss and thus a later version of the originary lost object (the breast).

When the phallus is referred to as the **SIGNIFIER OF DESIRE**, it is understood as having a symbolic role in the desires of the three protagonists of the Oedipal triangle – mother, father and child; it is the object to which desire is directed. It is thus not a real object, but an absent one (a fantasmatic object marked by loss), one that figures in a triangular signifying relation; it never really "belongs" to any of the three. So, in Parveen Adams' words, "What [the woman] lacks is not a penis as such, but the means to represent lack" (Adams 1978: 67). As a signifier of desire, the phallus represents the replacement of the immediate gratifications of infantile sexuality with a recognition of the self as a sexed, speaking, social subject.

All of these "stagings" of loss that produce the unconscious through a process of repression also fissure the subject as an ideal entity, that is, they produce a **SPLIT SUBJECT**. Strictly speaking, in Freud there is a split between two levels of being – the conscious life of the ego, or self, and the repressed desires of the unconscious. A relatively schematic model is implied by this division, in which guilty desires – forced down below the

134

surface of conscious awareness – cause the unconscious to come into being. The unconscious is radically distinct from rational conscious life – it is utterly *other*, strange, illogical and contradictory in its instinctual play of the drives and its ceaseless yearning for gratification. Lacanian psychoanalysis modifies (and multiplies) this split in terms of structural linguistics: the divided subject is produced in language as a constant dynamic of articulated difference.

Stephen Heath describes the process in this way:

> The passage into and in language divides and *in that division effects* the individual as subject. . . . The subject, that is, is not the beginning but the result of a structure of difference, of the symbolic order, and that result indexes a lack – the division – which is the constant "drama of the subject in language." . . . In short, there is a permanent performance of the subject in language itself.
>
> (Heath 1981: 117–18)

This split subject is distinct from the "individual" as conceived by **EGO PSYCHOLOGY**. The Lacanian emphasis on the articulation of subjectivity with social processes contrasts the normative, restrictive and developmental interpretations of ego psychology, which sees resistance as external to the already constituted and unified ego. The ego is conceived as an agency of adaptation, while for Lacanians resistance is internal, part of the constitution of the ego itself. They see the ego as the dynamic product of identifications, in a dialectical and continual process, whose result is, simply speaking, the formation of a love-object. While ego psychology seeks to bolster the unified subject by reinforcing the perception of a coherent self, Lacanian psychoanalysis implies a critique of this idealist unity by embedding contradiction and division in the very notion of the subject's formation.

The distinction comes down to a question of emphasis; once the unconscious and its mechanisms are seen to establish the fundamental discontinuity of psychic life, there can never be absolute certainty about empirical observation. Radically divided from objective experience, the dynamic unconscious is conceived as a site of desire, perpetually traversed by impulses which evade our conscious grasp. Theories of perception and cognition lose this radical heterogeneity of the unconscious, while it is that very difference from conscious life which defines the Lacanian perspective. A related concept is that of **PSYCHICAL REALITY**, a term used by Freud to designate the correlation of the world of the psyche and the material world, a relation that enables elements within the psyche to take on the force of reality for the subject. It is a concept intimately connected to unconscious wishes and, as Jean Laplanche and J.-B. Pontalis describe it, the "notion is bound up with the Freudian hypothesis about unconscious processes: not only do these processes take no account of external reality, they also replace it with a psychical one" (Laplanche and Pontalis 1973: 363). However, this does not simply mean an opposition between two kinds of reality; rather, unconscious wishes and their formation as fantasies are constantly implicated in the material life of the subject, while the relation between conscious and unconscious is one of disguised connections.

The split subject is also referred to as the **SUBJECT IN LANGUAGE** or the **SPEAKING SUBJECT**, making the connection between identity, subjectivity and language a fundamental feature of the unconscious. To say that the subject "performs in language" is to acknowledge the differing presence of the unconscious in every act of speech. The speaking self is an illusory (and elusive) unity that enables communication to take place, but beneath every speaking subject is the contradictory force of the unconscious articulating its own logic, its own language of desire. So when we speak there is never simply a complete, obvious or logical meaning to our words (because "our words" are always the sum of the words themselves and our statement of them). You the subject, as in the subject of a sentence, always takes up a somewhat arbitrary position when speaking. The pronoun "I" stands in for the ever-elusive subject, the speaking self.

To take the most often cited example, when I say "I am lying," the "I" in the sentence is fairly stable and coherent; but the "I" that pronounces the sentence (and throws its truthfulness into question along the way) is an always-changing, shifting force. For the sake of understanding, the "I" of the sentence and the one who produces/pronounces it are put into a unity that is of an imaginary kind. So there is a certain level of illusion about identity; we stabilize the shifting that happens in speaking in order to make communication possible. It is in this sense that the identity of the speaking subject, fully conscious, self-present and in command of its meanings, is a fictional construct.

Furthermore, cast in the terms of linguistically oriented psychoanalysis, the "I" of the statement (the subject of the *énoncé*) is telling the truth: it is a fact that what I say is untrue. But the I who produces the statement (the subject of the *énonciation*) is actually deceiving the listener, producing in deception a statement which appears as truth. And this is even further complicated, for the subject of the enunciation is, in fact, stating the truth as well: I am deceiving you (that is my wish). In deceiving, the subject of enunciation is being true to [his] desire. This contradictory shift and play of meanings is evidence of the unconscious at work. Stephen Heath demonstrates that the connection between signification, the unconscious and subject-formation is central to Lacan's thinking:

The unconscious is the fact of the constitution-division of the subject in language; an emphasis which can even lead Lacan to propose replacing the notion of the unconscious with that of the subject in language: "It is a vicious circle to say that we are speaking beings;

136

we are 'speakings', a word that can be advantageously substituted for the unconscious."

(Heath 1981: 79)

Finally, because it refuses to posit a pre-existent and specifically feminine (or masculine) essence, but rather describes and analyzes the processes by which **SEXUAL DIFFERENCE** is produced in human society, psychoanalysis has been taken up by feminists interested in understanding the cultural construction of sexuality and the implications of that for **FEMININE DIS-COURSE** – the articulation and expression of women's language, desire and subjectivity. In psychoanalysis, **FEMININITY** is seen as a category, produced psychologically and socially, rather than as a set of biological or anatomical features, and for this reason feminists (both men and women) find psychoanalysis useful in formulating alternative aesthetic and social practices.

In this light, Freud's familar characterization of the female sex as the "dark continent" is taken not as a restatement of the enduring myth of women's enigmatic and seductive essence, but as the posing of a question to be considered in analysis, and Freud himself is very clear on this: "In conformity with its peculiar nature, psychoanalysis does not try to describe what a woman is – that would be a task it could scarcely perform – but sets about inquiring how she comes into being" (Freud 1965: 116). Equally misunderstood is Lacan's famous phrase, "~~The~~ woman does not exist," because rather than denying the existence of actual women, it refers to the fact that there is no universal feminine essence, only a fantasy of femininity. As Jacqueline Rose explains,

As the place onto which lack is projected, and through which it is simultaneously disavowed, woman is a "symptom" for the man. Defined as such, reduced to being nothing other than this fantasmatic place, the woman does not exist. Lacan's statement . . . means, not that women do not exist, but that her status as an absolute category and guarantor of fantasy (exactly *The* woman) is false (~~The~~).

(Rose 1986: 72)

However, such a critique of **BIOLOGISM** can veer into a denial of the body altogether. For a number of feminist theorists the problem became one of retaining the concern with the constructedness of femininity (a process that parallels the emergence of subjectivity itself) while negotiating a space for the female body and reclaiming **JOUISSANCE** (sexual ecstasy or pleasure characterized by explosiveness, dissipation, the shattering of limits) from its phallic definition. Several French feminists propose theories of feminine writing based on a very specific conception of the female body; ironically, this has opened them up to the same critiques of essentialism leveled at the proponents of a universal, pre-existing feminine essence.

Julia Kristeva and Hélène Cixous see forces of resistance associated with

137

the imaginary register of the psyche, with pre-Oedipality, and with the maternal (feminine) body. Cixous asks, "What is female pleasure, where does it happen, how is it inscribed on her body, in her unconscious? And then how do we write it?" (Heath 1982: 111). Kristeva responds with the theory of a **SEMIOTIC CHORA** in special relation to both poetic language and the feminine, which, through its disordering of syntax and logical sequence and its emphasis on the rhythms, intonations and energies of pre-verbal discourse, constantly challenges and transforms the phallocentrism of the symbolic order. Luce Irigaray, a psychoanalyst who broke with Lacan's Ecole Freudienne, argues for a specifically **FEMININE LANGUAGE** that is based on an identity with the female anatomy; her "two-lipped discourse" challenges the unity of phallic symbolic representation with fluidity and multiplicity, thus indicating possible forms for the expression of female desire. Michelle Montrelay suggests that there is a specific, feminine unconscious that exists simultaneously with the masculine unconscious, thereby enabling her to adhere to the structures of the phallic economy while arguing for a specifically feminine jouissance based on "the 'set' of feminine drives." Thus, while maintaining the symbolic priority of the phallus, she posits a notion of woman not as "castrated," but as a "fullness" which has to be repressed, and in that plenitude lies the "ruin of representation."

For Mary Ann Doane, the terms of the body and of sexuality are not reducible to the merely physical (such as in the common-sense definition of "sexual response"), but are constructed in a matrix of symbolic and social relations. Still, she finds that an emphasis on the organization of psychic processes defined only in relation to a masculine subjectivity is in danger of leaving the female body out entirely. In Joan Copjec's words, there is a legitimate "fear of being deceived by the very theory through which we hope to be brought to truth" (Copjec 1986: 58). Doane therefore proposes that we "try to consider the relation between the female body and language, never forgetting that it is a relation between two terms and not two essences" (Doane 1981: 30–1). In order to do this, she suggests using the notion of **ANACLISIS** developed by psychoanalyst Jean Laplanche; this is the process whereby the early libidinal drives (such as the oral and anal drives) detach themselves from their original objects (the bodily organs) while these objects assume a symbolic, or fantasmatic, function. As we saw earlier, desire is born from this diversion, this "gap" in the drive, but the physical body must be there as a support for this process. As Robert Lapsley and Michael Westlake put it, "Although the body is not the cause of the psyche it nonetheless has a role in structuring it" (Lapsley and Westlake 1988: 102). Thus, in contrast to the theories of the French feminists, pre-Oedipal sexuality does not involve some pristine realm removed from the structures of symbolization; the body is *already* traversed by an organized network of fantasy relations and desiring symbols, even in the pre-Oedipal condition of infancy. Doane concludes that "Sexuality can only take form in a dissociation of subjectivity from the bodily function, but the concept of a bodily function is necessary in the explanation as, precisely, a support" (Doane 1981: 27).

The questions of femininity and female desire remain important issues for psychoanalytic theory to confront. Given that psychoanalysis describes the emergence of masculine subjectivity, but does so around the catalyst of sexual difference, it is critical to begin developing a theory of sexuality that does not privilege one sex over the other. Elizabeth Cowie points out that we must be able "to see 'woman' not as a given, biologically or psychologically, but as a category produced in signifying practices . . . or through signification at the level of the unconscious" (Cowie 1978: 60). Paradoxically, this is perhaps the most important feature of psychoanalysis – that it begins to chart the way for us to think in these terms, but it does so in such a way that a feminist challenge is absolutely necessary.

PSYCHOANALYTIC FILM THEORY

If any one text can be said to crystallize psychoanalytic thinking about the cinema, it is Christian Metz' landmark essay, "The Imaginary Signifier."[5] As the title implies, the cinema engages processes of the unconscious more than any other artistic medium – the very constitution of its signifier is imaginary. Unlike literary or pictorial arts – whose signifiers pre-exist the imaginative work of the reader or viewer (in the form of words on a page or images on a canvas) – films themselves only come into being through the fictive work of their spectators. Obviously, this does not mean that the film itself (in a material sense) does not pre-exist its viewing, but that its signifiers (its mode of meaning-production) are activated in the viewing. The film's images and sounds are not meaningful without the (unconscious) work of the spectator, and it is in this sense that every film is a construction of its viewer. In a way, "The Imaginary Signifier" is the primary text of psychoanalytic film theory – nearly every article on the subject makes some reference to Metz' work. The structuring question of the essay is this: "What contribution can . . . psychoanalysis make to the study of the cinematic signifier?" (Metz 1975: 28) and Metz seeks to answer it by showing how the cinema mobilizes techniques of the imaginary in order to (1) ensure the functioning of the cinematic apparatus; (2) create the conditions of reception specific to the film spectator; and (3) generate the peculiarly fantasmatic quality of cinematic signification.

Metz means imaginary in three ways, the first being in the ordinary sense of the word as "fictional" or "fictive" – films are imaginary stories represented by present images of absent objects and people. The second meaning has to do with the "imaginary" nature of the cinematic signifier. Because film depends on a high degree of perceptual activity (vision, sound and the perception of movement in an ordered sequence) while at the same time invoking a lesser degree of substantiality (filmed images and their spectators do not share the same time and space, as they do in the dramatic theater, for example), there is a pervasive sense of absence at the heart of its representation. Screen images are "made present in the mode of absence," offering us "unaccustomed perceptual wealth, but unusually profoundly stamped with unreality" (Metz 1975: 48).

The third meaning is more strictly psychoanalytic, as Metz refers specifically to the Lacanian "imaginary," that site of the initial constitution of the ego prior to the Oedipal moment (which, as noted, contains all of the relations of fantasy and desire that form the "initial core of the unconscious" (ibid.: 15)). But even at the very outset of the essay Metz is careful to avoid the characterization of the cinema as exclusively imaginary, stating that he will continually be concerned with "the intimately ramifying articulation of this imaginary with the feats of the signifier, with the semiotic imprint of the Law (here, the cinematic codes) which also marks the unconscious" (ibid.). In other words, the cinema is both a symbolic system and an imaginary operation, and any successful analysis will have to be poised in a dynamic relation between the two.

In the most general terms, psychoanalytic film theory grounds its description in an equivalence between the film-viewer and the dreamer, taking that archetypal production of unconscious fantasy, the **DREAM-WORK**, as analogous to the film itself. As symbolic fulfillments of unconscious wishes, dreams are structured "texts" that can be understood via an analysis of their **MANIFEST CONTENT** (the "story" told in the dream), in order to reveal the **LATENT CONTENT**, the **DREAM-WISH** (the unconscious and forbidden desire that generates the dream) beneath the seemingly random and confused collection of images. In *The Interpretation of Dreams* Freud demonstrates, through a process of decipherment (in which the various threads of dream-imagery are unravelled), the transforming and deforming processes of the dream-work which permit the unconscious wish to surface in a representation. These processes of the dream-work are called **PRIMARY PROCESSES**, and they consist of **CONDENSATION** (in which a whole range of associations can be represented by a single image), **DISPLACEMENT** (in which psychic energy is transferred from something significant to something banal, conferring great importance on a trivial item), **CONDITIONS OF REPRESENTABILITY** (in which it becomes possible for certain thoughts to be represented by visual images), and **SECONDARY REVISION** (in which a logical, narrative coherence is imposed on the stream of images). In the activity of unconscious production, they combine to transform the raw materials of the dream (bodily stimuli, things that happened during the day, dream-thoughts) into that hallucinatory "visual story" which is the dream itself.

The power of the film-dream analogy for film theory comes from the cinema's peculiar construction of its spectator as a semi-wakeful dreamer. Psychoanalytic film theory's emphasis on subjectivity as a process of construction implies that there can never be a realm of meaning fixed and independent of a signifying chain into which the subject is inserted. Because of this, the move from the analysis of meaning as a content to the analysis of meaning as a structuring process gives the unconscious new priority in the description of spectatorship. If meaning is always produced *for* a subject, psychoanalytic film theory's concern encompasses both the meaning of the film-text itself (the *énoncé*) and the production of that text (the *énonciation*), considering both film-maker and spectator as sources of that production. From this perspective, both author and viewer are conceived not only as individuals who make cognitive choices in forming conscious interpretations, but as processes in the production of desiring subjectivity, and this implies a global notion of the cinema as an institution, a social practice and a psychic matrix. If psychoanalysis can be said to address the problem of "interlocking subjectivities" caught up in a network of symbolic systems, psychoanalytic film theory addresses spectatorship as an integral part of this complicated weave.

Thus the spectator of the cinema is a desiring spectator, and within the psychoanalytic framework, both the viewing state that "constructs" this spectator and the film-text itself are seen to mobilize the structures of **UNCONSCIOUS FANTASY**. More than any other form, the cinema is capable of actually reproducing or approximating the structure and logic of dreams and the unconscious. From Freud we know that "fantasy" refers to the psychic production around an unconscious wish by means of an **IMAGINARY SCENE** in which which the subject/dreamer, whether depicted as present or not, is the protagonist. For French post-Freudians Laplanche and Pontalis, "[U]nconscious ideas are organized into phantasies or imaginary scenarios to which the instinct becomes fixated and which may be conceived as true *mises-en-scène* [stagings/performances] of desire" (Laplanche and Pontalis 1973: 475). Psychoanalytic film theory emphasizes the notion of production in its description, focussing on the ways in which the viewer is positioned, by means of a series of hallucinatory "lures," as the desiring producer of the cinematic fiction. According to this idea, then, when we watch a film we are somehow dreaming it as well; our unconscious desires work in tandem with those that generated the film-dream.

Three additional points about the notion of fantasy should be made. First, fantasy in this usage does not simply mean a fantastic or imaginary content that originates in the mind of the director (as some content-based psychological analyses would have us believe, say, in the case of an anti-clerical Hitchcock, for example). Rather, it is the result of an interactive relationship between the film and the spectator, in which the spectator both constructs the fantasy and at the same time is constituted by it in a complex relay of processes of projection (in which specific impulses, wishes and aspects of the self are imagined to be located in an object external to it) and identification (in which there is either an extension of identity into another, a borrowing of identity from another, or a confusion/fusion of identity with another). Second, fantasy is never simply wish-fulfillment, but a compromise formation in which (as we saw with the dream-work) repressed ideas can find expression only through censorship and distortion; the compromise is between desire and the law. Again Laplanche and Pontalis make this clear when they describe fantasy as an "imaginary scene . . . representing the fulfillment of a wish . . . in a manner that is distorted to a greater or lesser extent by defensive processes" (Laplanche and Pontalis 1973: 314). Finally, fantasy figures in the perpetual deferral rather than the satisfaction of desire (it is the representation of fulfillment, and not fulfillment *per se*). Lacan puts it this way: "the fantasy is the support of desire, it is not the object that is the support of the desire" (Lacan 1979: 185).

The cinema-spectator of psychoanalytic film theory is thus the central "mechanism" of the entire cinematic operation. The film-text – whose affinity with the dream is signaled by the fact that both are "stories told in images" that the subject recounts to itself – engages this viewer in a complex of pleasure and meaning by mobilizing deep-rooted structures of fantasy, identification and vision, and it does this through interlocking systems of narrativity, continuity and point-of-view. The result is that in every viewing of a film, spectators can be said to repeatedly "enunciate their own economy of desire" (Lapsley and Westlake 1988: 95). Discussion of psychoanalytic film theory will be organized around five core concepts: the apparatus, the spectator, enunciation, the gaze, and feminist theory.

THE CINEMATIC APPARATUS

Because the psychoanalytic constitution of the film-spectator also suggested ways of understanding the social impact of the cinema as an institution, Metz first made his claim for the psychoanalytic approach in terms of the cinema's institutional form. In "The Imaginary Signifier" he speaks of the "dual kinship" between the psychic life of the spectator and the financial or industrial mechanisms of the cinema in order to show how the reciprocal relations between the psychological and the technological components of the cinematic institution work to create in viewers not only a belief in the impression of reality offered by its fictions, but deep psychic gratification and a desire to continually return. It is worth citing the whole passage, as this intersection of the psychic and the social is at the core of the definition of the **CINEMATIC APPARATUS**:

> The cinematic institution is not just the cinema industry (which also works to fill cinemas, not to empty them). It is also the mental

142

machinery – another industry – which spectators "accustomed to the cinema" have internalised historically, and which has adapted them to the consumption of films. (The institution is outside us and inside us, indistinctly collective and intimate, sociological and psychoanalytic, just as the general prohibition of incest has as its individual corollary the Oedipus complex . . . or perhaps . . . different psychical configurations which . . . *imprint* the institution in us in their own way.) The second machine, ie, the social regulation of the spectator's metapsychology, like the first, has as its function to set up good object relations with films. . . . The cinema is attended out of desire, not reluctance, in the hope that the film will please, not that it will displease. . . . [T]he institution as a whole has filmic pleasure alone as its aim.

(Metz 1975: 18–19)

Broadly speaking, the term cinematic apparatus refers to the totality of interdependent operations that make up the cinema-viewing situation, including (1) the technical base (specific effects produced by the various components of the film equipment, including camera, lights, film and projector); (2) the conditions of film projection (the darkened theater, the immobility implied by the seating, the illuminated screen in front, and the light beam projected from behind the spectator's head); (3) the film itself, as a "text" (involving various devices to represent visual continuity, the illusion of real space, and the creation of a believable impression of reality); and (4) that "mental machinery" of the spectator (including conscious perceptual as well as unconscious and preconscious processes) that constitutes the viewer as subject of desire. Thus both technological *and* libidinal/erotic components intersect to form the cinematic apparatus as a whole, producing a definition of the entire cinema-machine that goes beyond films themselves to the whole range of operations involved in their production and consumption, and one that places the spectator – as unconscious desiring subject – at the center of the entire process. Another way of defining the apparatus is to consider it as the point of intersection of a number of relationships – relations of text, meaning, pleasure and spectator-position that crystallize and condense in the projection of a film.

The seminal texts in the theory of the apparatus are Jean-Louis Baudry's 1970 article, "The Ideological Effects of the Basic Cinematographic Apparatus" and the more fully psychoanalytic "The Apparatus: Metapsychological Approaches to the Impression of Reality in the Cinema" (1975).[6] Even though the cinematic apparatus is defined as a complex, interlocking structure across four distinct types of operation, from the perspective of psychoanalytic film theory the most salient feature of this apparatus is its construction of a **DREAM STATE**. Certain conditions make film viewing similar to dreaming: we are in a darkened room, our motor activity is reduced, our visual perception is heightened to compensate for our lack of physical movement. Because of this, the film spectator enters a **REGIME OF BELIEF** (where everything is accepted as real, and flimsy two-dimensional images have the uncanny substance of real bodies and things) that is like the condition of the dreamer. The cinema can achieve its greatest power of fascination over the viewer not simply because of its impression of reality, but more precisely because this impression of reality is intensified by the conditions of the dream; this is what is known as the **FICTION EFFECT**.

It is this fiction effect which allows the spectator to have the feeling that he or she is actually producing the cinematic fiction, dreaming the images and situations that appear on the screen. This is what makes film-going similar to other fantasy situations (daydreaming, dreaming, fantasizing), and provides the basis for the slippage between dreamer and viewer that is the hinge of psychoanalytic film theory. The cinema does, in fact, create an impression of reality, but this is a total effect – engulfing and in a sense "creating" the spectator – which is much more than a simple replica of the real. Another term for this constellation of features is the **SUBJECT EFFECT**, and it comes from the fact that Baudry, in his second essay, attributes film's impression of reality not to its verisimilitude but to an experience created in the viewer: "The entire cinematographic apparatus is activated in order to provoke this simulation: it is indeed a simulation of a condition of the subject, a position of the subject, a subject and not of reality" (Baudry, in Cha 1980: 60).

These conditions produce what Baudry calls "a state of **ARTIFICIAL REGRESSION**" (ibid.: 56). The totalizing, womblike effects of the film viewing situation represent, for him, the activation of an unconscious desire to return to an earlier state of psychic development, one before the formation of the ego, in which the divisions between self and other, internal and external, have not yet taken shape. For Baudry, this condition in which the subject cannot distinguish between perception (of an actual thing) and representation (an "image" that stands in for it) is like the earliest forms of satisfaction of the infant in which the boundaries between itself and the world are confused. Baudry says that the cinema situation reproduces the hallucinatory power of a dream because it turns a perception into something that looks like a **HALLUCINATION** – a vision with a compelling sense of reality of something that is, precisely, *not* there. But Baudry says that there is an important difference. Where Freud says that the dream is a "normal hallucinatory psychosis" of every individual, Baudry points out that film offers an "artificial psychosis without offering the dreamer the possibility of exercising any kind of immediate control" (ibid.: 58). Central to psychoanalytic film theory is the fact that the cinema's unique capacity to recreate the dream state makes the unconscious the primary factor in both our desire for the cinema and its reality effect.

144

In his account of the curious disjunction between two worlds experienced "upon leaving the movie theater," Roland Barthes also takes up the film viewer's heightened receptivity (a state something like the suggestibility of hypnosis) produced by the artificial regression of the fiction-effect. He says that we dream *before* becoming spectators, placed, as we are, in a pre-hypnotic "cinematic condition" within "an anonymous, indifferent cube of darkness," "a cinematographic cocoon" where we "shine with all the intensity of [our] desire" (Barthes 1975a: 1, 2). Invoking the split subject of psychoanalysis (the spectator is both in the story and "elsewhere"), Barthes connects filmic fascination with the lure of narcissism in early imaginary identifications (all terms to be taken up in relation to the spectator). More importantly, he suggests ways in which we can complicate our relation to the screen (we are "riveted to the representation" (ibid.: 3)), either by establishing a critical distance through Brechtian technique, or by multiplying the fascination through attention to the extra-cinematic surroundings.

The groundwork had already been laid for the spectator's centrality in the apparatus by the very article that brought the term "apparatus" to film theory – Baudry's earlier essay on "Ideological Effects." It was here that the relation between the camera and the viewing subject was posited as the site of ideological production, and that the spectator was shown to occupy a central and illusory position in the entire cinematic arrangement. Baudry first demonstrates how the idealist notion of a **TRANSCENDENTAL SUBJECT** – in which all objects are seen from a fixed point which is conceived to be the source of meaning, and this point is then held as an ideological unity, denying contradiction to maintain its illusory centrality and positing the philosophical subject of idealism – was transferred from the optical rules of monocular perspective in Renaissance painting to the mechanical base of the camera. He then analyzes the way the subject's sense of mastery is reinforced when the differences between frames are effaced in the name of a seamless illusion of reality, a continuous vision. The sense of dominance is even further maintained when the multiple perspectives implied by editing are synthesized into a coherent and mean-ingful whole by the subject. The ideological work of the apparatus is explained in terms of a duplicity: the subject feels like the source of meanings when in fact this subject is the effect of meanings.

What emerges here (in outline) is the specific function fulfilled by cinema as support and instrument of ideology. It constitutes the "subject" by the illusory delimitation of a central location – whether this be that of a god or of any other substitute. It is an apparatus destined to obtain a precise ideological effect, necessary to the domi-nant ideology: creating a fantasmatization of the subject, it collabor-ates with a marked efficacity in the maintenance of idealism. . . .

Everything happens as if, the subject himself being unable – and for a reason – to account for his own situation, it was necessary to substitute secondary organs . . . instruments or ideological formations capable of filling his function as subject. In fact, this substitution is only possible on the condition that the instrumentation itself be hidden or repressed.

(Baudry, in Cha 1980: 34)

This combination of technical, ideological and psychological operations returns us to the original definition of the apparatus, whose mode of functioning is brilliantly illustrated by the cinematic example of Dziga Vertov's *Man With a Movie Camera*.

In a film whose ostensible subject is a day in the life of a bustling Soviet city, all four areas of the apparatus are deftly put into motion, while the "man with a movie camera" connects the various "demonstrations" (of the apparatus and of daily life) and gives priority to the camera's (and the viewer's) eye. All aspects of the apparatus are mobilized in this film, which constantly reveals the process of its own making: it is as much about the construction of cinematic reality as it is about Soviet life, providing a powerful unmasking of those operations that the ideological work of the apparatus must suppress. The technical base is alluded to in the camera-man's activity; the camera, tripod, lenses and other technologies for record-ing and projecting are equally depicted. The conditions of reception are noted by sequences in the movie theater itself. The film-text has a kind of starring role, as editing is depicted in frames that are frozen in mid-motion, taken onto the editing table, surveyed, catalogued and spliced in sequences that foreground the hands and eyes of the editor. But most important are the viewers themselves – those who watch the film within the film as well as the depicted viewers – constantly sliding from documentary reality to constructed illusion, both fascinated and aware at the same time. More than a primer on cinematic techniques and methods, *Man With a Movie Camera* reinforces the spectator's central role in the cinematic apparatus, for while it demystifies its illusions in order to show how they are produced, it continually reaffirms the fact that the spectator's psychic participation is what makes the film exist.

THE SPECTATOR

The psychoanalytic conception of the cinema **SPECTATOR** is the matrix from which all other descriptions in the field flow. But this is a very particular kind of viewer, one quite different from that presupposed by other methodological approaches in film studies. Unlike the models of mass audience offered by empirical or sociological approaches to the cinema ("real" people who go to movies), and unlike the notion of a consciously

146

aware viewer provided by Formalist approaches (people who have conscious artistic ideas and interpretations about what they see), psychoanalytic film theory discusses film spectatorship in terms of the circulation of desire. The range of psychoanalytic concepts having to do with unconscious fantasy and the formation of (gendered) identity are enlisted to explain and describe the peculiar forms of imaginary projection and comprehension that characterize the cine-subject and the viewing state. Alain Bergala determines four areas of inquiry in the theory of the spectator: (1) What does the spectator desire in going to the cinema? (2) What kind of subject-spectator is constructed by the cinematographic apparatus? (3) What is the metapsychological "regime" of the spectator during the film's projection? (4) What is the spectator's position, strictly speaking, within the film itself? (in Aumont *et al.* 1983: 172–3). While each of these questions delimits a possible approach to spectatorship in terms of a theory of the unconscious, closer inspection reveals that they are all contingent on one another; a whole complex of intersecting features forms the psychoanalytically constructed viewer. Discussion of the apparatus went some way toward answering questions (1) and (2); the section on the gaze will deal more fully with question (4). Question (3), that of the metapsychological "regime," is the cornerstone of psychoanalytic theories of spectatorship, and will be discussed here.

Psychoanalytic film theory sees the viewer not as a person, a flesh-and-blood individual, but as an artificial construct, produced and activated by the cinematic apparatus. This spectator is conceived as a "space" that is both "productive" (as in the production of the dream-work or other unconscious fantasy structures) and "empty" (anyone can occupy it); to achieve this ambiguous duality, the cinema in some sense "constructs" its spectator along a number of psychoanalytic modalities that link the dreamer to the film viewer. But a film is not exactly the same thing as a dream; in order for the film spectator to become the subject of a fantasy that is not self-generated, a situation must be produced in which the viewer is "more immediately vulnerable and more likely to let his own fantasies work themselves into those offered by the fiction machine" (Augst 1981: 3). This process hinges on the distinction between the real person (as an individual) and the film viewer (as a construct), and psychoanalytic film theory draws on operations of the unconscious in order to explain it. Five intersecting factors go into the psychoanalytic construction of this viewer: (1) a state of regression is produced; (2) a situation of belief is constructed; (3) mechanisms of primary identification are activated (onto which secondary identifications are then "grafted"); (4) fantasy structures, such as the family romance, are put into play by the cinematic fiction; and (5) those "marks of enunciation" that stamp the film with authorship must be concealed.

We have already seen how the processes of the apparatus itself – and more specifically, the conditions of reception – induce a state of regression in the viewer which makes susceptibility to the cinematic fantasy come about. This also creates the context for the peculiar kind of belief that characterizes the viewing situation – the cinema spectator is first and foremost a credulous one. Using the psychoanalytic model of **FETISHISM** (strictly speaking, the child's maintenance of a belief in the maternal phallus in the face of the anxiety-inducing evidence of her castration), and drawing his discussion in part from the work of psychoanalyst Octave Mannoni, Metz describes belief in the cinema as a process of denial or **DISAVOWAL** – the mechanism, or mode of defense, invoked in fetishism, whereby the subject refuses to recognize the reality of a traumatic perception. Behind every incredulous spectator (who knows the events taking place on the screen are fictional) lies a credulous one (who nevertheless believes these events to be true); the spectator thus disavows what he or she knows in order to maintain the cinematic illusion. The whole effect of the film-viewing situation turns on this continual back-and-forth of knowledge and belief, this split in the consciousness of the spectator between "I know full well . . ." and "But, nevertheless . . . ," this "no" to reality and "yes" to the dream. The spectator is, in a sense, a double-spectator, whose division of the self is uncannily like that between conscious and unconscious.

"I know . . . but, nevertheless" is the structure of fetishism in psychoanalysis, for the subject disavows the lack interpreted as resulting from castration precisely by an imaginary belief in its fulfillment. Fetishism is different from negation, or total suppression, in that by virtue of its disavowal of difference, it continually evokes what it is meant to deny. Freud calls disavowal "a process which in the mental life of children seems neither uncommon nor very dangerous but which in an adult would mean the beginning of a psychosis" (Freud 1963: 188), and maintains that something can be learned from fetishism about the "splitting of the ego." Disavowal, as a response to castration anxiety, is not the reaction to a simple perception of a certain reality, but to the relation of two symbolic formations – the recognition of sexual difference and the fear of castration by the father. Fetishism is a process that allows the simultaneous interaction of two contradictory meanings, but it is a symbolic process at the level of the unconscious.

Linking this **SPLITTING OF BELIEF** to a primordial scenario in the life of the subject, Metz traces still another relation between cinema viewing and the unconscious. He says that whether one understands the scenario of castration as a symbolic drama that becomes a metaphor for all losses, both real and imaginary (as in Lacan), or takes it more literally (as in Freud), the process is the same.

Before this unveiling of a lack (we are already close to the cinematic signifier), the child . . . will have to double up its belief (another cinematic characteristic) and from then on forever hold two contradictory opinions. . . . In other words, it will, perhaps definitively, retain its former belief beneath the new ones, but it will also hold to its new perceptual observation while disavowing it on another level. . . . Thus is established the lasting matrix, the affective prototype of all the splittings of belief.

(Metz 1975: 68)

These issues have dramatic consequences for feminist criticism. Laura Mulvey interprets fetishism as one modality in the relationship between the spectator and the woman's image, while Jacqueline Rose challenges the repression of the feminine in this model of belief. Both will be considered more fully later, but here is a provisional suggestion about women's relation to the concept of fetishism. The scenario of fetishism is not about a real woman who lacks a real penis, but a structure in which symbolic relations, already constituted as meaningful, are put into play. Looking at the screen is not like looking at a "castrated" woman, but the structures of belief recapitulate the early psychic formation.

Perhaps the most complicated issue in the theory of the spectator is **IDENTIFICATION**; not only is there a distinction between primary and secondary identification in both psychoanalysis and film theory, but the definition of these is interpreted differently by Freud and Lacan, and later by Baudry and Metz, the two theorists to use the term the most comprehensively. Briefly, in psychoanalysis the simplest definition of the term involves a process of assimilation by the subject of an other, either in its totality (as in identifying with an individual), or partially (as in the assumption of a physical trait or characteristic). According to Laplanche and Pontalis, the subject "is transformed, wholly or partially, after the model the other provides. It is by means of a series of identifications that the personality is constituted and specified" (Laplanche and Pontalis 1978: 205).

Because identification, the earliest emotional tie in the life of the subject, plays a central role in the imaginary formation of the ego (in spite of the fact that Freud himself was never completely satisfied with either its definition or its place among other processes of the psyche), psychoanalytic film theory accords it a central place in its conception of the spectator's imaginary access to the film. Thus, for Alain Bergala,

[I]dentification is both the basic mechanism of the imaginary constitution of the ego (a founding function) and the core, the prototype of a number of subsequent psychical instances and processes through which the ego, once constituted, continues to differentiate itself (a matrix function).

(in Aumont *et al.* 1983: 174)

149

For Freud (provisionally), primary identification involves an early mode of the constitution of the self on the model of another person, and as such, an early form of affective relationship to an object, before there is any real distinction between self and object. It is pre-Oedipal, bound up with oral incorporation, and characterized by a certain amount of confusion between the ego and the other. It is distinct from the type of identification in Lacan's mirror phase, because for Lacan it is here that the dual relationship between the ego and the other, between subject and object (a relationship of similarity *and* difference) is established. This first differentiation of the subject begins on the basis of an identification with an image in an immediate, dual and reciprocal relation, but it depends, precisely, on a recognition of the self as distinct and distanced from the image. However, there is also a sense in which this is primary identification as well (the affinities between the descriptions make this clear).

Another way of clarifying the issue is to think in terms of the distinction between the ideal ego (associated with the pre-Oedipal and the imaginary) and the ego ideal (associated with the punitive paternal function in the Oedipal complex and emerging in the symbolic). Although these distinctions are not very clear in most of the literature, thinking of primary identification in relation to the ideal ego associates it with an early idealization of the self, while the processes involving the ego ideal concern identification-with parents, their substitutes, or collective ideals as models with which the subject attempts to conform, processes more aligned with secondary identification.

For Freud and Lacan, secondary identifications are those under the province of the Oedipal complex, in which the subject both constitutes itself in the Symbolic (the realm of language and culture) and establishes its singularity, its identity in relation to parents and cultural "others." Secondary identifications are always ambivalent, characterized by the complexity of contradictory feelings of love and hate. Parents can serve equally as objects of libidinal attachment (the desire to have) or objects of identification (the desire to be); what is important to retain is the idea that all future relationships will contain some element of identification, on the model of infantile **TRANSITIVISM** (for example, when a child attributes its own behavior to another, as when in seeing another child get hurt, it begins to cry).

What we commonly call "identification," when it is based on a kind of empathetic reaction to characters in a novel, play or film, is considered to be in the psychoanalytic realm of secondary identifications. But the issue of identification in the psychoanalytic sense is even more complex: Because psychoanalytic identification is concerned with unconscious processes of the psyche rather than with cognitive processes of the mind, consciously experienced empathy has very little to do with identification in the psychoanalytic sense (or in the cinema, for that matter). The difference might be put in the following way: *Empathy* = "I *know* how you *feel*"; knowledge and perception are its structuring categories. *Identification* = "I *see* as you see, from your *position*"; vision and psychic placement define its terms. While this might appear to some as the rigid splitting off of cognitive processes from those of the unconscious, it is absolutely crucial to maintain a distinction between these two levels of activity. Although cognition and the unconscious do interanimate (desire motivates conscious thought and, in certain cases, vice versa), the distinction between empathy and identification depends on a clear understanding of their separateness. One more thing to note (particularly in terms of the critiques of the way identification has been used by film theory) is that, far from establishing a unified subject, the imaginary identifications that constitute the ego do so in a complex grouping, "a real patchwork of disparate images" (Aumont *et al.*: 180), which has led Lacan to call the ego a "hodge-podge of identifications" (cited by Bergala, ibid.).

Metz defines **PRIMARY CINEMATIC IDENTIFICATION** as the spectator's identification with the act of looking itself:

> I am all-perceiving ... the constitutive instance ... of the cinematic signifier (it is I who make the film). ... [T]he spectator *identifies with himself*, with himself as a pure act of perception (as wakefulness, alertness): as condition of possibility of the perceived and hence as a kind of transcendental subject, anterior to every *there is*.
>
> (Metz 1975: 48–9)

This type of identification is considered primary because it is what makes all secondary cinematic identifications with characters and events on the screen possible. This process, both perceptual (the viewer sees the object) and unconscious (the viewer participates in a fantasmatic or imaginary way), is at once constructed and directed by the look of the camera and its stand-in, the projector. From a look that proceeds from the back of the head, then, "precisely where fantasy locates the 'focus' of all vision" (Metz 1975: 49), the spectator is given that illusory capacity to be everywhere at once, that power of vision for which the cinema is famous. In "Ideological Effects," Baudry describes this arrangement in a slightly more technological way: "[T]he spectator identifies less with what is represented, the spectacle itself, than with what stages the spectacle, makes it seen, obliging him to see what it sees; this is exactly the function taken over by the camera as a sort of relay" (Baudry, in Cha 1980: 34).

Metz relates this type of identification to the mirror phase by saying that primary cinematic identification is only possible because the viewer has already undergone the formative psychic process of this initial constitution of the ego. The film viewer's fictional participation in the unfolding of events is made possible by this first experience of the subject, that early moment in the formation of the ego when the small infant begins to distinguish objects as different from itself, and in so doing, begins to distinguish a self. What links this process to the cinema for Metz is the fact that it occurs in terms of visual images – what the child sees at this point (a unified image that is distanced and objectified) forms how he or she will interact with others at later stages in life. The fictive aspect is also crucial here – the perception of that "other" as a more perfect self is also a misperception, a misrecognition.

Part of film theory's correspondence between primary cinematic identification and the mirror phase, then, comes from the similarities between the infant in front of the "mirror" and the spectator in front of the screen, both being fascinated by and identifying with an imaged ideal, viewed from a distance. This early process of ego construction, in which the viewing subject finds an identity by absorbing an image in a mirror, is one of the founding concepts in the psychoanalytic theory of cinema spectatorship and the basis for its discussion of primary identification. According to this description, part of the cinema's fascination comes from the fact that while it allows for the temporary loss of ego (the film spectator "becomes" someone else), it simultaneously reinforces the ego (through invocation of the mirror phase). In a sense, the film viewer both loses him/herself, and refinds him/herself – over and over – by continually re-enacting the first fictive moment of identification and establishment of identity.

Another aspect of the mirror phase analogy that is a point of debate in psychoanalytic film theory has to do with the illusion of coherence and mastery suggested by the imaginary constitution of the ego (as a correlative to the spectator's position of illusory control). This can be traced back to Baudry's transcendental subject of the first article, in which "[b]oth specular tranquility and the assurance of one's own identity" (Baudry, in Cha 1980: 34) are produced in the spectator's position: "Meaning and consciousness" coalesce in a single point for the subject (ibid.: 30). In an article that critiques this notion of the spectator precisely because it neglects the ramifications of sexual difference and the female viewer, Mary Ann Doane defines the problematic: "Coherency of vision insures a controlling knowledge which, in its turn, is a guarantee of the untroubled centrality and unity of the subject' (Doane 1980: 28). But this is a misrecognition, brought on by those cinematic procedures which efface contradiction and difference. For Doane, "the pleasure of misrecognition ultimately lies in its confirmation of the subject's mastery over the signifier, its guarantee of a unified and coherent ego capable of controlling the effects of the unconscious" (ibid.).

The transformation for the subject in the mirror phase from a fragmented body-image to an image of totality, unity and coherence, is taken (by Baudry in his first article) to be reproduced for the spectator in the cinema. From this fantasy of integration associated with the mirror comes a conception of the cinema as an answer to our desire for plenitude – offering us fixed, coherent, non-contradictory worlds with the subject as the source of meaning. This concept of the spectator figured largely in an important theoretical debate in France in the 1970s (involving Baudry, Marcellin Pleynet, Jean-Patrick Lebel, Jean Narboni, Jean-Louis Comolli and others, and journals such as *Cinéthique*, *Cahiers du Cinéma* and *Tel Quel*) about the relationship of the apparatus, the subject and ideology. The political cast of the debate focussed on the possibilities for an alternative, materialist cinema, one which emphasized contradiction and those differences. effaced in the production of the transcendental subject (exemplified by the work of Godard and the Dziga Vertov Group, Jean-Marie Straub/Danielle Huillet and others). But this is a slightly different emphasis than the specifically psychoanalytic construction of the viewing subject under discussion here.

The unity in the strictly psychoanalytic sense places somewhat more emphasis on the imaginary constitution of the self in the Lacanian paradigm, "in which the imaginary, opposed to the symbolic but constantly imbricated with it, designates *the basic lure of the ego* [emphasis added], the definitive imprint of a *before* the Oedipus complex (which also continues after it) . . ." (Metz 1975: 15). In "Upon Leaving the Movie Theater" Barthes emphasizes the correlation between cinema viewing and this early narcissistic unity:

> A film image (sound included), what is it? A *lure*. This word must be taken in its psychoanalytic sense. I am locked in on the image as though I was caught in the famous dual relationship which establishes the imaginary. . . . Of course, the image maintains (in the subject that I think I am) a miscognition attached to the ego and to the imaginary. . . . I glue my nose on the mirror of the screen, to the imaginary other with which I identify myself narcissistically.
>
> (Barthes 1975a: 3)

However, Metz is always careful to emphasize the relation between this imaginary unity and the discordances of the symbolic, implicitly answering the critiques of totalizing by implying that it is not the theory that totalizes, but the interpretation of the theory. As he says,

> The imaginary of the cinema presupposes the symbolic, for the spectator must first of all have known the primordial mirror. But as the latter instituted the ego very largely in the imaginary, the second mirror of the screen, a symbolic apparatus, itself in turn depends on reflection and lack.
>
> (Metz 1975: 58–9)

Any form of identification in the cinema, then, pertains to a secondary psychoanalytic level, because it concerns a subject already constituted, one who has evolved past the undifferentiation of early childhood and acceded to the Symbolic Order, and therefore one who is able to "own" a look. For this reason, Metz makes the distinction between primary identification in the psychoanalytic sense and primary cinematic identification, which is the the spectator's identification with his own look. This form of identification has its roots in the mirror phase, but is not completely homologous to it: "The mirror is the site of primary identification. Identification with one's own look is secondary with respect to the mirror . . . but it is the foundation of the cinema and hence primary when the latter is under discussion" (Metz 1975: 58).

Further clarification might be found in the concept of **SECONDARY CINE-MATIC IDENTIFICATION**:

> As for identifications with characters, with their own different levels (out-of-frame character, etc.) they are secondary, tertiary cinematic identifications, etc; taken as a whole in opposition to the simple identification of the spectator with his own look, they constitute together secondary cinematic identification, in the singular.
>
> (Metz 1975: 58)

This concept of multiple points of identification provides a way out of the impasse of unity implied by the monolithic idea of primary identification, whether it be in terms of invoking the "multiple identifications" suggested by the structure of unconscious fantasy or in terms of a "variety of subject positions" suggested by some forms of alternative cinema. The first option, that suggested by fantasy, retains the force of the unconscious as the motor of spectatorship while challenging the idea that this *only* involves the assumption of a unified self-image. Freud's paper, "A Child is Being Beaten," (Freud 1963a) is the article used by film theorists to chart the way that, in Janet Bergstrom's words, "spectators are able to take up multiple identificatory positions, whether successively or simultaneously" (Bergstrom 1979a: 58). Freud demonstrates the possibilities for the subject of fantasy to participate in a variety of roles – sliding, exchanging and doubling in the interchangeable positions of subject, object and observer. He does this by engaging with different forms of the fantasy in terms of the linguistic pronouns they imply: "My father is beating the child," "I am being beaten by my father," and "A child is being beaten" (I am probably looking on). During the three stages of this fantasy, the subject (a woman) takes the place of the father who is doing the beating, the child being beaten, and the viewer of the scene. The subject of the fantasy thus becomes a mobile and mutable entity rather than a particular gendered individual, and sexuality takes on the variable quality implied by psychoanalysis (Freud's theory of bisexuality). The implications for feminist scholarship are quite clear.

The concept of **SPECTATOR-POSITIONING**, often referred to as **SUBJECT-**

154

POSITIONING, is another way of referring to the way the spectator is "placed" in (and by) the text and made to assume roles based on identificatory participation. It locates the ability to establish the coherence or meaning of a film in the unconscious, and refers to a "site" rather than an individual. Still, there is much confusion, and the exact distinction between subject-positioning and fantasy-identifications is not very clear, though subject-positioning is more aligned with the political project of a counter-cinema. The radical potential of a film can be considered in terms of its ability to "rupture" fixed positions of identification and the coherence of the subject's unified state. On the other hand, discussion of unconscious fantasy as a possible mode of dispersed identification has been largely considered in terms of the dominant narrative fiction film.

Further clarification comes from Stephen Heath. For him, films are not discrete formal entities, but "relations of subjectivity, relations which are not the simple 'property' of the film nor that of the individual-spectator but which are those of a subject production in which film and individual have their specific historical and social reality as such" (Heath 1979: 44). Considering the film-text as a process of production of subjectivity means incorporating a notion of spectator-positioning into the analysis of a film *and* tracing the possible ways identification might be engaged; Heath brings a historical dimension to this concept while retaining the radical force of the unconscious in the definition. However, he also seems to use subject-positioning interchangeably with identification, and this has contributed to the confusion. For example, in "Narrative Space" he describes the cinematic operation in terms of a "positioning" induced in the subject: the combined elements of perspectival representation, editing, narration and modes of identification produce a subject-position of coherence and unity. But he is also careful to unfix this definition with a corrective emphasis on process:

> What moves in film, finally, is the spectator, immobile in front of the screen. Film is the regulation of that movement, the individual as subject held in a shifting and placing of desire, energy, contradiction, in a perpetual retotalization of the imaginary (the set scene of image and subject). This is the investment of film in narrativization; and crucially for a coherent space, the unity of place for vision. Once again, however, the investment is in the process . . . the give and take of absence and presence, the play of negativity and negation, flow and bind. Narrativization, with its continuity, closes, and is that movement of closure that shifts the spectator as subject in its terms: the spectator is the *point* of the film's spatial relations – the turn, say, of shot to reverse shot – their subject passage.
>
> (Heath 1981: 53-5)

The fourth feature that characterizes the construction of the desiring

155

spectator (after regression, belief and identification) is the engagement of fantasy structures such as the **FAMILY ROMANCE**. This will be used as a model for the way that the cinema mobilizes unconscious productions in order to activate the fantasmatic participation of the viewer. In psychoanalysis, the term family romance refers to an early form of imaginative activity whereby the child fantasizes ideal parents to replace the actual ones, considered to be inferior. Fantasies of this sort involve modifying the parental relationships, as in being a foundling of royal birth, or being a bastard from the mother's illicit liaison with a noble father. Grounded in the Oedipal complex, they are seen to originate from the pressure exerted on the subject by the Oedipal situation. Both types of family romance are bound up with the subject's differentiation from its parents, and thus can be combined with other processes in the evolving structure of the ego. The fantasy of the foundling is asexual and involves the simple replacement of the existing parents by superior ones; the fantasy of the bastard emerges from increased knowledge of sexual difference and incorporates sexuality into the fictional production of origins.

Using phrases like "works of fiction" and "imaginative romances," Freud first coined the term to account for a primitive form of fictional activity by the subject. Both the psychoanalytic (relations of the familial) and the novelistic (the etymology of "romance") converge in this early type of fantasmatic work, discussed by Freud along the lines of daydreaming. As a narrated scene that the subject recounts to himself in a waking state, the daydream is a prototype for the production of imaginary worlds in an attempt to correct perceived reality. Its structure and form are indicative of all fantasy life (conscious or unconscious) in the sense that it is, as with the dream work, an imaginary scene, a fictive scenario, representing the fulfillment of an unconscious wish and designating the subject as protagonist. The family romance is a particular kind of fantasy that anticipates future, more complicated forms of fantasizing. Initially believed by Freud to be a pathological symptom of paranoia, it was later found to be a normal, and in fact universal, phenomenon of infantile life. The universality of a fantasy structure like the family romance is related to the *a priori* quality of generalization that Freud finds in the Oedipal complex, and by extension, in the unconscious.

Film studies uses family romance in two ways, two general emphases corresponding roughly to thematics (the family romance as narrated or represented content) and production process (the family romance, in its wish-fulfilling, reality-correcting function, as fictive generator of that narrated or represented content). These two areas intersect; a film's represented content is not simply a matter of social or ideological analysis, while the process of psychic production is not simply the domain of psychoanalysis. Stephen Heath and Geoffrey Nowell-Smith see melodrama as "an investment in a constant repetition of family romance fantasizing both in its themes and in its processes of relations and positions of the subject-speaker" (Heath and Nowell-Smith 1977: 119). By far the most interesting development of family romance in cinema is that of Stephen Heath in an article entitled "Screen Images: Film Memory." Where Freud's emphasis falls on specific childhood fantasies of noble parentage, Heath uses the concept to discuss film as a process of narrativization and memory. In both cases familial relations are the starting point for both fictive and fantasmatic production. Heath contrasts two theories of fiction in Freud, that of the family romance, in which "the fictioning production serves to regulate and unify, to hold tight in the imaginary" (Heath 1976: 39) and that of the fort-da game, in which the fiction is not simply one of coherent mastery, but is produced as a repetition of absence. Heath's point is that of the two types of fiction-making in Freud – one totalizing (as in day-dreams and the family romance), the other process-oriented (as in the continual return of a loss in the fort-da game) – the latter is most funda-mental to the cinema in its endless process of activating and recovering difference and absence. But the cinema produces its effects in a double movement: classical film narrative always works to bind the flow into "fictions of coherence," holding, suspending and fixing its process. This dialectical play enables Heath to state: "In a real sense, in the sense of this development and exploitation, novels and films have one single title (the title of the novelistic) – *Family Romance . . .*" (ibid.: 41).

Such a use of the family romance indicates something fundamental in fiction-making and the unconscious that replays itself in cinema-viewing, and this has everything to do with the spectator. Dream, fantasy and the cinema all have this in common: they are imaginary productions that have their source in unconscious desire, and the subject in all fantasmatic productions/projections (for which, here, the family romance is the proto-type) is invariably present. Freud concisely summarizes this function of the desiring subject: "His Majesty the Ego, the hero of all day-dreams and all novels" (Freud 1958: 51). In the cinema, it is precisely because this space of subjectivity is produced as an empty space, that the slippage which gives the viewer the sense of producing the cinematic fiction can take place. The family romance, as an early form of fictive activity, stages, at an unconscious level, participation in the fantasm in just such a way.

Before discussing how this is enabled through strategies of cinematic enunciation, two filmic examples will demonstrate the psychoanalytic con-struction of spectatorship. Carl Dreyer's *Vampyr* attempts to represent the supernatural, and it is able to create the ambivalent reality of dreams precisely because it constructs a viewing position which is analogous to that of the dreamer. By blurring the distinctions between fantasy and reality, present and past, perception and imagination, substance and phan-tom, *Vampyr* recreates the dream state of the cinema-viewing subject. According to Bertrand Augst,

the film doubles back on itself to explore and define the very conditions which characterize the elusive operations of cinema and of
the imaginary, establishing itself in this very process as the central
metaphor of the creative process.... It would appear that the film
was conceived as a metaphor for the mechanisms of the imaginary.

(Augst 1978: 6, 23)[7]

What we as viewers see (and what the central character, David Gray,
also sees) constantly eludes our grasp by defying all laws of realistic
representation; "the precarious balance between belief and disbelief is
tipped to the advantage of disbelief" (ibid.: 12). In *Vampyr*, phantoms
dance and disappear, familiar objects become uncannily "other," and
perceptions turn into hallucinations; the film dramatizes all of the conditions which produce the fiction effect – regression, splitting of belief,
primary cinematic identification, fantasy structures, and the effacement of
enunciative marks – in a mirroring of the subject-effect that encompasses
both characters and viewers alike.

No less a film about the unconscious, Alain Resnais' *Last Year at Marienbad* tells the story of a seduction that may have never happened. Appropriately titled – Jacques Lacan delivered the famous "Mirror Stage" paper
in Marienbad in 1936 – the film actively engages its viewer in assembling
its narrative, constructing its own reality apart from external categories.
Screenplay author Alain Robbe-Grillet said the film represented "an
attempt to construct a purely mental space and time," that of dream or
memory. Resnais' own interpretation is that the film is "about greater or
lesser degrees of reality," an interpretation among others (there are at least
eighteen possible accounts of what "happens" in the film), but one that
gets to the heart of the film. Because it is viewer-centered, the film works
subliminally to create a totally subjective experience by approximating the
intricate, non-linear structure of the mind. The most minimal of plots
involves three "characters" about whom we know nothing, only that they
exist in the space–time continuum that is the film. Suave-voiced Character
X tries throughout the film to convince Character A to come away with
him, to leave the frozen palace (resort?) inhabited by elegant, robotic
guests, and to leave Character M as well. As each spectator is led through
a self-constructed labyrinth of possibilities, it becomes clear that the only
reality is the film itself; the past has no reality beyond the moment it is
evoked while the characters and images have no status beyond their presence on the screen. More than anything, *Marienbad* dramatizes its status
as an apparatus for engaging fantasy, memory and desire, and ceasing to
function without the viewer, it creates an object-lesson in the theory of
film-spectatorship.

ENUNCIATION

The fifth element in the construction of the cinematic spectator has to do with "authorship" and its effacement. In order to give the spectator the impression that it is he or she who is producing the cinematic fantasm on the screen, something must happen to hide the "real" dreamer – the implied author of the film, its putative subject of desire – from view. The viewer must be made to forget that an external fiction is being watched, a fiction which has come from another source of desire. As Metz puts it, "I [the subject] espouse the filmmaker's look (without which no cinema would be possible)" (Metz 1975: 56). Psychoanalytic film theory turns to the concept of **ENUNCIATION** to describe this complicated process of slippage, but it uses the concept very differently than narratology does, largely because it is concerned with the place of the split subject of the unconscious in the enunciative operation. Psychoanalytic film theory thus connects what narratology describes as the viewer's assumption of narration ("The film seems to be narrated by the spectator himself, who becomes, in imagination, its discursive source," see p. 106 above) to desire and subjectivity. Enunciation is related to dreaming – as a fantasmatic, unconscious operation, and not as a cognitive process.

Psychoanalytic film theory borrows the concept of enunciation from structural linguistics, emphasizing the position of the speaking subject as one produced in division and implicated in the constant activity of the unconscious. In every verbal exchange there is both the *énoncé* (the statement, what is said, the language itself) and the *énonciation* (the process that produces the statement, how something is said, from what position it emanates). Consideration of enunciation as a process involves extra-linguistic determinations – social, psychological, unconscious – as well as the specific linguistic features of the language system mobilized by the speaker. As such, it points to the fundamental importance of the extra-linguistic in any act of communication, and therefore emphasizes subjectivity – the subject's place in language – as constitutive of the production of all utterances, of all human discursive exchange. According to French linguist Emile Benveniste, "what characterizes enunciation in general is the emphasis on the discursive relationship with a partner, whether it be real or imagined, individual or collective" (Benveniste 1971: 85). As elaborated in the notion of the split subject, when psychoanalysis is factored into this linguistic relationship, the *énonciation*, as a site of production, becomes infused with unconscious desire. Psychoanalytic film theory thus makes use of the concept as a way of describing both the "origin" of the film-fantasy (at the site of authorship) and its "appropriation" (at the site of spectatorship).

According to this logic, psychoanalytic film theory asserts that in every film there is always a place of enunciation – a place from which the cinematic discourse proceeds. The psychoanalytic model theorizes this as a position, not to be confused with the actual individual (the film-maker), and it is therefore not accessible to either cognitive theories or analyses of intentionality. The most substantial and suggestive argument for cinematic enunciation has been put forward by Raymond Bellour, mainly in his article, "Hitchcock: The Enunciator," and in his clarifications in an interview with Janet Bergstrom. In "Hitchcock: The Enunciator" Bellour uses an analysis of Hitchcock's *Marnie* to demonstrate the way in which the director uses his privileged position to represent his own desire, indicating how the "logical unfolding of the phantasy originat[es] in the conditions of enunciation" (Bellour 1977: 73). It is also here that he coins the terms **CAMERA-WISH** and **FILM-WISH** to designate that peculiar correspondence between the cinema and unconscious fantasy that is the cornerstone of psychoanalytic film theory. For Bellour, the system of cinematic enunciation is defined in the following way: "A subject endowed with a kind of infinite power, constituted as the place from which the set of representations are ordered and organized, and toward which they are channeled back. For that reason, this subject is the one who sustains the very possibility of any representation" (Bellour 1979a: 98). Already implicit in this definition is the *reciprocal* status of enunciation, for not only do the screen images emanate from a desiring source, they are returned (in order to be taken over) to an equally desiring source – the spectator. That is why, in the same interview, Bellour can expand on the kind of relay implied by the enunciative system that he analyzes in *Marnie*, noting how easily one can move through the alternation of different characters' points-of-view "to a central point from which all these different visions emanate: the place, at once productive and empty, of the subject-director" (ibid.). The operative concept here is the dialectic – the double movement by which the enunciative space is simultaneously productive and empty. It is in this sense that enunciation is used to describe both the textual articulation of the film-maker's desire across the visual field and the spectator's desire as it is engaged by this articulation.

Metz provides further clarification of how this space of cinematic enunciation becomes the position of cinematic vieweing in "History/Discourse: A Note on Two Voyeurisms,"[8] an article that connects the enunciative process to **VOYEURISM**, the libidinal aspect of pleasurable looking that is so central to psychoanalytic film theory's model of the cinema. In psychoanalysis, voyeurism applies to any kind of sexual gratification obtained from vision, and is usually associated with a hidden vantage point, such as a keyhole. (It is sometimes used interchangeably with **SCOPOPHILIA**, another term for the erotic component of seeing, because there is no precise distinction between the terms in the psychoanalytic literature. Generally speaking, both terms are invoked in the cinema where, obviously, the visual is dominant, but while scopophilia defines the general pleasure in looking, voyeurism denotes a specific perversion.) In film theory, this vantage point (created by the keyhole effect) becomes the source and end point in the enunciative relay that enacts the circulation of desire between the author, text and viewer. "If the traditional film tends to suppress all the marks of the subject of enunciation, *this is in order that the viewer may have the impression of being that subject himself*, but an empty, absent subject, a pure capacity for seeing" (Metz 1976: 24, emphasis added). In the film-theoretical description, in order for the cinematic fiction to both produce and maintain its fascinating hold on the spectator, it must appear as if the screen images are the expressions of the spectator's own desire. Or rather, as Bertrand Augst describes it, "The subject-producer must disappear so that the subject-spectator can take his place in the production of the filmic discourse" (Augst 1979: 51).

For his model of the cinema, Metz transforms the linguistic emphasis of enunciation into a concept of the enunciator as "producer of the fiction," indicating that process by which every film-maker organizes the image flow, choosing and designating the series of images, organizing the diverse views that make up the relay between the one who looks (the camera, the film-maker) and what is being looked at (the scene of the action). He then relates this to the spectator's voyeurism, conceived as an instance of "pure seeing," the capacity to wield the objectifying gaze without its exhibitionist component. Metz maintains that one of the primary operations of the classical narrative film (what distinguishes it as "classical" in fact), is the effacement or hiding of those marks of enunciation which point to the director's work of selecting and arranging shots – textual indicators that, in a sense, reveal the film-maker's hand. This work of masking over the discursive process is at the heart of the "invisible editing" or transparency of Hollywood cinema. Terms of enunciation theory are invoked to describe this process: the work of production is concealed by disguising the **DISCOURSE** – in which the source of enunciation is both marked and foregrounded, its reference point is the present tense, and the pronouns "I" and "you" are engaged – in order to present itself as **HISTORY (STORY)** – in which the source of enunciation is suppressed, the verb tense is an indefinite past of already completed events, and the pronouns engaged are "he," "she" and "it".

In an article accompanying Metz' essay in *Edinburgh 76 Magazine*, Geoffrey Nowell-Smith further clarifies the distinction:

> Discourse and history are both forms of enunciation, the difference between them lying in the fact that in the discursive form the source of the enunciation is present, whereas in the historical it is suppressed. History is always "there" and "then," and its protagonists are "he," "she," and "it." Discourse however, always contains, as its points of reference, a "here" and a "now" and an "I" and a "you".
>
> (Nowell-Smith 1976: 27)

In discourse the discursive relation is emphasized, while in history (story) the address is impersonal. In cinematic terms, the film – a constructed discourse logically emanating from a specific source – passes itself off as history – an impersonal narration that simply exists. In narratology's formulation, "The enunciative process transforms the discourse into an apparently self-generating story," but it does this (and this is the distinction), for psychoanalytic film theory, precisely so that it can have another subject of enunciation.

Some theories of radical political counter-cinema frame these filmmakers' challenges to the dominant cinema in terms of emphasizing the discursive marks in the enunciative process. Films that foreground discourse over history (through techniques such as disjunctive editing and direct address) are seen as politically progressive. In this context, any film by Godard could be analyzed in terms of the discursive authorial interventions (either those specifically by Godard or those produced textually) which disrupt the seamless and illusory fabrications of the (hi)story. But it is important not to confuse the two methods of analysis (that of narrative/linguistic theory and that of psychoanalysis); cinematic enunciation in its psychoanalytic usage involves unconscious processes rather than formal strategies. Psychoanalytic film theory deals with the production of desiring subjectivities – the author's, the spectator's – and thus conceives of enunciation as a process of circulation rather than focussing on its manifestation through specific textual instances.

So, in order for the spectator to assume the position of filmic enunciation, to have the impression that it is his/her own story being told, it must appear as if the fiction on the screen emerges from nowhere. Since, as Metz asserts, "history . . . is always (by definition) a story told from nowhere, told by nobody, but received by someone (without which it would not exist)," the invisible style which hides the work of the enunciator makes it seem like "it is . . . the receiver (or rather the receptacle) who tells it" (Metz 1976: 24). Accordingly, the effective functioning and the psychic engagement of the cinema as an apparatus are only possible on the basis of this concealment of its operations; in this way a "pseudo-viewer" is created, which every spectator can appropriate at will.

THE GAZE

The first and perhaps most direct way of discussing the constellation of issues surrounding the **GAZE** in cinema is through the concept of the **PRIMAL SCENE**. In psychoanalytic theory, the primal scene designates a traumatic infantile experience, a scenario of vision involving the child's observation of parental intercourse. Like all **PRIMAL FANTASIES** (that is, typical fantasy structures – such as those of intra-uterine existence, castration and seduction – responsible for the organization of psychic life) the primal scene is not necessarily based on an actual event. In fact, its status as "reality" (for the subject) is what led Freud to theorize unconscious fantasy in general, and to establish the concept of psychical reality as a way of accounting for both the dramatic impact these fantasies have in the life of the subject and the coherence, organization, autonomy and efficacy of the fantasy realm. For Freud, primal fantasies were proof that structures exist in the dimension of fantasy which are irreducible to lived experience; they can therefore be considered unconscious "schemata," or patterns structuring the imaginative life of the subject, which transcend both the individual's lived experience and personal imaginings. Like collective myths, primal fantasies are seen to represent a solution to whatever constitutes a major enigma for the child. They dramatize responses to questions of origins: the primal scene stages the emergence of the individual; the fantasy of seduction dramatizes the emergence of sexuality; fantasies of castration represent the origin of sexual difference.

Freud is very precise about the universality of these fantasies, giving special prominence to the primal scene:

> Among the wealth of unconscious phantasies of neurotics, and probably of all human beings, there is one which is seldom absent and can be disclosed by analysis concerning the watching of sexual intercourse between the parents. I call these phantasies, together with those of seduction, castration, and others, *primal phantasies*.
>
> (Freud 1963a: 103)

Elsewhere he speaks of the "constant sameness which as a rule characterizes the phantasies that are constructed [in] childhood, irrespective of how greatly or how little real experiences have contributed toward them" (Freud 1963b: 66). This description of the primal fantasy as a universal phenomenon, plus the fact that psychic meanings accrue to an event which may never have happened, gives Freud a basis for the theory of phylogenetic inheritance: primal fantasies are grounded in events which precede the individual and are transmitted historically from generation to generation. Thus they structure the psychic life not only of the individual but of the culture in general.

Freud elaborates the notion of the primal scene in his account of the case of the "Wolf Man." Through an analysis of the patient's terrifying dream he determined that the vision of parental intercourse was not an actual memory, but a reconstruction made plausible by the convergence of many details. Several things emerge from this analysis. First, parental coitus is generally interpreted by the child as paternal aggression; second, the scene gives rise to sexual excitation in the child, and this is often associated with danger and anxiety; third, within the context of an infantile sexual theory, the act is interpreted as anal intercourse.

But most important for our purpose is the fact that a disposition of elements (darkness, reduced motor capability, stability, and a witnessing position) situate the subject of the fantasy in a position of spectatorship remarkably like that in the cinema: "*It was night, I was lying in my bed*. This latter is the beginning of the reproduction of the primal scene" (Freud 1963b: 228). At an early stage in his work, Freud referred to all primal fantasies as scenes of archetypal scenarios by designating them as "primal scenes" regardless of their content. Yet only the fantasy structure involving the child's witnessing of parental coitus has retained the visual terminology of primal *scene*, and this is what makes it so productive an analogue to spectatorship in the cinema.

In "The Imaginary Signifier," Metz argues that the cinema's reactivation of the primal scene makes the unconscious component of film viewing much stronger than that in the theater. He attributes this to "certain precise features of the institution" (Metz 1975: 64), among which the keyhole effect, produced by those conditions of reception discussed earlier (and reintroduced in terms of voyeurism), is only the most graphic. Metz notes three main reasons for the affinity between the primal scene and cinema viewing. First, the spectator's solitude and enforced direction of energy toward the screen make the film audience more fragmented and isolated than the "temporary collectivity" of the theatrical spectacle. Second, because film is comprised of the representation of *absent* people and objects, what is seen is "more radically ignorant of its spectator" (ibid.: 63), while the actors in the theater can engage in a true reciprocal relation with the viewers (the spectator's voyeurism is matched by the actor's exhibitionism in "an authentic perverse couple" (ibid.)). Third, there is an important "segregation of spaces" involved in the cinema which enhances, and in fact depends on, the distance between the spectacle and spectator. The two spaces are absolutely separate realms. Thus, "[for] its spectator the film unfolds in that simultaneously quite close and definitively inaccessible 'elsewhere' in which the child *sees* the gambols of the parental couple, who are similarly ignorant of it and leave it alone, a pure onlooker whose participation is inconceivable" (ibid.: 64). In this way the primal scene is invoked to create an analogy between this specific production of a fantasy of origins and the psychic modalities of film spectatorship, and (again) to define the matrix of vision and desire which connects cinema viewing with unconscious activity.

The best discussion of the primal scene in relation to a specific film-text is Thierry Kuntzel's monumental textual analysis of Schoedsack and Pichel's *The Most Dangerous Game* (Kuntzel 1980a, 1980b). The first part, "The Film-Work, 2," has obvious affinities with Freud's dream analyses, tracing the work of the primary processes in a detailed, sixty-five-page exploration of every aspect of the film. He ends this article (which transforms a minor adventure film into a subtle demonstration of psychic processes) with a formulation of the film's spectator's unconscious position (he begins by

164

citing Metz): " 'Cinematic voyeurism, unauthorized scopophilia, is . . . in a direct line from the primal scene.' Uncanniness of *The Most Dangerous Game*: It puts into play, stages, my 'love' of the cinema; that is what I go to see (again) with each new film; my own desire – endlessly repeated – for re-presentation" (Kuntzel 1980a: 63). The second article, "Sight, Insight, and Power: Allegory of a Cave," involves a highly suggestive shot-by-shot analysis of a particular sequence's dramatization of the primal scene. The ending of this article ingeniously interfaces the description of a primal scene in Melanie Klein with both the characters in *The Most Dangerous Game* and the spectators beyond it: "For this ultimate spectator, who sees both scenes at once – and often sees them *better* than the first spectator, who is caught up in the scene and must conceal himself – to see is to have divine (in)sight" (Kuntzel 1980b: 109).

To take a filmic example, a primal scene episode in Godard/Miéville's *Numéro Deux*, involving a young girl's observation of a scene of anal inter-course by her parents in the kitchen, is rendered by a close-up of the child's face superimposed over an image of the couple. The single close-up of the child bleeds into one of the couple, so that we retroactively read the close-up as a scene of vision. In a striking compression of shot and reverse-shot – the viewer and the viewed within a single image – the act of witnessing the primal scene and its cinematic equivalent are rendered without a cut. This shot is rephotographed, solarized and visually manipulated, creating repeated invisible displacements of the scene. The voices of the diegetic parents combine with that of the film-maker (What did the child actually see? Was it violence or lovemaking? What does it mean to witness? How was the act interpreted? Did it actually happen?), provoking both a reflection on cinematic meaning-production and on the psychic components of film viewing as well.

Godard's intervention as authorial voice suggests another way of thinking about the gaze, a way of specifying its particular use by psychoanalytic film theory, and that is in terms of the connection between vision and enunciation. As Bellour establishes in his analysis of Hitchcock's function in *Marnie*, each film-maker appropriates and then designates "the look" in a specific way, and this is what characterizes a particular director's system of enunciation. The enunciative system is thus aligned with structures of looking in order to describe the way that vision and desire are organized in the construction of cinematic discourse. Through a demonstration of how Marnie is constituted as the object of the desiring gaze – of the male characters, Hitchcock himself, the camera and, by extension, the viewer – Bellour asserts that Hitchcock's power to delegate his look (the image-generating function) to the male characters (his fictional surrogates) inscribes them onto the "trajectory of virtual possession of the object" (Bellour 1977: 72). When Mark Rutland imagines Marnie, in a close-up that reveals that "he is daydreaming about this woman whose virtual image he has helped to create" (ibid: 71), her immediate appearance on the screen – in a space which is diegetically impossible for Mark to see – produces this conclusion:

> Mark's single-minded desire for Marnie is aroused by this relation-ship between himself and the image – Mark takes on Hitchcock's desire which Hitchcock can only realize through the camera [, an apparatus] which forbids him to exercise his desire through pos-session[,] thus permitting him to represent it.
>
> (ibid.: 71–2)

Bellour thus defines the place of the enunciator as that which monitors the different types of scopic relation to the object, classifying relative positions of the camera-look in relation to what is represented. Importantly, this is a relation of desire defined by masculine subjectivity, in which the woman is irrefutably positioned as the image-object of the gaze.

Another way of defining psychoanalytic film theory's conception of the gaze is in terms of the point-of-view and reverse-shot structures, editing figures that combine with the apparatus in the construction of the spectator as a fantasmatic entity. The association of enunciation and vision suggests the central position held by the textual organization of the gaze in produc-ing that slippage between author and viewer activated in spectatorship. The editing figures that accomplish this utilize the spectator's ability to construct an imaginary coherence – a filmic space–time dimension – by articulating a logic of viewer/viewed. In the classical model of the fiction film, narrative storytelling, seamless editing and secondary identifications (with characters) contribute to the production of an illusory world with its own internal consistency. Historically, it was through the joining of shot to shot in the construction of this fictional world that the cinema came to have its own method of constructing not only "reality" but its spectator as well. This is not to say that one-shot actualities (early news-reels) were devoid of meaning – to be sure, there are discursive relations within a single shot. But along with editing came the privileging, channel-ing and directing of those relations in the production of a viewing subjec-tivity that is markedly different from the viewer of one-shot actualities. Classical editing implies subjectivity – or its negotiation – by guiding the subjective processes toward a meaning-effect.

But while this spectator is constructed, as noted regarding enunciation, the work of the organizing principle (the "author") – a subject motivated by desire and external to the text which selected and arranged the shots into a composite fictional world – had to be rendered invisible. The rules of continuity were developed in order to maintain the impression of an imaginary coherence, permitting the spectator's belief in the integrity of the space, the logical sequence of time, and the "reality" of the fictive universe. The spectator's fictive participation thus hinges on a perceived spatial coherence – fragmentary images are given a logical consistency because they are subordinated to a causal sequence of narrative events. In "Narrative Space," Stephen Heath refers to this process as "the conversion of seen into scene," in which vision itself is dramatized, staged as a narrated (and therefore meaningful) spectacle before the viewer: "What is crucial is the conversion of seen into scene, the holding of signifier on signified: the frame, composed, centred, narrated, is the point of that conversion" (Heath 1981: 37).

The spectator's ability to construct a mentally continuous time and space out of fragmentary images is based on a system of looks, a structured relay of glances: (1) from the film-maker/enunciator/camera toward the pro-filmic event (the scene observed by the camera); (2) between the characters within the fiction; and (3) across the visual field from spectator to screen – glances that bind the viewer in a position of meaning, coherence, belief and power. It is these traversing gazes that are primarily negotiated through the reverse-shot and point-of-view structures, the central means by which "the look" is inscribed in the cinematic fiction. Most commonly applied to conversation situations, the **REVERSE-SHOT** structure implies an alternation of images between seeing and seen, the **POINT-OF-VIEW** shot anchoring the image in the vision and perspective of one or another character (and marked by greater or lesser degrees of subjective distortion). The spectator therefore identifies, in effect, with someone who is always off-screen, an absent "other" whose main function is to signify a space to be occupied (see the following discussion of suture). The reverse-shot structure enables the spectator to become a sort of **INVISIBLE MEDIATOR** between an interplay of looks, a fictive participant in the fantasy of the film. From a shot of one character looking, to another character looked at, the viewer's subjectivity is bound into the text.

Recalling the complex and ambivalent structure of secondary identifications in the Oedipal complex (the movement between the desire to have and the desire to be), Alain Bergala discusses the reverse-shot configuration in psychoanalytic terms:

> In films, the combined effects of the classical decoupage and point-of-view place the character in a similar situation [of ambivalence], sometimes subject of the look (he is the one who observes the scene, others), and sometimes as object of someone's look (another character or the omniscient spectator). It is through the mechanism of the look [*jeu des regards*] mediated by the camera, that the classical decoupage of filmic action offers the spectator in a very ordinary way, inscribed in the code, this regulated ambivalence of the fictional character in relation to the look of the spectator (to the other's desire).
>
> (in Aumont *et al.* 1963: 179)

Metz connects this relay of looks to identification by describing the trajectories of vision as so many "notches" in the complicated structure of spectatorial belief. He refers to the textual exchange of glances as "certain localized figures of the cinematic codes" that intersect with "primary cinematic identification, [that is] identification with one's own look" in the course of a film (Metz 1975: 58).

> As it happens (and this is already another "notch" in the chain of identifications) a character looks at another who is momentarily out-of-frame, or else is looked at by him. If we have gone one notch further, this is because everything out-of-frame *brings us closer to the spectator*, since it is the peculiarity of the latter to be out-of-frame (the out-of-frame character thus has a point in common with him: he is looking at the screen).
>
> (ibid.: 57)

He goes on to say that this off-screen character's look is reinforced by various techniques that establish point-of-view, either through camera position (as in the optical point-of-view shot) or through visual distortions such as blurring or soft-focus (as in the semi-subjective shot). However, he says, there are usually other elements, instead of camera placement, that signal the character's point-of-view, such as the logic of the narrative, an element of dialogue, or a previous shot. But most important from Metz' theoretical perspective is the fact that "the identification that founds the signifier is *twice relayed*, doubly duplicated in a circuit that leads it to the heart of the film along a line which . . . follows the inclination of the looks and is therefore governed by the film itself" (ibid.) Before "dispersing all over the screen in a variety of intersecting lines" made up of the looks of characters on the screen (a "second duplication"), the spectator's look ("the basic identification") must traverse ("'go through' as in crossing a strait") the look of the off-screen character (the "first duplication"), who is himself a spectator. Metz considers this off-screen character the "first delegate" of the spectator, and he describes this extremely complex operation in the following way: "By offering himself as a crossing for the spectator, he inflects the circuit followed by the sequence of identifications and it is only in this sense that he is himself seen: as we see through him, we see ourselves not seeing him" (ibid.).

Betrand Augst clarifies this by proposing an intricate, variable model that associates identification with a whole range of cinematic looks: "Identification plays a central role in the operations of the cinematographic apparatus because it regulates, balances, modulates the subtle shift of balance between the many regimes of belief which intervene continually in the process of production of the fiction-effect" (Augst 1978: 12). He thus provides the framework for Metz' demonstration of the impossible location constructed by these looks, and of the circuits of desire engaged by cinematic viewing. Identifications in the cinema are always partial, diffuse and imaginary, momentarily catching and suspending the spectator in a net of elusive glances, an invisible but powerful mirror which holds the viewer in a state of fascination.

Another concept in psychoanalytic film theory which is developed around the gaze is **SUTURE**. This is an extremely complicated idea, first formulated in 1966 by Jacques-Alain Miller (a student of Lacan's) to designate the relation of the subject to the chain of its own discourse, a concept meant to clarify the production of the subject in language. In 1969 Jean-Pierre Oudart applied the theory to the cinema, specifically with respect to the films of Robert Bresson, as a way of designating a particular type of relation between the look of the subject-spectator and the chain of filmic discourse. More generally (although the application of Oudart's thesis to films other than Bresson's has been problematic), the notion of suture applies to the different positions available to the spectator in relation to both screen space and off-screen space. Subsequent articles in English, such as Daniel Dayan's influential exposition of Oudart (Dayan 1974) and William Rothman's criticism of the Dayan-Oudart position (Rothman 1975), as well as Stephen Heath's careful explication of the concept in *Questions of Cinema* (1981) set the terms of the debate as it has been conceived by psychoanalytic film theory.

Seeking to clarify the relation of Miller's term to the unconscious production of the subject, Heath cites Lacan:

> The subject is thus nothing other than that which "slides in a chain of signifiers" (Lacan 1975: 48), its cause is the effect of language. . . .
> Veritable treasure of signifiers, the unconscious is structured as a language; psychoanalysis, the "talking cure," developing precisely as an acute attention to the movement of the subject in the signifying chain.
>
> (Heath 1981: 79)

He notes how Miller cites the division between *énoncé* and *énonciation* as evidence that "the subject is not one in its representation in language" (ibid.: 85). Suture becomes, then, the process whereby the subject is "stitched" into the chain of discourse which both defines and is defined by the work of the unconscious. But it is also used in the sense of suturing *over*, binding and making coherent that process which produces the subject: "Suture names not just a structure of lack but also an availability of the subject, a certain closure . . ." (ibid.). In this sense suture is understood as a process of masking, of taking over, of taking the place of, or as Heath puts it, "[T]he 'I' is a division but joins all the same, the stand-in is the lack in the structure but nevertheless, simultaneously, the possibility of a coherence, of the *filling in*" (ibid.: 86).

Oudart's claim is that the psychic processes which constitute subjectivity are reiterated in film by the process which binds the spectator into the coherence of its fictions, namely the reverse-shot structure. For him, the screen image offers the viewer an imaginary plenitude which recalls the infant's early experience of the mirror. This satisfaction, however, is immediately ruptured by the awareness of off-screen space, which, according to Oudart, invokes anxiety. The anxiety is allayed by the reverse-shot structure which, by "answering" the absence evoked by the empty space (with the vision of the character off-screen, the **ABSENT ONE**), "sutures" the spectator into the original experience of imaginary satisfaction. Dayan brings the concept of ideology to this operation, applying the theories of ideological masking found in Baudry's first article to the system of the suture activated in editing (see Baudry 1974–5). For him, the reverse-shot structure renders the discursive construction of the film invisible, thus producing a mystified subject who "absorbs an ideological effect without being aware of it." Rothman's criticism comes from a literal reading of the concept of spectator-positioning, claiming that the absent one does not exist in the viewing situation because spectators always know whose point-of-view is being represented. However, as has been established, whether it is called the absent one or not, there is *always* an invisible discursive agency in any cinematic construction. In a film, "someone looking" is always the *representation* of someone looking, and the notion of enunciative source connects this representation to desire.

Because Heath most fully explores the psychoanalytic underpinnings of the concept of suture, he is able to make the most reliable argument in support of it. For him the alliance of meaning and subjectivity in the "production" of a film always reiterates the psychoanalytic subject's emergence in the symbolic: "Crucially, what this realization of absence from the image at once achieves is the definition of the image as discontinuous, its production *as signifier*: the move from cinema to cinematic, cinema as discourse" (Heath 1981: 87). Finally, considered in the light of theories of suture, Metz' description (above) of the trajectory of gazes that bind the viewer into relations of desire and meaning provides at once a convincing argument for its existence and a suggestive proposal for its application.

The notion of **PLENITUDE** – the production of an ideal (and idealized) entity through cinematic processes – is extremely complicated; each theorist considers it somewhat differently. For this reason, critiques of the gaze have taken a variety of forms. The entire context of the debate involves the cinema's implication in the **SCOPIC REGIME**. Citing the absence at the center of all cinematic representation and relating this to both the fantasmatic processes of the imaginary and the signifying processes of the symbolic, Metz defines the scopic regime in the following way:

Cinema practice is only possible through the perceptual passions: the desire to see (= scopic drive, scopophilia, voyeurism) [and] the desire to hear (this is the "*pulsion invocante*" the invocatory drive). . . . [The]

visual and auditory drives have a stronger or more special relationship with the absence of their object . . . because, as opposed to other
sexual drives, the "perceiving drive" . . . concretely represents the
absence of its object in the distance at which it maintains it and
which is part of its very definition. . . . [But] what defines the specifically cinematic scopic regime is not so much the distance kept, the
"keeping" itself (first figure of the lack, common to all voyeurism),
as the absence of the object seen. . . . The cinema signifier . . . installs
a new figure of the lack.

(Metz 1975: 59, 60, 62, 63)

What distinguishes the cinema from other arts based on seeing and
hearing (painting, sculpture, architecture, music, opera, theater, etc.) is
this specific imaginary process by which the film provides "an extra
reduplication, a supplementary and specific turn to the screw bolting desire
to the lack" (ibid.: 61). Because the spectators and the actors never share
the same space, the register in which viewing subjectivity can be discussed
– the scopic regime – is much more connected to the intricate processes
of the unconscious than other forms of representation that invoke the
perceptual drives.

This "production of a viewing subjectivity" within the scopic regime
has been understood in two contrasting ways – either as a binding, totalizing operation or as one that implies a constant process of division and
lack. Each option suggests a different idea of how the cinematic apparatus
affects its viewer as psychoanalytic subject. Two main objections characterize the arguments about the relation between the cinematic apparatus and
the gaze – those regarding its affinities with the mirror phase (and the
subjective consequences implied) and those regarding its failure to acknowledge sexual difference as a category. In some cases the second premise
derives from the first. For example, in "Misrecognition and Identity,"
Mary Ann Doane carefully traces the concept of identification (both primary and secondary) as it is posited by both Laura Mulvey and Metz,
challenging the notion of a coherent position of mastery and, at the same
time, finding either an exclusion of the feminine or an incorporation into
patriarchal definitions. The structures of seeing outlined by psychoanalytic
theories of the apparatus – scopophilia/voyeurism, fetishism and primary
identification – have necessarily been determined in terms of masculine
subjectivity; they are not ideologically neutral, removed from the context
of sexual definitions. She concludes:

To speak of identification and the cinema . . . [is] to trace another
way in which the woman is inscribed as absent, lacking, a gap,
both on the level of cinematic representation and on the level of its
theorization. As long as it is a question of mastery of the image, of

171

representation and self-representation, identification must be considered in relation to . . . the problematic of sexual difference.

(Doane 1980: 31)

In "The Cinematic Apparatus: Problems in Current Theory," Jacqueline Rose suggests just such a way of thinking identification in its multiple possibilities, pointing to the bisexual disposition of each individual implicit in Freud's concept of the drives. She says that his essay, "A Child is Being Beaten," "demonstrates that male and female cannot be assimilated to active and passive and that there is always a potential split between the sexual object and the sexual aim, between the subject and object of desire" (Rose 1986: 210). Bisexuality can be productively incorporated into a notion of the apparatus, destabilizing its imputed constitution of a coherent subject ("an imaginary, essentially passive cohesion" (ibid.: 200)) and allowing possible alternative, gendered identifications, available to both masculine and feminine subjects. This is a move (she suggests in her critique of Metz) which is not only possible but necessary:

To redefine [the concept of disavowal] as the question of sexual difference is necessarily to recognise its phallic reference: how woman is structured as image around this reference and how she thereby *comes* to represent the potential loss and difference which underpins the whole system (and it is the failure to engage with this that is the problem with Metz's . . . work). What classical cinema performs or "puts on stage" is this image of woman as other, dark continent, and from there what escapes or is lost to the system; at the same time that sexuality is frozen into her body as spectacle, the object of phallic desire and/or identification.

(ibid.: 210–11)

Rose's more complex (and more Lacanian) critique of Metz is found in "The Imaginary," where she skilfully develops the groundwork for an argument in six parts that she summarizes at the end of the chapter (ibid.: 195–7). Among her points of critique, she notes that the illusion at the basis of the subject "seeing itself seeing itself" is produced by the activity of the critic and not by the specular situation; she concludes that Metz needs to relate his consideration of the "all-perceiving subject" more explicitly to his discussion of scopic perversion. In addition, she claims, Metz does not account for the ambivalent use of the word "screen" in Lacan, where it provides not only the function of a mirror, but that of a veil ("the simultaneous sign of the barrier between the subject and the object of desire"). She concludes by demonstrating how Metz' assertion that the cinema is more "imaginary" than other arts can be challenged: what he claims about the illusory capacity of the cinema's "presentified absence" is equally applicable to any pictorial representation. Rose bolsters her point with a quote from Lacan, who uses the story of Zeuxis and Parrhasios and their drawing/painting on a wall to show that "in order to dupe a human subject: 'what one presents to her or him is a painting of a veil, that is to say, something beyond which she or he demands to see' " (ibid.: 197).

In "The Avant-Garde and Its Imaginary," Constance Penley's discussion of the gaze critiques the idealist notion of the subject posited by the apparatus, while her criticisms are more fully developed in "Feminism, Film Theory, and the Bachelor Machines." In this latter article she provides a comprehensive interpretation and evaluation of the work of Doane, Copjec and Rose, positing, like Rose, a notion of the subject's multiple and shifting identifications found in the fantasy structure as a way of incorporating sexual difference into the theory of the apparatus.

One of the most sophisticated psychoanalytic critiques comes from Joan Copjec, whose argument (across a series of complex articles) entails a precise and subtle understanding of Lacan. In "The Delirium of Clinical Perfection" she says that the concept of the gaze, as the founding look of the camera "with which the spectator identifies in an act that establishes his identity as the condition of the possibility of the perceived" (Copjec 1986: 60), "is not governed solely by recognition of a total image with which one can then identify oneself. Instead this relation remains one of alterity in which there is a measure of nonrecognition, nonencounter, and anxiety" (ibid.: 64). The other articles, culminating in "The Orthopsychic Subject," provide a thoroughgoing critique of the entire apparatus of the gaze, the only argument (with the possible exception of Rose) to come from completely within the parameters of Lacanian psychoanalysis. Arguing that film theory's conception of the gaze is dependent on psychoanalytic (and presumed masculine) structures of voyeurism and fetishism, Copjec claims instead that the gaze arises out of linguistic assumptions that, in turn, shape the psychoanalytic concepts from a matrix of division. For example,

[T]he law does not construct a subject who simply and unequivocally has a desire, but one who *rejects* its desire, one who wants not to desire it. The subject is thus split from its desire, and desire itself is conceived as something – precisely – unrealized.

(Copjec 1989: 61)

Film theory's introduction of the "subject" by means of the concept of narcissism elides this difference – a division implicit in the Lacanian gaze which "splits the subject that it describes." Moreover, that splitting demonstrates "why the speaking subject *cannot* ever be totally trapped in the imaginary" (ibid.: 67).

The Lacanian gaze is conceived at an invisible point where something appears to be missing from the representation, and thus takes on a "terrifying alterity that prohibits the subject from seeing itself in the representation" (ibid.: 69). Copjec concludes:

> In film theory the subject identifies with the gaze as the signified of the image and comes into existence as the realization of a possibility. In Lacan, the subject identifies with the gaze as the signifier of the lack that causes the image to languish. The subject comes into existence, then, through a desire which is still considered to be the *effect* of the law, but not its *realization*.
>
> (ibid.: 70)

According to Copjec, in order to be more commensurate with the Lacanian model that it invokes, film theory will have to take this into account.

FEMINIST FILM THEORY

The most substantial challenges to psychoanalytic film theory (from within an acceptance of, and an argument for, the psychoanalytic method) come from **FEMINIST THEORY**. Questions posed to psychoanalytic film theory as the result of feminist inquiries and scholarship – precisely around sexual difference – operate a necessary corrective to its naturalized patriarchal assumptions. As discussed, psychoanalytic film theory posits the cinema as a fantasmatic production which mobilizes primary processes in the circulation of desire. The cinematic apparatus constructs its spectator and then structures the screen relationship along psychoanalytic modalities of fantasy, the scopic drive, fetishism, narcissism and identification. Conventionally, it is the woman's image, existing to be looked at (and to be desired) that is offered to the male spectator-consumer who possesses the gaze. If psychoanalytic film theory describes the production of a masculine cine-subject whose desire is activated and constantly displaced, then it is clear that feminist criticism has its work cut out for it.

The text that established the psychoanalytic framework for feminist film theory was Laura Mulvey's 1975 article, "Visual Pleasure and Narrative Cinema,"[9] in which she asserted that "the unconscious of patriarchal society has structured film form" in such a way that the "socially established interpretation of sexual difference . . . controls images, erotic ways of looking, and spectacle" (Mulvey 1975: 6). She argues for an interpretive use of psychoanalysis that will reveal the ways in which every cinematic operation (and particularly those processes associated with the gaze – identification, voyeurism and fetishism) reinscribes the subjective structures of patriarchy. Beyond this, the article calls upon psychoanalysis to assist in the "destruction of pleasure as a radical weapon" (ibid.: 7), something necessary if women are to attain both power over their representations and an autonomous symbolic form, "a new language of desire" (ibid.: 8) articulated by and through the cinema.

174

Mulvey's argument is basically this: spectatorship in the cinema is organized along gender lines, creating an active (male) spectator in control of a passive (female) screen-object. The operations of spectacle and narrative combine to dictate specific masculine and feminine viewing positions according to a standard which is implicitly male: "Cinematic codes create a gaze, a world, and an object, thereby producing an illusion cut to the measure of desire" (Mulvey 1975: 17). The cinema makes its appeal to the spectator's unconscious along two lines, that of scopophilia (in which an active subject derives pleasure in looking at a passive object) and that of narcissism/ego-libido (in which a sense of self is reconfirmed in the unity of the screen image). Both activities are connected to the earliest forms of satisfaction, related either to the erotics of the gaze as the basis for voyeurism (this corresponds to the keyhole effect noted by Metz) or to the fascination of the mirror phase (which Metz invokes in his discussion of primary identification). But then Mulvey goes on to say that in the cinema these activities become uniquely available to the male, because "in a world ordered by sexual imbalance, pleasure in looking has been split between active/male and passive/female. . . . Woman [is posited] as image, man as bearer of the look" (ibid.: 11). "An active/passive heterosexual division of labor" (ibid.: 12) defines the parameters of *both* narrative and spectacle: the male protagonist (who is the viewer's stand-in) advances the action in the three-dimensional world of the fiction; the female, as image, is aligned with spectacle, space and screen.

Yet within the psychoanalytic framework, the female also signifies the threat of castration, evoking in the male a reaction of defense. There are two textual options for averting the anxiety caused by the woman's image – **SADISM** (domination through narrative subjugation, in which the woman is investigated and either punished or saved) and fetishism (overvaluation, in which the glamorized figure of the woman – or a body part – is offered, luminous and spectacular, as an "image in direct erotic rapport with the spectator" (ibid.: 14)). By orchestrating its three looks (the camera, the characters, the spectator), the cinema produces a specific, eroticized image of the woman, naturalizing the "masculine" position of the spectator and the pleasures that entails. Thus modes of cinematic looking and identification inevitably impose a masculine point-of-view on the spectator, while the powerful erotic impact of the highly coded woman's image connotes "to-be-looked-at-ness [and] cinema builds the way she is to be looked at into the spectacle itself" (ibid.: 17). For Mulvey, the possibility of destabilizing the voyeuristic gaze (whose varied parameters she traces throughout the article) represents the most promising option for an alternative cinematic practice. Whatever limitations there are to Mulvey's model, she was the first theorist to seriously consider the implications of gender in the processes of cinema-spectatorship, and because of that, she defined the terrain on which feminist film theory would subsequently debate its issues.

That terrain was, in fact, already implicit in the project of psychoanalytic film theory from the start, specifically for two reasons. Because there is no gender-neutral representation, the question of woman's place within that representation was immediately posed, and because the recognition of sexual difference is the cornerstone of psychoanalytic theory, psychoanalysis automatically implies a consideration of femininity (not as a content, but as a "position" which is produced). Feminist scholarship around these issues can be considered from the standpoint of three general areas – each posed in terms of female subjectivity and desire: Feminine spectatorship, female enunciation and feminist textual practice.

Mulvey's model had brought the issue of gender into spectatorship in terms of a description of a masculine position of viewing, implicitly arguing that the entire apparatus of classical cinema operated according to masculine standards that objectified and dominated the woman. Thus the question of the **FEMALE SPECTATOR** became the first line of investigation for feminists. Gaylyn Studlar, for example, counters Mulvey by arguing that the

> cinematic apparatus and the masochistic aesthetic offer identificatory positions for [both] male and female spectators that reintegrate psychic bisexuality, offer the sensual pleasures of polymorphous sexuality, and make the male and female one in their identification with and desire for the pre-Oedipal mother.
>
> (Studlar 1988: 192)

Mulvey herself subsequently corrected her position in an essay on *Duel in the Sun*, stating that while her earlier article determined that in dominant cinema there is always "a 'masculinisation' of the spectator position regardless of the actual sex (or possible deviance) of any real live moviegoer" (Mulvey 1981: 12), the possibilities for female spectatorship must nevertheless be considered. Maintaining her argument that pleasure in looking is associated with early libidinal experiences, she concludes that the female spectator "temporarily accepts 'masculinisation' in memory of her 'active' phase" (ibid.: 15). The feminine position of viewing thus necessarily involves identification with an alien masculine gaze – a psychic borrowing of "transvestite clothes."

Mary Ann Doane's *The Desire to Desire* conceptualizes the **FEMALE GAZE** (and the female spectator's position) in films explicitly and institutionally addressed to women. Taking as her object the "woman's film," "in its obsessive attempt to circumscribe a place for the female viewer," (Doane 1987: 37) Doane considers the way the address to a female audience involves a contradictory pressure on the psychical mechanisms of voyeurism and fetishism. She finds that

> when one explores the margins of the major masculine scenarios

informing the theories of the cinematic apparatus [scenarios which "theorists such as Metz and Baudry often appeal to . . . as if they were sexually indifferent"], one discovers a series of scenarios which construct the image of a specifically feminine subjectivity and spectatorial position as well.

(Doane 1987: 20)

She concludes that films which attempt to trace female subjectivity and desire in both their subject-matter and in their modes of address do so in terms of fantasies traditionally associated with the feminine: **MASOCHISM** – the sexual perversion in which the subject derives pleasure from having pain inflicted, the passive component of sadism; **HYSTERIA** – the type of neurosis in which psychical conflict is either expressed symbolically through bodily symptoms or phobically, through anxiety attached to a specific object; **PARANOIA** – the delusional psychosis expressed through fantasies of persecution, erotomania, grandeur, jealousy and the like, in which the delusions are organized into a coherent, internally consistent system; and **NEUROSIS** – the defensive conflict forming the basis of psychoanalysis, which can be understood as the theory of neurotic conflict and its modes.

Another concept associated with female spectatorship is the **MASQUER-ADE**. Conventionally defined by Joan Rivière as the assumption of "feminine" traits to disguise an underlying masculine preference (or exaggerating these traits to foreground their constructedness), the concept has been taken up by feminist film theorists, first by Claire Johnston in her analysis of *Anne of the Indies* and then by Mary Ann Doane in two articles on spectatorship, to analyze the representations of femininity in the cinema. Stephen Heath points out that Rivière's paper poses the question of feminine identity rather than purporting to answer it: "In the masquerade the woman mimics an authentic – genuine – womanliness but then authentic womanliness is such a mimicry, *is* the masquerade ('they are the same thing'); to be a woman is to dissimulate a fundamental masculinity, femininity is that dissimulation" (Heath 1986: 49). In her analysis, Johnston concludes that Rivière shows "how homosexuality/heterosexuality in the subject results from the interplay of conflicts rather than a fundamental tendency," (Johnston 1975a: 41) in order to demonstrate the way that *Anne of the Indies* "poses the possibility of a genuinely bi-sexual disposition while remaining a male myth" (ibid.: 42). The film is thus read as a parable for patriarchal culture's repression of the feminine.

In "Film and the Masquerade" and "Masquerade Reconsidered," Doane uses the concept to further focus her work on spectatorship. Both articles explore the possibilities available to the female spectator – who finds herself either too close (absorbed in her own image as the object of narcissistic desire) or too far (assuming the alienated distance necessary to identification with the male voyeur) – in relation to the classical text.

Either position involves the imperilment of female subjectivity – for the woman, a perpetual loss of sexual identity in the act of viewing. But although Doane must conclude that in dominant cinema the woman possesses a gaze which does not see, she stops short of asserting the total impossibility of woman as subject of the gaze. There are still pleasures available to the female viewer, pleasures, for example, in the masquerade's "potential to manufacture a distance from the image which is manipulable, producible, and readable by the woman" (Doane 1982: 87), pleasures to be gotten from a liberating dislocation of the feminine gaze. Doane asserts that female spectatorship is never *entirely* foreclosed, repressed or irretrievable; even in its negation it is produced – as is femininity itself – as a position, a position empowered (by the very activity which produces it) to suggest a radical challenge to dominant modes of vision. In "Masquerade Reconsidered," she suggests other destabilizing options related to the masquerade such as the "game," the "joke" and "fantasy," defining her entire project as a reconceptualization of the gaze in its relation to a general theory of feminine subjectivity.

One more point about the female spectator needs to be made. Both Freud's and Lacan's theories of the unconscious establish the fact that sexuality is never a given; in no way can it be automatically assumed. Both masculinity and femininity are constituted in symbolic and discursive processes, and this implies that sexuality itself is not a content, but a set of positions that are reversible, changing, conflictual. Because of this, we can never complacently assume or attribute a fixed sexual identity; for theories of spectatorship, a more precise concept of the female viewer is needed to incorporate this fact.

One possibility can be found in specifying the different levels on which the female spectator is addressed. E. Ann Kaplan provides a useful formulation along these lines by suggesting a distinction between three types of female viewer: (1) the historical spectator – the actual person in the audience at the time of the film's release; (2) the hypothetical spectator – the subject constructed by the film's textual strategies, its modes of address and its activation of psychoanalytic processes such as voyeurism and identification; and (3) the contemporary female spectator – whose reading of the film might be inflected by a feminist consciousness which suggests alternate interpretations, meanings "against the grain" (Kaplan 1985: 40–3). While psychoanalytic film theory addresses the second level, it can never ignore the other two. At the same time, the film analyst must be able to discern which forms of address actually engage psychoanalytic processes in the construction of subjectivity and which work at a different level of functioning (the distinction between "empathy" and "identification" resurfaces here). Because it is concerned precisely with this necessary mediation between the psychic and the social, feminist work on spectatorship continues to provide some of the most comprehensive and engaging uses of psychoanalytic film theory to date.

Just as feminist theory introduced gender into concepts of spectatorship, so too did it posit a consideration of the feminine in theories of cinematic authorship. As noted, psychoanalytic film theory connects authorship to enunciation, defining the film-maker as the subject of desire and implying a masculine enunciative position. This presents some complex problems for defining **FEMALE ENUNCIATION**. Raymond Bellour's work on Hitchcock as a model for enunciative theory demonstrated, at the level of the text, that the 'Hitchcockian system of enunciation . . . crystallizes around the desire for the woman" (Bellour 1977: 85). Bellour is explicit about the problems this raises for conceptualizing a feminine enunciative space:

> [T]here always exists, more or less masked or more or less marked, a certain place of enunciation . . . the place of a certain subject of discourse and consequently of a certain subject of desire. . . . The classical American cinema is founded in a systematicity which oper-ates very precisely at the expense of the woman . . . by determining her image . . . in relation to the desire of the masculine subject. . . . [This is] a perspective which always collapses the representation of the two sexes into the dominant logic of a single one.
>
> (Bellour 1979: 99, 97)

The questions posed by feminist film theory are these: if the psychoana-lytic conception of authorship is defined (and therefore bound) by a struc-ture in which enunciation is determined by masculine subjectivity and desire, does this preclude any concept of female enunciation? Likewise, if enunciation eliminates intentionality as a category in its construction of authorship, how can the textual presence of a "feminine discourse" be found, how can a "female voice" be located?

In an effort to define the female author as one who attempts to originate the representation of her own desire, feminist scholarship has taken two routes. The first has been through an examination of work by women directors within the Hollywood system (such as Dorothy Arzner), analyzing texts for the manifestation of a feminine discourse that erupts from within the regulated confines of the classical film. The second involves an analysis of (mainly) contemporary works by what can be considered a "feminist avant-garde," film-makers whose strategies of subversion of the dominant cinematic codes are articulated in works that comprise an alternative feminist tradition. In either case, the contradiction of female enunciation applies. While the attempt to theorize authorship as a position (rather than an individual) is the cornerstone of enunciative theory, the "discovery" or re-evaluation of women directors has been motivated mainly by the fact that *they were/are women*. The interest in actual women *per se* would seem, then, to be in direct contradiction with the move to designate the *textual* production of gendered authorship. In order to avoid validating the common verities that enunciative theory denies (the author as the punctual source of meaning, intentionality defining the text, the pure expressivity of a woman's voice, grounded in biology or essence, manifesting itself in a film), feminist scholarship must forge a new definition of female enunciation which mediates between sexual difference and authorial voice.

It is possible that the concept of enunciation can offer a means of theorizing feminine subjectivity, in fact, by allowing the categories of author, spectator and text to be rethought from the standpoint of female desire. As a mode of analysis for the systematic organization of patterns of looking, enunciation can enable the understanding of how a woman film-maker might negotiate the disparate visions of the text. As a means of interpreting the film-viewing process, enunciation can allow the conceptualization of possibilities for feminine spectatorship. And as a method of designating textual instances, enunciation can make visible the ways in which female desire might be articulated and addressed within a particular film.

Another set of issues raised for psychoanalytic film theory by feminists are those around **FEMINIST TEXTUAL PRACTICE** and feminine discourse. In seeking to define and specify an alternative "language of desire," feminist scholarship began looking at the avant-garde practice of women filmmakers in order to see how female authorship might be textually manifested and inscribed. This was, in some cases, preceded by focussed feminist work on the classical text as a way of elaborating more precisely how the voice of patriarchy (and thus its opposition or subversion) came to be articulated cinematically. The most important of these studies analyzed the Oedipal narrative, demonstrating how the narrative and symbolic problematic of sexual difference both motivated the characters and structured film form. Thus Bellour's analysis of *North by Northwest* (1979), Heath's analysis of *Touch of Evil* (1979), and the *Cahiers du Cinema* collective analysis of *Young Mister Lincoln* (1972) all examined the textual inscription of the Oedipal trajectory, while articles by Pam Cook/Claire Johnston and Elizabeth Cowie paid particular attention to the place of sexuality in the overall symbolic content of the narrative.

In a chapter of *Alice Doesn't* entitled "Desire in Narrative," Teresa de Lauretis discusses the Oedipal configuration in both literary and cinematic narratives: "The Oedipus of psychoanalysis is the *Oedipus Rex*, where myth is already textually inscribed, cast in dramatic literary form, and thus sharply focused on the hero as mover of the narrative, the center and term of reference of consciousness and desire" (de Lauretis 1985: 112). In an effort to define a place for the woman within the narrative, to drive a wedge between fictionalizing and its patriarchal foundations, and after an extensive analysis of the way in which Oedipal logic is seen to structure a variety of texts, she concludes:

What I have been arguing for . . . is an interruption of the triple
track by which narrative, meaning, and pleasure are constructed from
[Oedipus'] point of view. The most exciting work in cinema and in
feminism today is not anti-narrative or anti-Oedipal; quite the
opposite. It is narrative and Oedipal with a vengeance, for it seeks
to stress the duplicity of that scenario and the specific contradiction
of the female subject in it, the contradiction by which historical
women must work with and against Oedipus.

(de Lauretis 1985: 157)

Proposals for a kind of cinematic textual resistance link the work of
psychoanalytically informed textual analysis to the specific practice of
women film-makers. The works of Chantal Akerman, Marguerite Duras,
Laura Mulvey/Peter Wollen, Lizzie Borden, Sally Potter and Yvonne
Rainer, among others, are all seen in the light of the challenges they offer
to dominant cinematic structures of vision, narrative and address. While,
most often, these film-makers do not *explicitly* address psychoanalysis, their
films resume many of the issues central to feminist film theory. At the end
of her critical assessment of the work of Claire Johnston, Janet Bergstrom
points out that textual analyses of the classical film "have shown consistently how women function in different but equally crucial ways to insure
narrative, to position the enunciation" (Bergstrom 1979b: 30). She formu-
lates the question of an alternative feminist cinematic practice in terms of
"how feminine discourse, feminine desire, may organize filmic enunciation,
how feminine discourse might constitute textual logic differently" (ibid.).
Chantal Akerman's films provide a particularly powerful demonstration of
that rearticulation.

Jeanne Dielman, 23 quai du Commerce, 1080 Bruxelles is a three-hour film
which traces the daily tasks of a (typical?) woman in real time by means
of a minimalist, almost hyper-realist *mise-en-scène*. The woman, a widow who
incorporates daily prostitution into her rigidly defined household schedule
(making breakfast, sending her son to school, making the bed, shopping,
having sex, getting paid, making dinner, taking a walk, etc.), is watched
by the relentless and distanced camera. In speaking of this pervasive, un-
narrativized look which structures the film, Akerman outlines her enunciative stance:

You *know* who is looking; you always know what the point of view
is, all the time. It's always the same. But still . . . it was not a neutral
look. . . . I didn't go in too close, but I was not *very* far away. . . .
The camera was not voyeuristic in the commercial way because you
always knew where I was. You know, it wasn't shot through the
keyhole.

(Akerman 1977: 119)

And in speaking of the register of secondary looks she says,

> It was never shot from the point of view of the son or anyone else. It's always me. Because the other way is manipulation. The son is not the camera; the son is her son. If the son looks at his mother, it's because you asked him to do it. So you should look at the son looking at the mother, and not have the camera in place of the son looking at the mother.
>
> (Akerman 1979: 119)

In systematically avoiding the point-of-view shot (and its complement, the reverse-shot, so central to the classical film), and simultaneously foregrounding her own "view," Akerman can be seen to reinscribe those marks of enunciation that the dominant cinema works to efface, and she does so on both the primary and secondary identificatory levels at once. By asserting that the logic of vision which organizes the shots and disperses the gaze is emphatically her own, Akerman reinserts herself into the enunciative process, and does so as a woman. It is precisely around an "unrepresentable desire" that the film builds its climax, leaving the viewer to contemplate that which can*not* be seen – and this contemplation inevitably raises questions about femininity itself. In this way Akerman is able to appropriate that articulation of desire and vision that defines enunciation, in a film that exemplifies (in her words) *"la jouissance du voir"* (the ecstasy of seeing).

Psychoanalytic film theory, and feminist theory in particular, have described the ways in which it is necessary to theorize the relation of the woman's body to discourse, keeping in mind that the symbolic construction of sexuality provides a means of thinking this body in terms other than those of biology or mystical essence. Because of this, feminist film-makers interested in "re-imag[in]ing" the woman have found ways to incorporate the notions of desire and language into their films. In Mary Ann Doane's words, "The most interesting and productive . . . films dealing with the feminist problematic are those which elaborate a new syntax, thus 'speaking' the female body differently, even haltingly or inarticulately from the perspective of a classical syntax" (Doane 1981: 34). As this account of psychoanalytic film theory has demonstrated, "speaking" cinematically is not a simple task: there is a whole constellation of complex, interrelated psychic processes that combine in the production of what is, in the final analysis, the cinematic circulation of (authorial, spectatorial and textual) desire.

NOTES

1 Some of the following discussion is indebted to Terry Eagleton's extremely useful summary discussion of psychoanalysis in *Literary Theory: An Introduction* (Minneapolis: University of Minnesota Press, 1983): 151–93.

2 This (and the following description) rely in part on the excellent work of Shakespeare scholar Joel Fineman, as presented in his seminar at U.C. Berkeley in 1978, and in Colin MacCabe's "Presentation of 'The Imaginary Signifier'," *Screen* 16 (2) (Summer 1975): 7–13. It should be noted that although the description of these "moments" appears to be linear, this is, in fact, not the case. The Lacanian paradigm sees these points as constantly interacting, continually reflecting on the subject both in earlier and later stages of the formation of identity; the process of desire is retroactive, circular and infinite.

3 This definition, and some of the others, rely in part on Jean Laplanche and J.-B. Pontalis, *The Language of Psychoanalysis* (New York: W. W. Norton, 1973).

4 Some unexpected corroboration for this process comes in the form of a catalogue ad for a Giant Crib or Playpen Mirror: "**See the Baby?** This huge mirror was developed by a learning consultant, to entertain as well as teach. Baby can wake up and practice talking to someone, get a self-image by seeing his whole body, watch his developing motor skills" (Lillian Vernon Catalogue).

5 This article also appears in a book of collected essays by Metz, *The Imaginary Signifier: Psychoanalysis and the Cinema* (Bloomington: Indiana University Press, 1982): 3–87. References will be made to the translation in *Screen* (1975) which is augmented by excellent notes by Colin MacCabe and Ben Brewster.

6 Both essays are found in Phil Rosen (ed.), *Narrative, Apparatus, Ideology* (New York: Columbia University Press, 1986): 286–98 and 299–318, as well as in Theresa Hak Kyung Cha (ed.), *Apparatus* (New York: Tanam Press, 1980): 25–37 and 41–62, from which citations will be taken.

7 Theresa Cha's *Apparatus* collection is "illustrated" with a conceptual piece by Cha herself (she was a performance and video artist) in which stills from *Vampyr* are used. (Other illustrations include stills from *Man With a Movie Camera* throughout the book, as well as photos illustrating the work of Jean-Marie Straub and Danielle Huillet on their film, *Moses and Aaron*.)

8 This article was originally published in *Edinburgh 76 Magazine*, pp. 21–5, which is the text we are citing. It also appears in Metz, *The Imaginary Signifier*, under the title "Story/Discourse: A Note on Two Kinds of Voyeurism." The original version can also be found in John Caughie (ed.), *Theories of Authorship* (London: Routledge & Kegan Paul, 1981).

9 For a critique of Mulvey see D. N. Rodowick, "The Difficulty of Difference," *Wide Angle* 5 (1) (1982): 4–15, and Gaylyn Studlar, *In the Realm of Pleasure* (Urbana: University of Illinois Press, 1988).

V

FROM REALISM TO
INTERTEXTUALITY

A clear trajectory takes us from the emphasis on realism, in the film theory of the 1950s and early 1960s, to a relativization and even attack on realism in the name of reflexivity and intertextuality in the late 1960s, 1970s and 1980s. This trajectory takes us from an "ontological" interest in cinema as the phenomenal depiction of real-life "existents," to an analysis of filmic realism as a matter of aesthetic convention and choice. The emphasis shifted to art as **REPRESENTATION**, i.e. likeness, picture, copy, model, a word whose resonances were at once verbal/literary and visual, aesthetic, semiotic, theatrical and political. (All these meanings, as W. J. T. Mitchell points out (in Lentricchia 1990) have in common a triangular relationship whereby a representation is of something or someone, by something or someone, and to someone). Film theory thus gradually transformed itself from a meditation on the film object as the reproduction of pro-filmic phenomena into a critique of the very idea of mimetic reproduction. Film came to be seen as text, utterance, speech act, not the depiction of an event but rather an event in itself, one which participated in the production of a certain kind of subject.

The purpose of this part will be to chart the terminological ramifications of this overall shift from issues of realism to issues of representation and intertextuality. The term **REALISM** is of course an uncommonly elastic one, heavily laden, as we have seen, with millennial encrustations from antecedent debates in philosophy and literature. Within art criticism, the term realism, while ultimately rooted in the occidental mimetic idea that art imitates reality, gains programmatic significance only in the nineteenth century, when it comes to denote a movement in the figurative and narrative arts dedicated to the observation and accurate representation of the contemporary world. A neologism coined by nineteenth-century French writers and artists, realism was originally linked to an oppositional attitude toward romantic and neo-classical models in fiction and painting. The aim of this movement, which attained its most coherent formulation in France but had echoes and parallels elsewhere, was, in Linda Nochlin's words, "to give a truthful, objective and impartial representation of the real world, based on meticulous observation of contemporary life" (Nochlin 1971: 13). The realist novels of writers like Balzac, Stendhal, Flaubert and George Eliot brought intensely individualized, seriously conceived characters into typical contemporary social situations. The realist impulse was accompanied by a social dimension in the form of an implicit teleology of democratization which facilitated the emergence of "more extensive and socially inferior human groups to the position of subject matter for problematic-existential representation" (Auerbach 1953: 491).

CINEMATIC REALISM

Without involving ourselves in the intellectual morass usually triggered by attempts at a rigorous definition of the term "realism," we can posit several broad tendencies within the debate around **CINEMATIC REALISM**. Some definitions of cinematic realism have to do with the aspiration of an author or school to create an innovatory representation, seen as a corrective to dominant canons or to antecedent literary or cinematic decorum. This corrective can be stylistic – as in the French New Wave attack on the artificiality of the "tradition of quality" – or social – Italian neo-realism aiming to show post-war Italy its true face – or both at once – Brazilian Cinema Novo revolutionizing both the social thematics and the cinematic procedures of antecedent cinema. Other definitions of realism bear on the question of verisimilitude, the putative adequation of a fiction to deeply ingrained and widely disseminated cultural models of "believable stories" and "coherent characterization." Related definitions have to do with a text's degree of conformity to *generic* codes; the crusty conservative father who resists his show-crazed daughter's entrance into show-business can "realistically" be expected, in a backstage musical, to applaud her apotheosis at the end of the film. Another related definition of realism involves readerly or spectatorial belief, a realism of subjective response, rooted less in mimetic accuracy than in a strong desire to believe on the spectator's part. Psychoanalytically inflected theorists such as Baudry and Metz, as we have seen, stressed the metapsychological aspects of this desire, whereby the combination of verisimilar cinematic representationalism and a fantasy-inducing spectatorial situation conspire to project the spectator into a dream-like state where interior hallucination is confused with real perception. A purely Formalist definition of realism, finally, would emphasize the conventional nature of all fictional codes, and would posit realism simply as a constellation of stylistic devices, a set of conventions that at a given moment in the history of an art, manages, through the fine-tuning of illusionistic technique, to crystallize a strong feeling of authenticity.

The semiotic interrogation of the issue of cinematic realism takes places against the backdrop of those critical views which posited the cinema as essentially or *intrinsically* realist. The mechanical means of photographic

185

reproduction, for both Kracauer and Bazin, assured the essential "objectivity" of film. That the photographer, unlike the painter or poet, cannot work in the absence of a model, was presumed to guarantee an ontological bond between the photographic representation and what it represents. Since photochemical processes involve an indexical link between the photographic analogon and its referent, cinematography bears unimpeachable witness to "things as they are." Thinkers as diverse as Panofsky, Kracauer, Bazin and Pasolini emphasize film as an "art of reality" and even Metz, in his early work, contrasted the "arbitrary" and "unmotivated" linguistic sign with the "analogous" and "motivated" photographic image.

IDEOLOGY AND THE CAMERA

In the wake of the events of May 1968, the French film journals *Cahiers du Cinéma* and *Cinétique* sought to extrapolate Althusser's theoretical practice in order to forge a scientific understanding of the cinema as an ideological apparatus. Theorists such as Marcelin Pleynet, Jean-Louis Baudry and Jean-Louis Comolli questioned the idealization of the cinema's presumably inherent truth-telling capabilities, claiming that bourgeois ideology was built into the cinematic apparatus itself. Jean-Louis Baudry argued, in "The Ideological Effects of the Basic Cinematographic Apparatus," that the apparatus must be examined in the context of the ideology which produced it as an effect, contending that the specificity of the cinematic apparatus as a mode of representation and as a material practice consisted in its way of literally realizing the very processes by which the subject is constructed in ideology. The specific function of the cinema, as support and instrument of ideology, was to constitute the subject by the illusory delimitation of a central location, thus creating a "phantasmization" of the subject and collaborating in the maintenance of bourgeois idealism (Baudry, in Rosen 1986). Marcelin Pleynet pointed out (in Harvey 1978: 159) that the technology of the camera was conditioned by the **CODE OF RENAISSANCE PERSPECTIVE**, i.e. the convention of pictorial representation developed by the Renaissance painters of the quattrocento, who noted that the perceived size of objects in nature varies proportionally with the square of the distance from the eye.

The quattrocento painters incorporated this code into their paintings in order to project three-dimensional space onto a flat two-dimensional surface, thus producing the impression of depth, an innovation which ultimately led to impressive *trompe-l'oeil* effects. As absorbed into the camera, this code functioned, as Marcelin Pleynet put it, "to rectify" any anomoly in perspective, so as to reproduce in its full authority the code of specular vision as it was defined by Renaissance humanism."[1] By incorporating the *perspectiva artificialis* into its reproductive apparatus, the camera gave expression to the "centered space" of the "transcendental subject"; the image converged toward a vanishing point, implying a privileged and unitary vantage point directed from an imaginary outside space. Rather than simply recording reality, the camera conveys the world already filtered through a bourgeois ideology which makes the presumably free and unique individual subject the focus and origin of meaning. The code of perspective, furthermore, produces the illusion of its own absence; it "innocently" denies its status as representation and passes off the image as if it were actually a kind of "piece of the world."

Film semioticians spoke of the **IMPRESSION OF REALITY** engendered by the cinema, triggered by (a) the perspectival analogy of the photographic image, (b) persistence of vision and (c) the **PHI-EFFECT** or "phenomenon of apparent movement," i.e. the perceptual-cognitive mechanism by which the mind posits continuities of movement even when perceiving, as in the cinema, nothing more than a series of static images. Thanks to the *phi-effect*, shifting configurations of light and shadow are received as the equivalent of material tangible movement. Jean-Paul Fargier argued that the impression of reality was a constitutive part of the ideology produced by the cinematic apparatus: "[The screen] opens like a window, it is transparent. This illusion is the very substance of the specific ideology secreted by the cinema" (Fargier, in *Screen Reader I*: 28). In "Cinema/Ideology/Criticism," Jean-Louis Comolli and Jean Narboni argued from within an Althusserian framework that

> what the camera registers in fact is the vague, unformulated, untheorized, unthought-out world of the dominant ideology . . . reproducing things not as they really are but as they appear when refracted through the ideology. This includes every stage in the process of production: subject, "styles," forms, meanings, narrative traditions; all underline the general, ideological discourse.
>
> (in *Screen Reader I*: 4–5)

Subsequent commentators were quick to censure such a view as monolithic and ahistorical, based on a naively realist epistemology which virtually equated perception itself with ideology, thus leading to a quasi-puritanical condemnation of the apparatus as an all-powerful "influencing machine" against which all resistance was vain. (The despair of subverting the apparatus was not without correlation to a certain decline and defeatism of the left in the period – the early 1970s – during which the theories were being formulated.) This monolithic model of the cinema failed to allow for possible modifications of the apparatus, for "tricking" or distorting perspective, for procedures which might "dephantasmize" the spectator, or for "readings" which might subvert the model. Coming from an anti-semiotic perspective, Noel Carroll argued in *Mystifying Movies* (1988) that the concept of subject positioning was superfluous to political-ideological analysis, since the subject's subordination to the reigning social order was better explained by what Marx called the "dull compulsion of economic relations" than by any hypothesis concerning subject-construction.

THE CLASSIC REALIST TEXT

The impression of reality in the cinema, semioticians argued, was also reinforced by conventions of narrative construction. The notion of **CLASSICAL CINEMA**, first formulated by Bazin but subsequently extended and critiqued by others, denotes a set of formal parameters involving practices of editing, camera-work and sound. Classical cinema evokes the reconstitution of a fictional world characterized by internal coherence, plausible and linear causality, psychological realism, and the appearance of spatial and temporal continuity. This continuity was achieved, in the classical period of the Hollywood film, by an etiquette for introducing new scenes (a choreographed progression from establishing shot to medium shot to close shot); conventional devices for evoking the passage of time (dissolves, iris effects); conventional techniques to render imperceptible the transition from shot to shot (position matches, direction matches, movement matches, and inserts to cover up unavoidable discontinuities); and devices for implying subjectivity (subjective shots, shot-reaction shots, eyeline matches, empathetic music). The classical realist film stood for **TRANSPARENCY**, i.e. the attempt to efface traces of the "work of the film," making it pass for "natural," and thus reproducing the vague and non-theorized world of common sense, i.e. of dominant ideology in Althusser's sense. Film semioticians also drew on Barthes notion of fictional **REALITY EFFECTS**, i.e. the artistic orchestration of apparently inessential details as guarantors of authenticity, designed, in the Barthesian perspective, to engender a tacit acquiescence in the ideology of verisimilitude. The representational accuracy of the details was less important than their role in creating the optical illusion of truth. By effacing the signs of their production, "dominant" cinema persuaded spectators to take constructed simulations as transparent renderings of the real.

It was through such procedures, by combining the codes of visual perception introduced in the Renaissance with the codes of narration dominant in the nineteenth century, that the classical fiction film acquired the emotional power and diegetic prestige of the realistic novel. Indeed, in its dominant mode, the cinema prolonged the aesthetic regime and the social function of the nineteenth-century mimetic novel. It was within this perspective that Colin MacCabe spoke of the **CLASSIC REALIST TEXT**, definable as a literary or filmic text in which a clear hierarchy orders the discourses composing the text, a hierarchy defined in terms of an empirical notion of truth. Dominant cinema inherited from the nineteenth-century novel a precise kind of textual structuration which positioned the reader/

spectator in a specific way. Classical texts privileged certain discourses over others; the narration provided a metalanguage, a site of unquestioned authority from which the other discourses might be tested, rejected or approved. The classic text was reactionary not because of any mimetic inaccuracies but rather because of its authoritarian subjection of the spectator.

David Bordwell, meanwhile, argued that MacCabe's view of the novel was simplistic in comparison to the more nuanced Bakhtinian notion of the novel as the privileged site of heteroglossia or the competition of discourses. Both building on and critiquing the work of the cine-semiologists, Bordwell argued that commonplaces about "transparency" and invisibility were unhelpful in dealing with the narrational procedures of the classical film. In *Narration in the Fiction Film*, Bordwell delineates these procedures in so far as they concern the classical Hollywood cinema. Combining issues of denotative representation and dramaturgical structure, Bordwell highlights the ways in which **CLASSICAL HOLLYWOOD NARRATION** constitutes a particular configuration of normalized options for representing the story and manipulating style. The classical Hollywood film, he argues, presents psychologically defined individuals as its principal causal agents, struggling to solve a clear-cut problem or to attain specific goals, the story ending either with a resolution of the problem or a clear achievement or non-achievement of the goals. Causality revolving around character provides the prime unifying principle, while spatial configurations are motivated by realism as well as compositional necessity. Scenes are demarcated by neo-classical criteria – unity of time, space and action. Classical narration tends to be omniscient, highly communicative and only moderately self-conscious. If time is skipped over, a montage sequence or scrap of dialogue informs us; if a cause is missing, we are informed about its absence. Classical narration poses as an "editorial intelligence" that selects certain stretches of time for full-scale treatment, pares down others, and presents others in a highly compressed fashion, while presumably scissoring out inconsequential events. Classical style, meanwhile, (1) treats film technique as a vehicle for the syuzhet's transmission of fabula information; (2) encourages the spectator to construct a coherent, consistent time and space of the fabula action, and (3) consists of a limited number of technical devices organized into a stable paradigm and ranked probabilistically according to syuzhet demands. (Lighting, for example, may be "high-lit" or "low-key," three-point or single-source, diffuse or concentrated. In a comedy, high-key lighting is more probable.)

CINEMATIC ECRITURE

One term very much in circulation in the entire post-war period is **ECRITURE**, or writing. Indeed, one might easily chart the major developments in post-war intellectual history, at least in France, by the successive inflections given to this term. Already in *Le Degré Zéro de la Littérature (Writing Degree Zero*, 1953; trans. 1968), Barthes distinguished between **LANGUE/ STYLE** and *écriture*, where *langue* represents the "horizon" of the very possibility of writing, style is the mark of individuality, and *écriture* represents the process of expressive negotiation between the social generality of language and style as a kind of personal repertory of devices. In 1960, Barthes distinguished between **ECRIVANTS** (writers), i.e. those for whom writing is transitive, a means to an end, and **ECRIVAINS** (authors), i.e. those for whom writing is a self-purposeful activity, an end in itself. But alongside the literary and philosophical discussion of *écriture*, film discourse too became oriented toward the constellation of concepts revolving around "writing" and "textuality." The **GRAPHOLOGICAL TROPE**, i.e. the metaphor which compares film-making to a kind of writing, has dominated film theory and criticism, especially in France, since the 1950s, from Astruc's "caméra-stylo" (camera-pen) to Metz' discussion of "cinema and écriture" in *Language and Cinema*. The French New Wave directors were especially fond of the scriptural metaphor, scarcely surprising given that many of them began as writer-critics who saw writing articles and making films as alternative forms of expressive *écriture*. Indeed, the New Wave itself formed part of a discursive continuum of experimentation which included the *nouveau roman*, absurdist theater and other experiments in music and the arts. The writing metaphor, in any case, facilitated a displacement of interest from realism to textuality, from the situation or characters depicted to the act of writing itself.

AUTEURISM was defined by André Bazin in "La Politique des Auteurs" (1957) as the analytical process of "choosing in the artistic creation the personal factor as a criterion of reference, and then postulating its permanence and even its progress from one work to the next."[2] Auteurism was fueled by successive waves of European "art cinema" and by independent 16mm production. The auteurists extended the notion of individual authorship, obvious in the case of such clearly artistic directors as Eisenstein or Cocteau, to mainstream studio directors such as Hitchcock and Hawks. While auteurism in one sense resuscitated a romanticism discarded both by the other arts and by the most advanced theory, its project of seeking out and constructing authorial personalities did at least introduce a kind of system, however problematic, into the realm of film studies. This systematic side of auteurism made it apparently reconcilable with a hybrid called **AUTEUR-STRUCTURALISM**, exemplified by such books as Geoffrey Nowell-Smith's *Visconti* (1968) and Peter Wollen's *Signs and Meaning in the Cinema* (1969). The auteur-structuralists put the director's name in quotation marks, to emphasize their view of the author as critical construct rather than an originary, biographical flesh-and-blood person.

Both structuralism and post-structuralism relativized the notion of the

190

author as the sole originating and creative source of the text. For Barthes, the "author" became a kind of by-product of writing. The author was never more than the instance writing, just as linguistically the subject "I" is nothing more than the instance saying "I". Barthes spoke, somewhat demogogically, of the "death of the author" and the consequent "birth of the reader" (Barthes 1977: 148). Foucault, meanwhile, foresaw a future "pervasive anonymity of discourse." The film author, as a consequence of the post-structuralist attack on the originary subject, tended to shift from being the generating source of the text to becoming merely a term in the process of reading and spectating, a space where discourses intersect, a shifting configuration produced by the intersection of a group of films with historically constituted ways of reading and viewing.

Since the concept of writing is performative, rather than one of mere transcription, it implicitly undermines the mimetic view which regards the work as a mirror-like reflection of pre-existing reality. For Barthes and the contributors to *Tel Quel*, **ECRITURE** evoked avant-garde literary practices, as well as the philosophical concept elaborated by Jacques Derrida. Saussurean linguistics, Derrida argued, systematically devalued writing; while the voice is seen as the source and sign of truth and presence, writing is regarded as secondary and derivative. But for Derrida *écriture* refers to whatever resists the centrifugal force of logocentric discourse of speech-as-presence, undoing logocentrism through the tropings of textuality. **DECONSTRUCTION**, for Derrida (although Derrida himself employed the term but rarely) was the critical activity which drew out the contradictory logics of sense and implication within philosophical or literary texts. By calling attention to the figurative gestures of the text, deconstruction exposed the extent to which all that was consciously excluded from the text, all that was pushed to the margins, was in fact necessary to its organization. Derridean deconstruction undercuts the binary structures on which logocentric thought is presumed to be based: reality/appearance, inside/outside, subject/object, destabilizing dualisms by disrupting the illusion of priority which coalesces around one of the terms.

FROM "WORK" TO "TEXT"

Semioticians preferred to speak not of films but of texts. The concept of text (etymologically "tissue," "weave") tended to emphasize the film not as an imitation of reality but rather as an artifact, a construct. The term had the corollary effect of a cultural upgrading for the cinema; in a single terminological stroke, film-as-text took on all the prestige of literature. In "From Work to Text," Barthes distinguished between the **WORK**, defined as the phenomenal surface of the object, for example the book one holds in one's hand, i.e. writing read as a completed product conveying an intended and pre-existent meaning, as opposed to the **TEXT**, defined as a

191

methodological field of energy, an ongoing production absorbing writer and reader together. "We now know," Barthes writes, "that the text is not a line of words releasing a single 'theological' meaning (the 'message' of an Author-God) but a multi-dimensional space in which a variety of writings, none of them original, blend and clash" (Barthes 1977: 146).

Barthes further distinguished in *S/Z* between the **READERLY TEXT** ("lisible") and the **WRITERLY TEXT** ("scriptible"), or better between readerly and writerly approaches to texts. The readerly approach privileges those values sought and assumed in the classic text – organic unity, linear sequence, stylistic transparency, conventional realism. The readerly text posits authorial mastery and readerly passivity. To the author as God responds the critic as "the priest whose task is to decipher the Writing of the god" (Barthes 1974: 174). The writerly text, in contrast, stimulates and provokes an active reader, sensitive to contradiction and heterogeneity, aware of the work of the text. It transforms its consumer into a producer, foregrounding the process of its own construction and promoting the infinite play of signification.

In his *S/Z*, a work often regarded as the premier work of post-structuralist literary criticism, Barthes inventories the codes necessary to the production of the classical "readerly" text, in this case the Balzac novella *Sarrasine*. The illusion of realism, for Barthes, is founded on the integrated functioning of five codes or "voices." (The paradoxical achievement of *S/Z* was to call attention both to the clasical readerly features of the Balzacian text and to its multi-voiced and writerly nature.) Among these codes are the following: (1) the **HERMENEUTIC CODE**; (2) the **PROAIRETIC CODE**; (3) the **SEMIC CODE**; (4) the **SYMBOLIC CODE**; and (5) the **REFERENTIAL CODE**. Barthes rather perversely highjacks the word "hermeneutic" (from Greek *hermeneuein*, "to interpret") from the classical discipline of **HERMENEUTICS** – the philosophical and exegetical tradition of interpretation – to refer to the hermeneutic code, i.e. inculation of the enigma, the question to be pursued throughout the text, in sum all the units whose function it is to articulate in various ways a question, its response, and the variety of chance events which either formulate the question or delay its answer; or even, constitute an enigma and lead to its solution. While Barthes compares the hermeneutic code to the Voice of Truth – the solution of the enigma constituting the moment of revelation – the function of the hermeneutic code is to delay revelation, to dodge the moment of truth by setting up obstacles, stoppages, deviations. The hermeneutic code regulates the pacing of the pleasures afforded by the text, engaging the reader/spectator in what Barthes calls the "narrative striptease," delaying final disclosure until the ultimate moment.

The hermeneutic code engenders a set of tactics and devices as part of this narrative sleight-of-hand. The **SNARE** is a deliberate evasion of the truth, a tease or implication that sends the reader/spectator up false alleyways of meaning. The **EQUIVOCATION** mingles truth and snare; while focussing attention on the enigma, it also helps to thicken it. The **PARTIAL ANSWER** exacerbates the expectation of truth much as partial disrobing exacerbates the desire for total nudity. The **SUSPENDED ANSWER** constitutes an aphasic stoppage of the disclosure; the answer is hinted at then veered away from. **JAMMING** refers to the acknowledgment of the insolubility of the enigma. While the classical text often ends with a complete disclosure or decipherment of the truth, the modernist text is fond of an anti-climactic jamming.

Because literary and cinematic realism are so closely allied, all of these tactics and devices find their analogies in film. The "snare" in *Sarrasine* consists of Balzac's description of La Zambinella's "dainty little foot" to suggest that "he" is a woman. The Brazilian TV serial *Grande Sertão: Veredas*, similarly, misleads the tele-spectator with regard to the protagonist's gender. Coppola's *The Conversation* ensnares the spectator by playing on our assumption that the young couple being spied upon, simply because they are young and attractive, *must* be innocent. Hitchcock, in *The Lodger*, "ensnares" the spectator by calculatedly casting suspicion on the titular figure through Gothic lighting, sinister dialogue and misleading narrative coincidences. Just as Balzac's text lies by referring to "him" as "her," Hitchcock lies in the mendacious flashback in *Stage Fright*. "Jamming" occurs, meanwhile, when films emphasize the insolubility of an enigma, for example when Buñuel in *Exterminating Angel* refuses to explain the inability of the aristocratic guests to leave the mansion. The psychiatrist's final explanation in *Psycho*, for its part, pretends to offer a full and final disclosure, but here the very pretense of full explanation is itself a kind of snare. The sheriff's question: "Then who *is* buried in Norman's mother's grave?" constitutes a classic example of "equivocation," designed to thicken the enigma by providing a false orientation to the truth. The final disclosure of *Psycho* attains its horrific impact almost entirely through the multiplication of hermeneutic devices planted, rather like land mines, throughout the territory of the text. All the false leads and evasions which the text has fashioned magnify the spectator's anticipation and curiosity so that the revelation of the answer both fulfills expectations, and surprises. The text, according to Barthes, tries to lie "as little as possible," a compunction which gives rise to double meaning, making the hermeneutic code in this sense comparable to an oracular discourse which conceals as much as it reveals.

The revelation of the truth generally comes at the end of the classical narrative, leading Barthes to compare the hermeneutic narrative to the grammatical sentence, where closure depends on full "predication" of subject and object. The classical hermeneutic sentence/narrative states a subject and elicits curiosity about the predicate, but delays their conjunction by lying and equivocating. For the reader/spectator, the hermeneutic code fosters curiosity. In *Sarrasine*, the enigma begins with the title, which poses the question: "Who is Sarrasine?" The title of *Citizen Kane*, similarly, raises the question – "Who is Citizen Kane?" – a question quickly supplanted by the question: "What is the meaning of 'Rosebud'?" Welles offers us partial truths, but systematically excludes us from plenitude. The young Kane appears on the sled in the snow, but nothing prods the spectator to connect that sight with the word "Rosebud." Enigmas, finally, are not always so clearly related to questions of suspense or the ambiguities of character. The enigma in an avant-garde film such as *Wavelength* is the simple one of the simulated zoom's ultimate destination, the truth of which is both disclosed and hidden by the pun of the title.

Barthes' proairetic code refers to the code of actions. **PROAIRESIS**, for Aristotle, was the ability to rationally determine the result of actions. Thus the proairetic code refers to the logic of actions as they are governed by the laws of narrative discourse. Barthes elsewhere offers an example from a James Bond film, *Goldfinger*. Bond hears a telephone ring; the proairetic code ensures that an orderly sequence of narrative actions will ensue. Bond will answer the phone, wait for a reply, converse, hang up and act according to the message received (Barthes 1977). The code of actions pertains to sequential narrative and its parceling out of gestures into comprehensible segments; it forms the main armature of the readerly text. The actions named by the proairetic code can be trivial (a phone call, a knock at the door) or momentous (a declaration of love, a murder, an elopement). The code of actions functions in conjunction with the other codes to produce a legible coherent narrative.

The code of actions has historically received the bulk of attention in both ancient and modern accounts of narrative form. Aristotle in the *Poetics* defines actions, rather than character, as the fundamental prerequisite for narrative. Barthes sees proairetic sequences as artificial constructs of reading which gain definitive characteristics only through the act of naming them: "kissing sequences," "murder sequences," "walk-in-the garden sequences." The code of actions in the cinema would touch on such questions as: (a) what actions are considered legitimate objects of filmic representation?; (b) what actions are conventionally prescribed (or proscribed) for specific situations?; and (c) how much of each action is to be shown? The first question has to do with what Metz calls the **VRAISEMBLABLE** (literally, the "true-seeming" or verisimilar) i.e. the evolving norms concerning what is deemed worthy of narrative representation. Films often annex new territory for the *vraisemblable*. Godard's early films, for example, constantly defied the constraints of the *vraisemblable* by showing characters using public lavatories, a kind of "action" which antecedent cinema would have regarded as out of bounds (obscene) or lacking in interest. The second question has to do with audience expectations, a kind of internalized calculus of narrative probabilities, and a film's readiness or lack of readiness to satisfy such expectations. The third question, concerning how much of an action is to be shown, has to do with the spatial and temporal coordinates of the filmic representation of actions. Metz' Grand Syntagmatique attempts to introduce a minimum of rigor into this issue: are complex human events such as a dinner to be rendered by a conventionalized cinematic shorthand or explored in what one imagines to be their "real" duration? Should the murder of a policeman be staged so as to include all the crucial details or should it be evoked stenographically, in a fragmented fashion, as in *Breathless*?

Barthes' semic code has to do with **CONNOTATION**, i.e. a second level of meaning linked to the affective or emotive associations attached, for example, to a word or proper name. (For example, the connotations of "spring," for Northern Europeans, include "renewal," "fresh flowering" and so forth.) The semic code for Barthes designates the constellation of fictive devices that thematize persons, objects and places. The semic code associates specific signifiers with a name, a character or a locale. Barthes calls semic connotation a form of "noise" which both names and dissimulates the truth, the rich ambiguity of which gives texture to the fiction. The semic code is premised on a high degree of cultural repetition, whereby connotative signification has been habitually associated with given cultural objects. The telephone in the films of the Italian Fascist period "white telephone films," for example, came to connote "bourgeois milieu" and "decadence." The jukebox in 1950s Hollywood films connotes "teenage hangout."

In practice, it is often difficult to separate the semic codes from Barthes' next category, the **CULTURAL (REFERENTIAL) CODES**, i.e. those codes making explicit or implicit reference to "what everyone knows," to the conventional wisdom about time, medicine, history, in short to "common sense." (Barthes elsewhere refers to doxa, i.e. the "voice of the natural," everything that "goes without saying," current opinion, repeated meaning.) In her "*S/Z* and *Rules of the Game*," an analysis of the Renoir film from a Barthesian perspective, Julia Lesage correlates the cultural codes with the film's title: "Renoir presents explicitly the rules governing marriage and adultery in high society, the rules of the hunt, the rules governing relations between masters and servants, and the rules governing peer relationships (courtesy, friendship, honor, jealousy, gossip) among masters and servants." Renoir's theme, Lesage argues, is the suffocating, all-pervasive influence of the "rules of the game." Renoir both delineates and "denaturalizes" the quotidian rituals and behavioral codes obtaining between de la Chesnayes, among the servants, and between the two groups (Lesage, in Nichols 1985).

Barthes' fifth category, the symbolic codes, bears on culturally determined antitheses which seem to allow for no mediation between terms. In the background of Barthes' notion of the symbolic is the crucial role of binary oppositions within Lévi-Straussean anthropology, i.e. of cultural oppositions forming part of the "symbolic economy" of a myth, a culture, a text. The play of the symbolic is worked out in terms of the culture as a whole, with its taken-for-granted oppositions such as male/female and nature/culture. The symbolic code maps out the fields of antitheses in which culture articulates meaning through the differential representation of symbolic identities so that the oppositions appear natural, inevitable and non-linguistic. *Sarrasine*, as Barthes points out, both assumes and subverts the symbolic binarism of gender by attributing male or female qualities to its characters quite irrespective of their "actual" sexual identity, and by deliberately miscuing the reader in terms of the gender of the titular character. Lesage, in her extrapolation of the five codes to *Rules of the Game*, finds the following antinomies: nature/civilization; sincerity/lies; organic life/artifacts; life/death; outdoors/indoors; lower-class/upper-class; servants/masters; female/male; wildlife/property; greenhouse/manor; and childishness/maturity.

THE CONTRADICTORY TEXT

A number of theoreticians have tried to align a version of Derridean deconstruction with dialectical materialism. Jean-Louis Baudry, in "Writing, Fiction, Ideology" (trans. *Afterimage* 5, Spring 1974), spoke of the revolutionary "text of *écriture*" as being characterized by (1) a negative relation to narrative; (2) a refusal of representationality; (3) a refusal of an expressive notion of artistic discourse; (4) a foregrounding of the materiality of signification; (5) a preference for non-linear, permutational or serial structures.[3] In a 1969 article "Cinema/Ideology/Criticism" (in Nichols 1985), meanwhile, Comolli and Narboni proposed a taxonomy concerning the possible relations between a film and dominant ideology, ranged in seven categories – the summary terms are ours – moving from (a) **DOMINANT FILMS**, i.e. those films thoroughly imbued with dominant ideology; (b) **RESISTANT FILMS**, which attack the dominant ideology on the level both of the signified and of the signifier; (c) **FORMALLY RESISTANT FILMS**, those films which, while not explicitly political, practice formal subversion; (d) **CONTENT-ORIENTED POLITICAL FILMS**, explicitly political and critical films – for example those of Costa-Gavras – whose critique of the ideological system is undermined by the adoption of dominant language and imagery; (e) **FISSURE FILMS**, i.e. films which superficially belong to dominant cinema but where an internal criticism opens up a "rupture"; (f) **LIVE CINEMA I**, i.e. films depicting social events critically but which fail to challenge the cinema's traditional ideologically conditioned method of depiction; and (g) **LIVE CINEMA II**, direct cinema films which simultaneously depict contemporary events critically and question traditional representation.

The Narboni/Comolli category (e) was by far the most productive of interpretative analyses. The notion of the "contradictory text" allowed for a link to the Lacanian/Althusserian conception of the "split" human subject. Critics of the contradictory text were drawn to what Bordwell (1989: 219) calls "San Andreas fault" metaphors: "cracks," "gaps," "crevices" and "fissures." Paul Willemen pointed out that "gaps and fissures" analyses soon became quite predictable, leading to the "familiar conclusion that the 'text' under analysis is full of contradictory tensions, requires active readers and produces a variety of pleasures."[4] But one might argue that the problem derives less from the contradictory text model *per se*, or from the "symptomatic" interpretative project generally, than from the failure to move beyond purely formal parameters to link textual contradictions to the larger socio-historical contradictions which pervade text, context and spectator. Bakhtin's critique of the Formalists, in this sense, can be extrapolated to apply to any de-historicizing view of textual systems. Although the Formalists described **TEXTUAL CONTRADICTION** in metaphors redolent of social struggle – "combat," "struggle" and "conflict" – their approach was ultimately *only* metaphorical, for literary contradiction tended to remain in a hermetically sealed world of pure textuality. But in *The Formal Method in Literary Scholarship*, as Graham Pechey points out, Bakhtin/Medvedev take the Formalist metaphors seriously – especially those terms which easily resonate with class struggle and insurrection, terms such as "revolt," "conflict," "struggle" and "destruction" – but make them apply equally to the text and to the social itself.[5]

The semiotic view of the contradictory text might be usefully strengthened, then, by the Bakhtinian concept of **HETEROGLOSSIA**, i.e. a notion a competing languages and discourses applying equally to "text" and "context." The role of the artistic text, within a Bakhtinian perspective, is not to represent real life "existents" but to stage the conflicts, the coincidences and competitions of languages and discourses, inherent in heteroglossia. The languages of heteroglossia, Bakhtin argues, in terms that recall Metz' affirmations about mutually displacing filmic codes, may be "juxtaposed to one another, mutually supplement one another, contradict one another and be inter-related dialogically" (Bakhtin 1981: 292). The Bakhtinian formulation is especially appropriate to films which rather than represent "real" humanly purposeful events within an illusionistic aesthetic, simply stage the clash of languages and discourses: one thinks of Godard-Gorin's *Tout Va Bien* with its structuring tripartite play of ideological languages (that of capital, the Communist Party, and the Maoists) or of Yvonne Rainer's *The Man Who Envied Women* with its horizontal juxtaposition and vertical superimposition of a wide gamut of voices and discourses (theoretical texts, film clips, news photos, advertisements, snippets of dialogue). Such films practice what Bakhtin called the "mutual illumination of

197

languages," languages which intersect, collide and mutually relativize one another.

Within a Bakhtinian translinguistic approach, a conflictual heteroglossia pervades text and context, producer and reader/spectator. The text is rendered contradictory by the diversity of readings generated by readers who are situated in time and space, who hold power or lack power, each approaching the text from a specific dialogical angle. Working out of a Marxist-inflected "cultural studies" tradition, Stuart Hall, in his influential essay "Encoding/Decoding" (Hall *et al.* 1980), develops his theory of **PRE-FERRED READINGS**. Hall sees texts (in this case televisual texts) as susceptible to diverse readings based on political-ideological contradiction, and posits three broad reading strategies in relation to dominant ideology: (1) the **DOMINANT READING** produced by a viewer situated to acquiesce in the dominant ideology and the subjectivity it produces; (2) the **NEGOTIATED READING** produced by the viewer who largely acquiesces in dominant ideology, but whose situation provokes specific "local" critical inflections; and (3) the resistant reading produced by those whose social situation places them in a directly oppositional relation to dominant ideology.

THE NATURE OF REFLEXIVITY

Given the ideological limitations of dominant cinema, some analysts such as Peter Wollen called for an aggressive **COUNTER-CINEMA**. Wollen's schema pitted mainstream cinema against a counter-cinema, best exemplified by the work of Godard, in the form of seven binary features: (1) **NARRATIVE INTRANSITIVITY**, i.e. the systematic disruption of the flow of the narrative rather than narrative transitivity; (2) **ESTRANGEMENT** rather than identification (through distanced acting, sound/image disjunction, direct address, etc.); (3) **FOREGROUNDING** versus transparency (systematic drawing of attention to the process of construction of meaning); (4) **MUL-TIPLE DIEGESIS** instead of single diegesis; (5) **APERTURE**, narrative opening instead of closure and resolution, the narrative tying up of loose ends; (6) **UNPLEASURE**, a text resisting the habitual pleasures of coherence, suspense and identification; and (7) **REALITY** instead of fiction (the critical exposure of the mystifications involved in filmic fictions).

Wollen's schema was obviously indebted to the theories of Bertolt Brecht, and it was no accident that many film analysts in the late 1960s and 1970s turned with enthusiasm to the theories of the German dramatist. Brecht's **EPIC THEATER** rejected classical theater, instead calling for a narrative structure which was interrupted, fractured, digressive. The overall mode was one of argumentation rather than of representation. The spectator was to remain outside of the drama rather than to be drawn in. Character was seen as an epiphenomenon of social process rather than the expression of individual will and desire. The dominant narrative strategy was one of montage, the juxtaposition of self-contained units rather than of organic growth and the evolution of a homogeneous structure. Apart from the general goals of Brechtian theater – laying bare the causal network of events, the cultivation of an active, thinking spectator, the defamiliarization of alienating social realities, the emphasis on social contradiction, and the immanence of meaning, Brecht also proposed specific techniques to achieve those goals: the refusal of heroes/stars, direct address to the spectator, depsychologization. In terms of acting, Brecht argued for a double distanciation, between the actor and the part, and between the actor and the spectator. Brecht also argued for the use of **GESTUS**, i.e. the "mimetic and gestural expression of social relationships between people in a given period," by which a play might evoke domination, submission, arrogance, humility and self-deprecation based on social position. The *gestus* provided exaggerated ideological gestures evocative of larger historical relationships. (The mechanical way that Doctor Strangelove's right arm automatically stiffens into a Nazi salute, in the Kubrick film, might be cited as an effective instance of *gestus*.)

Brecht also proposed a theater productive of **ALIENATION EFFECTS**, i.e. deconditioning devices by which the lived social world is "made strange." Brechtian alienation effects go beyond Formalist "defamiliarization" in that they trigger a series of social and ideological disruptions which remind us that representations are *socially* produced. Rather than an aesthetic device opening up the doors of perception, the alienation effect is an instrument for reconceiving and ultimately changing, social reality itself. With Brecht, the issue of "alienation" was closely tied to a dialectical analysis of **ALIENATION** – the process by which human beings, in a Marxist perspective, lose control of their labor power, their products, their institutions and their lives. Bourgeois normality, for Brecht, numbs human perception and masks the contradictions between professed values and social realities; whence the need for an art which would free socially conditioned phenomena from the "stamp of familiarity," and reveal them as striking, as calling for explanation, as other than natural. (Although Brecht devised these techniques to demystify capitalist society, they have functioned as well to critique bureaucratic-communist societies, as for example in Wajda's *Man of Marble*.)

Brecht proposed an aesthetic of heterogeneity, characterized by what he called the **RADICAL SEPARATION OF THE ELEMENTS** – a structurating technique which functioned both "horizontally," i.e. each scene would be radically separated from its "neighboring" scenes, and "vertically," in that each "track" was to exist in tension with other tracks. The Brechtian aesthetic set scene against scene and track – music, dialogue, lyric – against track. Music and lyrics, for example, were designed to mutually discredit rather than complement each other. Along with a "horizontal" autonomy of clearly demarcated scenes, then, Epic Theater develops a "vertical" tension between the diverse strata or tracks of the text. Godard/Miéville's *Numéro Deux* exacerbates this tension by having multiple images play with and against one another within the rectangle of the screen, and by having the distinct temporalities of the different tracks enter into fecund interaction and "dialogue." The implications of these Brechtian ideas were taken up not only by film theorists and analysts, but also by innumerable film-makers like Jean-Luc Godard, notably by Tomas Guttierez Alea, Alain Tanner and Herbert Ross. (The work of Douglas Sirk, like Brecht a product of the Weimar theatrical scene, was reread by film analysts as a storehouse of alienation effects, even though audiences at the time rarely recognized them as such.)

Brecht proposed, finally, a thoroughgoing **REFLEXIVITY** – the principle that art should reveal the principles of its own construction, to avoid the "swindle" of suggesting that fictive events were not "worked at" but simply "happened." Brechtian theater, in this spirit, revealed not only the sources of the lighting and the scaffolding of the sets, but also the narrative and aesthetic principles subtending the text. Indeed, in all the debates revolving around art and politics, **REFLEXIVITY** formed a key term. The term was first borrowed from philosophy and psychology, where it originally referred to the mind's capacity to be both subject and object to itself within the cognitive process, but was extended metaphorically to the arts to evoke the capacity for self-reflexion of any medium or language. In the broadest sense, **ARTISTIC REFLEXIVITY** refers to the process by which texts fore-ground their own production, their authorship, their intertextual influences, their textual processes, or their reception.

The penchant for reflexivity must be seen as symptomatic of the metho-dological self-scrutiny typical of contemporary thought, its tendency to examine its own terms and procedures. Thus we find reflexivity forming part of diverse fields and universes of discourse – in linguistics' concern with the reflexive capacity of natural languages, in psychoanalysis' method of relying on verbally transmitted self-reflexions, in cybernetics' use of the reflexive concept of "feedback." The broad notion of reflexivity generated a swirling galaxy of satellite terms pointing to specific dimensions of reflex-ivity. The terms associated with reflexivity, as Luiz Antonio Coelho points out, belong to morphological families with prefixes or roots deriving from the "auto" family, the "meta" family, the "reflect" family, the "self" family and the "textuality" family.[6] Thus in art and literature we find a proliferation of critical terms designating reflexive practices: **SELF-CONSCIOUS FICTION** (Robert Alter) designates those novelists (e.g. Cerv-antes, Fielding, Machado de Assis) who call attention to the novel's status as artifact; **METAFICTION** (Waugh 1984) is defined as fiction about fiction that comments on its own narrative or linguistic identity; and **NARCISS-ISTIC NARRATIVE** is "the figural adjective designating this textual self-awareness" (Hutcheon 1984: 1); **ART OF EXHAUSTION** (John Barth) refers to art premised on the virtual impossibility of novelty in the contemporary period; **ANTI-ILLUSIONISM** refers to novels or films which take a conscious stance against the realist tradition of representation by foregrounding improbabilities of plot, character or language: **SELF-REFERENTIALITY** designates any entity or text which refers or points to itself; **MISE-EN-ABYME** refers to the infinite regress of mirror reflections to denote the literary, painterly or filmic process by which a passage, a section or sequence plays out in miniature the processes of the text as a whole. The **AUTO-DESIGNATION OF THE CODE**, finally, refers to a textual situation in which the act of communication is reproduced within the structure of the message itself.

THE POLITICS OF REFLEXIVITY

Much polemic has revolved around the issue of what might be called the **POLITICAL VALENCE OF REFLEXIVITY**. While Anglo-American cultural criticism has often seen reflexivity as a sign of the postmodern, a point at which an "art of exhaustion" has little left to do except contemplate its own instruments or render homage to past works of art, the left wing of film theory, especially that influenced by Althusser as well as Brecht, has seen reflexivity as a *political* obligation. A major thrust of the Althusserian movement in cultural studies was the critique of realism, and the tendency, in the early phase, was simply to equate "realist" with "bourgeois" and "reflexive" with "revolutionary." The terms "Hollywood" and "dominant cinema" became code words for "retrograde" and "passivity-inducing." The identity of "deconstructive" and "revolutionary," meanwhile, led in the pages of journals such as *Cinétique* to the rejection of virtually all cinema, past and present, as "idealist." But both of these equations call for close examination. Reflexivity and realism, first of all, are not necessarily antithetical terms. A novel such as Balzac's *Lost Illusions*, and a film like Godard's *Tout Va Bien*, can be seen as at once reflexive *and* realist, in that they illuminate the everyday lived realities of the social conjunctures from which they emerge, while also reminding the readers/spectators of the constructed nature of their own representation. Rather than strictly opposed polarities, realism and reflexivity are interpenetrating tendencies quite capable of coexisting within the same text. It would be more accurate to speak of a "coefficient" of reflexivity or realism, while recognizing that it is not a question of a fixed proportion. Godard-Miéville's *Numéro Deux*, for example, displays a simultaneously high coefficient of both realism and reflexivity.

Illusionism, meanwhile, has never been monolithically dominant even in the mainstream fiction film. The coefficient of reflexivity varies from genre to genre (musicals like *Singin' in the Rain* are classically more reflexive than social realist dramas like *Marty*), from era to era (in the contemporary

201

epoch reflexivity is fashionable, even *de rigueur*), from film to film by the same director (Woody Allen's *Zelig* is more reflexive than *Another Woman*); and even from sequence to sequence within the same film. Even the most paradigmatically realist texts – as Barthes' reading of *Sarrasine* and *Cahier's* reading of *Young Mr Lincoln* demonstrate – are marked by gaps and fissures in their illusionism. Few classical films perfectly fit the abstract category of transparency often taken to be the norm in mainstream cinema. Nor can one simply assign a positive or negative value to realism, or reflexivity, as such. Marx's interest in Balzac suggests that realism is not inherently reactionary. What Jakobson calls **PROGRESSIVE REALISM** has been used as an instrument of social criticism in favor of the working class (*Salt of the Earth*), women (*Julia*) and by emergent Third World nations (*Barren Lives* and *Battle of Algiers*). Brecht's theories pointed the way beyond the false dichotomy of realism and reflexivity, since Brechtian reflexivity clearly attempts to enlist self-referential narrative procedures in the service of revolutionary aims. The Brechtian approach assumes the compatibility of reflexivity as an aesthetic strategy and realism as an aspiration. Brecht distinguished between realism as "laying bare society's causal network" – a goal realizable within a reflexive, modernist aesthetic – and realism as a historically determinate set of conventions. His critique of realism centered on the ossified conventions of the nineteenth-century novel and naturalist theater, but not on the goal of truthful representation.

The generalized equation of the reflexive with the progressive is also problematic. Texts may foreground their own procedures or not; the contrast cannot always be read as a political one. Jane Feuer speaks, in relation to the musical, of **CONSERVATIVE REFLEXIVITY**, i.e. the reflexivity characterizing films, such as *Singin' in the Rain*, which foreground cinema as an institution, which emphasize spectacle and artifice, but ultimately within an illusionistic aesthetic which has little to do with subversive, demystificatory or revolutionary purposes or procedures. The reflexivity of a certain avant-garde, similarly, is eminently cooptable within an "artsy" Formalism. One might speak, similarly, of the **POSTMODERN REFLEXIVITY** of commercial television, which is often reflexive and self-referential, but whose reflexivity is, at most, ambiguous. *The Letterman Show* is relentlessly reflexive, but almost always within a kind of cynical, pervasive ironic stance which looks with a jaundiced eye at all political position-taking. Many of the distancing features characterized as reflexive in Godard's films also seem to typify many television shows: the designation of the apparatus (cameras, monitors, switches), the "disruption" of narrative flow (via commercials); the juxtaposition of heterogeneous slices of discourses; the mixing of documentary and fictive modes. Yet rather than trigger "alienation effects," television is often simply alienating in a different sense. The commercial interruptions that disrupt fiction programming, for example, are not intended to make the tele-spectator think but rather to feel and to buy. The self-referential humor signals to the spectator that the commercial is not to be taken seriously, and this relaxed state of expectation renders the viewer more permeable to the commercial message.

INTERTEXTUALITY

One of the by-products of the semiotic approach to film was to question realism by emphasizing the coded, constructed nature of the filmic artifact. Art was seen as a discourse, responding not to reality but to other discourses. Julia Kristeva defined film and other artistic discourses as **SIGNI-FYING PRACTICES**, i.e. as differentiated signifying systems. Elaborating on the Kristevan conception, Stephen Heath explicated the phrase as follows:

> *signifying* indicates the recognition of film as a system of series of systems of meaning, film as articulation. Practice stresses the process of this articulation . . . it takes film as a work of production of meanings and in so doing brings into the analysis the question of the positioning of the subject within that work, its relation to the subject, what kind of "reader" and "author" it constructs. Specific is the necessity for analysis to understand film in the particularity of the work it engages, the differences it sustains with other signifying practices.[7]

The word practice came with Althusserian-Marxist overtones of the processes of transformation of a determinate raw material into a determinate product. Film thus involved the active production of meaning rather than a neutral relay or transfer of meaning. Both Kristeva and Heath called for a shift in attention, therefore, to the signifier and to the enunciating subject. Kristeva defines the text as **PRODUCTIVITY**, as a production involving both producer and reader/spectator, often taking the form of the deconstruction of systematicity and of communicative functions. Kristeva gave the name **SIGNIFIANCE** to the work of differentiation and confrontation practices in language, referring both to the productive work of the signifier and the productive reading whereby the producer and receiver of the text deconstruct its sense.

The term **INTERTEXTUALITY** began as Kristeva's translation of the Bakhtinian notion of **DIALOGISM**. Bakhtin defines dialogism as "the necessary relation of any utterance to other utterances." (An "utterance," for Bakhtin, can refer to any "complex of signs," from a spoken phrase to a poem, or song, or play or film.) Bakhtin sees dialogism as a defining characteristic of the novel, cognate with its openness to the social diversity of speech types. The word "dialogism" in Bakhtin's writings progressively accretes meanings and connotations without ever losing this central idea of "the relation between the utterance and other utterances." Bakhtin traces **LITERARY DIALOGISM** as far back as the Socratic dialogues, with their agonic staging of the contest of two competing discourses, and continuing with the dialogic and polyphonic texts of Rabelais, Cervantes, Diderot and Dostoevsky, which Bakhtin opposes to "monologic" and "theological" texts which unproblematically assert a single truth. The concept of dialogism suggests that every text forms an intersection of textual surfaces. All texts are tissues of anonymous formulae embedded in the language, variations on those formulae, conscious and unconscious quotations, conflations and inversions of other texts. In the broadest sense, intertextual dialogism refers to the infinite and open-ended possibilities generated by all the discursive practices of a culture, the entire matrix of communicative utterances within which the artistic text is situated, and which reach the text not only through recognizable influences but also through a subtle process of dissemination.

In her study of the literary avant-garde, Kristeva explores the dialogic character of texts by Sollers, Burroughs and Joyce as evolving from a literary tradition which articulates a complex, composite system, a montage of heterogeneous discourses within a single text. For Kristeva, as for Bakhtin, every text forms a "mosaic of citations," a palimpsest of traces, where other texts may be read, although Kristeva tends to limit her attention to erudite texts. The concept of intertextuality is not reducible to matters of "influence" by one writer on another, or by one film-maker on another, or with "sources" of a text in the old philological sense. Kristeva defines intertextuality in *La Révolution du Langage Poétique* as the transposition of one or more system of signs into another, accompanied by a new articulation of the enunciative and denotative position. Michael Riffaterre, meanwhile, defines intertextuality as the reader's perception of the relations between a text and all the other texts that have preceded or followed it.[8] Thus the intertext of a film such as Kubrick's *The Shining* could be said to consist of all the genres to which the film refers, for example the horror film and the melodrama, but also to that class of films called literary adaptations, with the attendant literary affiliates, such as the Gothic novel, and extending to the entire canon of Kubrick films, Jack Nicholson films, and so forth. The intertext of the work of art, then, may be taken to include not just other artworks in the same or comparable form, but also all the "series" within which the singular text is situated.

The conceptual necessity of the intertext is foregrounded in Lévi-Strauss' analysis of native American myths. The anthropologist found that a particular myth could be comprehended only in relation to a vast system of other myths, social practices and cultural codes. The individual story came to be seen as a fragment, existing in extended articulation with other systems, such as kinship structures, village planning, body art (tattooing), as well as with other myths. Eco speaks of **INTERTEXTUAL FRAMES**, i.e. the diverse frames of reference invoked in the reader, which authorize and orient interpretation, the filling in of gaps and fissures in the text, guiding the reader's inferences about the story and the characters by providing intertextual cues. Intertextuality is a valuable theoretical concept in that it relates the singular text principally to other systems of representation rather than to an amorphous "context" anointed with the dubious status and authority of "the real" or "reality." In order even to discuss the relation of a work to its historical circumstances, we are obliged to situate the text within its intertext and then relate both text and intertext to the other "systems" and "series" which form its context.

Bakhtin spoke of what he called the **DEEP GENERATING SERIES** of literature, i.e. the complex and multi-dimensional dialogism, rooted in social life and history, comprising both primary (oral) and secondary (literate) genres, which engendered literature as a cultural phenomenon. The "semantic treasures Shakespeare embedded in his works," Bakhtin writes:

> were created and collected through the centuries and even millennia: they lay hidden in the language, and not only in the literary language, but also in those strata of the popular language that before Shakespeare's time had not entered literature, in the diverse genres and forms of speech communication, in the forms of a mighty national culture (primarily, carnival forms) that were shaped through millennia, in theatre-spectacle genres (mystery plays, farces, and so forth) in plots whose roots go back to prehistoric antiquity, and, finally, in forms of thinking.

> (Bakhtin 1986: 5)

The Bakhtinian reformulation of the problem of intertextuality must be seen as an "answer" both to the purely intrinsic Formalist and structuralist paradigms of linguistic theory and literary criticism, as well as to sociologistic paradigms interested only in extrinsic class-biographical and ideological determinations. Bakhtin attacks the limitation of the literary scholar-critic's interest exclusively to the "literary series," arguing for a more diffuse dissemination of ideas as interanimating all the "series," literary and non-literary, as they are generated by what he calls the "powerful deep currents of culture." Literature, and by extension the cinema, must be understood within what Bakhtin calls the "differentiated unity of the epoch's entire culture" (1986: 5).

Dialogism operates, then, within all cultural production, whether literate or non-literate, verbal or non-verbal, highbrow or lowbrow. The contemporary film artist, within this conception, becomes the orchestrator, the amplifier of the ambient messages thrown up by all the series – literary, painterly, musical, cinematic, commercial and so forth. A film like *The Band Wagon*, as Geoffrey Nowell-Smith points out (in *Narremore*, 1991: 16–18), is a virtual melting-pot of "high" and "low" artistic discourses, with references to ballet, folk art, Broadway, Faust, Mickey Spillane and *film noir*. This inclusive view of intertextuality would see a film like Woody

Allen's *Zelig* as the site of intersection of innumerable intertexts, some specifically filmic (newsreels, archival material, home movies, television compilation films, "witness" documentaries, cinema verité, film melodrama, psychological case-study films like *Spellbound*, "fictive documentaries" like *F for Fake*, and more immediate fiction-film predecessors like Warren Beatty's *Reds*); others literary (the Melvillean "anatomy"), and some broadly cultural (Yiddish theatre, Borscht-Belt Comedy). The film's originality, paradoxically, lies in the audacity of its imitation, quotation and absorption of other texts, its ironic hybridization of traditionally opposed discourses.[9]

Partially inspired by Bakhtin's notion of the generating series, Kristeva distinguished between the **PHENO-TEXT**, i.e. the "outside" or "remainder" of the *signifiance* of the text, the "flat" surface of its structured signification, but which bears traces of the productivity of the **GENO-TEXT**, i.e. the process of productivity itself, the "operation of the generation of the pheno-text." While the pheno-text is "available" for formal, linguistic analysis, the geno-text has to do with the play of signifiers before meaning. To study the geno-text is to study the operations of textuality itself.

TRANSTEXTUALITY

Building on Bakhtin and Kristeva, Gerard Genette in *Palimpsestes* (1982) proposed a more inclusive term, **TRANSTEXTUALITY**, to refer to "all that which puts one text in relation, whether manifest or secret, with other texts." Genette posits five types of transtextual relations. He defines **INTER-TEXTUALITY**, more restrictively than Kristeva, as the "effective co-presence of two texts" in the form of quotation, plagiarism and allusion. Although Genette largely restricts himself to literary examples, one might easily imagine filmic instances of the same procedures. **QUOTATION** can take the form of the insertion of classic clips into films: Peter Bogdanovich quotes Hawks' *The Criminal Code* in *Targets*; Godard quotes Resnais' *Night and Fog* in *A Married Woman*. Films like Resnais' *Mon Oncle d'Amérique*, as well as *Dead Men Don't Wear Plaid* and *Zelig* make the citation of pre-existing film sequences a central structuring principle. **ALLUSION**, meanwhile, can take the form of a verbal or visual evocation of another film, hopefully as an expressive means of commenting on the fictional world of the alluding film. Godard in *Contempt* alludes, through a title on a movie theater marquee, to Rossellini's *Voyage in Italy*, a film by one of Godard's favorite directors which recounts, like *Contempt* itself, the slow undoing of a couple. Even an actor can constitute an allusion, as in the case of the Boris Karloff character in *Targets*, seen as the embodiment of old-style Gothic horror, the essential dignity of which Bogdanovich contrasts with anonymous contemporary mass murder. A cinematic technique can constitute an allusion: the iris-in to an informer in *Breathless*, or the use of Griffith-style masking in *Jules and Jim*, allude by the calculatedly archaic nature to earlier periods of film history, while the subjectivized camera movements and point-of-view structurings in Brian de Palma's *Body Double* allude to the strong intertextual influence of Alfred Hitchcock.

Indeed, Genette's highly suggestive categories tempt one to coin additional terms within the same paradigm. One might speak of **CELEBRITY INTERTEXTUALITY**, i.e. filmic situations where the presence of a film or television star or celebrity intellectual evokes a genre or cultural milieu (Truffaut in *Close Encounters of a Third Kind*, Norman Mailer in Godard's *King Lear*, Marshall McLuhan in *Annie Hall*). **GENETIC INTERTEXTUALITY** would evoke the process by which the appearance of the sons and daughters of well-known actors and actresses – Jamie Lee Curtis, Liza Minelli, Melanie Griffith – evokes the memory of their famous parents. **INTRATEXTUALITY** would refer to the process by which films refer to themselves through mirroring, microcosmic, and *mise-en-abyme* structures, while **AUTO-CITATION** would refer to an author's self-quotation, as when Vincent Minelli cites his own *The Bad and the Beautiful* within *Two Weeks in Another Town*. **MENDACIOUS INTERTEXUALITY** would evoke those texts, e.g. the pseudo-newsreels of *Zelig* or the ersatz Nazi films in *Kiss of the Spider Woman*, which invent a pseudo-intertextual reference.

PARATEXTUALITY, Genette's second type of transtextuality, refers to the relation, in literature, between the text proper and its "paratext" – titles, prefaces, postfaces, epigraphs, dedications, illustrations, and even book jackets and signed autographs. The paratext is constituted by all the accessory messages and commentaries which come to surround the text and which at times become virtually indistinguishable from it. The notion leads, as Genette admits, to a mine of unanswerable questions. Do the original chapter titles evoking *The Odyssey*, included in the subscribers' pre-publication of Joyce's *Ulysses* but withdrawn in the final version, but which came to orient the reading of the novel, form part of the text of that novel? The question, then, is one of closure, of the lines of demarcation between text and *hors-texte*.

It is intriguing to speculate concerning the relevance of such a category to film. Do widely quoted prefatory remarks by a director at a film's first screening form part of a film's paratext? What about reported remarks by a director about a film, such as Godard's celebrated characterization of *Numéro Deux* as a "remake of *Breathless*"? How should we regard the original variant versions of films, about which there is often much fanfare in the press, which resonate, as it were, around the edges of a text, as in the case of Erich von Stroheim's original 42-reel version of *Greed*, or the longer versions of Bertolucci's *1900* or Scorsese's *New York, New York*? Widely reported information about the budget of a film can inflect critical reception, as in the case of Coppola's *Cotton Club*, where reviewers found that the film-maker had achieved very little in relation to an enormous budget, or, as in the case of Spike Lee's *She's Gotta Have It*, that the film-maker achieved a good deal despite a very low budget? What about authorized scripts of screenplays, such as Nabokov's screenplay to *Lolita*, which show variance from the film as released? What about the program notes distributed at press screenings which often orient journalistic responses to commercial films? All these questions, operating on the margins of the official text, impinge on the issue of a film's paratext.

METATEXTUALITY, Genette's third type of transtextuality, consists of the critical relation between one text and another, whether the commented text is explicitly cited or only silently evoked. Genette cites the relation between Hegel's *Phenomenology of Mind* and the text that it constantly evokes without explicitly mentioning: Diderot's *Le Neveu de Rameau*. Transferring our attention to the cinema, the avant-garde films of the New American Cinema offer metatextual critiques of classical Hollywood cinema. Michael Snow's *Wavelength*, for example, both alludes to and refused the conventional "suspense" of Hollywood thrillers, as if it were stretching a single Hitchcock dolly-shot into a 45-minute simulated zoom shot covering the space of a Manhattan loft. The multiple refusals of Hollis Frampton's *nostalgia* – of plot development, of movement in the shot, of closure – suggest a mocking critique of the expectations triggered by conventional narrative films. In practice, it should be pointed out, it is not always easy to distinguish Genette's metatextuality from his fifth category of "hypertextuality" (the relation between a text and an anterior text which it transforms or modifies).

ARCHITEXTUALITY, Genette's fourth category of transtextuality, refers to the generic taxonomies suggested or refused by the titles or infratitles of a text. Architextuality has to do with a text's willingness, or reluctance, to characterize itself directly or indirectly in its title as a poem, essay, novel, film. In literature, Genette points out, critics often refuse a text's self-designation, arguing, for example, that a certain "tragedy" by Corneille is not "really" a tragedy. (Juri Lotman, in the same vein, speaks of **GENRE MISTAKES**, situations where critics are induced into misattributing a given generic status to a film, and thus confusing the film's textual characteristics.) A text's refusal to designate itself homogeneously, meanwhile, often provokes debate about the text's "real" genre or conflation of genres. (A Bakhtinian approach would allow for the multi-generic status of a text.) Fielding's characterization of *Joseph Andrews* as a "comic epic poem in prose" or Godard's description of *Contempt* as a "tragedy in long shot" (a scrambling of Chaplin's famous definition of tragedy as close-up and comedy as long-shot) are designed to prod the critics/readers/spectators toward more complex responses.

Some film titles align a text with literary antecedents. *Sullivan's Travels* evokes Swift's *Gulliver's Travels* and, by extension, the satiric mode. The title of Woody Allen's *Midsummer Night's Sex Comedy* begins by alluding to

Shakespeare and ends with a comic fall into prurience, all the while echoing Bergman's *Smiles of a Summer Night*. Coppola's *Apocalypse Now* offers a disenchanted 1970s variation on a famous utopian theatrical performance of the 1960s, the Living Theater's *Paradise Now*. Other titles signal a sequel: *Return of . . . Son of . . . Rocky V*. The graphic and linguistic unconventionality of the titles of many avant-garde films – Paul Sharits' *T.O.U.C.H.I.N.G.* – announce a similar unconventionality in cinematic approach. Although a film need not designate itself as, first and foremost, a film, certain reflexive film-makers have chosen to accentuate the obvious in their titles: Mel Brook's *Silent Movie*, Bruce Conner's *A Movie*. The extended literary "subtitles" of certain films: *Doctor Strangelove: Or How I Learned to Stop Worrying and Love the Bomb; A Married Woman: Fragments of a Film Made in 1964* – finally, suggest a kind of rapprochement with literary practices.

HYPERTEXTUALITY, Genette's fifth type of transtextuality, is extremely suggestive for film analysis. Hypertextuality refers to the relation between one text, which Genette calls hypertext, to an anterior text or **HYPOTEXT**, which the former transforms, modifies, elaborates or extends. In literature, the *Aeneid*'s hypotexts include *The Odyssey* and *The Iliad*, while the hypotexts of Joyce's *Ulysses* include *The Odyssey* and *Hamlet*. Both the *Aeneid* and *Ulysses* are hypertextual elaborations of a single hypotext – *The Odyssey*. Virgil recounts the adventures of Aeneas in a manner generically and stylistically inspired by Homeric epic. Joyce transposes the central mythos of *The Odyssey* into twentieth-century Dublin. Both operate transformations on pre-existing texts. The term hypertextuality is rich in potential application to the cinema, and especially to those films which derive from pre-existing texts in a way more precise and specific than that evoked by the term intertextuality. Filmic adaptations of celebrated novels, for example, are hypertexts derived from pre-existing hypotexts which have been transformed by operations of selection, amplification, concretization and actualization. The diverse filmic adaptations of *Madame Bovary* (Renoir, Minelli) or of *La Femme et le Pantin* (Duvivier, von Sternberg, Buñuel) can be seen as variant hypertextual "readings" triggered by an identical hypotext. Indeed, the diverse prior adaptations can come to form part of the hypotext available to a film-maker coming relatively "late" in the series.

Hypertextuality calls attention to all the transformative operations that one text can operate on another text. Travesty, for example, irreverently devalorizes and "trivializes" a pre-existing "noble" text. Buster Keaton mocks the lofty humanitarian platitudes of *Intolerance* in *The Three Ages*. Mel Brooks rewrites the Hitchcockian text, with a distinct style and elocution, in *High Anxiety*. Many Brazilian comedies parodically re-elaborate Hollywood hypotexts whose production values they both resent and admire. Other hypertextual films simply update earlier works while accentuating specific features of the original. The Morissey/Warhol collaboration *Heat* (1972) transposes the plot of Billy Wilder's *Sunset Boulevard* (1950) into 1970s

Hollywood, filtering the original through a gay-camp sensibility. Elsewhere the transposition is not of a single film but of an entire genre. Kasdan's *Body Heat* (1981) evokes the corpus of 1940s *film noir* in terms of plot, character and style, in such a way that a knowledge of *film noir* becomes, as Noel Carroll points out, a privileged hermeneutic grid for the cine-literate spectator.[10] A more expansive conception of hypertextuality might include many of the films generated by the Hollywood combinatory: remakes like *Invasion of the Body Snatchers* (1978) and *The Postman Always Rings Twice* (1981); sequels like *Psycho II* (1983); revisionist Westerns like *Little Big Man* (1970); generic pastiches and reworkings like Scorsese's *New York, New York* (1977); and parodies like Mel Brooks' *Blazing Saddles* (1974). Most of these films assume spectatorial competence in diverse generic codes; they are calculated deviations meant to be appreciated by discerning connoisseurs.

The only film actually discussed by Genette in *Palimpsestes* is Herbert Ross' *Play It Again, Sam* (1972). The film's title, as Genette himself points out, functions as a contract of cinematic hypertextuality for those film-lovers who recognize (or misrecognize) the most celebrated phrase associated with *Casablanca* (1942). The film too "plays it again," i.e. plays again, in its fashion, the "song" which is *Casablanca*. The Allan Felix character (Woody Allen) dreams of emulating a fictive model with whom he has virtually nothing in common. The same text and situation become travesty merely through the substitution of actors, and the ironic distance that separates him from his prototype.[11]

DISCOURSE

The term **DISCOURSE** has successfully accumulated many significations. In the pre-semiotic period, the word denoted the ordered exposition in speech or writing on a particular theme or subject. But with the advent of structuralism and semiotics, the word came to crystallize the concerns of a wide variety of disciplines, becoming the point of intersection for a diversity of inquiries. In linguistics, **DISCOURSE** refers to any organized use of language above the sentence. But within this broad notion, one can posit diverse tendencies. Discourse can refer, for example, to any set of utterances constituting a speech event (conversation, song, poem, speech, sermon, interview). In *Problems in General Linguistics*, Benveniste focusses on the interrelational nature of discourse. Exploring the role and function of pronouns, Benveniste argues that a word such as "I" only gains meaning within the ephemeral circumstances of discourse. The person who functions as speaker one moment functions as a listener the next. Both pronouns and verbs become active as signs, then, only within **DISCOURSE**, which Benveniste defines as "every utterance (verbal or written) assuming a speaker and a hearer, and in the speaker, the intention of influencing the other in some way" (Benveniste 1971: 208–9). (As we saw in Part III, Benveniste's distinction between *histoire* and *discours*, the former involving an utterance from which all markers of enunciation have been effaced, and the latter involving an utterance where such markers are present, has been highly productive within film theory and analysis.)

Sociolinguistics, meanwhile, explores the embeddedness of speech-events within a given social or cultural formation. We can distinguish, in this context, between the text as a concrete semiotic object or complex of signs with a socially ascribed unity and discourse as referring to the social-semiotic processes within which texts are embedded. **DISCOURSE ANALYSIS** refers to the search for linguistic regularities, such as "cohesion," within discourses. Within a more politicized tradition, discourse analysis, as practiced by feminist sociolinguists as well as by everyday language linguists such as Pêcheux and Halliday, pays attention to the ways that assymetrical arrangements of power impinge on everyday language use, the manner in which social inequalities are reinforced, contested or negotiated within language.

DISCOURSE also forms a key term in the writings of the French philosopher and historian Michel Foucault. Discourse, for Foucault, is more than a set of statements; rather, it has social materiality and ideological particularity, and is always imbricated with power. Following Nietzsche, Foucault gives the name **GENEALOGY** to his method of analyzing the nature and development of modern forms of power. Rather than analyze culture in semiological terms of "systems of signs," Foucault sees culture as a social constellation of sites of powers. Thus Foucault grounds discourse in relations of power, and specifically in the forms of power embodied in specialized and institutionalized languages.

Foucauldian genealogy is concerned with **DISCURSIVE REGIMES**, i.e. the processes, procedures and apparatuses whereby truth and knowledge are produced. "Truth," within a Foucauldian perspective, is a construct exploited and struggled over by contending groups. Foucault studies discourse first as a historical phenomenon. The analysis of discourse for Foucault involves research into the historical conditions – the power relations – which facilitated, but did not wholly determine, their emergence. Foucault speaks of **DISCURSIVE FORMATIONS**, i.e. the linguistic practices and institutions that produce the knowledge claims, usually correlatable with a disseminated power, within which we exist socially. Discourses for Foucault have a maieutic function; they bring cultural objects into being by naming them, defining them, delimiting their field of operation. These objects of knowledge then become linked to specific practices, for example those of the criminologist, the psychiatrist, the administrator, the legislator. Practices realize and set the conditions for discourse, while discourse, reciprocally, feeds back utterances which facilitate practice. The concept of discursive formation, although influenced by Marxism, marked a sharp

211

break from Marxist conceptions of state-centered power. While classical Marxism saw power and repression as emanating from the bourgeois state, Foucault conceives of power as omnipresent, dispersed across the plural relationalities of the social field. Unlike earlier forms of power, modern power is continuous, capillary and productive. Foucault's critique had the paradoxical result of seeming on the one hand to offer a way out of the impasses of more determinist forms of Marxism, while on the other positing a disciplinary society where power was so pervasive and all-infiltrating as to be virtually "unseizable."

Foucault's analyses of power had relevance not only to the analysis of cinema as an institution, but also to films themselves and their relation to the spectator. Up to this point, however, cinema studies has shown less interest in the "post-structuralist" Foucault than in the equally post-structuralist Lacan. In *Film Theory: An Introduction* (1988), Robert Lapsley and Michael Westlake point out some of the problems in extrapolating Foucauldian theory for the cinema: (1) Foucault never explained how change occurs, how one discourse or regime comes to cede place to another (a subject about which Marxism had more precise ideas); (2) Foucault's concepts had more obvious bearing on issues cinema "shared" with other media such as literature, for example issues of authorship and realism, than with specifically cinematic issues; and (3) Foucault's claim that the subject was produced within discourse was not accompanied by any explanation of how exactly the subject was formed.

Despite Foucault's failure to analyze the role of communications media in transmitting discourse and power relations, film analysts have made occasional use of certain Foucauldian concepts. Dana Polan makes effective use of Foucauldian categories in his study of "power and paranoia" in the American cinema of the 1940s, demonstrating the ways that "homefront narratives" serve to discipline aberration: "the discourse of the war effort encourages a microphysics of power in which citizen spies on citizen, where everyone lives under the scrutiny of a relentless look" (Polan 1986: 78).

While it is difficult to point to a Foucauldian film theory, a number of critics have examined specific films in terms of Foucault's analysis of institutions. They have drawn, for example, on Foucault's concept of the **PANOPTIC REGIME**, i.e. a regime of synoptic visibility designed to facilitate a "disciplinary" overview of a prison population, best exemplified in the design of prisons after Bentham's **PANOPTICON**, i.e. rings of backlit cells encircling a central observation tower. Since the panopticon installs an assymetrical, unidirectional gaze – the scientist or warden can see the inmates but not vice versa – it has been compared to the voyeuristic situation of the film spectator. L. B. Jeffries, at the beginning of *Rear Window*, overseeing the world from a sheltered position, subjecting his neighbors to a controlling gaze, becomes the warden-spectator, as it were, in a private panopticon, where he observes the wards ("small captive shadows in the cells of the periphery") of an imaginary prison. Foucault's description of the cells of the panopticon – "so many cages, so many small theatres, in which each actor is alone, perfectly individualized and constantly visible" – in some ways describes the scene exposed to Jeffries' glance.

Power, for Foucault, is best understood not in the macropolitical terms of class and state, but in the micropolitical terms of the networks of power relations within local institutions. Dan Armstrong uses a Foucauldian framework to show how the documentarian Frederick Wiseman explores in his *oeuvre* a continuum of social institutions spreading out from the prison to the larger society, demonstrating "an extensive rationality and economy of power at work shaping, normalizing and objectifying subjects for the purposes of social utility and control." The normalizing forms of institutional power revealed in Wiseman's "carceral archipelago," Armstrong argues, correspond closely to Foucault's notion of dividing practices, i.e. methods of observation, classification and objectification in which the subject is divided (both within herself and from others) and thus regulated and dominated. Armstrong divides Wiseman's work into three clusters of films, each investigating a different political dynamic: confinement and punishment in *Titticut Follies* and *Juvenile Court*; assistance in *Hospital* and *Welfare*; and the "productive" disciplines of school, the military, religion and work in *High School*, *Basic Training*, *Essene* and *Meat*. Wiseman thus anatomizes the societal production of docile individuals while at the same time underlining the partial failure of this attempt to instrumentalize the subject.[12]

SOCIAL SEMIOTICS

Both structuralism and post-structuralism had in common the habit of "bracketing the referent," i.e. insisting more on the interrelations of signs than on any correspondence between sign and referent. In their critique of realism, both structuralism and post-structuralism occasionally went to the extreme of detaching art from all relation to social and historical context. But not all theorists accepted the pan-semiotic vision of what Edward Said called "wall-to-wall" text. The constructed, coded nature of artistic discourse, some argue, hardly precludes all reference to reality. Even Derrida, whose writing was often used to justify a wholesale rejection of all truth-claims, protested that his view of text and context "embraces and does not exclude the world, reality, history . . . it does not suspend reference" (in Norris 1990: 44). Filmic like literary fictions inevitably bring into play everyday assumptions not only about space and time but also about social and cultural relationships. If language structures the world, the world also structures and shapes language; the movement is not uni-directional. History inflects the structure, the socially lived system of differences that is language.

One of the challenges to semiotics has been to forge a link between text and context, to avoid the twin traps of an empty Formalism and a deterministic sociologism. In this final section, we will look at two currents within the semiotic tradition which try to forge this link: semio-pragmatics and Bakhtinian translinguistics.

The goal of **SEMIO-PRAGMATICS**, a movement especially associated with the names of Franco Casetti and Roger Odin, is to study the production and the reading of films in so far as they constitute programmed social practices. In linguistics, pragmatics consists of that branch of linguistics concerned with what transpires between the text and its reception, i.e. the ways in which language produces meaning and influences its interlocutors. Semio-pragmatics prolongs Metz' speculations, in "The Imaginary Signifier," concerning the active role of the spectator whose look brings the film into existence. Semio-pragmatics is less interested in a sociologistic study of actual spectators than in the psychic disposition of the spectator during the film experience, not spectators as they are in life, but spectators as the film "wants" them to be. Within this perspective, both the production and the reception of film are institutional acts involving roles shaped by a network of determinations generated by the larger social space. In *Dentro lo Squardo: Il Film e il suo Spettatore* (1986), Franco Casetti explores the ways that films signal the presence and assign a position to the spectator, inducing him/her to follow an itinerary. While early film semiotics saw the spectator as a relatively passive decoder of pre-established codes, Casetti sees the spectator as active "interlocutor" and interpretant.

The "space of communication" (Odin 1983) constituted by producer and spectator together is highly diverse, ranging from the pedagogic space of the classroom, the familial space of the home movie, to the fictional-entertainment space of mass-mediated culture. Much of the history of the cinema has consisted of a steady perfecting of the technique, language and conditions of reception for the requirements of fictionalization. In western societies, and increasingly in all societies, the space of fictional communication is becoming the dominant space. **FICTIONALIZATION** refers to the process by which the spectator is made to resonate to the fiction, the process which moves us and leads us to identify with, love or hate the characters. Odin divides this process into seven distinct operations: (1) **FIGURATIVIZATION**, the construction of audio-visual analogical signs; (2) **DIEGETICIZATION**, the construction of a fictive "world"; (3) **NARRATIVIZATION**, the temporalization of events involving antagonistic subjects: (4) **MONSTRATION**, the designation of the diegetic world, be it "actual" or "constructed," as "real"; (5) **BELIEF**, the split regime whereby the spectator is simultaneously aware of being at the movies and experiencing the perceived film "as if" it were real; (6) **MISE-EN-PHASE** (literally the "placing-in-phase" or "phasing-in" of the spectator), i.e. the operation which enlists all the filmic instances in the service of the narration, mobilizing the rhythmic and musical work, the play of looks and framing, to make the spectator vibrate to the rhythm of the filmic events; and (7) **FICTIVIZ-ATION**, i.e. the intentional modality which characterizes the status and the positioning of the spectator, who sees the enunciator of the film not as an originary self but as fictive. The spectator knows that he/she is witnessing a fiction which will not reach him/her personally, an operation which has the paradoxical result of allowing the film thus to touch the spectator in the very depths of the psyche. The **FICTION FILM**, for Odin, is that film conceived in order to foster all seven of the foregoing operations. The **NON-FICTION FILM**, in this perspective, refers to those films which block some or all of the fictionalizing operations.

Odin also speaks of a new kind of spectator shaped by the postmodern communications environment. Taking as an example Giorgio Moroder's musical "actualization" in 1984 of Fritz Lang's *Metropolis* (1926), Odin foregrounds processes, such as colorization, which "de-realize" the film, rendering it as "surface." (Odin's analysis is easily extrapolable for music-video.) Instead of the usual tertiary structure of film, narration and spectator, we find a dual structure in which the film acts directly on the spectator, who vibrates not to a fiction but rather to variations of rhythm, intensity and color, to what Baudrillard calls "plural energies," and "fragmentary intensities." This mutation of social space generates a "new spectatorial economy," product of the crisis of the "grand narratives of legitimation" (Lyotard 1979; trans. 1984) and the "end of the social" (Baudrillard 1983), and a new spectator less alert to "stories" than to the energetic discharge of the flux of music and images. Communication gives way to communion.

Jean Baudrillard, meanwhile, in work that both extends and revises semiotic and Marxist theory, while incorporating the anthropological theories of Marcel Mauss and Georges Bataille, argues that the contemporary world of mass-mediated commodification entails a new economy of the sign, and a consequently altered attitude toward representation. This new era is characterized by **SEMIURGY** – the process by which the production and proliferation of mass-mediated signs has replaced the production of objects as the motor of social life and as a means of social control. In "The Precession of Simulacra," (Baudrillard 1983a), Baudrillard posits four stages through which representation has passed on its way to unqualified simulation; a first stage in which the sign "reflects" a basic reality; a second stage in which the sign "masks" or "distorts" reality; a third stage in which the sign masks the *absence* of reality; and a fourth stage in which the sign becomes mere **SIMULACRUM**, i.e. a pure simulation bearing no relation whatsoever to reality. With **HYPER-REALITY**, the sign becomes more real than reality itself. The disappearance of the referent and even of the signified leaves in its wake nothing but an endless pageant of empty signifiers.

Baudrillard's critics, such as Douglas Kellner and Christopher Norris, accuse him of "sign fetishism." For Kellner (1989) Baudrillard is a "semiological idealist" who abstracts signs from their material underpinnings, while Norris (1990) describes Baudrillard's project as resulting in an "inverted Platonism," a discourse that systematically promotes what for Plato were negative terms (rhetoric, appearance, ideology) over their positive counterparts. The descriptive fact that we currently inhabit an unreal world of mass-media manipulation and hyper-real politics for Norris does not mean that no alternative is possible.

Baudrillard, along with Fredric Jameson and François Lyotard, is one of the major theorists of a theoretical construct called **POSTMODERNISM**. While a semiotic lexicon is hardly the place to define such an epoch-making and epoch-defining term, we can at least sketch out some of the features of the debate. The term "postmodernism" itself, as many analysts have pointed out, has been "stretched" to breaking point, showing a protean capacity to change meaning in different national and disciplinary contexts, coming to designate a host of heterogeneous phenomena, ranging from details of architectural décor to broad shifts in societal or historical sensibility. For Dick Hebdige (1988), postmodernism resembles Saussure's view of language as a system "without positive terms." Hebdige discerns three "founding negations" within postmodernism: (1) the negation of totalization, i.e. an antagonism to discourses which address a transcendental subject, define an essential human nature, or proscribe collective human goals; (2) the negation of teleology (whether in the form of authorial purpose or historical destiny); and (3) the negation of utopia (i.e. a scepticism about what Lyotard calls the "grands récits" of the west, the faith in progress, science, or class struggle). In his preface to *The Anti-Aesthetic* (1983), Hal Foster distinguishes between neo-conservative, anti-modernist, and critical postmodernisms, arguing, finally, for a **RESISTANCE POST-MODERNISM**, i.e. a postmodern "culture of resistance" as a "counter-practice not only to the official culture of modernism but also to the 'false narrativity' of a reactionary postmodernism" (Foster 1983: xii of preface).

While some analysts find Baudrillardian-style postmodernism defeatist and politically acquiescent, others posited the postmodern as the locus of a struggle over and within representation. Bakhtinian translinguistics, although not formulated with postmodernism in mind, in this sense is relevant to contemporary debates. In books such as *The Formal Method in Literary Scholarship* and *The Dialogical Imagination*, Bakhtin reformulates the question of "realism" in a manner compatible with post-structuralism. Human consciousness and artistic practice, Bakhtin argues, do not come into contact with existence directly but through the medium of the surrounding ideological world. Literature, and by extension cinema, does not so much refer to or call up the world as represent its languages and discourses. Rather than a reflection of the real, or even a refraction of the real, art is a refraction of a refraction, i.e. a mediated version of an already textualized socio-ideological world. By bracketing the question of "the real" and instead emphasizing the artistic representation of languages and discourses, Bakhtin relocates the question so as to avoid what literary theorists call the **REFERENTIAL ILLUSION**, i.e. the idea that texts "refer back" to some pre-existing anecdotal nucleus or truth. Bakhtin's formulation avoids a naively "realistic" view of artistic representation, then, without acceding to a "hermeneutic nihilism" whereby all texts are seen as nothing more than an infinite play of signification. Bakhtin rejects naive formulations of realism, in other words, while never abandoning the notion that artistic representations are at the same time thoroughly and irrevocably imbricated in the social, precisely because the discourses that are represents are *themselves* social and historical.

A number of film analysts (notably Vivian Sobchack, Margaret Morse, Paul Willemen, Kobena Mercer, Mary Desjardins, Patricia Mellenkamp and Robert Stam) have deployed Bakhtinian categories as a way to forge links and homologies between a "textualized" world of social discourses and the "world of the text." Bakhtin coined the term **CHRONOTOPE** – literally "space–time" – to refer to the constellation of distinctive temporal and spatial features of specific genres which function to evoke the existence of a life-world independent of the text and its representations. In "Forms of Time and Chronotope in the Novel," Bakhtin (1981) suggests that time and space in the novel are intrinsically connected since the chronotope "materializes time in space." The chronotope mediates between two orders of experience and discourse, the historical and the artistic, providing fictional environments where historically specific constellations of power are made visible. Through the idea of the chronotope, Bakhtin shows how concrete spatio-temporal structures in literature – the atemporal otherworldly forest of romance, the "nowhere" of fictional utopias, the roads and inns of the picaresque novel – limit narrative possibility, shape characterization and mold a discursive image of life and the world. These concrete spatio-temporal structures in the novel are correlatable with the real historical world but not equatable with it because they are always mediated by art; the represented world, however realistic and truthful, can never be chronotopically identical with the real world it represents.

Although Bakhtin does not refer to the cinema, his category seems ideally suited to it as a medium where "spatial and temporal indicators are fused into one carefully thought-out concrete whole." Bakhtin's description of the novel as the place where "time thickens, takes on flesh, becomes artistically visible" and where "space becomes charged and responsive to the movements of time, plot and history" seem in some ways even more appropriate to film than to literature, for whereas literature plays itself out

217

within a virtual, lexical space, the cinematic chronotope is quite literal, splayed out concretely across a screen with specific dimensions and unfolding in literal time (usually 24 frames per second), quite apart from the fictive time–space constructed by specific films. A number of analysts have deployed the notion of the chronotope to historicize the discussion of space, time and style in the cinema. In her "Lounge Time: Post-War Crises and the Chronotope of Film Noir," Vivian Sobchack extends chronotopic analysis to *film noir* as a cinematic space/time chronotopically linked to the post-war crisis in values.[13] Chronotopes, Sobchack argues, are not merely the spatio-temporal backdrop for narrative events but also the literal and concrete ground from which narrative and character emerge as the temporalization of human action. The diacritical contrast which structures *film noir*, for Sobchack, is between the impersonal, discontinuous rented space of cocktail lounge, nightclub, hotel and roadside cafe on the one hand, and the familiar, unfragmented secure space of domesticity on the other. The chronotope of *noir*, Sobchack argues, perversely celebrates the repressed hysteria of a post-war cultural moment when domestic and economic coherence were fractured, spatializing and concretizing a "freedom" at once attractive, frightening and ultimately illusory.

Bakhtinian translinguistics provides other conceptual categories which ease the passage from the textual to the extra-textual. In "The Problem of Speech Genres" (Bakhtin 1986), Bakhtin provides extremely suggestive concepts susceptible to extrapolation for the analysis of cinema. Bakhtin here elaborates his conception of a continuum of speech genres, which move from the **PRIMARY SPEECH GENRES,** relatively simple forms like everyday greetings or the literary aphorism, to **SECONDARY SPEECH GENRES**, more complex genres of literary and scientific discourse, from oral epic to the multi-volume treatise. The spectrum of speech genres thus ranges all the way from "the short rejoinders of ordinary dialogue" through everyday narration, the military command, to all the literary genres (from the proverb to the multi-volume novel) and other "secondary speech genres" such as major genres of social-cultural commentary and scientific research. The secondary complex genres draw from the primary genres of unmediated speech communion and influence them as well in a process of constant back-and-forth flow. A translinguistic approach to speech genres in the cinema might correlate the primary speech genres – familial conversation, dialogue among friends, chance encounters, boss–worker exchange, classroom discussion, cocktail party banter, military commands – with their secondary cinematic mediation. It would analyze the etiquette by which the classical Hollywood film, for example, deals with typical speech situations such as two-person dialogue (usually by the conventional ping-pong of shot/counter-shot), dramatic confrontations (the verbal stand-offs of the Western and the gangster film), as well as with the more avant-gardist subversions of that etiquette. Godard's entire career constitutes a protracted attack on the conventional Hollywood decorum for handling discursive situations in the cinema, whence his refusal of the canonical back-and-forth of over-the-shoulder shots for dialogue in favor of alternative approaches: pendulum-like lateral tracks (*Le Mépris*), lengthy single-shot sequences (*Masculin, Feminin*), and unorthodox positioning of the bodies of the interlocutors (*Vivre sa Vie*).

In the social life of the utterance, be that utterance a verbally proffered phrase, a literary text, a comic strip or a film, each "word" is subject to rival pronunciations and "social accents." Bakhtin and his collaborators invented an entire cluster of terms to evoke the complex social and linguistic codes governing these rival pronunciations and accents (most of the terms have simultaneous verbal and musical connotations). Bakhtin used the term **MULTI-ACCENTUALITY** to refer to the capacity of the sign to change meaning depending on the circumstances of use as defined by dialogic interaction. The appropriateness of these terms to the cinema becomes obvious when we remember that the fiction film, and especially the sound film, can be seen as the *mise-en-scène* of actual speech situations, as the visual and aural contextualization of speech. Sound cinema is perfectly qualified to render what Bakhtin calls **INTONATION**, that phenomenon which lies on the border of the verbal and the non-verbal, the spoken and the non-spoken, and which "pumps the energy of the real life situation into the discourse," imparting "active historical movement and uniqueness."[14] The cinema is superbly equipped to present the extra-verbal aspects of linguistic discourse, precisely those subtle contextualizing factors evoked by "intonation." In the sound-film, we not only hear the words, with their accent and intonation, but also witness the facial or corporeal expression which accompanies the words – the posture of arrogance or resignation, the raised eyebrow, the look of distrust, the ironic glance which modifies the ostensible meaning of an utterance – in short all those elements which discourse analysts have taught us to see as so essential to social communication.

In a brief but extremely suggestive passage in *The Formal Method in Literary Scholarship*, Bakhtin offers another conceptual tool for dealing with the intersection of language with history and power. He speaks of *Taktichnost* or **SPEECH TACT**, as referring to a "formative and organizing force" within everyday language-exchange. Tact refers to the "ensemble of codes governing discursive interaction" and is "determined by the aggregate of all the social relationships of the speakers, their ideological horizons, and finally, the concrete situation of the conversation" (Bakhtin and Medvedev 1985: 95–6). The notion of "tact" is extremely suggestive for film theory and analysis, applying literally to the verbal exchanges within the diegesis, and figuratively to the "tact" involved in the metaphorical dialogue of genres and discourses within the text, as well as to the "dialogue" between film and spectator. Tact evokes as well the power relations between film and audience. Does the film assume distance or a kind of intimacy? Does the film lord it over the audience in the manner of Hollywood "block-busters" and "superspectacles" (the terms themselves imply arrogance or aggression), or is it obsequious and insecure? Film dramaturgy has its special tact, its ways of suggesting, through camera placement, framing and acting, such phenomena as intimacy or distance, camaraderie or domination, in short all the social and personal dynamics operating between interlocutors.

Under the combined pressure of Bakhtinian translinguistics, Derridean deconstruction, Lyotardian postmodernism and Baudrillardian simulation theory, it is now clear that semiotics as a project of methodological unification has been radically recast, within an altered context. Theoretical projects are now more modest, less totalizing. While film theory developed in the 1960s and 1970s on the basis of concepts borrowed from the human sciences (linguistics, psychoanalysis), in the 1980s and 1990s we find a renewed interest in the specific nature and history of the cinema itself, and especially in its relation to a socially and historically situated spectator traversed by gender, race, ethnicity, class and sexuality. Many analysts have abandoned French-inspired methods in favor of studies rooted in Germanic Critical Theory or Anglo-American Cultural Studies. But none of these movements are exempt from the influence of semiotics; they are rich in the traces and vestiges, the conceptual vocabulary and methodological presuppositions, of semiotics. Although semiotics may no longer be the imperious fashion it once was, all the currently fashionable movements owe a good deal to it and would quite possibly not exist had semiotics not prepared the ground. Semiotics has become diasporic, scattered and dispersed among a plurality of movements. The project now, perhaps, is to forge a critical and theoretical practice which would synthesize the interdisciplinary thrust of first-phase (structuralist) semiotics with the critique of mastery and the unified subject characteristic of post-structuralism, all combined with a translinguistic "social semiotic" alert to the cultural and political inflections of the "life of signs in society."

NOTES

1 Marcelin Pleynet, "Economical-Ideological-Formal," cited in Harvey (1978: 159).
2 See André Bazin, "On the *politique des auteurs*" (April 1957), in Jim Hillier (ed.) *Cahiers du Cinéma: The 1950s: Neo Realism, Hollywood, New Wave*, Cambridge: Harvard University Press, 1985.
3 See Jean-Louis Baudry, "Ecriture/Fiction/Idéologie," in *Tel Quel* 31 (Autumn 1967), trans. Diana Matias in *Afterimage* 5 (Spring 1974): 22–39.
4 Paul Willemen, "For Information: Cinéaction," *Framework* 32/3 (1986): 227.
5 See Graham Pechey, "Bakhtin, Marxism and Post-Structuralism," in *Literature, Politics and Theory*, London: Methuen, 1986.

6 Unpublished thesis on reflexivity in television, Media Ecology Department, New York University, 1989.

7 Stephen Heath, "*Jaws*, Ideology and Film Theory," in Nichols (1985) vol. II.

8 See Riffaterre (1979) and (1982).

9 See Robert Stam and Ella Shohat, "*Zelig* and Contemporary Theory: Meditation on the Chameleon Text," *Enclitic* 9/1–2 (17/18) (Fall 1987). Also in Robert Stam, *Subversive Pleasures* (Baltimore: Johns Hopkins, 1989).

10 See Noel Carroll, "The Future of Allusion: Hollywood in the Seventies (and Beyond)," *October*, 20 (Spring 1982): 51–81.

11 For more on filmic extrapolations of Genette's categories, see Stam (1985).

12 Dan Armstrong, "Wiseman's Realm of Transgression: *Titticut Folliwes*, the Symbolic Father and the Spectacle of Confinement," *Cinema Journal* 29 (1) (Fall 1989).

13 Unpublished essay given me by the author.

14 See V. N. Volosinov [M. M. Bakhtin], "Discourse in Life and Discourse in Poetry: Questions of Sociological Poetics," in Ann Shukman (ed.) *Bakhtin School Papers* (Russian Poetics in Translation, 10, Oxford: RPT Publications, 1983): 18.

BIBLIOGRAPHY

Adams, Parveen (1978) "Representation and Sexuality," *m/f* 1: 65–82.
Akerman, Chantal (1977) "Interview with *Camera Obscura*," *Camera Obscura* 2 (Fall): 118–21.
Allen, Robert (ed.) (1987) *Channels of Discourse: Television and Contemporary Criticism*, Chapel Hill: University of North Carolina Press.
Althusser, Louis (1970) *For Marx*, New York: Vintage Books.
Altman, Rick (ed.) (1980) *Yale French Studies Cinema/Sound* 60, New Haven: Yale University Press.
— (1984) "A Semantic/Syntactic Approach to Film Genre," *Cinema Journal* 23: 6–18.
— (1987) *The American Film Musical*, Bloomington: Indiana University Press.
Andrew, Dudley (1984) *Concepts in Film Theory*, New York: Oxford University Press.
Auerbach, Erich (1953) *Mimesis: The Representation of Reality in Western Literature*, Princeton: Princeton University Press.
Augst, Bertrand (1979) "The Order of [Cinematographic] Discourse," *Discourse* 1: 39–57.
Aumont, Jacques (1989) *L'oeil Interminable: Cinéma et Peinture*, Paris: Librairie Seguier.
Aumont, Jacques and Leutrat, J. L. (1980) *Théorie du Film*, Paris: Albatross.
Aumont, Jacques and Marie, Michel (1989) *L'Analyse des Films*, Paris: Nathan-Université.
Aumont, Jacques, Bergala, Alain, Marie, Michel, and Vernet, Marc (1983) *Esthétique du Film*, Paris: Fernand Nathan.
Bailble, Claude, Marie, Michel, and Ropars-Wuilleumier, Marie-Claire (1974) *Muriel, Histoire d'une Recherche*, Paris: Galilée.
Bailey, R. W., Matejka, L. and Steiner, P. (eds) (1978) *The Sign: Semiotics Around the World*, Ann Arbor: Michigan Slavic Publications.
Bakhtin, Mikhail (1981) *The Dialogical Imagination*, trans. Michael Holquist, ed. Caryl Emerson and Michael Holquist, Austin: University of Texas Press.
— (1986) *Speech Genres and Other Late Essays*, trans. Vern W. McGee, ed. Caryl Emerson and Michael Holquist, Austin: University of Texas Press.
Bakhtin, Mikhail and Medvedev, P. M. (1985) *The Formal Method of Literary Scholarship*, trans. Albert J. Wehrle, Cambridge, MA: Harvard University Press.
Bal, Mieke (1985) *Narratology: Introduction to the Theory of Narrative*, Toronto: University of Toronto Press.
Balázs, Béla (1952) *Theory of the Film*, London: Dennis Dobson.
Barthes, Roland (1967a) "Science versus Literature," *Times Literary Supplement*, 28 September.

—— (1967b) *Elements of Semiology*, (1964) trans. Annette Lavers and Colin Smith, New York: Hill & Wang.

—— (1968) *Writing Degree Zero*, trans. Annette Lavers and Colin Smith, New York: Hill & Wang.

—— (1972) *Mythologies*, New York: Hill & Wang.

—— (1974) *S/Z*, New York: Hill & Wang.

—— (1975a) "Upon Leaving the Movie Theater," *Communications* 23; reprinted in Theresa Hak Kyung Cha (ed.) (1980) *Apparatus*, New York: Tanan Press.

—— (1975b) *The Pleasure of the Text*, New York: Hill & Wang.

—— (1977) *Image/Music/Text*, New York: Hill & Wang.

—— (1980) *Camera Lucida*, New York: Hill & Wang.

—— (1985) *The Grain of the Voice*, New York: Hill & Wang.

Baudrillard, Jean (1983a) *Simulations*, trans. Paul Foss, Paul Patton and Philip Bletchman, New York: Semiotext(e).

—— (1983b) *In the Shadow of the Silent Majorities . . . or the End of the Social and Other Essays*, New York: Semiotext(e).

—— (1987) *Forget Foucault*, New York: Semiotext(e).

—— (1988) *The Ecstasy of Communication*, New York: Semiotext(e).

Baudry, Jean-Louis (1974–5) "Ideological Effects of the Basic Cinematographic Apparatus" [*Cinethique* 7–8 (1970)] *Film Quarterly* 28(2) (Winter): 39–47. In Cha (ed.) (1980) and Rosen (ed.) (1986).

—— (1976) "The Apparatus: Metapsychological Approaches to the Impression of Reality" [*Communications* 23 (1975)] *Camera Obscura* 1 (Fall): 104–28. In Cha (ed.) (1980) and Rosen (ed.) (1986).

Bazin, André (1967) *What is Cinema?*, vols I and II, Berkeley: University of California Press.

Bellour, Raymond (1977) "Hitchcock: The Enunciator," *Camera Obscura* 2 (Fall): 66–91.

—— (1979a) "Alternation, Segmentation, Hypnosis: An Interview," *Camera Obscura* 3/4 (Summer): 70–103.

—— (1979b) "Psychosis, Neurosis, Perversion," *Camera Obscura* 3/4 (Summer): 104–32.

—— (1979c) *L'Analyse du Film*, Paris: Albatross.

Bellour, Raymond (ed.) (1980) *Le Cinéma Américain: Analyses de Films*, 2 vols, Paris: Flammarion.

Benveniste, Emile (1971) *Problems in General Linguistics*, trans. Mary Elizabeth Meek, Coral Gables: University of Miami Press.

Bergala, Alain (1975) *Pour une Pédagogie de l'Audiovisual*, Paris: Ligne Française de l'Enseignement.

—— (1977) *Initiation à la Sémiologie du Récit en Images*, Paris: Ligne Française de l'Enseignement.

Bergstrom, Janet (1979a) "Enunciation and Sexual Difference," *Camera Obscura* 3/4 (Summer): 30–65.

—— (1979b) "Rereading the Work of Claire Johnston," *Camera Obscura* 3/4 (Summer): 20–30.

Bettetini, Gianfranco (1968) *Cinema: Lingua e Escritura*, Milan: Bompiani.

—— (1971) *L'Indice del Realismo*, Milan: Bompiani.

—— (1984) *La Conversazione Audiovisua*, Milan: Bompiani.

Black, David Alan (1986) "Genette and Film: Narrative Level in the Fiction Cinema," *Wide Angle* 8(3/4): 19–26.

Bonitzer, Pascal (1976) *Le Regard et la Voix*, Paris: Union Générale d'Editions.

Booth, Wayne (1983) *The Rhetoric of Fiction*, Chicago: University of Chicago Press.

Bordwell, David (1985) *Narration in the Fiction Film*, Madison: University of Wisconsin Press.

—— (1988) "ApProppriations and ImProprieties: Problems in the Morphology of Film Narrative," *Cinema Journal* 27(3): 5–20.

—— (1989) *Making Meaning: Inference and Rhetoric in the Interpretation of the Cinema*, Cambridge, MA: Harvard University Press.

Bordwell, David, Staiger, Janet, and Thompson, Kristin (1985) *The Classical Hollywood Cinema*, New York: Columbia University Press.

Branigan, Edward R. (1984) *Point of View in the Cinema: A Theory of Narration and Subjectivity in Classical Film*, The Hague: Mouton.

—— (1985) "Formal Permutations of the Point-of-View Shot," *Screen* 16(3): 54–64.

Brecht, Bertolt (1964) *Brecht on Theatre*, trans. John Willett, New York: Hill & Wang.

Bremond, Claude (1979) *Logique du Récit*, Paris: Editions du Seuil.

Browne, Nick (1979) "Introduction," *Film Reader* 4: 105–7.

—— (1982) *The Rhetoric of Film Narration*, Ann Arbor: University of Michigan Press.

Brunette, Peter and Wills, David (1989) *Screen/Play: Derrida and Film Theory*, Princeton: Princeton University Press.

Burch, Noel (1973) *Theory of Film Practice*, New York: Praeger.

Burgoyne, Robert (1990a) "The Cinematic Narrator: The Logic and Pragmatics of Impersonal Narration," *Journal of Film and Video* 42(1): 3–16.

—— (1990b) *Bertolucci's 1900: A Narrative and Historical Analysis*, Detroit: Wayne State University Press.

Cahiers du Cinéma (eds) (1972) "John Ford's *Young Mister Lincoln*," *Screen* 13(3) (Autumn): 5–94.

Carroll, John M. (1977) "A Program for Film Theory," *Journal of Aesthetics and Art Criticism* (1988) 35(3) (Fall).

Carroll, Noel (1988) *Mystifying Movies: Fads and Fallacies of Contemporary Film Theory*, New York: Columbia University Press.

Casetti, Francesco (1986a) *Dentro lo Squardo, il Filme e il suo Spettatore*, Rome: Bompiani; French trans. (1990) *D'Un Regard l'Autre: Le Film et Son Spectateur*, Lyon: Presses Universitaires de Lyon.

—— (1986b) "Antonioni and Hitchcock: Two Strategies of Narrative Investment," *SubStance* 51: 69–86.

—— (1990) *D'Un Regard l'Autre*, Lyon: Presses Universitaires de Lyon.

Caughie, John (ed.) (1981) *Theories of Authorship*, London: Routledge & Kegan Paul.

Cha, Theresa Hak Kyung (ed.) (1980) *Apparatus*, New York: Tanam Press.

Château, Dominique, Gardies, André and Jost, François (1981) *Cinéma de la Modernity: Films, Théories*, Paris: Klincksieck.

Chatman, Seymour (1978) *Story and Discourse: Narrative Structure in Fiction and Film*, Ithaca, NY: Cornell University Press.

—— (1986a) "Review of *Narration in the Fiction Film*," *Wide Angle* 8(3–4): 139–41.

—— (1986b) "Filter, Center, Slant, and Interest-Focus," *Poetics Today* 7(2): 189–204.

—— (1990) *Coming to Terms: The Rhetoric of Narrative in Fiction and Film*, Ithaca, NY: Cornell University Press.

Chion, Michel (1982) *La Voix au Cinéma*, Paris: *Cahiers du Cinéma*/Editions de l'Etoile.

—— (1985) *Le Son au Cinéma*, Paris: *Cahiers du Cinéma*/Editions de l'Etoile.

—— (1988) *La Toile Trouée*, Paris: *Cahiers du Cinéma*/Editions de l'Etoile.

Chomsky, Noam (1957) *Syntactic Structures*, Hague: Mouton.

224

—— (1975) *Language and Mind*, New York: Harcourt Brace.

Cixous, Hélène and Clement, Catherine (1975) *La Jeune Née*, Paris: Union Générale d'Editions.

Colin, Michel (1985) *Langue, Film, Discours: Prolégomènes à une Sémiologie Générative du Film*, Paris: Klincksieck.

Collet, Jean, Marie, Michel, Percheron, Daniel, Simon, Jean-Paul and Vernet, Marc (1975) *Lectures du Film*, Paris: Albatross.

Comolli, Jean-Louis (1985) "Technique and Ideology: Camera, Perspective, Depth of Field," in Bill Nichols (ed.) *Movies and Methods*, Berkeley: University of California Press.

Communications 23 (1975) Special Issue on "Psychanalyse et Cinéma".

Communications 38 (1983) Special issue on "Enonciation et Cinéma."

Cook, Pam (ed.) (1985) *The Cinema Book*, London: British Film Institute.

Copjec, Joan (1982) "The Anxiety of the Influencing Machine," *October* 23 (Winter): 43–59.

—— (1986) "The Delirium of Clinical Perfection," *Oxford Literary Review* 8(1–2): 57–65.

—— (1989) "The Orthopsychic Subject: Film Theory and the Reception of Lacan,' *October* 49 (Summer): 53–71.

Coward, Rosalind (1976) "Lacan and Signification: An Introduction," *Edinburgh 76 Magazine*: 6–20.

Cowie, Elizabeth (1978) "Woman as Sign," *m/f* 1: 49–63.

—— (1984) "Fantasia," *m/f* 9: 71–105.

Culler, Jonathan (1975) *Structuralist Poetics: Structuralism, Linguistics and the Study of Literature*, Ithaca, NY: Cornell University Press.

—— (1980) "Fabula and Syuzhet in the Analysis of Narrative,' *Poetics Today* 1(3): 27–37.

—— (1981) *The Pursuit of Signs: Semiotics, Literature, Deconstruction*, Ithaca, NY: Cornell University Press.

—— (1982) *On Deconstruction: Theory and Criticism after Structuralism*, Ithaca, NY: Cornell University Press.

Dayan, Daniel (1974) "The Tutor-Code of Classical Cinema," *Film Quarterly* 28(1) (Fall): 22–31.

de Lauretis, Teresa (1985) *Alice Doesn't: Feminism, Semiotics, Cinema*, Bloomington: Indiana University Press.

—— (1987) *Technologies of Gender*, Bloomington: Indiana University Press.

Deleuze, Gilles (1986) *Cinema 1: The Movement-Image*, trans. Hugh Tomlinson and Barbara Habberjam, London: Athlonè Press.

—— (1989) *Cinema 2: The Time-Image*, trans. Hugh Tomlinson and Robert Galeta, Minneapolis: University of Minnesota Press.

Derrida, Jacques (1976) *Of Grammatology*, Baltimore, MD: Johns Hopkins University Press.

—— (1978) *Writing and Difference*, Chicago: University of Chicago Press.

—— (1981a) *Positions*, Chicago: University of Chicago Press.

—— (1981b) *Dissemination*, trans. Barbara Johnson, Chicago: University of Chicago Press.

Doane, Mary Ann (1980) "Misrecognition and Identity," *Cine-tracts* 11 (Fall): 25–32.

—— (1981) "Woman's Stake: Filming the Female Body," *October* 17 (Summer): 23–36.

—— (1982) "Film and the Masquerade: Theorising the Female Spectator," *Screen* 23(3–4) (September–October): 74–88.

—— (1987) *The Desire to Desire*, Bloomington: Indiana University Press.

—— (1988–9) "Masquerade Reconsidered: Further Thoughts on the Female Spectator," *Discourse* 11(1) (Fall/Winter): 42–54.

Doane, Mary Ann, Mellencamp, Patricia and Williams, Linda (eds) (1984) *Re-Vision: Essays in Feminist Film Criticism*, Frederick, MD: University Publications of America and the American Film Institute.

Dolezel, Lubomir (1980) "Truth and Authenticity in Narrative," *Poetics Today* 1(3): 7–26.

Dreyfus, Hubert L. and Rabinow, Paul (1982) *Michel Foucault: Beyond Structuralism and Hermeneutics*, Brighton: Harvester Press.

Eagle, Herbert (1981) *Russian Formalist Film Theory*, Ann Arbor: Michigan Slavic Publications.

Eagleton, Terry (1983) *Literary Theory: An Introduction*, Minnneapolis: University of Minnesota Press.

Eco, Umberto (1976) *A Theory of Semiotics*, Bloomington: Indiana University Press.

—— (1979) *The Role of the Reader: Explorations in the Semiotics of Texts*, Bloomington: Indiana University Press.

—— (1986) *Semiotics and the Philosophy of Language*, Bloomington: Indiana University Press.

Edinburgh 76 Magazine (1976) *Psychoanalysis/Cinema/Avant-Garde* 1.

Ehrlich, Victor (1981) *Russian Formalism: History-Doctrine*, New Haven and London: Yale University Press.

Eikhenbaum, Boris (ed.) (1982) *The Poetics of Cinema*, in *Russian Poetics in Translation* 9, trans. Richard Taylor, Oxford: RPT Publications.

Ellis, John M. (1989) *Against Deconstruction*, Princeton: Princeton University Press.

Elsaesser, Thomas (1983) "Ellipsis in Film," unpublished paper presented at Urbino, Italy, Conference on Semiotics of Film (Summer).

Erens, Patricia (1977) "Sunset Boulevard: A Morphological Analysis," *Film Reader* 2.

Fell, John (1977) "Vladimir Propp in Hollywood," *Film Quarterly* 30 (Spring).

Feuer, Jane (1982) *The Hollywood Musical*, Bloomington: Indiana University Press.

Fink, Guido (1982) "From Showing to Telling: Off-screen Narration in the American Cinema," *Littérature d'América* 3(12): 5–37.

Fiske, John (1989) *Understanding Popular Culture*, Boston: Unwin Hyman.

Flitterman-Lewis, Sandy (1987) "Psychoanalysis, Film, and Television," in *Channels of Discourse*, ed. Robert Allen, Chapel Hill: University of North Carolina Press, 172–210.

—— (1990) *To Desire Differently: Feminism and the French Cinema*, Urbana: University of Illinois Press.

Foster, Hal (ed.) (1983) *The Anti-Aesthetic: Essays on Postmodern Culture*, Port Townsend, WA: Bay Press.

Foucault, Michel (1971) *The Order of Things: An Archeology of the Human Sciences*, New York: Pantheon.

—— (1978) *The History of Sexuality*, New York: Pantheon.

—— (1979) *Discipline and Punishment: Birth of the Prison*, New York: Vintage Books.

Freud, Sigmund (1954) *The Origins of Psychoanalysis: Letters to Wilhelm Fleiss*, New York: Basic Books.

—— (1958) *On Creativity and the Unconscious*, New York: Harper & Row.

—— (1959) *Beyond the Pleasure Principle*, New York: Bantam.

—— (1963a) *Sexuality and the Psychology of Love*, New York: Collier Books. Originally published 1919.

—— (1963b) *Three Case Histories*, New York: Collier Books.

—— (1963c) "Instincts and the Vicissitudes," in *General Psychological Theory*, New York: Collier Books.

—— (1965) *New Introductory Lectures*, New York: W. W. Norton.

Galan, F. W. (1984) "Film as Poetry and Prose: Viktor Shklovsky's Contribution to Poetics of Cinema," *Essays in Poetics*: 95–104.

Garroni, Emilio (1972) *Progetto di Semiotica*, Bari: Laterza.

Gaudreault, André (1987) "Narration and Monstration in the Cinema," *Journal of Film and Video* 39 (Spring): 29–36.

—— (1988) *Du Littéraire au Filmique: Système du Récit*, Paris: Meridiens-Klincksieck and Montreal: Laval.

—— (1989) " 'Je' Narratorial, Je Actorial," unpublished manuscript.

Gaudreault, André and Jost, François (1990) *Le Récit Cinématographique*, Paris: Nathan.

Genette, Gerard (1976) *Mimologiques: Voyages en Cratylie*, Paris: Seuil.

—— (1980) *Narrative Discourse: An Essay in Method*, Ithaca, NY: Cornell University Press.

—— (1982a) *Figures of Literary Discourse*, New York: Columbia University Press.

—— (1982b) *Palimpsestes: La Littérature au Second Degré*, Paris: Seuil.

—— (1988) *Narrative Discourse Revisited*, trans. Jane E. Lewin, Ithaca, NY: Cornell University Press.

Godzich, Wlad (1985) "Foreword," in Thomas Pavel, *The Poetics of Plot*, Minneapolis: University of Minnesota Press.

Greimas, Algirdas Julien (1966) *Sémantique Structurale*, Paris: Larousse.

—— (1971) "Narrative Grammar: Units and Levels," *Modern Language Notes* 86: 793–806.

—— (1970) *Du Sens*, Paris: Seuil.

Greimas, Algirdas Julien and Tesniere, Lucien (1966) *Elements of Structural Syntax*, Paris: Klincksieck.

Gunning, Tom (1991) *D. W. Griffith and the Origins of American Narrative Film*, Urbana: University of Illinois Press.

Hall, Stuart, Hobson, Dorothy, Lowe, Andrew and Willis, Paul (1980) *Culture, Media, Language*, London: Hutchinson.

Harris, Roy and Taylor, Talbot J. (1989) *Landmarks in Linguistic Thought: The Western Tradition from Socrates to Saussure*, London: Routledge.

Harvey, Sylvia (1978) *May 68 and Film Culture*, London: British Film Institute.

Heath, Stephen (1975) "Films and System: Terms of Analysis," Part I, *Screen* 16(1) (Spring): 7–77; Part II, *Screen* 16(2) (Summer): 91–113.

—— (1976) "Screen Images: Film Memory," *Edinburgh 76 Magazine*: 33–42.

—— (1978) "Difference," *Screen* 19(3) (Autumn): 50–127.

—— (1979) "The Turn of the Subject," *Cine-tracts* 7/8 (Summer/Fall): 32–48.

—— (1981) *Questions of Cinema*, Bloomington: Indiana University Press.

—— (1982) *The Sexual Fix*, London: Macmillan.

—— (1986) "Joan Rivière and the Masquerade," in *Formations of Fantasy*, ed. Victor Burgin, James Donald and Cora Kaplan, London: Methuen, 45–61.

Heath, Stephen and de Lauretis, Teresa (eds) (1980) *The Cinematic Apparatus*, London: Macmillan.

Heath, Stephen and Mellencamp, Patricia (eds) (1983) *Cinema and Language*, Frederick, MD: University Publications of America.

Heath, Stephen and Nowell-Smith, Geoffrey (1977) "A Note on 'Family Romance'," *Screen* 18(2) (Summer): 118–19.

Hebdige, Dick (1979) *Subculture: The Meaning of Style*, London: Methuen.

—— (1988) *Hiding in the Light*, London: Routledge.

Henderson, Brian (1983) "Tense, Mood and Voice in Film," *Film Quarterly* (Fall): 4–17.

Hodge, Robert and Kress, Gunther (1988) *Social Semiotics*, Ithaca, NY: Cornell University Press.

Hutcheon, Linda (1984) *Narcissistic Narrative: the Metafictional Paradox*, London: Methuen.

Irigaray, Luce (1977) "Woman's Exile: Interview," *Ideology and Consciousness* 1 (May).

—— (1985a) *Speculum of the Other Woman*, Ithaca, NY: Cornell University Press.

—— (1985b) *This Sex Which is Not One*, Ithaca, NY: Cornell University Press.

Jakobson, Roman (1971) *Selected Writings*, vols I–IV, The Hague: Mouton.

Jakobson, Roman and Halle, Morris (1956) *Fundamentals of Language*, The Hague: Mouton.

Jameson, Fredric (1972) *The Prison-house of Language: A Critical Account of Structuralism and Russian Formalism*, Princeton: Princeton University Press.

—— (1981) *The Political Unconscious: Narrative as a Socially Symbolic Act*, Ithaca, NY: Cornell University Press.

Johnston, Claire (1973) *Notes on Women's Cinema*, London: Society for Education in Film and Television.

—— (1975a) "Femininity and the Masquerade, *Anne of the Indies*," in *Jacques Tourneur*, ed. Claire Johnston and Paul Willemen, London: British Film Institute, 36–44.

Johnston, Claire (ed.) (1975b) *The Work of Dorothy Arzner: Toward a Feminist Cinema*, London: British Film Institute.

Johnston, Claire and Cook, Pam (1974) "The Place of Women in the Cinema of Raoul Walsh," in *Raoul Walsh*, ed. Phil Hardy, Colchester: Vineyard Press, 93–110.

Johnston, Sheila (1985) "Film Narrative and the Structuralist Controversy," in *The Cinema Book*, ed. Pam Cook, London: British Film Institute, 222–50.

Jost, François (1983) "Narration(s): en deçà et au-delà," *Communications* 38: 192–212.

—— (1987) *L'Oeil-caméra – entre Film et Roman*, Lyon: Presses Universitaires.

Kaplan, E. Ann (1982) *Women in Film Noir*, London: British Film Institute.

—— (1985) "Reply to Linda Williams," *Cinema Journal* 24(2) (Winter) 40–3.

—— (1990) *Psychoanalysis and the Cinema*, London: Routledge.

Kaplan, E. Ann (ed.) (1983) *Regarding Television*, Frederick, MD: University Publications of America.

Kinder, Marsha (1989–90) "The Subversive Potential of the Pseudo-Iterative," *Film Quarterly*: 2–16.

Kitses, Jim (1969) *Horizons West*, London: Secker & Warburg/British Film Institute.

Kozloff, Sarah (1988) *Invisible Storytellers*, Berkeley: University of California Press.

Kristeva, Julia (1969) *Semeiotike: Recherches pour une Semanalyse*, Paris: Editions du Seuil.

—— (1980) *Desire in Language*, New York: Columbia University Press.

—— (1984) *Revolution in Poetic Language*, New York: Columbia University Press.

Kuhn, Annette (1982) *Women's Pictures: Feminism and Cinema*, London: Routledge.

—— (1984) "Women's Genres: Melodrama, Soap Opera, and Theory," *Screen* 25(1) (1) (January–February): 18–28.

Kuntzel, Thierry (1980a) "The Film-Work, 2," *Camera Obscura* 5 (Spring): 6–69.

—— (1980b) "Sight, Insight, and Power: Allegory of a Cave," *Camera Obscura* 6 (Fall): 90–110.

Lacan, Jacques (1975) *Seminar XX*, reprinted in Juliet Mitchell and Jacqueline Rose (eds) (1982) *Feminine Sexuality: Jacques Lacan and the Ecole Freudienne*, New York, W. W. Norton.

—— (1977) *Ecrits: A Selection*, New York: W. W. Norton.

—— (1979) *The Four Fundamentals of Psycho-Analysis*, New York: W. W. Norton.

Lagny, Michele, Ropars-Wuilleumier, Marie-Claire and Sorlin, Pierre (1976a) *Octobre: Ecriture et Idéologie*, Paris: Albatross.

—— (1976b) *La Révolution Figurée: Film, Histoire, Politique*, Paris: Albatross.

Laplanche, J. and Pontalis, J.-B. (1973) *The Language of Psychoanalysis*, trans. Donald Nicholson-Smith, New York: Norton.

Lapsley, Robert and Westlake, Michael (1988) *Film Theory: An Introduction*, Manchester: Manchester University Press.

Lebel, J. P. (1971) *Cinéma et Idéologie*, Paris: Editions Sociales.

Lemon, Lee T. and Reis, Marion J. (eds) (1965) *Russian Formalist Criticism: Four Essays*, Lincoln, Nebraska: Nebraska University Press.

Lentricchia, Frank and McLaughlin, Thomas (eds) (1990) *Criticial Terms for Literary Study*, Chicago: University of Chicago Press.

Lévi-Strauss, Claude (1967) *Structural Anthropology*, trans. Claire Jacobson and Brooke Grundfest Schoepf, Garden City, NY: Doubleday.

—— (1969) *The Raw and the Cooked*, trans. John and Doreen Weightman, New York: Harper & Row.

Lotman, Jurij (1976) *Semiotics of Cinema*, trans. Mark E. Suino, Ann Arbor: Michigan Slavic Contributions.

Lovell, Terry (1980) *Pictures of Reality: Aesthetics, Politics and Pleasure*, London: British Film Institute.

Lyon, Elisabeth (1980) "The Cinema of Lol V. Stein," *Camera Obscura* 6: 6–41.

Lyotard, Jean-François (1984) *The Postmodern Condition*, trans. Geoff Bennington and Brian Massumi, Manchester: Manchester University Press.

MacCabe, Colin (1985) *Tracking the Signifier: Theoretical Essays: Film, Linguistics, Literature*, Minneapolis: University of Minnesota Press.

Macksey, Richard and Donato, Eugenio (eds) (1972) *The Structuralist Controversy*, Baltimore, MD: Johns Hopkins University Press.

Mannoni, Octave (1969) *Clefs pour l'Imaginaire*, Paris: Editions du Seuil.

Marie, Michel and Vernet, Marc (1990) *Christian Metz et la Théorie du Cinéma*, Paris: Meridiens-Klincksieck.

Marks, Elaine and de Courtivron, Isabelle (eds) (1980) *New French Feminism*, Amherst: University of Massachusetts Press.

Martinez-Bonati, Felix (1981) *Fictive Discourse and the Structures of Literature*, Ithaca, NY: Cornell University Press.

Matejka, Ladislav and Titunik, Irwin R. (eds) (1976) *Semiotics of Art: Prague School Contributions*, Cambridge, MA: MIT Press.

Metz, Christian (1971, 1972) *Essais sur la Signification au Cinéma*, vols I and II, Paris: Klincksieck.

—— (1974a) *Film Language: A Semiotics of the Cinema*, New York: Oxford University Press.

—— (1974b) *Language and Cinema*, The Hague: Mouton.

—— (1975) "The Imaginary Signifier," *Screen* 16(2) (Summer): 14–76.

—— (1976) "History/Discourse: Note on Two Voyeurisms," *Edinburgh 76 Magazine*: 21–5.

—— (1977) *Essais Sémiotiques*, Paris: Klincksieck.

—— (1979) "The Cinematic Apparatus as Social Institution: An Interview," *Discourse* 1 (Fall): 6–37.

—— (1982) *The Imaginary Signifier: Psychoanalysis and the Cinema*, Bloomington: Indiana University Press.

—— (1991) *L'Enonciation impersonelle ou le Site du Film*, Paris: Klincksieck.

Miller, Jacques-Alain (1977–8) "Suture," *Screen* 18(4) (Winter): 24–34.

Mitchell, Juliet (1975) *Psychoanalysis and Feminism*, New York: Vintage Books.

Mitchell, Juliet and Rose, Jacqueline (eds) (1982) *Feminine Sexuality: Jacques Lacan and the Ecole Freudienne*, New York: W. W. Norton.

Montrelay, Michelle (1978) "Inquiry into Femininity," *m/f* 1: 83–101.

Mulvey, Laura (1975) "Visual Pleasure and Narrative Cinema," *Screen* 16(3) (Autumn): 6–18.

—— (1981) "Afterthoughts on 'Visual Pleasure and Narrative Cinema' inspired by *Duel in the Sun*," *Framework* 15–17: 12–15.

—— (1989) *Visual and Other Pleasures*, Bloomington: Indiana University Press.

Nasemore, James and Brantlinger, Patrick (eds) (1991) *Modernity and Mass Culture*, Bloomington: Indiana University Press.

Nash, Mark (1976) "*Vampyr* and the Fantastic," *Screen* 17(3): 29–67.

Nattiez, J. J. (1975) *Fondements d'une Sémiologie de la Musique*, Paris: Union Générale d'Editions.

Neale, Steve (1985) *Cinema and Technology: Image, Sound, Colour*, Bloomington: Indiana University Press.

Nichols, Bill (1981) *Ideology and the Image*, Bloomington: Indiana University Press.

Nichols, Bill (ed.) (1985) *Movies and Methods*, vols I and II, Berkeley: University of California Press.

Nochlin, Linda (1971) *Realism*, Harmondsworth: Penguin Books.

Noguez, Dominque (ed.) (1973) *Cinéma, Théorie, Lectures*, Paris: Klincksieck.

Norris, Christopher (1982) *Deconstruction: Theory and Practice*, London and New York: Methuen.

—— (1987) *Derrida*, Cambridge, MA: Harvard University Press.

Norris, Christopher and Benjamin, Andrew (1988) *What is Deconstruction?*, New York: St Martin's Press.

Nowell-Smith, Geoffrey (1968) *Visconti*, Garden City, NY: Doubleday.

—— (1976) "A Note on History/Discourse," *Edinburgh 76 Magazine*: 26–32.

Odin, Roger (1977) "Dix Années d'Analyses Textuelles de Films. Bibliographie Analytiques," special issue of *Linguistique et Sémiologie*, 3.

—— (1983) "Pour une Sémio-Pragmatique du Cinéma," *Iris*, 1(1).

O'Sullivan, Tim, Fiske, John, Hartley, John and Saunders, Danny (1983) *Key Concepts in Communication*, London and New York: Methuen.

Oudart, Jean-Pierre (1977–8) "Cinema and Suture," *Screen* 18(4) (Winter): 35–47.

Palmer, R. Barton (ed.) (1989) *The Cinematic Text: Methods and Approaches*, New York: AMS Press.

Panofsky, Erwin (1939) *Studies in Iconology*, Oxford: Oxford University Press.

Pasolini, Pier Paolo (1976) "The Cinema of Poetry," in Bill Nichols, *Movies and Methods* I, Berkeley: University of California Press.

Pavel, Thomas (1985) *The Poetics of Plot: The Case of English Renaissance Drama*, Minneapolis: University of Minnesota Press.

Peirce, Charles Sanders (1931) *Collected Papers*, vols I–VIII, ed. Charles Hartshorne and Paul Weiss, Cambridge, MA: Harvard University Press.

Penley, Constance (1977) "The Avant-Garde and Its Imaginary," *Camera Obscura* 2 (Fall): 2–33.

—— (1985) "Feminism, Film Theory, and the Bachelor Machines," *m/f* 10: 39–59.

—— (1989) *The Future of an Illusion: Film, Feminism and Psychoanalysis*, Minneapolis: University of Minnesota Press.

BIBLIOGRAPHY

Penley, Constance (ed.) (1988) *Feminism and Film Theory*, London: Routledge.

Piaget, Jean (1970) *Structuralism*, trans. and ed. Chaninah Maschler, New York: Harper/Colophon.

Pines, Jim and Willemen, Paul (1989) *Questions of Third Cinema*, London: British Film Institute.

Plato (1963) *The Republic*, in *The Collected Dialogues of Plato*, ed. Edith Hamilton and Huntington Cairns, New York: Pantheon.

Polan, Dana (1986) *Power and Paranoia: History, Narrative and the American Cinema, 1940–1950*, New York: Columbia University Press.

Prince, Gerald (1987) *A Dictionary of Narratology*, Lincoln: University of Nebraska Press.

Propp, Vladimir (1968) *Morphology of the Folk Tale*, Austin: University of Texas Press.

—— (1976) "Study of the Folktale: Structure and History," *Dispositio* 1(3): 277–92.

Riffaterre, Michel (1979) *La Production du Texte*, Paris: Editions du Seuil.

—— (1982) *Sémiotique de la Poésie*, Paris: Editions du Seuil.

Rimmon-Kenan, Shlomith (1983) *Narrative Fiction: Contemporary Poetics*, London: Methuen.

Rivière, Joan (1966) "Womanliness as Masquerade," in *Psychoanalysis and Female Sexuality*, ed. Hendrik M. Ruitenbeek, New Haven, CT: College and University Press, 209–20.

Rodowick, D. N. (1982) "The Difficulty of Difference," *Wide Angle* 5(1): 4–15.

—— (1988) *The Crisis of Political Modernism: Criticism and Ideology in Contemporary Film Theory*, Urbana: University of Illinois Press.

Ropars-Wuilleumier, Marie-Claire (1981) *Le Texte Divisé*, Paris: Presses Universitaires de France.

Rose, Jacqueline (1986) *Sexuality in the Field of Vision*, London: Verso.

Rosen, Philip (ed.) (1986) *Narrative, Apparatus, Ideology: A Film Theory Reader*, New York: Columbia University Press.

Rothman, William (1975) "Against 'The System of the Suture'," *Film Quarterly* 29(1) (Fall): 45–50.

Ryan, Marie-Laure (1981) "The Pragmatics of Personal and Impersonal Narration," *Poetics* 10: 517–39.

—— (1984) "Fiction as a Logical, Ontological and Illocutionary Issue," *Style* 18(2): 121–39.

Ryan, Michael (1982) *Marxism and Deconstruction: A Critical Articulation*, Baltimore, MD: Johns Hopkins University Press.

Ryan, Michael and Kellner, Douglas (1988) *Camera Politica: The Politics and Ideology of Contemporary Hollywood Film*, Bloomington: Indiana University Press.

Saussure, Ferdinand de (1966) *Course in General Linguistics*, trans. Wade Baskin, New York: McGraw Hill.

Schaeffer, Pierre (1966) *Traité des Objets musicaux*, Paris: Editions du Seuil.

Schefer, Jean-Louis (1981) *L'Homme Ordinaire du Cinéma*, Paris: Gallimard.

Scholes, Robert (1974) *Structuralism in Literature: An Introduction*, New Haven, CT: Yale University Press.

Screen Reader I (1977) London: SEFT.

Screen Reader II (1981) London: SEFT.

Sebeok, T. A. (ed.) (1960) *Style in Language*, Cambridge, MA: Harvard University Press.

Shklovsky, Victor (1927) "Poetry and Prose in Cinema," in *Poetika Kino*, Leningrad: Kinopechat. Also in *The Poetics of Cinema*, ed. Richard Taylor, Oxford: RTL Publications, 1982.

231

Shohat, Ella and Stam, Robert (1985) "The Cinema after Babel: Language, Difference, Power," *Screen* 26(3–4) (May-August).

Silverman, Kaja (1983) *The Subject of Semiotics*, New York: Oxford University Press.

—— (1985) "A Voice to Match: The Female Voice in Classical Cinema" *Iris* 3(1): 57–70.

—— (1988) *The Acoustic Mirror: The Female Voice in Psychoanalysis and Cinema*, Bloomington: Indiana University Press.

Spivak, Gayatri Chakravorty (1987) *In Other Worlds: Essays in Cultural Politics*, New York: Routledge.

Stam, James H. (1976) *Inquiries into the Origin of Language*, New York: Harper & Row.

Stam, Robert (1985) *Reflexivity in Film and Literature: From Don Quixote to Jean-Luc Godard*, Ann Arbor: University of Michigan Press.

—— (1989) *Subversive Pleasures: Bakhtin, Cultural Criticism and Film*, Baltimore, MD: Johns Hopkins University Press.

Studlar, Gaylyn (1988) *In The Realm of Pleasure*, Urbana: University of Illinois Press.

Thompson, Kristin (1981) *Ivan the Terrible: A New Formalist Analysis*, Princeton: Princeton University Press.

—— (1988) *Breaking the Glass Armor*, Princeton: Princeton University Press.

Todorov, Tzvetan (1977) *The Poetics of Prose*, Ithaca, NY: Cornell University Press.

Ulmer, Gregory (1985) *Applied Grammatology*, Baltimore, MD: Johns Hopkins University Press.

Vanoye, Francis (1989) *Récit Ecrit/Récit Filmique*, Paris: Nathan.

Vernet, Marc (1988) *Figures de l'Absence*, Paris: Cahiers du Cinéma.

Volosinov, V. N. (1973) *Marxism and the Philosophy of Language*, trans. Ladislav Matejka and I. R. Titunik, Cambridge, MA: Harvard University Press.

Vygotsky, Lev (1987) *Thought and Language*, Cambridge, MA: MIT Press.

Waugh, Patricia (1984) *Metafiction: the Theory and Practice of Self-conscious Fiction*, London: Methuen.

Weis, Elizabeth and Belton, John (1985) *Theory and Practice of Film Sound*, New York: Columbia University Press.

Wide Angle (1986) 8(3–4) "Narrative/Non-narrative," Baltimore, MD: Johns Hopkins University Press.

Williams, Linda (1981) *Figures of Desire*, Urbana: University of Illinois Press.

—— (1984) " 'Something Else Besides a Mother': *Stella Dallas* and the Maternal Melodrama," *Cinema Journal* 24(1) (Fall): 2–27.

Williams, Raymond (1983) *Keywords: A Vocabulary of Culture and Society*, New York: Oxford University Press.

Williamson, Judith (1978) *Decoding Advertisements: Ideology and Meaning in Advertising*, London: Marion Boyars.

Wilson, George M. (1986) *Narration in Light*, Baltimore, MD: Johns Hopkins University Press.

Wollen, Peter (1969) *Signs and Meanings in the Cinema*, Bloomington and London: Indiana University Press.

—— (1982) *Readings and Writings: Semiotic Counter Strategies*, London: Verso.

Wright, Will (1975) *Sixguns and Society*, Berkeley: University of California Press.

Xavier, Ismail (1977) *O Discurso Cinematografico*, Rio de Janeiro: Paz e Terra.

—— (1983) *A Experiencia do Cinema*, Rio de Janeiro: Graal.

INDEX OF TERMS

236

Clinical
Hypertension

SECOND EDITION

in Practice

Sern Lim

University Department of Medicine, City
Hospital NHS Trust, Birmingham, UK

© 2003, 2007 Royal Society of Medicine Press Ltd

2003 First edition

2007 Second edition

Published by the Royal Society of Medicine Press Ltd

1 Wimpole Street, London W1G 0AE, UK

Tel: +44 (0) 20 7290 2921

Fax: +44 (0) 20 7290 2929

Email: publishing@rsm.ac.uk

Website: www.rsmpress.co.uk

British Library Cataloguing in Publication Data

A catalogue record for this book is available from the British Library

ISBN 1-85315-659-0

ISSN 1473 6845

Distribution in Europe and Rest of World:

Marston Book Services Ltd

PO Box 269

Abingdon

Oxon OX14 4YN, UK

Tel: +44 (0) 1235 465 500

Fax: +44 (0) 1235 465 555

Email: direct.order@marston.com

Distribution in Australia and New Zealand:

Elsevier Australia

30–52 Smidmore Street

Marrickville NSW 2204

Australia

Tel: + 61 2 9517 8999

Fax: + 61 2 9517 2249

Email: service@elsevier.com.au

Distribution in the USA and Canada:

Royal Society of Medicine Press Ltd

c/o BookMasters, Inc

30 Amberwood Parkway

Ashland, Ohio 44805, USA

Tel: +1 800 247 6553 / +1 800 266 5564

Fax: +1 419 281 6883

E-mail: order@bookmasters.com

Typeset by Phoenix Photosetting, Chatham, Kent

Printed and bound in Spain by Liberdúplex

Foreword

The guidelines for the management of hypertension have progressively redefined this condition over the last few decades. Systemic hypertension, as it is now defined, encompasses a larger proportion of the population, but its significance as a cardiovascular risk factor is by no means diminished. Indeed, hypertension remains the major risk factor for cardiovascular morbidity and mortality. It is perhaps not surprising, therefore, that some of the largest clinical studies in recent years have been devoted to the management of high blood pressure. The data from these studies have prompted the release of new practice guidelines by the British Hypertension Society, the Joint British Societies and a further update by the National Institute for Health and Clinical Excellence.

This second edition of *Clinical Hypertension in Practice* builds on the strengths of the previous edition, with a new, young, dynamic author. The succinct description of the epidemiology, pathophysiology and clinical management of patients with hypertension is complemented by a clear summary of contemporary practice guidelines. This second edition should be of clear value to general practitioners, hospital doctors, students and nurses.

Gregory YH Lip

Professor of Cardiovascular Medicine
University Department of Medicine
City Hospital, Birmingham
UK

About the author

Hoong Sern Lim MD MRCP (London) is a Specialist Registrar in Cardiology at the West Midlands Deanery, UK. He has interests in clinical (diabetes, hypertension and heart failure) and basic science research (vascular biology), and has published numerous times on these subjects. He is a member of the European Society of Cardiology's Working Group on Pathogenesis of Atherosclerosis.

Preface

Interest in the arterial pulse and blood pressure date back hundreds, if not thousands of years. However, it was not until the pioneering work of Hales in 1733 and the description of stethoscopic sounds by Korotkoff in 1905 (and no less significant contributions of many others in the intervening years) that blood pressure measurement became established. These pioneering works thus allowed the study of the arterial blood pressure to grow from anecdotal to objective. Epidemiological studies that followed only a few decades later established high blood pressure as a major risk factor for cardiovascular disease.

Hamilton, Thompson and Wisniewski first published a clinical trial on the treatment of high blood pressure in 1964. This study signalled the beginning of an era of large placebo-controlled trials in the treatment of hypertension, which coincided with the development of new antihypertensive therapy, most notably the calcium channel blockers, angiotensin-converting enzyme inhibitors and angiotensin II receptor blockers. These clinical trials have shaped, and continue to shape, contemporary clinical guidelines. Indeed, the British Hypertension Society guidelines for the management of hypertension have undergone several revisions since Swales chaired the working party that prepared the Society's first report in 1989.

This book provides an overview of the historical, pathophysiological and clinical aspects of hypertension. The chapters on the diagnosis and management (both pharmacological and non-pharmacological) incorporate the British Hypertension Society (2004) and the Joint British Societies (2005) guidelines, and the most recent guidance update by the National Institute for Health and Clinical Excellence (NICE) and British Hypertension Society in 2006.

Sern Lim
September 2006

Contents

1. Historical background

The description of a 'hard pulse disease' dates back as far back as 2600 BC. In 1555, Joseph Struthius first described a primitive method of quantifying blood pressure by determining the number of objects that have to be placed to suppress the arterial pulsation. However, it was not until the series of experiments by Stephen Hales in the early 1700s that the basis of blood pressure measurement became established. Hales measured pressure in the leg and neck vessels of various animals and meticulously documented his observations. For example:

> 'In the larger horse and ox, the blood pressure is higher and the pulse slower than in the smaller sheep and dog'
> 'With blood loss, the pulse quickens and weakens and the blood pressure falls'
> 'Horses died when the blood pressure fell below 2 feet of blood'
> 'Blood pressure is increased during systole'

In the 1830s, with only a candle, a spoon, some acid (to distinguish phosphate from albumin) and pioneering clinical-pathological studies, Richard Bright was able to demonstrate the link between albuminuria, a hardened pulse and hypertrophy of the heart, particularly affecting the left ventricle. However, he had no means to quantify the blood pressure. This link between blood pressure and 'Bright's disease' (nephritis) was only described later by Frederick Mohamed in the 1870s with his modified sphygmograph. With his sphygmograph, Mohamed was able to document the presence of 'morbid arterial tension' in the absence of albuminuria. He called this 'chronic Bright's disease without albuminuria', now more familiar to us as essential hypertension. Mohamed also noted changes in the pulse waveform in persons with elevated arterial pressure and the elderly ('the tidal wave is prolonged and too much sustained'), which formed the basis of 'premature arterial senility'.

During this period, William Gull and Henry Sutton (in 1872) described the pathological changes in the kidneys in advanced stages of Bright's disease. They called the lesions 'arterio-capillary fibrosis', corresponding to arteriosclerosis of today. They also noted the presence of these lesions in other organs, including the heart, which was always hypertrophied. Gull and Sutton considered the arterio-capillary fibrosis an affection of the whole arterial system. Hence, the clinical and pathological changes in hypertensive disease were recognized by the end of the 19th century, and the study of arterial blood pressure was ready for the transition from the anecdotal to the objective.

The early years of the 20th century witnessed the introduction of the cuff sphygmomanometer and the seminal work by Nikolai Korotkoff. In 1905, Korotkoff presented his new method of measuring blood pressure at a scientific seminar of the Imperial Military Medical Academy in St Petersburg, Russia. In his studies, Korotkoff used Riva-Rocci's technique, first proposed in 1896, which involved an arm-encircling inflatable elastic cuff, a rubber bulb to inflate the cuff and a mercury sphygmomanometer. Riva-Rocci used this apparatus to measure systolic blood pressure by palpating the radial pulse. In 1897, Hill and Barnard reported a similar arm-encircling inflatable cuff apparatus to measure systolic blood pressure using a needle pressure gauge instead of palpation. Korotkoff's method, however, was a significant improvement over these other two techniques as it allowed measurement of diastolic blood pressure and, with the auscultatory technique, offered greater accuracy. Indeed, systolic blood pressure by Korotkoff's techniques was consistently 10–12 mmHg higher than the palpation method because generation of the pulse required filling of the vessel.

Korotkoff's contribution proved to be the catalyst in hypertension research. His method was widely received and quickly became a standard medical procedure. By 1916, data had been presented to show the relationship between risk of death and systolic blood pressure in asymptomatic individuals. Numerous epidemiological studies followed, clearly documenting the risk of high blood pressure.

At the same time, the treatment of hypertension developed apace. Early use of sodium thiocyanate and sympathectomy in the early 20th century to treat high blood pressure was unsurprisingly unpopular. The first major breakthrough came serendipitously when researchers working with the antibiotic sulphanilamide noted increased diuresis in their patients, which led to the development of chlorothiazide in the 1950s. Also in the 1950s and '60s, Sir James Black, building upon the work by Raymond Ahlquist in 1948 on adrenergic receptors, pioneered research into pharmacological intervention of the adrenergic system, which culminated in the development of beta-blockers. The first beta-blocker, propranolol, was introduced in 1964. The development of angiotensin-converting enzyme (ACE) inhibitors also started in the 1960s when an ACE inhibitor prototype was isolated from the Brazilian pit viper venom. In 1975, Cushman and Ondetti manipulated the carboxypeptidase A inhibitor and produced the first synthetic inhibitor of ACE, captopril.

By the middle part of the 20th century, the growing epidemiological data on the hazards of high blood pressure and emergence of (then untested) therapeutic agents set the scene for clinical trials for the treatment of asymptomatic patients with hypertension. In 1958, Hamilton and colleagues started the recruitment of patients for the first controlled trial with ganglion-blocking drugs (later replaced with methyldopa) and thiazide diuretics. Their landmark study of 61 patients was published in 1964 and demonstrated the benefit of blood pressure treatment. It was followed by a series of (much larger) studies, which have shaped contemporary guidelines for the treatment of blood pressure and hypertension.

Further reading

Beevers DG. The 40th anniversary of the publication in 1964 of the first trial of the treatment of uncomplicated, severe hypertension by Hamilton, Thompson and Wisniewski. *J Hum Hypertens* 2004; **18**: 831–3.

Shevchenko YL, Tsitlik JE. 90th anniversary of the development by Nikolai S Korotkoff of the auscultatory method of measuring blood pressure. *Circulation* 1996; **94**: 116–18.

2. Blood pressure and hypertension

Blood pressure and cardiovascular risk
Prevalence of hypertension
Aetiology of hypertension

Blood pressure and cardiovascular risk

Hypertension is a common problem and a major preventable cardiovascular risk factor. Worldwide prevalence estimates for hypertension may be as high as a billion individuals, with deaths attributable to hypertension estimated to be approximately 1.7 million deaths per year. The prevalence (and incidence) of hypertension and associated morbidity and mortality are likely to rise with the increasing epidemic of obesity and as the population ages.

In the vast majority, hypertension is asymptomatic until complications occur. These complications include cerebrovascular disease, heart disease, peripheral vascular disease, renal failure and retinopathy – target organ damage. The benefit of blood pressure (BP) lowering is now well established, but the 'rule of halves' still dominates – roughly half of patients with hypertension are identified; only half of them are actually treated; and only half of these have adequate blood pressure control (Figure 2.1).

> Complications of hypertension include stroke, heart disease, peripheral vascular disease, renal failure and retinopathy

Defining hypertension and cardiovascular risk

Hypertension can be defined pragmatically as 'that level of BP above which the use of antihypertensive treatment does more good than harm'. This level will vary from patient to patient and balances the risks of untreated hypertension with those of long-term exposure to antihypertensive drugs and their side-effects. Hence, the diagnosis and treatment of hypertension must be individualized – the higher the patient's cardiovascular disease (CVD) risk, the greater the (absolute) benefit of BP reduction and the lower the threshold for BP treatment will be accordingly.

Indeed, this recognition of high BP in the context of a patient's overall CVD risk is central to the current recommendations by the second Joint British Societies guidelines, which advise antihypertensive treatment based on the 10-year CVD risk (replacing the previous coronary heart disease (CHD) risk) of ≥ 20% according to the current Joint British Societies risk assessment chart (Figure 2.2, inside front cover). There is a strong 'additive' effect of other risk factors such as diabetes, hyperlipidaemia, smoking and gender to the overall risk profile and thus a multifactorial approach should be considered. The charts are based on the Framingham risk function and specify three levels of 10-year CVD risk: ≥30%, ≥20% and ≤10%, which are equivalent to a CHD

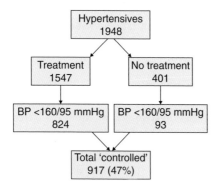

Figure 2.1
Hypertension in general practice in England, illustrating the 'rule of halves'. (Adapted from Poulter et al. Blood Pressure 1996; **5**: 209–15.)

risk of 23%, 15% and 8% respectively. These three groups are represented by three colour bands on the chart for easy use. The information needed to assess scores is shown in Table 2.1.

Table 2.1
Use of the Joint British Societies CVD risk chart (see inside front cover)

Information needed:	Age
	Sex
	Systolic BP (mmHg)
	Smoking status
	Serum cholesterol (any units)
	HDL cholesterol (same units as serum cholesterol)

The 10-year absolute CVD risk now replaces the CHD risk assessment. The CVD end-points include fatal/non-fatal myocardial infarction or angina plus stroke (fatal/non-fatal stroke and intracerebral haemorrhage) or transient ischaemic attack. Diabetes status is no longer included into the risk chart as most patients with diabetes have estimated 10-year CVD risk of ≥20%, and therefore considered at high risk.

Blood pressure should be considered in the context of overall cardiovascular risk

---

From a population perspective, hypertension is defined as sustained systolic BP between 140 and 159 mmHg or sustained diastolic BP between 90 and 99 mmHg. The British Hypertension Society (BHS) and the American Joint National Committee on prevention, detection, evaluation, and treatment of high BP (JNC-VII) guidelines are concordant in this regard. However, the broader blood pressure classification remains divergent between guidelines (see Table 2.3).

Hypertension and cardiovascular risk

There almost appears to be a dose–response relationship between hypertension and the risk of stroke or CHD; conversely, the reduction of BP by antihypertensive treatment reduces the risk of stroke and heart attacks (Figure 2.3).

In 1990, MacMahon et al. analysed nine prospective longitudinal observational studies from North America and Europe consisting of untreated middle-aged and predominantly (96%) male populations, totalling 4.2 million person-years of observation. After a mean follow-up of 10 years, this meta-analysis confirmed the positive, continuous, independent association of stroke and coronary risk with high BP throughout its range. The data suggest that a 5–6 mmHg reduction in the average level of diastolic BP would be associated with an approximately 40% reduction in stroke and a 20–25% reduction in CHD. Crucially, there was no evidence of a threshold between 'normal' BP and the pressure associated with higher risk. Furthermore, there was very little evidence in untreated populations of a so-called 'J-curve', where increased risk might be seen in individuals with low BPs. A more recent meta-analysis of 61 prospective studies by Lewington et al. reaffirms this dose–response relationship between blood pressure and cardiovascular mortality.

Reducing the average level of diastolic BP by 5–6 mmHg would give a 40% reduction in stroke and a 20–25% reduction in CHD

A lower level of risk appears to be present in women, at least below the age of 55 years. Also, in the Eastern Stroke and Coronary Heart Disease Collaborative Research Group study (1998) a different ratio between heart attacks and strokes is seen among Far Eastern populations.

In the Multiple Risk Factor Intervention Trial, a cross-tabulation of systolic and diastolic BPs found that relative risk of CHD would increase progressively as follows:

- 1.0 with optimal levels of BP (regular systolic BP <120 mmHg, diastolic BP <80 mmHg)
- 3.23 in isolated diastolic hypertension (diastolic BP >100 mmHg, systolic BP <120 mmHg)

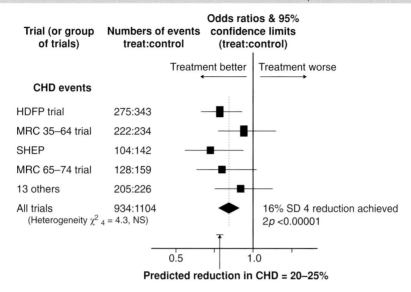

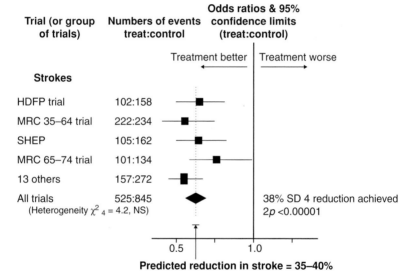

Figure 2.3
The effect of treating hypertension on the risk of suffering from coronary heart disease or stroke. CHD, coronary heart disease.

- 4.19 in people with isolated systolic hypertension (systolic BP >160 mmHg and diastolic BP <80 mmHg)
- 4.57 in those with a combined increase of both systolic and diastolic BP (systolic BP >160 mmHg, diastolic BP >100 mmHg).

This is illustrated in Figure 2.4. The corresponding rise of stroke risk is also shown.

There has been some debate on the relative importance of systolic and diastolic blood pressure, but in practice systolic blood pressure

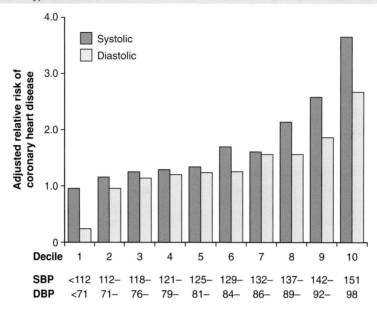

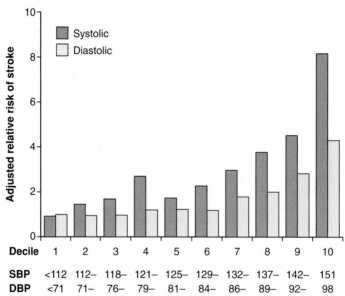

Figure 2.4
How increasing systolic and diastolic blood pressures affect the relative risk of coronary heart disease and stroke. SBP, systolic blood pressure; DBP, diastolic blood pressure. (Adapted from Stamler *et al. Arch Int Med* 1993; **153**: 598–615; He *et al. J Hypertens* 1999; **17**: 7–13.)

should be regarded as the more important. In epidemiological studies both systolic and diastolic blood pressure are important risk factors for cardiovascular disease. Certainly, systolic blood pressure is a better predictor of cardiovascular mortality and morbidity even correcting for underlying diastolic blood pressure. Figure 2.4 clearly shows the greater effect of systolic blood pressure compared to diastolic on relative risk of CHD.

Geoffrey Rose and the population approach to cardiovascular risk

In a population, BP is a continuous variable, distributed in a roughly normal (or Gaussian) manner. There are not two separate groups of individuals (that is, those with and without hypertension) but a continuous range of BP from the lowest to the highest, with the majority of individuals falling somewhere in the middle. Although those with very high blood pressures are individually at very high risk of stroke and CHD, there are relatively few of them. Treating all these patients with severe hypertension would have little impact on the number of strokes and heart attacks occurring in the population as a whole, as most strokes and heart attacks occur in those with only mildly elevated or even normal BP. On the other hand, small reductions in BP of the population as a whole may result in greater numbers of cardiovascular events in the population. This population strategy is based on the axiom by the British epidemiologist Geoffrey Rose that 'a large number of people at small risk may give rise to more cases than a small number of people at high risk'.

> BP is a continuous variable distributed in a fairly normal manner. There are not two groups – people with and without hypertension – but a continuous range of BPs with most people falling somewhere in the middle

The 'population approach' to managing hypertension suggests that reducing the mean BP of the population as a whole by only a few mmHg using public health measures (such as reducing salt intake and increasing exercise) would significantly reduce the rate of stroke and CHD when compared to a strategy of achieving large reductions in BP in only a few individuals with severe hypertension.

However, contemporary medical practice has evolved from a single risk factor approach to an emphasis on CVD risk, which incorporates the assessment of multiple risk factors. This led to a recent re-examination of Rose's classic axiom by Manuel and colleagues. They reported on the estimated effectiveness of the population strategy compared to a single risk factor approach (in this case, targeting lipid-lowering treatment in patients with high cholesterol levels) and a cardiovascular risk approach (targeting treatment at patients with the highest CVD risk). Based on their results, the strategy of targeting individuals at highest CVD risk was by far the most effective. Their study lends support to the current recommendations for a CVD risk guided approach to the management of patients with cardiovascular risk factors, including hypertension.

> The strategy of targeting individuals at highest CVD risk is by far the most effective

Prevalence of hypertension

Using a definition of a systolic BP >140 mmHg or a diastolic BP >90 mmHg or current treatment with antihypertensive medication, the prevalence of hypertension in the US population varies from 4% in 18–29-year-olds to 65% in those aged 80 years and over. Data from the Birmingham Factory Screen project are illustrated in Figure 2.5. This shows the rise in blood pressure with age, as well as ethnic differences.

Nevertheless, hypertension is not distributed evenly in the community, and even in the UK there are variations with geography. For example, in a survey of 24 large towns, the lowest mean BP was found in Shrewsbury, while the highest was in Dunfermline where the BP (systolic/diastolic) was on average 17/11 mmHg higher.

Systolic blood pressure also rises steadily with increasing age, and the prevalence of hypertension including isolated systolic hypertension (systolic BP ≥ 160/diastolic BP <90 mmHg) is more than 50% in those aged

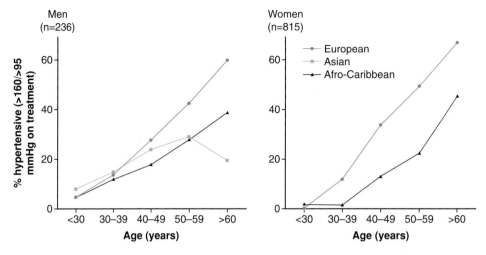

Figure 2.5
How age, gender and ethnicity affect hypertension. (Adapted from Lane *et al. J Hum Hypertens* 2002; **16**: 267–73.)

over 60 years. Isolated systolic hypertension is the predominant form of hypertension found in the older population (Figure 2.6). In premenopausal women, hypertension has a lower prevalence in women than in men, but beyond the age of 65 years, the mean systolic BP in women at least approaches that seen in older men, and has occasionally been reported

to be even higher, with overall prevalence estimated at 30–50% in women aged 65 years or older. Indeed, hypertension is an important contributor to morbidity and mortality in postmenopausal women in Western countries (Figure 2.7).

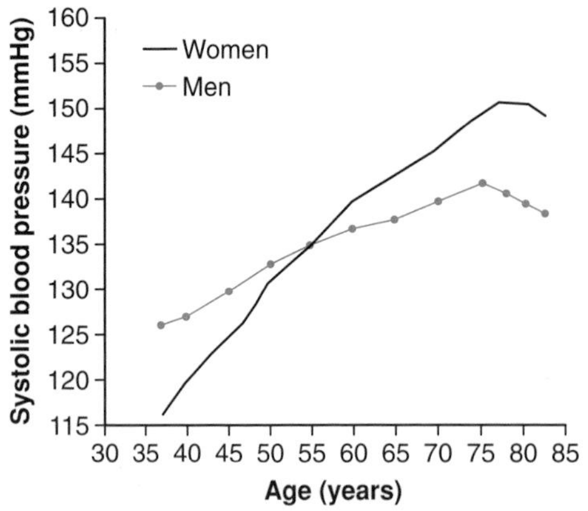

Many patients with 'high normal' blood pressure levels will progress to overt hypertension. In the Framingham Heart Study, 9845 non-hypertensive patients were followed up for 4 years, and their blood pressures were initially classified as: optimum (SBP<120 and DBP<80 mmHg), normal (SBP 120–9 or DBP 80–4 mmHg) or high normal (SBP 130–9 or DBP 85–9 mmHg). The proportions progressing to >140/90 are illustrated in Table 2.2.

These findings support recommendations for monitoring individuals with high normal BP once a year, and monitoring those with normal blood pressure every 2 years, and they emphasize the importance of weight control as a measure for primary prevention of hypertension. Indeed, the American guidelines highlight this increased risk of developing hypertension among individuals with blood pressure of 120–139 mmHg systolic and 80–89

Figure 2.6
Cross-sectional age trend of systolic hypertension in men and women. (Adapted from Kannel WB. *Am Heart J* 1999; **138**: s 205.)

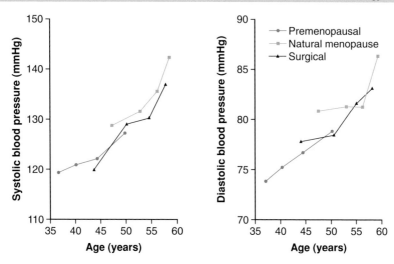

Figure 2.7
The influence of the menopause on blood pressure. The adjusted blood pressure rise with age was steeper in postmenopausal women. (Adapted from Staesson *et al.* *J Hum Hypertens* 1989; **3**: 427–33.)

mmHg diastolic with the designation of 'pre-hypertension' (Table 2.3).

Aetiology of hypertension

The vast majority (>95%) of patients with hypertension have primary or essential (idiopathic) hypertension, where there is no immediate underlying cause (Figure 2.8). This definition is somewhat misleading in that all hypertension clearly has a cause, albeit one due to the interplay of complex genetic and environmental factors.

Even in so-called 'essential hypertension', lifestyle influences such as salt and potassium intake, alcohol, dietary factors and exercise can contribute to raised BP, as do gender, ethnic origin and body mass index. Acute stress can cause a rise in BP, but there is little evidence of

Table 2.2
Progression to hypertension in the Framingham Heart Study (Adapted from Vasan *et al.* *Lancet* 2001; **358**: 1682–6)

	Baseline BP (mmHg)	% progressing to >140/90 mmHg over 4 years
Age 35–64	<120 and <80	5.1%
	120–9 or 80–4	18.1%
	130–9 or 85–9	39.4%
Age 65–94	<120 and <80	18.5%
	120–9 or 80–4	29.2%
	130–9 or 85–9	52.5%

Table 2.3 (a)
The definitions and classification of BP levels (BHS-IV, 2004)

Category	Systolic BP (mmHg)	Diastolic BP (mmHg)
Optimal	<120	<80
Normal	<130	<85
High normal	130–139	85–89
Grade 1 hypertension (mild)	140–159	90–99
Grade 2 hypertension (moderate)	160–179	100–109
Grade 3 hypertension (severe)	≥180	≥110
Isolated systolic hypertension:		
Grade 1	140–159	<90
Grade 2	≥160	<90

When a patient's systolic blood pressure and diastolic blood pressure fall into different categories, the higher category should apply. BP, blood pressure.

Table 2.3 (b)
Classification of blood pressure in adults (JNC-VII)

Blood pressure classification	Systolic blood pressure (mmHg)	Diastolic blood pressure (mmHg)
Normal	<120	And <80
Pre-hypertension	120–139	Or 80–89
Stage 1 hypertension	140–159	Or 90–99
Stage 2 hypertension	≥160	Or ≥100

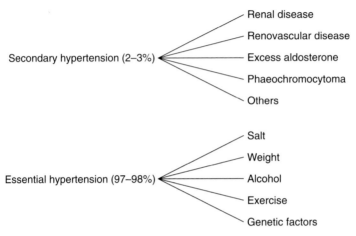

Figure 2.8
Essential and secondary hypertension.

a causal effect of chronic stress on BP. The so-called 'Barker hypothesis' suggests that fetal influences, particularly birth weight, may be a determinant of adult BP. For example, small babies are more likely to have high BP as adolescents and to be hypertensive as adults.

> The majority of patients with hypertension have primary or essential hypertension

In a small minority of patients, hypertension is 'secondary', or due to an underlying disease usually involving the kidneys or endocrine system (see Chapter 4). Effective treatment of the underlying condition can sometimes abolish the hypertension.

Further reading

Colhoun HM, Dong W, Poulter NR. Blood pressure screening, management and control in England: results from the health survey for England 1994. *J Hypertens* 1998; **16:** 747–52.

Eastern Stroke and Coronary Heart Disease Collaborative Research Group. Blood pressure, cholesterol, and stroke in eastern Asia. *Lancet* 1998; **352:** 1801–7.

JBS 2: Joint British Societies' guidelines on prevention of cardiovascular disease in clinical practice. *Heart* 2005; **91:** 1–52.

Lewington S, Clarke R, Qizilbash N, et al. Age-specific relevance of usual blood pressure to vascular mortality: a meta-analysis of individual data for one million adults in 61 prospective studies. Prospective Studies Collaboration. *Lancet* 2002; **360:** 1903–13.

Manuel DG, Lim J, Tanuseputro P, et al. Revisiting Rose: strategies for reducing coronary heart disease. *BMJ* 2006; **332:** 659–62.

Rosenthal T, Oparil S. Hypertension in women. *J Hum Hypertens* 2000; **14**: 691–704.

Seedat YK. Hypertension in developing nations in sub-Saharan Africa. *J Hum Hypertens* 2000; **14**: 739–47.

Seventh Report of the Joint National Committee on Prevention, Detection, Evaluation and Treatment of High Blood Pressure. *Hypertension* 2003; **42**: 1206–52.

Singh RB, Suh IL, Singh VP, *et al.* Hypertension and stroke in Asia: prevalence, control and strategies in developing countries for prevention. *J Hum Hypertens* 2000; **14**: 749–63.

Ueshima H, Zhang XH, Choudhury SR. Epidemiology of hypertension in China and Japan. *J Hum Hypertens* 2000; **14**: 765–9.

Williams B, Poulter NR, Brown MJ, *et al.* Guidelines for management of hypertension: report of the fourth working party of the British Hypertension Society. *J Hum Hypertens* 2004; **18**: 139–85.

World Health Organisation. International Society Guidelines for the Management of Hypertension. Guidelines Subcommittee. *J Hypertens* 1999; **17**: 151–83.

3. Pathophysiology

Cardiac output and peripheral resistance
Arterial stiffness
Renin–angiotensin system
Autonomic nervous system
Hypercoagulability
Endothelial dysfunction
Other factors

The pathophysiology of hypertension is complex, and the subject of much uncertainty. In most cases (95%), no clear single identifiable cause is found and the condition is labelled 'essential hypertension'. A small number of patients (between 2% and 5%) have an underlying secondary disease as the cause of their hypertension.

Many physiological mechanisms are involved in the maintenance of normal blood pressure (BP), and pathophysiological abnormalities in these systems might play a part in the development of essential hypertension. The factors that influence BP include:

- salt intake
- physical activity
- obesity and insulin resistance
- the renin–angiotensin system
- the sympathetic nervous system.

Additional factors proposed include:

- genetics
- endothelial dysfunction (including changes in mediators, such as endothelin and nitric oxide)
- hypercoagulability

- low birth weight
- intrauterine nutrition
- neurovascular anomalies.

Their relative roles may differ between individuals and ethnic groups. For example, there is a high prevalence of insulin resistance in the peoples of South Asia, which can be associated with obesity, diabetes and lipid abnormalities – the so-called 'metabolic syndrome'.

> Hypertension has a complex pathophysiology with most cases exhibiting no clear single identifiable cause, though abnormalities in the physiological mechanisms involved in maintaining normal BP may play a part in its development

Cardiac output and peripheral resistance

Normal BP depends upon a balance between the cardiac output and peripheral vascular resistance. In essential hypertension, cardiac output is normal but peripheral resistance is raised. The latter is determined by the state of small arterioles, the walls of which contain smooth muscle cells, and not by large arteries or the capillaries.

In early hypertension, especially in younger patients, BP elevation may be caused by a raised cardiac output related to sympathetic overactivity (peripheral resistance is not raised). Compensatory vasoconstriction of resistance vessels (arterioles) prevents the raised pressure being transmitted to the capillary bed where it would substantially affect cell homeostasis. This initial response of the vasculature to mild to moderate elevations of blood pressure is probably mediated by endogenous vasoconstrictors such as angiotensin and endothelin. However, prolonged smooth muscle constriction induces structural changes in these arterioles, with vessel wall thickening possibly mediated by angiotensin, which leads to an irreversible rise in peripheral resistance. The intracellular calcium concentration found in smooth muscle cells is responsible for this contraction, and explains the vasodilatory effect of calcium channel blockers.

> In very early hypertension, raised BP may be caused by a raised cardiac output related to sympathetic overactivity

Auto-regulation in hypertension

In chronic hypertension, the lower limit of auto-regulation of cerebral blood flow is shifted towards higher BPs, with impairment of the tolerance to acute hypotension. For example, in normotensive subjects, the upper limit of auto-regulation can be a mean arterial pressure of 120 mmHg (or about 160/100 mmHg), but in individuals whose vessels are hypertrophied by longstanding hypertension, it may be substantially higher.

In very severe hypertension, such as is seen in hypertensive emergencies, intense peripheral vasoconstriction results in a rapid rise in BP and a vicious cycle of events that includes ischaemia of the brain and peripheral organs. This ischaemia stimulates neurohormone and cytokine release, exacerbating the vasoconstriction and ischaemia, further increasing BP and leading to target organ damage. In addition, myointimal proliferation in the vasculature can make the situation worse, as may disseminated intravascular coagulation. Furthermore, renal ischaemia leads to the activation of the renin–angiotensin system causing a further rise in BP and microvascular damage.

With rapid and severe rises in BP, the process of auto-regulation fails, leading to a rise in pressure in the arterioles and capillaries, causing vascular damage. This disruption of the endothelium allows plasma constituents (including fibrinoid material) to enter the vessel wall, narrowing or obliterating the lumen

in many tissue beds. The level at which fibrinoid necrosis occurs is dependent upon the baseline BP. In the cerebral circulation, this can lead to the development of cerebral oedema and the clinical picture of hypertensive encephalopathy.

In addition to protecting the tissues against the effects of hypertension, auto-regulation maintains perfusion during the treatment of hypertension via arterial and arteriolar vasodilatation.

However, excessive falls in BP below the auto-regulatory range can lead to organ ischaemia. The arteriolar hypertrophy induced by chronic hypertension means target organ ischaemia will occur at a higher BP than in previously normotensive subjects (Figure 3.1).

> Rapid and severe rises in BP can cause auto-regulation to fail, followed by vascular damage caused by a rise in pressure in the arterioles and capillaries

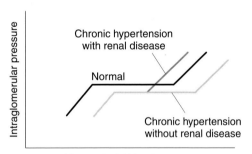

Figure 3.1
Auto-regulatory mechanism to maintain relatively constant organ blood flow across a range of blood pressures. Intraglomerular pressure (renal blood flow) is illustrated in this case, with a rightward shift in the auto-regulatory curve (light blue line). Hence, rapid and excessive blood pressure reduction into the 'normal' range may compromise renal function. Also highlighted here is the narrowed auto-regulation range (dark blue line) in patients with renal disease (more sensitive to increased blood pressure). (Adapted from Palmer BF. Renal dysfunction complicating the treatment of hypertension. *N Engl J Med* 2002; **347**: 1256–61.)

Arterial stiffness

Arterial stiffness describes the mechanical properties of the arterial system. These mechanical properties can be inferred by various methods, including quantification of compliance (or distensibility) and pulse wave velocity (the time taken for a pressure wave to travel a known distance). The latter is widely used to characterize the 'stiffness' of the artery, based on the principle that the pulse wave travels faster in stiffer arteries.

In older patients and patients with hypertension and diabetes, changes in the arterial wall (e.g. elastin to collagen ratio and glycation of connective tissue) result in 'stiffening' of the arterial tree. The consequent increase in pulse wave velocity is associated with earlier pulse wave reflection at branch points. The earlier return of these reflected waves augments the systolic instead of diastolic pressure wave, resulting in increased systolic pressure and reduced diastolic pressure in the central arterial circulation (aorta and large vessels).

The recent CAFÉ study (a substudy of the ASCOT) demonstrated significantly higher central arterial blood pressure in the atenolol-based group compared to the amlodipine-based antihypertensive regime, despite similar blood pressure reduction measured at the brachial artery. These differences may explain the higher rates of cardiovascular events with atenolol treatment in the ASCOT study.

Renin–angiotensin system

The renin–angiotensin system is probably the most important of the endocrine systems controlling BP. The kidney's juxtaglomerular apparatus secretes renin in response to glomerular underperfusion or a reduced salt intake. Renin is also released in response to stimulation from the sympathetic nervous system. Renin is responsible for converting renin substrate (angiotensinogen) to angiotensin I, a physiologically inactive substance that is rapidly converted to angiotensin II in the lungs by angiotensin-converting enzyme (ACE). Angiotensin II is a potent vasoconstrictor and thus causes a rise in BP. It also stimulates the release of aldosterone from the adrenal zona glomerulosa, which results in both sodium and water retention (Figure 3.2).

There are also important non-circulating 'local' renin–angiotensin epicrine or paracrine systems in the kidney, the heart and the arterial tree which also control BP and may have important roles in regulating regional blood flow.

Although the circulating renin–angiotensin system may have a pathophysiological role, this endocrine system is not a direct or the sole cause of hypertension. This is especially evident in the elderly or in Afro-Caribbean patients, who have low levels of renin and angiotensin II; drugs which block the renin–angiotensin system are less effective in such patient groups (Table 3.1). None the less, the renin–angiotensin system is an important target for the treatment of hypertension.

Table 3.1
Drugs which block the renin system (beta-blockers, ACE inhibitors and angiotensin receptor blockers) tend to be less effective in patients with low renin and angiotensin levels

Low renin states:	
Anephrics	Older patients
Patients with Conn's syndrome	Afro-Caribbean patients
Patients with liquorice-induced hypertension	Patients with type 2 diabetes

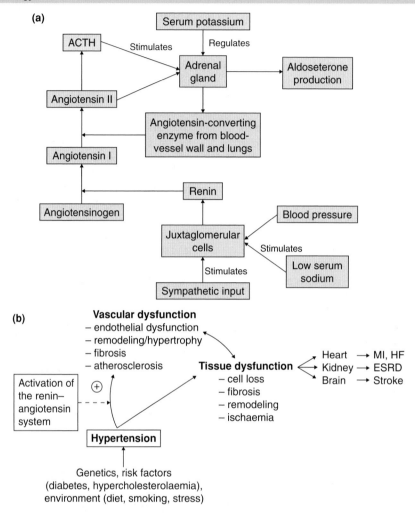

Figure 3.2
(a) The renin–angiotensin–aldosterone system. (b) The renin–angiotensin drives the pathology in hypertension. ACTH, adrenocorticotropic hormone; ESRD, end stage renal disease; HF, heart failure; MI, myocardial infarction. (Adapted from Weir *et al.* *Am J Hypertens* 1999; **12**: 205S–35; Timmermans *et al.* *Pharmacol Rev* 1993; **45**: 205–51.)

Autonomic nervous system

The autonomic nervous system plays an important role in the pathophysiology of hypertension, and is key to maintaining a normal BP. For example, sympathetic nervous system stimulation can cause both arteriolar constriction and arteriolar dilation, depending on whether or not the receptors are excitatory or inhibitory.

The autonomic nervous system is important in the mediation of short-term changes in BP in response to stress and physical exercise. However, adrenaline (epinephrine) and noradrenaline (norepinephrine) may not have a clear role in the aetiology of hypertension, though drugs used for the treatment of hypertension do block the sympathetic nervous system and have a well-established therapeutic role. There is more likely to be a complex interaction between the autonomic nervous system and the various neuroendocrine systems (including the renin–angiotensin system), together with other factors, including circulating sodium volume.

> The autonomic nervous system has a central role in hypertension pathophysiology, maintaining a normal BP and mediating short-term changes in BP in response to stress and physical exercise

Hypercoagulability

While the blood vessels are exposed to high pressures in hypertension, paradoxically, the main complications of hypertension (stroke and myocardial infarction) are thrombotic rather than haemorrhagic – the so-called thrombotic paradox of hypertension (or 'Birmingham paradox') (Figure 3.3). Increasing evidence suggests that patients with hypertension demonstrate abnormalities of:

● vessel walls (endothelial dysfunction or damage)
● blood constituents (abnormal levels of haemostatic factors, platelet activation and fibrinolysis)
● blood flow (rheology, viscosity and flow reserve).

The fulfilment of the three components of Virchow's triad for thrombogenesis suggests that hypertension confers a prothrombotic or

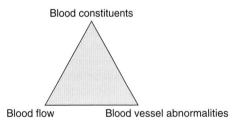

Blood constituents

Blood flow   Blood vessel abnormalities

Figure 3.3
Virchow's triad of thrombogenesis. Abnormalities of all three components of Virchow's triad are present in hypertension; hypertension confers a prothrombotic state.

hypercoagulable state, which appears to be related to the degree or severity of target organ damage. These abnormalities can be related to long-term prognosis and in addition, may be altered by antihypertensive treatment.

Endothelial dysfunction

Vascular endothelial cells play a key role in cardiovascular regulation by producing a number of potent local vasoactive agents, including the vasodilator molecule nitric oxide (NO) and the vasoconstrictor peptide endothelin. Dysfunction of the endothelium, therefore, may lead to alteration in vascular tone and arterial blood pressure. Indeed, endothelial damage or dysfunction is well-described in human essential hypertension.

Modulation of the endothelial function is an attractive therapeutic option in attempting to minimize some of the important complications of hypertension. Clinically effective antihypertensive therapy appears to restore impaired production of nitric oxide, but does not seem to restore the impaired endothelium-dependent vascular relaxation or vascular response to endothelial receptors. This indicates that such endothelial dysfunction is primary and becomes irreversible once the hypertensive process has become established.

Vasoactive substances

Many vasoactive systems and mechanisms that affect sodium transport and vascular tone are involved in maintaining normal BP. For example, endothelin is a powerful, vascular, endothelial vasoconstrictor, which may produce a 'salt-sensitive' rise in BP. It also activates local renin–angiotensin systems. Bradykinin is a potent vasodilator, which is inactivated by an angiotensin-converting enzyme. Consequently, treatment with ACE inhibitors may exert some of their effect by blocking bradykinin inactivation.

Endothelial-derived relaxant factor, which is now known to be nitric oxide (NO), is produced by arterial and venous endothelium and diffuses through the vessel wall into the smooth muscle causing vasodilatation. The production of NO also modulates the thrombotic balance and may limit the prothrombotic tendencies in hypertension described above.

Nevibolol, a novel beta-blocker with NO-modulating effects, has been shown to be an effective blood pressure-lowering agent, but it is unclear if the NO-modulating effects confer any additional benefits. It is possible that this property may limit the side-effects associated with beta-blockers, for example impotence, which is common with other beta-blockers.

Atrial natriuretic peptide (ANP) is a hormone secreted from the atria of the heart in response to increased blood volume. The effect of ANP is to increase sodium and water excretion from the kidney. Modulation of this hormone has been a target for agents such as omapatrilat, a vasopeptidase inhibitor, with the aim of treating hypertension and heart failure. However, data from randomized studies were disappointing, emphasizing the complexity and unpredictability of neurohormonal modulation.

> Many vasoactive systems and sodium transport-affecting mechanisms are involved in maintaining normal BP, such as endothelin and bradykinin

Other factors

Angiogenesis

Abnormal angiogenesis has been demonstrated in hypertensive animal models as well as in different stages of hypertension in humans. In hypertension, there seems to be an impaired ability for vascular growth resulting from structural alteration of the microvascular network, which includes capillary rarefaction, increased arteriolar length and tortuosity. These alterations in the microvasculature appear at very early stages of hypertension, and increasing evidence points to the possibility

that abnormal angiogenesis may contribute causally to hypertension.

Sodium transport

The transport of sodium across vascular smooth muscle cell walls could influence BP via its interrelationship with calcium transport.

Insulin sensitivity

Several 'classic' risk factors, such as obesity, glucose intolerance, diabetes mellitus and hyperlipidaemia, tend to cluster together. The frequent association of these risk factors led to the suggestion of a clinical syndrome, now termed the metabolic syndrome. Obesity and insulin resistance (generally defined by high levels of insulin in the face of normal or high glucose levels), is widely regarded as a central feature of this syndrome. However, some hypertensive patients who are not obese display resistance to insulin. The metabolic syndrome, which is especially prevalent in South Asians (who are at high risk of ischaemic heart disease), could explain why the hazards of cardiovascular risk are synergistic or multiplicative rather than simply additive. In view of the well-documented associations between these risk factors, the presence of hypertension should prompt the search for other risk factors (e.g. diabetes and dyslipidaemia).

Genetic factors

Human essential hypertension is a complex, multifactorial, quantitative trait under polygenic control. Over the last decade several strategies have been used to dissect the genetic determinants of hypertension. Separate genes and genetic factors have been linked to the development of essential hypertension, but multiple genes probably contribute to the development of the disorder in a particular individual. It is rare that a specific genetic mutation can cause hypertension and the condition is twice as common in subjects with one or two hypertensive parents. Genetic factors account for approximately 30% of the variation in BP in various populations.

In the quest for a gene (or genes) for hypertension, the study of rare monogenic forms of hypertension has been the most successful. Attempts to identify the multiple genes involved in the more common polygenic form of hypertension have been much more difficult. Many laboratories use rat models of genetic hypertension where some of the complexity of studying human hypertension can be removed, but whether such information can be applied to large populations of hypertensive patients remains debatable. Numerous crosses between hypertensive and normotensive rat strains have produced several quantitative trait loci for blood pressure and other related phenotypes such as left ventricular hypertrophy, stroke, insulin resistance and kidney failure.

Intrauterine influences

Fetal influences, particularly birth weight, may be a determinant of BP in adult life, although the precise pathophysiological mechanisms are still uncertain. For example, babies with a low birth weight are more likely to have higher BPs during adolescence and to be hypertensive as adults.

The Barker hypothesis states that small-for-age babies are also more likely to have metabolic abnormalities that have been associated with the later development of hypertension and cardiovascular disease, such as insulin resistance, diabetes mellitus, hyperlipidaemia and abdominal obesity. This hypothesis has been applied to the South Asian population to explain the increased cardiovascular risk in this population.

Another interpretation suggests that genetic factors may explain the Barker hypothesis. For example, mothers with above average BP in pregnancy give birth to smaller babies who subsequently develop above average BP themselves and eventually hypertension. It is entirely likely that the similarity of BPs in mother and child are genetic and in a modern 'healthy' society, unrelated to intrauterine under-nutrition.

Further reading

Blann AD, Lip GYH. The endothelium in atherothrombotic disease: assessment of function, mechanisms and clinical implications. *Blood Coag Fibrinolys* 1998; **9**: 297–306.

Eriksson JG, Forsen T, Tuomilehto J, *et al*. Early growth and coronary heart disease in later life: longitudinal study. *BMJ* 2001; **322**: 949–53.

Gibbons GH. The pathophysiology of hypertension: the importance of angiotensin II in cardiovascular remodeling. *Am J Hypertens* 1998; **11**: 177S–181S.

Lee WK, Padmanabhan S, Dominiczak AF. Genetics of hypertension: from experimental models to clinical applications. *J Hum Hypertens* 2000; **14**: 631–47.

Le Noble FAC, Stassen FRM, Hacking WJG, *et al*. Angiogenesis and hypertension. *J Hypertens* 1998; **16**: 1563–72.

Lip GYH. Hypertension and the prothrombotic state. *J Hum Hypertens* 2000; **14**: 687–90.

Lip GYH, Blann AD. Does hypertension confer a prothrombotic state? Virchow's triad revisited. *Circulation* 2000; **101**: 218–20.

Nicholls MG, Robertson JI. The renin–angiotensin system in the year 2000. *J Hum Hypertens* 2000; **14**: 649–66.

Roseboom TJ, van der Meulen JH, van Montfrans GA, *et al*. Maternal nutrition during gestation and blood pressure in later life. *J Hypertens* 2001; **19**: 29–34.

Ross R. The pathogenesis of atherosclerosis: a perspective for the 1990s. *Nature* 1993; **362**: 801–9.

Safar ME, Levy BI, Struijker-Boudier H. Current perspectives on arterial stiffness and pulse pressure in hypertension and cardiovascular disease. *Circulation* 2003; **107**: 2864–9.

Sagnella GA. Atrial natriuretic peptide mimetics and vasopeptidase inhibitors. *Cardiovasc Res* 2001; **51**: 416–28.

Schlaich MP, Schmieder RE. Left ventricular hypertrophy and its regression: pathophysiology and therapeutic approach: focus on treatment by antihypertensive agents. *Am J Hypertens* 1998; **11**: 1394–404.

Spieker LE, Noll G, Ruschitzka FT, *et al*. Working under pressure: the vascular endothelium in arterial hypertension. *J Hum Hypertens* 2000; **14**: 617–30.

4. Target organ damage

Cerebrovascular disease
Heart
Large vessel arterial disease
Kidney and renal failure
Retinopathy

Table 4.1
Definite and possible risk factors for stroke

Definite	Possible
Hypertension	Lipid level
Atrial fibrillation	Salt consumption
Coronary heart disease	Low potassium diet
Diabetes	Low vitamin C diet
TIA	Fibrinogen
Smoking	
Carotid disease	
Alcohol excess	

The natural history of high blood pressure (BP) can be regarded as having two stages. Initially, hypertension can develop as a risk factor, without significant local organ damage or symptoms. Later, this can shift towards significant target organ damage with cardiovascular symptoms. This can manifest itself as blocking effects (atherothrombotic plaques causing coronary, cerebrovascular or peripheral artery disease) or 'bursting' effects (cerebral haemorrhage, aortic dissection or heart failure).

Cerebrovascular disease

Stroke is one of the most devastating consequences of hypertension, and can result in significant disability as well as in premature death. Definite and possible stroke risk factors are summarized in Table 4.1.

Strokes account for about 12% of all deaths, and about 25% of all strokes occur in patients younger than 65 years. After standardizing for age, men aged 40–59 years with a systolic BP of 160–180 mmHg are approximately four times more likely to suffer a stroke during the next eight years when compared to men with a systolic BP of 140–159 mmHg. An average reduction of just 9/5 mmHg in BP results in a 34% reduction in the incidence of stroke

whereas a reduction of 19/10 mmHg results in a 56% lower incidence of stroke.

Strokes account for 12% of deaths, with 25% of all strokes affecting the under-65 age group. Men with a systolic BP of 160–180 mmHg are around four times more likely to have a stroke than men with a systolic BP of 140–159 mmHg

In patients with hypertension, about 80% of strokes are ischaemic, caused by intra-arterial thrombosis or embolization from the heart and large arteries. The remaining 20% are due to haemorrhagic causes, which may also be related to very high BP. In the UK 40% of all strokes are estimated to be linked to a systolic BP of 140 mmHg or more. The relation between prior blood pressure control and odds ratio for stroke is illustrated in Figure 4.1. Stroke recurrence after transient ischaemic attack (TIA) or minor stroke is also greater with higher blood pressures (Figure 4.2).

Strokes and the elderly

Elderly hypertensive patients are particularly prone to developing all types of stroke and often sustain multiple small, asymptomatic cerebral infarcts, leading to progressive loss of intellectual function and dementia. Indeed, the recent SYT-EUR study convincingly showed that treatment of isolated systolic hypertension, which is generally more frequent in the elderly, resulted in the prevention of dementia at follow-up (Table 4.2).

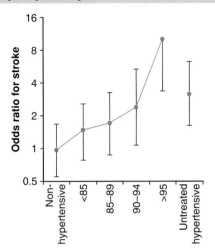

Figure 4.1
Prior blood pressure control and odds ratio for stroke.
(Adapted from Du et al. Br Med J 1997; **314:** 272–6.)

Table 4.2
The Syst-Eur dementia substudy (Adapted from Forette
et al. Lancet 1998; **352:** 1347–51)

	Placebo	Active	p value
Number in trial	1180	1238	
All dementia	21	11	<0.05
Alzheimer's	15	8	NS
Mixed	4	3	NS
Vascular	2	0	NS

atrial fibrillation are additional to the risk of stroke. In the low risk arm of the third Stroke Prevention in Atrial Fibrillation study (SPAF-3), even a history of previous hypertension increased the risk of stroke nearly four-fold, despite aspirin therapy. In view of the significant risk of stroke, patients with hypertension and atrial fibrillation should be considered for anticoagulation.

Strokes and atrial fibrillation

Hypertension is also associated with an increased risk of atrial fibrillation, which is the most common sustained cardiac rhythm disorder. The presence of both hypertension and

Heart

Coronary heart disease

Fatal coronary heart disease (CHD) is seven times more common among hypertensives than a fatal stroke, and is the major population

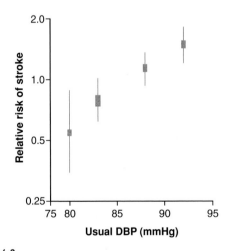

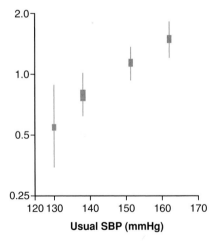

Figure 4.2
Stroke recurrence after transient ischaemic attack (TIA) or minor stroke. DBP, diastolic blood pressure; SBP, systolic blood pressure. (Adapted from Rogers et al. Br Med J 1996; **313:** 147.)

consequence of hypertension. Early trials of hypertension treatment provided convincing evidence for reductions in the risk of stroke but little evidence of benefit on coronary heart disease. However, these studies were not adequately powered to evaluate the impact of blood pressure treatment on CHD events. Indeed, subsequent larger controlled trials confirmed the benefit of blood pressure reduction on CHD events, although the reduction of coronary thrombosis is less impressive. Nevertheless, analysis of the large treatment trials suggests that adequate treatment of hypertension reduces the risk of heart attack by approximately 25%, although this is based on BP reduction with thiazides and beta-blockers, rather than the newer antihypertensive drugs.

Left ventricular hypertrophy

As a result of the increased afterload placed on the heart by high BP, the mass of the left ventricular muscle increases. While this is initially a compensatory response, increased muscle mass outstrips its oxygen supply. When left ventricular hypertrophy (LVH) is coupled with the reduced coronary vascular reserve in hypertension, it can result in myocardial ischaemia even with patent epicardial coronary arteries.

Thus, beyond a certain point, LVH secondary to hypertension becomes a major risk factor for myocardial infarction, stroke, congestive cardiac failure and sudden death. This increased risk is in addition to that imposed by hypertension itself. Hypertensives with LVH are also at an increased risk of developing cardiac arrhythmias (atrial fibrillation, ventricular arrhythmias) and atherosclerotic vascular disease (coronary and peripheral artery disease). Indeed, for a given level of BP, and if LVH is present, the prognosis is three or four times worse, especially for cardiac failure and stroke (Table 4.3).

Pathogenesis of LVH

The mechanisms promoting the development of LVH remain uncertain. The basic underlying mechanism may be an increase in ventricular wall stress and pressure workload on the left ventricle. Thus, with an increase in afterload as a result of hypertension, the heart responds with an increase in wall thickness. There is, however, a poor correlation between left ventricular wall thickness and BP. In addition, the pathogenesis of LVH has been shown to be influenced by demographic factors, such as age, sex, race and body habitus; exogenous factors, such as dietary salt intake and alcohol consumption; and neurohumoral substances, such as activity of the renin–angiotensin–aldosterone system, the sympathetic system, growth hormone and insulin. Several mechanisms have also been postulated for the role of the renin–angiotensin system in the pathogenesis of LVH. First,

Table 4.3

Relative risks of cardiovascular events and risk with increments in LV mass from Framingham data (Levy *et al.* Prognostic implications of echocardiographically determined left ventricular mass in the Framingham Heart Study. *N Engl J Med* 1990; **322**: 1561–6)

	Relative risk (95%CI) for 50 g increase in LV mass	
	Men	Women
CVD events	1.49(1.20–1.88)	1.57(1.20–2.04)
Cardiovascular mortality	1.73(1.19–2.52)	2.12(1.28–3.49)
Total mortality	1.49(1.14–1.94)	2.01(1.33–2.81)

All values have been adjusted for age, antihypertensive medications and standard CVD risk factors including blood pressure. LV, left ventricular; CVD, cardiovascular disease.

angiotensin II has direct and widespread vasoconstrictor actions, with effects on left ventricular afterload and myocardial ischaemia. Second, angiotensin II can also indirectly stimulate myocyte hypertrophy via its interaction with sympathetic tone, and in addition could be trophic to myocytes. This may stimulate fibroblastic proliferation and collagen formation; these factors are involved in the development of LVH (Table 4.4).

> The factors affecting the development of LVH remain unclear. The basic underlying mechanism may be an increase in ventricular wall stress and pressure workload on the left ventricle

Table 4.4
Possible adverse features of left ventricular hypertrophy

- Mismatch of blood supply and non-vascular tissue resulting in a relatively 'starved' subendocardial region
- Increased basal myocardial oxygen demand due to increased mass and wall stress
- A heightened likelihood of ventricular arrhythmias, perhaps related to the presence of fibrous tissue
- A markedly reduced coronary flow reserve, with abnormalities in the ability to dilate coronary arteries, resulting in increased cardiac ischaemia

Screening for LVH

A commonly used screening test for LVH in hypertensive patients is the 12-lead electrocardiogram (ECG). The usual criteria are those proposed by Sokolow and Lyon, that is, the sum of the S wave in lead V1 and the R wave in leads V5 or V6 on the ECG >35 mm. Nevertheless, LVH may be identified by electrocardiography in only 5–10% of hypertensive patients, while echocardiography is a far more sensitive investigation, identifying LVH in around 50% of untreated hypertensive patients. The various ECG criteria used for defining LVH are summarized in Table 4.5.

LVH and cardiac arrhythmias

LVH is also a risk factor for the development of cardiac arrhythmias, the most common being atrial fibrillation and ventricular arrhythmias. The presence of atrial fibrillation is important as this arrhythmia is associated with a five-fold increase in mortality and may often require long-term antiarrhythmic and antithrombotic therapy. Also, ventricular arrhythmias have important implications for the risk of sudden death in these patients. The mechanisms for sudden death are complex and may include malignant cardiac arrhythmias, including increased ventricular ectopics and nonsustained ventricular tachycardia. However, this risk of sudden death is independent of arterial pressure. Electrophysiological mechanisms for

Table 4.5
Electrocardiographic criteria for the diagnosis of left ventricular hypertrophy

Criterion	Measurement	Author(s) and year of description
R wave in aVL	R aVL	Sokolow and Lyon 1949
Sokolow–Lyon	SV1 + R (V5 or V6)	Sokolow and Lyon 1949
Cornell	RaVL + SV3	Casale et al. 1985
Cornell Voltage Duration Product	RaVL + SV3 × QRS duration	Molloy et al. 1992
Cornell/QRS II	RaVL + SV3/Total QRS voltage in lead II	Denarié et al. 1998
Lewis	RI – RIII + SIII – SI	Lewis 1914
RI + SIII	RI + SIII	Gubner and Ungerleider 1943

arrhythmogenesis in left ventricular hypertrophy (LVH) are summarized in Table 4.6.

Table 4.6
Electrophysiological mechanisms for arrhythmogenesis in left ventricular hypertrophy (LVH)

- Re-entry mechanisms related to myocardial fibrosis in LVH
- Myocardial ischaemic areas, perhaps related to reduced coronary reserve (as coronary artery disease is often not present)
- Ventricular myocyte stretching and arterial wall tension in the hypertrophied heart
- Increased sympathetic nervous system activity

LVH is a risk factor in developing cardiac arrhythmias, such as atrial fibrillation – associated with a five-fold increase in mortality – and ventricular arrhythmias

Heart failure as a complication of LVH

Heart failure is another complication commonly associated with LVH and hypertension. In the Framingham study, the presence of LVH on the ECG is associated with a substantially increased risk of heart failure. The way in which hypertension results in heart failure is unclear, but may occur as a result of pressure overload, for example the excessive demand of afterload on an otherwise normal heart. LVH may also result in impaired cardiac function that is secondary to diastolic dysfunction, subendocardial ischaemia and an inefficient cardiac rhythm due to frequent arrhythmias or even atrial fibrillation. A final mechanism is the association with coronary artery disease, which may result in cardiac ischaemia (with ventricular impairment or 'hibernation') or myocardial infarction (Figure 4.3).

Antihypertensive drugs and LVH

It should be emphasized that LVH is preventable with the use of antihypertensive therapy and improved control of hypertension. In fact, almost every antihypertensive drug is capable of reducing cardiac mass and reversing LVH if therapy is maintained for long enough. The reduction in left ventricular mass also correlates with the reduction in mean arterial pressure.

Not all antihypertensive drugs result in the regression of LVH in a similar fashion. For example, angiotensin-converting enzyme (ACE)

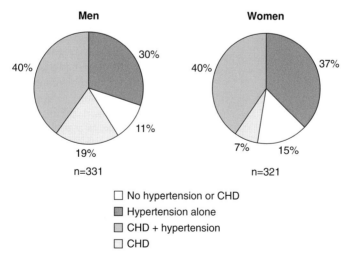

Figure 4.3
Prevalence of coronary heart disease and hypertension in chronic heart failure as seen in the Framingham Heart Study. CHD, coronary heart disease.

inhibitors appear more effective in the regression of LVH than beta-blockers and diuretics (Figure 4.4). By contrast, directly acting vasodilators, such as minoxidil and hydralazine, have little impact on LVH. The effects of left ventricular mass reduction often parallel the reduction in BP as a result of treatment. There is also evidence that cardiac arrhythmias, myocardial ischaemia and impaired ventricular filling diminish in parallel to the reduction in left ventricular mass and the regression of LVH. In the Framingham study, for example, patients with a reduction in LVH showed a decrease of at least 25% in cardiovascular mortality over four years, the effect being most beneficial in men.

In the recent Losartan Intervention For Endpoint reduction in hypertension (LIFE) trial in 'high risk' patients with essential hypertension and ECG evidence LVH, the primary composite endpoint was reduced by 13% with the angiotensin receptor blocker losartan compared to atenolol, and was virtually the result of a

25% stroke reduction by losartan. In addition, there was a 25% reduction in cases of new diabetes in patients treated with losartan compared with atenolol.

> Not all antihypertensive drugs operate in the same way to reduce LVH; for example, ACE inhibitors appear to be more effective than beta-blockers and diuretics, while directly acting vasodilators have little impact

Heart failure

Convincing evidence from prospective epidemiological studies suggests that heart failure may be caused by high BP and can be prevented by its control. For example, the Framingham study suggested that high BP was the principal cause of heart failure; subjects with BP >160/95 mmHg had a six-fold higher incidence of heart failure than those with BP <140/90 mmHg. Heart failure has a poor long-term prognosis, and New York Heart Association (NYHA) Grade IV heart failure has a worse prognosis than some cancers, with a one year mortality of >50%. Heart failure in association with untreated hypertension over many years can slowly be replaced by 'normal' BP as the left ventricular muscle progressively fails.

Hypertension is associated with structural changes in the heart that result in increased passive stiffness and impaired diastolic relaxation. This compromises cardiac filling during diastole and reduces cardiac output, resulting in heart failure. Conventional belief suggests that as a result of reduced diastolic filling, left ventricular filling becomes more dependent on heart rate and atrial contribution. Thus, during tachycardia or atrial fibrillation, which reduces diastolic filling time and atrial contribution, stroke volume may be significantly reduced, with consequent increase in end-diastolic pressure and pulmonary oedema. However, rate-lowering drugs such as beta-blockers have not been tested in large clinical trials in patients with heart failure and normal left ventricular ejection fraction.

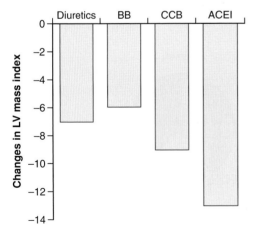

Figure 4.4
Reversal of left ventricular hypertrophy in essential hypertension – meta-analysis data showing changes in left ventricular mass index with different classes of antihypertensive agent. BB, beta-blockers; CCB, calcium channel blockers; ACEI, angiotensin-converting enzyme inhibitors. (Adapted from Schmeider et al. JAMA 1996; **275**: 1507–13.)

Other contributory factors include exercise-induced subendocardial ischaemia, which can produce 'exaggerated' impairment of diastolic relaxation of the hypertrophied myocardium, and finally, hypertension in association with renal artery stenosis can cause 'flash' pulmonary oedema, which can be corrected by treatment of the renal artery stenosis.

Large vessel arterial disease

Peripheral vascular disease (PVD) is associated with a high cardiovascular morbidity and mortality. Intermittent claudication is the most common symptomatic manifestation of PVD, but is also an important predictor of cardiovascular death, increasing it three-fold, and increasing all-cause mortality by two to five times.

Hypertension is a common and important risk factor for vascular disorders, including PVD. About 2–5% of hypertensive patients have intermittent claudication at presentation and the prevalence increases with age. Similarly, 35–55% of patients with PVD at presentation also have hypertension. Patients who suffer from hypertension with PVD have a greatly increased risk of myocardial infarction and stroke. Many patients with PVD also have renal artery stenosis, which may contribute to their hypertension. Unless specifically investigated for, this often remains undiagnosed (Figure 4.5).

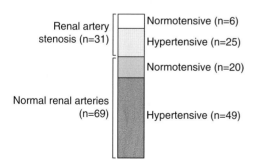

Figure 4.5
Renal artery stenosis in peripheral vascular disease.
(Adapted from Wachtell *et al. J Hum Hypertens* 1996; **10**: 83–5.)

> The most common symptom of PVD is intermittent claudication, and it also increases the chances of cardiovascular death three-fold

Hypertension is also a major risk factor for aneurysmal dilation of the aorta (thoracic and abdominal). High pulsatile wave stress and atheromatous disease can lead to dissection of the aorta, which carries a high short-term mortality. Extracranial carotid artery disease is also more common in hypertensive patients and is one of the mechanisms by which hypertension leads to the increased risk of stroke.

Despite these well-recognized associations, none of the large antihypertensive treatment trials have adequately studied the benefit of BP reduction on the incidence of PVD and aortic aneurysms. There is an obvious need for such outcome studies to correlate the effect of BP reduction on the incidence of these arterial diseases, especially since the two conditions are commonly encountered together, but the association is often neglected.

> The majority of aortic aneurysms occur in patients with hypertension, where high pulsatile wave stress and atheromatous disease can result in dissection of the aorta

Kidney and renal failure

Renal dysfunction is often found in hypertensive patients and malignant hypertension frequently leads to progressive renal failure. There is some controversy as to whether or not mild-to-moderate essential hypertension leads to renal failure. It may be that patients who develop renal failure in fact have hypertension secondary to renal disease, rather than vice-versa.

In the Renfrew community project, individuals with raised BP had a higher frequency of ECG evidence of left ventricular enlargement assessed by the Minnesota code and slightly larger cardiothoracic ratios on chest X-ray. In sharp contrast, serum creatinine as an index of renal damage did not differ when comparing hypertensive patients to normotensive patients. If serum creatinine is an index of hypertensive target organ damage as LVH is, then higher serum creatinine levels would be expected in hypertensive patients. Thus the relationship between hypertension and the kidney is qualitatively rather than quantitatively different from the link between hypertension and cardiac or cerebral damage.

Proteinuria

In hypertensive patients, the presence of proteinuria is prognostically important and associated with a roughly two-fold increase in cardiovascular mortality (Figure 4.6). Microproteinuria has been considered to be evidence of early BP-induced kidney damage. Relationships have been found between microproteinuria and the left ventricular mass on echocardiography.

In the INTERSALT (International Study of Salt and Blood Pressure) project, no relationship was found between the height of the systolic or diastolic BP and the amount of protein in urine. This may be related to the large number of non-BP related causes of proteinuria (non-specific), including fever, heart failure, changes in posture, vigorous exercise and trauma.

There are no reported cases of benign essential hypertensive patients with normal serum creatinine levels and no proteinuria who subsequently went on to develop renal failure. This is in sharp contrast to the relationship between hypertension and its cardiovascular and cerebral complications where uncomplicated benign hypertension frequently leads to the development of heart attacks or strokes. These data strongly suggest that only those patients with primary renal disease will progress to develop end-stage renal failure (Figure 4.7).

Possible mechanisms of renal damage in hypertension

Several hormones, some of which have a renal origin, are involved in the maintenance of BP, renal blood flow and renal function. Most of these mechanisms explain why kidney diseases

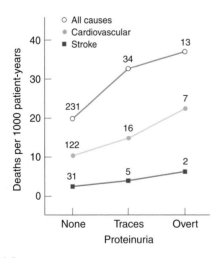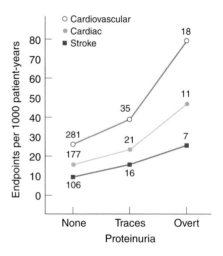

Figure 4.6

The left panel shows age- and gender-adjusted death rates according to the level of proteinuria. The right panel shows the age- and gender-adjusted fatal and non-fatal event rates according to the level of proteinuria. (From De Leeuw et al. Prognostic significance of renal function in elderly patients with isolated systolic hypertension: results from the Syst-Eur trial. *J Am Soc Nephrol* 2002; **13**: 2213–22.)

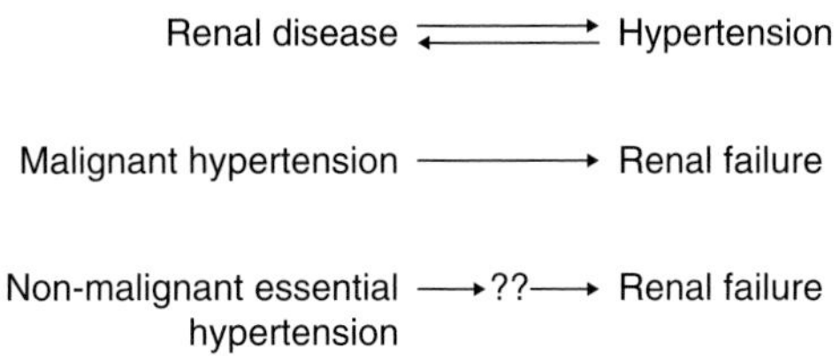

Renal disease ⇄ Hypertension

Malignant hypertension ⟶ Renal failure

Non-malignant essential ⟶??⟶ Renal failure
hypertension

Figure 4.7
Hypertension and the kidney – the development of end-stage renal failure.

cause raised BP rather than vice versa. Some patients with hypertension-induced atheromatous disease of their renal arteries might be expected to develop renal impairment but that is not due to intrinsic kidney damage.

Other possible mechanisms include effects of cardiovascular drugs, such as a reduction of cardiac output and renal blood flow due to beta-blockade and a reduction of renal plasma flow in patients treated with ACE inhibitors while in a state of intravascular volume depletion. The vast majority of these patients with benign essential hypertension will not develop any renal damage whether they are treated or untreated.

> Several hormones help maintain BP, renal blood flow and renal functions, and most explain why kidney diseases cause raised BP rather than vice versa

Evidence from treatment trials

Among hypertensive patients, renal damage is rare compared to heart attacks and strokes, and the number of renal events encountered in the randomized trials of treatment is very small. There is a definite lack of difference in renal endpoints in treated versus untreated hypertensive patients, with a tiny number of cases developing renal impairment.

Participants in the MRC trial of mild hypertension (including a cohort from Renfrew) had their serum urea levels measured at

baseline and were restudied after three years; there was no difference at the outset between those patients who were randomized either to placebo, propranolol, or bendrofluazide treatment (Figure 4.8). A tendency to develop a rise in serum creatinine has been noted in African Americans with hypertension. However, it was striking that the relationship between BP at screening and subsequent renal impairment was very weak compared with the close relationship between BP and the subsequent development of heart attack and strokes.

In a meta-analysis of 10 trials involving 26,521 individuals, Hsu found that among patients enrolled into clinical trials with non-malignant hypertension and without renal dysfunction at baseline, treated patients did not have a lower risk of renal dysfunction. Therefore, this meta-analysis questions the link between benign essential hypertension and renal failure in patients without renal disease.

In contrast, the benefit of blood pressure lowering in ameliorating the progression of renal disease is well demonstrated. A meta-analysis of patients with chronic renal disease and albuminuria suggests better outcomes with systolic blood pressures of less than 130 mmHg and indeed, analysis of the Modification of Diet in Renal Disease study suggests that patients with proteinuria (>1 g/24 hours) may benefit from reduction of blood pressure to less than 125/75 mmHg. Hence, a blood pressure goal of 130/80 mmHg for patients with renal disease is recommended by international guidelines.

> Limited evidence exists that controlling BP in non-malignant essential hypertension influenced renal function in patients without renal disease. However, blood pressure reduction in patients *with* renal disease retards the progression of renal dysfunction

Retinopathy

Hypertension leads to vascular changes in the eye, referred to as hypertensive retinopathy.

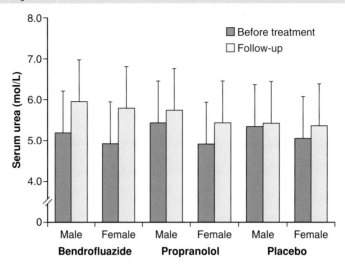

Figure 4.8
Changes in blood urea levels over five years. Data are from the Medical Research Council (MRC) trial. (Adapted from MRC Working Party on Mild Hypertension. *Br Med J* 1986; **293**: 988–92.)

These changes have been classified by Keith, Wagener and Barker into four grades, which correlate with prognosis (Tables 4.7 and 4.8). Malignant hypertension, the most severe form, is clinically defined as raised BP in association with bilateral retinal flame-shaped haemorrhages, and/or cotton wool spots and/or hard exudates, with or without papilloedema.

Table 4.7
The Keith, Wagener, Barker classification

Grade I	Grade II	Grade III	Grade IV
● Benign hypertension ● Mild narrowing or sclerosis of the retinal arterioles ● No symptoms ● Good general health	● More marked hypertensive retinopathy ● Moderate to marked sclerosis of the retinal arterioles ● Exaggerated arterial light reflex ● Venous compression at arteriovenous crossings ● Blood pressure higher and more sustained than Group 1 ● (Asymptomatic) ● Good general health	● Mild angiospastic retinopathy ● Retinal oedema, cotton-wool spots and haemorrhages ● Sclerosis and spastic lesions of retinal arterioles ● Blood pressure often high and sustained ● (Symptomatic)	● Malignant hypertension ● All the features in Grades I–III plus optic disc oedema ● Cardiac and renal functions may be impaired ● Reduced survival

Table 4.8

Keith, Wagener, Barker classification – patient survival (Adapted from Keith NM, Wagener HP, Barker NW. Some different types of essential hypertension: their course and prognosis. *Am J Med Sci* 1939; **196**: 332–43)

Years follow-up	Patient survival (%)			
	Grade I	Grade II	Grade III	Grade IV
1	90	88	65	21
3	70	62	22	6
5	70	54	20	1

Further reading

Dahlof B, Pennert K, Hansson L. Reversal of left ventricular hypertrophy in hypertensive patients: a meta-analysis of 109 treatment studies. *Am J Hypertens* 1992; **5**: 95–110.

Dahlof B, Devereux RB, Kjeldsen SE, *et al.* Cardiovascular morbidity and mortality in the Losartan Intervention For Endpoint reduction in hypertension study (LIFE): a randomized trial against atenolol. *Lancet* 2002; **359**: 995–1003.

Levy D, Anderson KM, Savage DD, *et al.* Echocardiographically detected left ventricular hypertrophy: prevalence and risk factors: the Framingham Heart Study. *Ann Intern Med* 1988; **108**: 7–13.

Lip GYH, Felmeden DC, Li-Saw-Hee FL, *et al.* Hypertensive heart disease: a complex syndrome or a hypertensive 'cardiomyopathy'? *Eur Heart J* 2000; **21**: 1653–65.

Rigaud AS, Seux ML, Staessen JA, *et al.* Cerebral complications of hypertension. *J Hum Hypertens* 2000; **14**: 605–16.

Schmieder RE, Messerli FH. Hypertension and the heart. *J Hum Hypertens* 2000; **14**: 597–604.

Schmieder RE, Martus P, Klingbeil A. Reversal of left ventricular hypertrophy in essential hypertension: a meta-analysis of randomized double-blind studies. *JAMA* 1996; **275**: 1507–13.

Schmieder RE, Schlaich MP, Klingbeil AU, *et al.* Update on reversal of left ventricular hypertrophy in essential hypertension (a meta-analysis of all randomized double-blind studies until December 1996). *Nephrol Dial Transplant* 1998; **13**: 564–9.

5. Clinical assessment

Clinical assessment
Investigation of all patients with hypertension
Investigation for secondary causes of hypertension

Clinical assessment

The assessment of the hypertensive patient should include (Table 5.1): confirmation of the diagnosis, assessment of the patient for the underlying cause(s) and target organ damage, identification of concomitant cardiovascular risk factors (to assess overall CVD risk) and identification of compelling indications and contraindications.

The most important aspect of the management of a patient presenting with high blood pressure (BP) is to confirm the diagnosis of hypertension. Multiple measurements of BP over a period of time may show that BP levels fall over time so that a significant number of

patients can no longer be regarded as hypertensive. Some patients develop high BP in relation to hospital or clinical attendance, the so-called 'white-coat' effect. Patients with white-coat hypertension do not need antihypertensive therapy but do need careful monitoring as these patients may exhibit minor vascular changes and eventually develop overt hypertension in the future. Ambulatory BP monitoring devices have assisted the diagnosis of this condition, with the typical high BPs when the patient is attending the doctor/hospital and virtually normal BPs when the patient is away from the doctor/hospital.

It is a fundamental error to condemn a patient to decades of medication based on only one or two casual BP measurements. Except for hypertensive emergencies or those in high-risk groups (including those exhibiting hypertensive target organ damage), it is good practice to take multiple BP readings over a few months while pursuing non-pharmacological measures before instituting drug therapy.

> Multiple measurements of BP are advisable to diagnose hypertension, as a prelude to drug treatments

BP measurement

Despite the important management decisions based upon it, BP measurement in clinical practice is fraught with inaccuracy. Variation in BP readings might occur owing to factors in the patient (biological variation) or problems involving the observer (measurement variation). Frequent observer retraining and a meticulous technique are vital. In an individual patient, BP can vary considerably. BP tends to be highest first thing in the morning and lowest at night, and is higher in cold weather and after consuming caffeine, tobacco or alcohol.

All adults should have BP measured routinely at least every five years until the age of 80 years. Those with high-normal values (135–139/85–89 mmHg) and those who have had high

---

Table 5.1
Assessment of hypertensive patients

- Causes of hypertension, e.g. renal disease, endocrine causes
- Contributory factors, e.g. obesity, salt intake, excess alcohol intake
- Complications of hypertension, e.g. previous stroke, left ventricular hypertrophy
- Cardiovascular risk factors, e.g. smoking, family history
- Contraindications to specific drugs, e.g. asthma (beta-blockers), gout (thiazides)

readings at any time previously should have BP re-measured annually. Seated BP recordings are generally sufficient, but standing BP should be measured in elderly or diabetic patients to exclude orthostatic hypotension.

> BP readings should be treated with some caution as a multiplicity of factors can skew the results

Measurement devices

The most accurate device for a non-invasive BP measurement is a well-cared-for mercury manometer; however, mercury is likely to be outlawed in the near future, owing to safety concerns. Aneroid manometers are inaccurate unless regularly calibrated. In the future, it is likely that most BP readings will be made with electronic oscillometric devices, although currently only a few such machines have been carefully validated or certified for clinical use. For example, many devices have failed the British Hypertension Society (BHS) and/or the Association for the Advancement of Medical Instrumentation (AAMI) criteria, although the OMRON HEM 705 CP, OMRON M4 & UA-767 (A&D) have passed. Unfortunately, many devices are marketed without accuracy testing. (For full recommendations of the European Society of Hypertension on blood pressure measuring devices, see O'Brien et al. Blood pressure measuring devices: recommendations of the European Society of Hypertension. Br Med J 2001; 322: 531–6, or visit the British Hypertension Society website: www.bhsoc.org for devices that have been tested according to the BHS protocol.)

> Equipment must be regularly calibrated to ensure accuracy of BP measurements

Measurement technique

It is important that the correct sized cuff is used when measuring BP: the width of the air bladder should be equal to about two-thirds the distance from the axilla to the antecubital fossa and it should encompass at least 80% of the upper arm. The use of too small a cuff will result in an overestimation of the BP. Conversely, oversized cuffs will underestimate the BP.

The patient should be seated in a quiet room with the arm supported at the same level as the heart. The cuff should be inflated to about 20 mmHg above the systolic pressure as indicated by the disappearance of the radial pulse. It should then be deflated at 2–4 mmHg/s and the systolic pressure recorded at the first appearance of the ausculatory sounds, while the diastolic pressure is indicated by the disappearance of the sounds (phase V) (Figure 5.1).

Multiple measurements and monitoring

Management decisions should be made based on readings taken on several occasions over a period of time. An average reading of several measurements taken at separate visits is more accurate than measurements taken at a single visit. In uncomplicated mild hypertension, the average of two readings per visit at monthly intervals over 4–6 months should be used to guide the decision to treat. In more severe hypertension, prolonged observation is not necessary or warranted before treatment. The average BP is only one factor determining cardiovascular risk in uncomplicated mild hypertension. Any formal estimation of CVD risk should heed the consideration of age, sex, smoking habit, diabetes, total cholesterol:high-density lipoprotein (HDL) cholesterol ratio and family history in addition to BP, as described later.

Systolic or diastolic BP?

In practice, systolic BP should be regarded as the more important. Both systolic and diastolic BP are highly correlated, and outcome trials of antihypertensive treatment based on thresholds of diastolic or systolic BP have shown similar reductions in cardiovascular events. Nevertheless, systolic BP is a better predictor of cardiovascular prognosis, correcting for

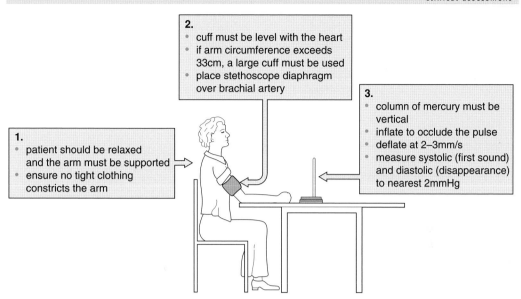

2.
- cuff must be level with the heart
- if arm circumference exceeds 33cm, a large cuff must be used
- place stethoscope diaphragm over brachial artery

3.
- column of mercury must be vertical
- inflate to occlude the pulse
- deflate at 2–3mm/s
- measure systolic (first sound) and diastolic (disappearance) to nearest 2mmHg

1.
- patient should be relaxed and the arm must be supported
- ensure no tight clothing constricts the arm

Figure 5.1
Proper measurement of 'sitting' blood pressure.

underlying diastolic BP. The 2004 British Hypertension Society guidelines recommend a BP treatment target of 140/90 mmHg; this means 140 mmHg systolic or 90 mmHg diastolic in uncomplicated hypertension.

> Systolic BP is a better indicator of cardiovascular risk than diastolic BP

Ambulatory blood pressure monitoring

It is difficult to provide firm guidance on evidence for the use of ambulatory blood pressure monitoring (ABPM) to guide treatment, as all outcome trials in hypertension have been based on surgery or clinic BP, not ABPM. ABPM provides numerous measurements over a short time and reduces variability and measurement error when compared to the average of a limited number of clinic readings. BP by ABPM correlates more closely with evidence of target organ damage.

ABPM may be indicated in the following circumstances:

- when BP shows unusual variability
- in hypertension resistant to drug therapy, defined as BP >150/90 mmHg on a regimen of three or more antihypertensive drugs
- when symptoms suggest the possibility of hypotension
- to diagnose white-coat hypertension.

It is not necessary or feasible to perform ABPM to exclude white-coat hypertension in all hypertensive patients. The term 'white-coat hypertension' has been widely used to describe regular hypertension in the clinic with consistent normotension by ABPM. In these patients, there is a systematic clinic–ABPM difference in the population that is related to the level of clinic BP, and white-coat hypertension is considered to be present only when the clinic–ABPM difference exceeds the population average difference. This white-coat hypertension should be suspected in patients who demonstrate persistently elevated BP yet have little or no evidence of end-organ damage, or who develop symptoms of hypotension on even small doses of antihypertensive drugs.

White-coat hypertension may not need treatment, but should be kept under observation, as many do develop changes in endothelial function, intima thickness, echocardiography that are intermediate between normotensive patients and overt hypertensive patients.

> Ambulatory blood pressure monitoring (ABPM) can be used to provide additional readings for BP, but not to exclude white-coat hypertension

Thus, patients left untreated on the basis of ABPM will need to be followed up, with reassessment of BP and cardiovascular risk at least once-yearly. The annual reassessment may require repeated ABPM measurement.

When interpreting ABPM results, the average daytime BP should be used for treatment decisions, not the average 24-hour BP. Any BP measured by ABPM is systematically lower than surgery or clinic measurements in hypertensive and normotensive people. Thus an ABPM average daytime BP would be expected to be equivalent to 10/5 mmHg lower than the office BP, and both treatment thresholds and targets should be adjusted accordingly.

BP measurement at home

Evidence on the role of self-measurement of BP is less extensive than for ABPM, but many of the same considerations apply. As in ABPM, home blood pressure measurements tend to be systematically lower than clinic BP and BP of ≥135/85 mmHg should be considered the hypertension range.

Patient assessment – beyond blood pressure

The primary purpose of the assessment is to exclude secondary causes (see Table 5.3). Although accounting for fewer than 5% of hypertensive patients, secondary causes of hypertension should be excluded as they are often either correctable or represent serious

underlying disease. Renal and endocrine disease or concomitant medication (such as oestrogen-containing contraceptive pills or non-steroidal anti-inflammatory drugs) account for the majority of the secondary causes of hypertension.

The second purpose is to establish the individual's level of absolute risk. A patient who has had a myocardial infarction is at high risk of further cardiovascular events, and as such will require treatment at lower blood pressure levels. Evidence of hypertensive target organ damage, such as left ventricular hypertrophy (LVH), proteinuria or severe retinopathy are also high-risk features with a lower threshold for blood pressure treatment. Hence, each new patient requires a thorough clinical assessment. A full cardiovascular examination should be accompanied by simple investigations: (i) blood biochemistry for urea and electrolytes, serum creatinine, fasting glucose and cholesterol; (ii) urinalysis for blood, protein and glucose; and (iii) an electrocardiogram (ECG) (Table 5.2).

Thirdly, the individual patient should be assessed for other concomitant conditions or co-morbidities as this will guide antihypertensive therapy. For example, beta-blockers, which are not be recommended for the initial treatment of hypertension, are indicated in patients with heart failure due to

---

Table 5.2

Routine investigations in hypertensive patients (see text for more details)

- Urine strip test, e.g. for protein and blood, which may indicate underlying renal disease
- Serum creatinine and electrolytes, which may raise a clinical suspicion of renal disease, Conn's syndrome, etc.
- Blood glucose, e.g. for associated diabetes
- Total serum:HDL cholesterol, which would allow associated hyperlipidaemia to be treated as part of overall cardiovascular risk prevention
- ECG, e.g. for diagnosis of associated rhythm abnormalities, myocardial infarction, LVH, etc.

left ventricular systolic dysfunction (see Chapter 6). Therefore, antihypertensive therapy may be individualized based on the presence of specific compelling indications or contraindications.

The need for further investigations such as chest X-ray, urine microscopy and culture, renal ultrasound and echocardiography should be individualized. An echocardiogram is valuable to confirm or refute the presence of LVH when the ECG shows 'high' left ventricular voltage without T-wave abnormalities, as is often the case in young patients.

The absolute risk is the probability (range 0 to 1) that an individual will experience the specified outcome during a specified period. The relative risk (RR) is the number of times more likely (RR > 1.0) or less likely (RR < 1.0) an event is to happen in one group compared to another. It is analogous to the odds ratio (OR) when events are rare, and is the ratio of the absolute risk for each group (definition from *Clinical Evidence*).

Investigation of all patients with hypertension

The basic investigations should include blood biochemistry for urea and electrolytes, serum creatinine, fasting glucose and cholesterol, urinalysis for blood, protein and glucose and an ECG.

Urinalysis

Proteinuria and microscopic haematuria might result from renal arteriolar fibrinoid necrosis in patients with malignant hypertension, and also occur in patients with non-malignant hypertension and hypertensive nephrosclerosis. In those cases where proteinuria is present, for a given BP level, the risk of death is roughly doubled. Glycosuria may indicate coincident diabetes mellitus.

Proteinuria and microscopic haematuria may also indicate:

- intrinsic renal disease
  - —glomerulonephritis
  - —polycystic kidney disease
  - —pyelonephritis
- urological malignancy.

Haematology

Anaemia in a hypertensive patient may be due to renal impairment. Polycythaemia may be seen in patients with chronic obstructive airways disease, Cushing's syndrome, alcohol excess and, very rarely, renal carcinoma. Plasma viscosity or erythrocyte sedimentation rate should be measured if there is a suspicion of some underlying vasculitic disease.

Biochemical investigations

Serum sodium concentration may be raised or in the high-normal range in patients with primary hyperaldosteronism (Conn's syndrome). In patients with secondary hyperaldosteronism, as occurs in chronic renal failure, serum sodium concentration can be low or low-normal. Low serum sodium levels are also produced by high doses of diuretics; occasionally profound hyponatraemia may be encountered in combination therapy, such as Moduret (amiloride and hydrochlorothiazide).

Serum potassium concentration is usually low or low-normal in patients with Conn's syndrome, but the most common cause of hypokalaemia is diuretic therapy. Hyperkalaemia may be found in renal failure or with the use of some antihypertensive drugs such as the angiotensin-converting enzyme (ACE) inhibitors or the potassium-sparing diuretics (e.g. spironolactone or amiloride).

> Different serum sodium concentrations indicate different conditions such as Conn's syndrome (high-normal) or secondary hyperaldosteronism (low or low-normal)

Life-threatening hyperkalaemia has been described in patients receiving an ACE inhibitor who then opted to consume a salt substitute (Lo-Salt), which contains potassium chloride instead of sodium chloride. Monitoring of electrolytes is also important with the use of diuretics and ACE inhibitors; in particular, ACE inhibitors and potassium-sparing diuretics should not be used together unless very careful monitoring of serum potassium is undertaken.

Serum urea and creatinine concentrations should be monitored as hypertension may cause renal impairment and renal diseases cause hypertension. A graph plotting the reciprocal of the serum creatinine against time may give an indication of the rate of deterioration of renal function, and hence predict the need for intervention and renal dialysis. Increasingly, laboratories are now reporting estimated glomerular filtration rates, which allows direct assessment of renal function over time. Of note, a rise in serum creatinine early after the initiation of an ACE inhibitor is common. In a review of 12 clinical trials by Bakris and Weir, a rise in serum creatinine of up to 30% that stabilizes within the first two months of ACE inhibitor therapy is associated with long-term preservation of renal function. Based on this study, ACE inhibitors should not be withdrawn in patients with a minor (<30%) rise in serum creatinine.

Primary hyperparathyroidism, which is associated with hypertension, causes a raised serum calcium concentration with a low serum phosphate concentration. As with serum potassium, these results may be affected by the use of diuretic therapy, which modestly raises serum calcium.

Hyperuricaemia is found in about 40% of hypertensive patients, in association with renal impairment. Serum uric acid rises with increased alcohol ingestion or the use of thiazide diuretics. Raised gamma-glutamyl transferase levels strongly suggest an excessive alcohol intake, assuming that other intrinsic liver diseases have been excluded.

Elevated serum cholesterol and triglyceride levels with low high-density lipoprotein (HDL) cholesterol levels are synergistic risk factors that need to be assessed in all hypertensive patients and treated if necessary. They may also be elevated very slightly by the use of some antihypertensive agents, such as the thiazide diuretics and non-selective beta-blockers. Concomitant cardiovascular risk factors are common in patients with hypertension (Figure 5.2) and should be actively sought and treated.

Two-fifths of hypertensive patients have hyperuricaemia in association with renal impairment

Electrocardiography

The ECG should be a routine investigation in all hypertensive patients, providing a baseline with which later changes may be compared. An ECG may show evidence of underlying ischaemic heart disease and is useful to screen for the presence of LVH. However, a normal ECG does not exclude the presence of LVH and there is a strong case for using echocardiography to more regularly diagnose cardiac enlargement.

The diagnosis of LVH by electrocardiogram has been described previously (see Chapter 4). The presence of LVH provides clear evidence of end-organ damage and a three- to four-fold excess mortality, and indicates the need for aggressive BP control. The prognosis is even worse if the 'strain' pattern of ST inversion is also seen in leads V5 and V6.

Despite not being able to exclude LVH, ECGs should be used more frequently to diagnose cardiac enlargements

Investigation for secondary causes of hypertension

Secondary causes of hypertension are listed in Table 5.3. These should be considered in selected patient populations (Table 5.4).

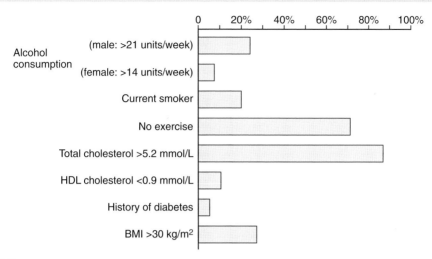

Figure 5.2
Concomitant risk factors in hypertensive patients. HDL, high-density lipoprotein; BMI, body mass index. (Adapted from Poulter *et al. Blood Pressure* 1996; **5**: 209–15.)

Table 5.3
Secondary causes of hypertension

Endocrine:
—Cushing's syndrome
—Conn's syndrome
—phaeochromocytoma
—hyper/hypothyroidism
—acromegaly
—hypercalcaemia
—carcinoid
—exogenous hormones, e.g. contraceptive pill, glucocorticoids
Renal:
—glomerulonephritis
—diabetic nephropathy
—polycystic kidney disease
—renal artery stenosis (fibromuscular or atherosclerotic)
Coarctation of the aorta
Raised intracranial pressure
Pregnancy-induced hypertension
Alcohol and drug abuse
Acute stress

Table 5.4
Patients who require further investigations

● The young (aged <40 years)
● Those with severe hypertension (diastolic blood pressure >120 mmHg)
● Those with resistant or uncontrolled hypertension
● Those with a suspicion of underlying pathology (i.e. secondary hypertension)

trigger further analyses including urinary microscopy for red and white cell casts to exclude glomerulonephritis and vasculitis. This should prompt referral to specialist services. Similarly, specialist referral should be considered in patients with dipstick proteinuria and urinary protein:creatinine ratio of > 100 mg/mmol. Of note, renal dysfunction in patients with diabetes should not be immediately assumed to represent diabetic nephropathy, especially in the absence of other concomitant microvascular disease (e.g. retinopathy).

Renal disease

Urinalysis and renal ultrasound are crucial for the diagnosis of renal disease. The identification of persistent unexplained haematuria should

Renal ultrasonography is useful in demonstrating renal anatomy, for example, hydronephrosis, abnormal polycystic kidneys, or diminished renal size. A unilateral, smooth, small kidney may indicate renal artery stenosis. In patients with intrinsic renal disease the kidneys may appear 'bright' on ultrasonography. Renal ultrasound may be justified in patients with hypertension and renal bruit, abnormal renal function, severe deterioration in renal function with ACE inhibitors and recurrent hospital admissions with 'flash' pulmonary oedema.

Phaeochromocytoma

Phaeochromocytomas are catecholamine-producing neuroendocrine tumours arising most commonly in the adrenal glands. The prevalence of phaeochromocytoma among patients with hypertension is low (<1%), but the consequences of a missed diagnosis are often fatal. Hence a high index of suspicion is required and should be supported by biochemical testing. Symptoms and signs are usually non-specific and include headaches, flushing, palpitations, sweats and sometimes even postural hypotension.

Twenty-four-hour urine collections for catecholamines and vanillyl mandelic acid (VMA) are traditionally used for the diagnosis of phaeochromocytoma. However, more recent data suggest higher sensitivity with measurement of plasma and urinary metanephrines.

Primary aldosteronism

Primary aldosteronism is characterized by hypertension, suppressed plasma renin activity (PRA) and increased plasma aldosterone concentration (PAC). Conn's syndrome refers to an uncommon subtype of primary aldosteronism due to an underlying aldosterone-secreting adenoma. A more common subtype, however, is idiopathic hyperaldosteronism characterized by bilateral hyperplasia of the zona glomerulosa. Using a high PAC:PRA ratio in the presence of high PAC (values dependent on local laboratories), the prevalence of primary aldosteronism may be as high as 12% of patients referred to a tertiary centre. The prevalence is higher in patients with more severe hypertension. PAC:PRA ratio should therefore be considered for patients with resistant hypertension.

Cushing's syndrome

Investigations for Cushing's syndrome should be conducted in all patients with a 'cushingoid' appearance (a plethoric round face, hirsutism, central obesity with red abdominal striae, thin skin and easy bruising). In addition, screening for Cushing's syndrome may be considered in obese patients with uncontrolled glucose and hypertension (especially in association with hypokalaemia).

Random cortisol assays can be misleading and should not be routinely performed. Assessment

Table 5.5
Key issues to consider in imaging

Factors to consider:
- intravenous urography is no longer used in the investigation of hypertension
- renal angiography is the gold standard for the diagnosis of renal artery stenosis, although the procedure does carry some risk
- magnetic resonance (MR) renal angiography is replacing renal angiography as the investigation of choice to diagnose renal artery stenosis
- computed tomography (CT) or magnetic resonance imaging (MRI) can be used for the localization of phaeochromocytomas or adrenal tumours causing aldosterone excess, but beware of non-hormone-secreting incidentalomas detected on CT or MRI
- standard renal radioisotope imaging now has little to offer in the investigation of hypertension
- radioisotope imaging may also be useful in the localization of phaeochromocytomas using scans with metaiodo-benzylguanidene (MIBG scan)
- iodo-cholesterol radioisotope imaging has little value in the diagnosis of aldosterone-secreting adrenal adenomas
- echocardiography is primarily of use in the investigation of structural heart disease, including valvular heart disease and left ventricular dysfunction

of the 24-hour urinary free cortisol (multiple 24-hour collections are generally recommended) and overnight dexamethasone (1 mg) suppression test are useful initial biochemical tests. Clinical suspicion or abnormal biochemical tests should prompt specialist referral as the diagnosis poses significant diagnostic challenge. Imaging tests should not be requested without concomitant biochemical evaluation (Table 5.5).

Acromegaly and hyperparathyroidism

Acromegaly may be suspected from the patient's clinical features; it is investigated through glucose tolerance testing, with measurement of growth hormone and insulin-like growth factor-1 (IGF-1) levels, and imaging of the pituitary fossa. Primary hyperparathyroidism is diagnosed by the presence of a normal or raised parathyroid hormone concentration in the presence of a raised serum calcium concentration.

Further reading

JBS 2: Joint British Societies' guidelines on prevention of cardiovascular disease in clinical practice. *Heart* 2005; **91**: 1–52.

O'Brien E, Waeber B, Parati G, *et al*. Blood pressure measuring devices: recommendations of the European Society of Hypertension. *BMJ* 2001; **322**: 531–6.

Seventh Report of the Joint National Committee on Prevention, Detection, Evaluation and Treatment of High Blood Pressure. *Hypertension* 2003; **42**: 1206–52.

Williams B, Poulter NR, Brown MJ, *et al*. Guidelines for management of hypertension: report of the fourth working party of the British Hypertension Society. *J Hum Hypertens* 2004; **18**: 139–85.

Young Jr WF. Primary aldosteronism – changing concepts in diagnosis and treatment. *Endocrinology* 2003; **144**: 2208–23.

6. Treatment

Cardiovascular risk and
   antihypertensive therapy
Non-pharmacological management
Pharmacological management
Multifactorial interventions to prevent
   cardiovascular disease
Resistant hypertension
Combination antihypertensive therapy
Clinical guidelines

There is almost a dose–response relationship between increasing stroke and coronary risk with increasing blood pressure (BP), while evidence from clinical trials suggests that BP lowering is associated with a marked reduction in cardiovascular events. Therefore, there is no doubt that patients at high risk of cardiovascular events require aggressive BP lowering.

The current approach to the management of hypertension is to take into account the patient's individual characteristics in terms of concomitant disease and risk factors, as well as social and economic considerations, in deciding on the most appropriate therapy.

> Many factors must be taken into account when deciding on appropriate treatment for a hypertensive patient

This chapter provides an overview of the management of hypertension, predominantly based upon the 2004 British Hypertension Society guidelines. These 2004 guidelines, however, preceded the publication of several landmark clinical trials. More recently, the National Institute of Clinical Excellence (NICE) has taken the data from these clinical trials into consideration and issued a partial update on the previous guidelines.

Cardiovascular risk and antihypertensive therapy

Absolute blood pressure and absolute cardiovascular risk

The individual's blood pressure level, presence of other cardiovascular risk factors (e.g. diabetes and dyslipidaemia) or atherosclerotic vascular disease (e.g. coronary heart disease, stroke or peripheral vascular disease) determines the risk of cardiovascular disease (CVD). The threshold for initiating treatment should reflect these clinical factors.

The British Hypertension Society and Joint British Societies consider the following patient groups at high risk of CVD:

- patients with persistently high blood pressure ($\geq$ 160/100 mmHg)
- cardiovascular complications (e.g. previous stroke or coronary disease)
- target organ damage (e.g. left ventricular hypertrophy (LVH))
- type 1 and type 2 diabetes
- renal dysfunction
- total cholesterol:HDL cholesterol ratio >6 or inherited dyslipidaemia.

Therefore, further risk assessment is not required and antihypertensive treatment should be initiated even for patients with 'mild' hypertension (140–159/90–99 mmHg).

For patients with hypertension without these high-risk features, the decision to start antihypertensive treatment should be guided by further CVD risk assessment. Intuitive estimates of absolute risk are very inaccurate, and while risk estimation is improved when additional risk factors are simply counted, it is significantly more accurate when all major risk factors are counted and weighted using risk functions derived from epidemiological studies, most commonly the Framingham risk function.

> Even mild hypertension must be treated if the patient has additional cardiovascular problems

Risk assessment

The 1999 British Hypertension Society guidelines used the Joint British Societies recommendations on preventing coronary heart diseases (CHD), which included a computer program (the 'Cardiac risk assessor') and a CHD risk chart, both of which are based on the Framingham risk function. The second Joint British Societies guidelines now recommend a move away from CHD risk to the more global CVD risk. The latter includes the risk of stroke (fatal/non-fatal stroke, intracerebral haemorrhage and transient ischaemic attack (TIA), in addition to coronary events). The new CVD charts are also based on the Framingham risk function and specify three levels of 10-year CVD risk: $\geq 30\%$, $\geq 20\%$ and $\leq 10\%$, which are equivalent to CHD risk of 23%, 15% and 8% respectively. These three groups are represented by three colour bands on the chart for easy use (see Chapter 2, Table 2.1).

The targeting of antihypertensive treatment at absolute (CVD) risk is underpinned by evidence from meta-analyses of outcome trials. These studies show that the relative risk reduction by antihypertensive treatment is approximately constant, with a 38% reduction in stroke and 16% reduction in coronary events. In patients with mild hypertension, treatment reduces cardiovascular complications by approximately 25%. Treatment of patients at a 10-year CVD risk of $\geq 20\%$ corresponds to a number needed to treat (NNT) for five years of 40 (i.e. treatment of 40 patients for five years to prevent one cardiovascular complication). Assessment of CVD risk also guides the use of aspirin or statins in hypertensive patients. Decisions on treatment at lower levels of CVD risk will be influenced by the patient's attitude

to treatment, and the benefit anticipated from treatment.

It is recommended that all patients with average BP 140–159 or 90–99 mmHg should be offered antihypertensive drug treatment if:

- there is any complication of hypertension or target organ damage, or diabetes
- the 10-year CVD risk is $\geq 20\%$ despite advice on non-pharmacological measures. (Source: British Hypertension Society, 2004)

> Treatment of hypertensive patients can reduce the risk of strokes by 38% and of coronary events by 16%

Monitoring

The British Hypertension Society guidelines recommend that when a decision is reached not to treat a patient with mild hypertension, it is essential to continue observation and monitoring of their BP, at least yearly. Certainly, in about 10–15% of patients, BP levels rise in five years to levels clearly requiring treatment. Age is obviously an important consideration, and risk should be reassessed at yearly intervals. Non-pharmacological measures should be encouraged, to lower BP and cardiovascular risk.

> Yearly monitoring of BP is essential, even in mildly hypertensive patients

Thresholds for intervention

Antihypertensive therapy should be started as follows:

- Accelerated (malignant) hypertension (papilloedema, fundal haemorrhages and exudates) or impending cardiovascular complications: admit for immediate treatment.
- BP $\geq 220/120$ mmHg: treat immediately.
- BP 200–219/110–119 mmHg: confirm over 1–2 weeks, then treat.

- BP 160–199/100–109 mmHg:
  —cardiovascular complications/target organ damage or diabetes (type 1 or 2) present: confirm over 3–4 weeks, then treat
  —cardiovascular complications/target organ damage or diabetes (type 1 or 2) absent: non-pharmacological advice, re-measure weekly and treat if BP persists at these levels over 4–12 weeks.
- BP 140–159/90–99 mmHg:
  —cardiovascular complications/target organ damage or diabetes (type 1 or 2) present: confirm and treat
  —cardiovascular complications/target organ damage or diabetes (type 1 or 2) absent: non-pharmacological advice, re-measure at monthly intervals.
- If mild hypertension persists, estimate 10-year CVD risk formally using the second Joint British Societies CVD risk chart. Treat if the estimated 10-year CVD risk ≥ 20%. (Source: British Hypertension Society, 2004)

Non-pharmacological management

Before a patient is commenced on antihypertensive medication, it is always appropriate to attempt non-pharmacological measures to lower BP, except in a few high-risk cases where they should be applied in parallel. Certainly, non-pharmacological measures can be synergistic with drugs, e.g. salt restriction and the use of diuretics. Elderly and Afro-Caribbean patients are examples where such an approach may be useful. Benefits of non-pharmacological methods are listed in Table 6.1.

> Non-pharmacological methods of lowering BP should be attempted first

A number of lifestyle modifications (e.g. weight reduction, salt and alcohol restriction and regular exercise) may produce significant falls in BP and can also improve other cardiovascular risk factors.

Table 6.1
Benefits of non-pharmacological methods to treat hypertension

- Lowers blood pressure as much as drug monotherapy
- Reduces the need for drug therapy
- Enhances the antihypertensive effect of drugs
- Reduces the need for multiple drug regimens
- Favourably influences overall cardiovascular risk

The epidemiologists would advocate that a population strategy could potentially prevent the rise in BP with age, reduce the prevalence of hypertension and need for drug therapy, and reduce overall cardiovascular risk in a population. The public health initiatives for such a strategy include a diet that is:

- high in fruit and vegetables
- high in legumes and whole grains
- high in fat-free and low-fat dairy products, poultry, fish, shellfish and meat products
- high in all essential nutrients
- reduced in salt
- reduced in total fat, saturated fat and cholesterol
- low in alcohol (with no more than 2–3 units per day)
- calorie-controlled to prevent or correct obesity.

In individual patients, changes in diet and lifestyle do lower BP and may also reduce cardiovascular risk.

> Sensible diet leads to lower blood pressure

Conversely, failure to adopt these measures may attenuate the response to antihypertensive drugs. Clear verbal and written advice should be provided for all hypertensive patients and also for those with high-normal BP or a strong family history.

The British Hypertension Society guidelines suggest that in patients with mild hypertension but no cardiovascular complications or target organ damage, the response to these measures may be observed up to 6 months. In patients with severe hypertension, non-pharmacological measures should also be instituted in parallel with drug treatment, and should be backed up by simple written information. Effective implementation of these non-pharmacological measures requires enthusiasm, knowledge, patience and considerable time spent with patients and other family members. A summary of the recommendations in the British Hypertension Society guidelines is as follows:

Measures that lower BP:

- weight reduction
- reduced salt intake
- reduced alcohol consumption
- physical exercise
- increased fruit and vegetable consumption
- reduced total fat and saturated fat intake.

Measures to reduce cardiovascular risk:

- stop smoking
- replace saturated fat with polyunsaturated and monounsaturated fats
- increase oily fish consumption
- reduce total fat intake.

Weight reduction

Weight reduction results in BP reduction of about 2.5/1.5 mmHg for each kilogram lost and, in addition, could also improve lipid profile and insulin resistance. Pharmacological intervention to improve weight loss is generally only recommended as part of an overall treatment plan in patients with obesity with cardiovascular risk factors, including hypertension. Orlistat is preferable to sibutramine as the latter increases blood pressure and is not recommended for patients with hypertension. Orlistat, however, is associated with significant gastrointestinal effects intrinsic to its mechanism of action (orlistat reduces absorption of fat molecules).

More recently, the novel endocannabinoid receptor CB1 antagonist rimonabant has been shown to enhance weight loss (again, as part of an overall treatment plan) compared to placebo. This is associated with significant improvement in risk factor profile, including blood pressure lowering, improvement in dyslipidaemia and glycaemic control. Rimonabant has also been shown to improve smoking cessation rates although it is currently only licensed for the treatment of obesity.

Salt reduction

Salt reduction from a daily average of 10 g to 5 g (5 g ≈1 teaspoon) can lower average BP by about 5/3 mmHg, and is particularly effective in the elderly and those with higher initial BP levels. In most people eating a western diet, dietary sodium intake is grossly in excess of that required for good health. Hypertensive patients should thus be advised to avoid adding salt to cooking or at the table. Vast quantities of salt are contained in processed foods such as bread (one slice contains 0.5 g), some breakfast cereals and flavour enhancers such as stock cubes or manufactured sauces, and should be avoided. Salt substitutes containing potassium chloride may be beneficial, but can cause life-threatening hyperkalaemia when combined with angiotensin-converting enzyme (ACE) inhibitors or potassium-sparing diuretics. Almost certainly, salt restriction may be useful in combination with antihypertensive therapy.

Alcohol consumption

Alcohol intake should generally be limited to <21 units per week. Hypertensive patients should be advised to limit their alcohol intake to 21 units per week for men and 14 units per week for women. Chronic excessive alcohol intake is associated with hypertension as well as other adverse cardiac effects, e.g. atrial fibrillation or alcoholic cardiomyopathy. Binge drinking is associated with an increased risk of stroke. Consumption of smaller amounts of alcohol, up to the recommended limit, may protect against CHD and should not be discouraged.

Regular exercise

Exercise on a regular basis should be encouraged, and the type of exercise should be 'regular and dynamic' (e.g. brisk walking) rather than 'isometric' (e.g. weight training). For example, three vigorous training sessions per week may be appropriate for fit younger patients, or brisk walking for 20 minutes each day for older patients. Indeed, 30–45 minutes of modest aerobic exercise, such as a brisk walk or a swim, three times a week would produce a modest fall in BP.

Fruit and vegetable consumption

Increased fruit and vegetable consumption, from two to seven portions daily, lowers BP in hypertensive patients by 7/3 mmHg. This effect may be a consequence of increased potassium intake. When this is done in combination with an increase in low-fat dairy products and a reduction of saturated and total fat, BP falls may be larger, averaging 11/6 mmHg in hypertensive patients and 4/2 mmHg in those with high-normal BP.

Smoking cessation

Cigarette smoking substantially increases cardiovascular risk, and is a greater threat than mild hypertension. Hypertensive patients who smoke should be given advice and help to stop smoking. The use of nicotine replacement therapies approximately doubles the smoking cessation rate.

Saturated fat consumption

Serum cholesterol is additive to the risk of CVD. All patients should be advised to reduce saturated fat and cholesterol intake and to use polyunsaturated and monounsaturated fats instead. Most diet changes will only reduce serum cholesterol by an average of 6%, and there are great difficulties in implementing and sustaining these measures. Thus, many will need aspirin and statin treatment in addition to non-pharmacological measures.

Pharmacological management

It is now well established that hypertension confers an increased risk of heart attacks and strokes, and treatment of high BP reduces this risk. There is a wide variety of antihypertensive agents, although most can be classified into one of five major classes. Each of these drug classes has merits and disadvantages, as well as ancillary properties that influence the choice for a particular patient. In addition, many patients require more than one agent to control their BP, so the choice of sensible combination therapy with appropriate synergistic effects of the drugs becomes important.

Choice of drug

The ideal drug should have a predictable dose–response curve, as well as an acceptable, recognized side-effect profile. The issue of 24-hour control has also increasingly been recognized as important. BP tends to be highest first thing in the morning and this is when the majority of cardiac events occur. A short-acting drug, even if taken the evening before, may have worn off by the time the patient rises in the morning, whereas a drug with a longer half-life will still be protecting the patient.

A drug with a long half-life also has the advantage of only being taken once daily which improves compliance, especially given that up to 30% of patients miss at least one dose weekly. For example, the ACE inhibitor trandolapril maintains >50% of its activity 48 hours after the last dose.

As the purpose of treating hypertension is to reduce the incidence of hypertensive complications, particularly CHD and stroke, the ideal drug should have trial evidence to show that it achieves these ends as well as simply lowering BP.

For each major class of antihypertensive drug there are indications and contraindications for use in specific patient groups. When none of the special considerations apply, the least expensive drug with the most supportive trial evidence – a low dose of a thiazide diuretic – should be preferred.

> The ideal drug is a once-daily drug giving 24-hour control, prolonging protection and reducing the risk of patients missing a dose

Clinical studies

Recent long-term double-blind studies have compared the major classes of antihypertensive drugs (thiazides, beta-blockers, calcium antagonists, ACE inhibitors and alpha-blockers) and showed no consistent or important differences as regards antihypertensive efficacy, side-effects or quality of life.

Overall, these outcome trials have shown significant reductions in stroke by 38%, in coronary events by 16% (less than the 20–25% reduction that is predicted from epidemiological observations) and in cardiovascular mortality by 21%. However, there were differences in the average response between drug classes that were linked to age and ethnic group. The absolute benefit from treatment is smaller in women than men, but this is compatible with their lower cardiovascular risk.

Until recently, there were few trials that compared different classes of drugs directly with regard to reduction in cardiovascular events. However, differences between regimens based on different drug classes are now becoming evident.

> Recent clinical trials suggest differences between classes of drugs in reducing cardiovascular events

Thiazide diuretics

Thiazide diuretics act to reduce the reabsorption of sodium and chloride in the early part of the distal convoluted tubule of the kidney. This results in the delivery of increased amounts of sodium to the distal tubule where some of it is exchanged for potassium. The net result is

increased excretion of sodium, potassium and water. Circulating volume is diminished, reducing preload on the heart and thereby lowering cardiac output and BP. With long-term therapy, autoregulation by the body's compensatory mechanisms results in vasodilatation, reduction of peripheral vascular resistance and return of the cardiac output to normal. Thiazides may also have some direct vasodilatory properties. Newer thiazide-like agents such as indapamide may have ancillary direct effect on the myocardium, resulting in regression of LVH.

Thiazides are rapidly absorbed orally and produce a prolonged diuresis. Loop diuretics exert their effects on the loop of Henle and when combined with thiazide diuretics, especially metolazone may result in profound diuresis due to 'sequential nephron blockade'. Hence, combined use of different diuretics requires greater monitoring of patients.

There is no reason not to start treatment with a diuretic in the uncomplicated hypertensive and in fact many clinicians would advocate their use. While there is a flat dose–response curve in terms of blood pressure lowering effect, the side-effect profile is significantly increased at higher doses and low doses should, therefore, be used. Maximal response is obtained at relatively low doses, such as 12.5 mg hydrochlorothiazide or 1.25–2.5 mg bendroflumethiazide. Further increases in dose simply increase side-effects with little further effect on BP. Thus, higher doses of thiazide diuretics (bendroflumethiazide >2.5 mg or hydrochlorothiazide >25 mg daily) are unnecessary and should not be used. On the whole, standard doses of thiazides lower BP as much as other first-line antihypertensives. In some patient groups, e.g. Afro-Caribbean patients and elderly patients, thiazides are particularly effective. Conversely, however, they tend to be less effective in younger Caucasian patients.

There is little to choose between the various thiazides, although it seems prudent to use agents such as hydrochlorothiazide and bendroflumethiazide, which have been proven to be effective at low doses in clinical trials. Newer agents, such as indapamide, have fewer metabolic side-effects and as mentioned above, may even regress hypertensive LVH on echocardiography.

> Use of thiazides leads to increased excretion of sodium, potassium and water, and lowers cardiac output and BP

Clinical studies of thiazide diuretics

Thiazides are one of the classes of antihypertensives that have been extensively tested in large clinical trials. In early trials, thiazides reduced the incidence of stroke by the 40% expected from epidemiological studies, although the reduction in CHD was disappointing. This was perhaps due to the adverse metabolic effects of the large doses used. More recent trials using lower doses have demonstrated impressive reductions in both strokes and heart disease, especially in the elderly. The reduction in coronary events in trials based on low-dose thiazides has been significantly larger, at 28%, than those in trials of regimens based on high-dose thiazide or beta-blocker. Low-dose thiazide-based regimens also significantly reduced cardiovascular and all-cause mortality. The larger benefit on coronary events observed in these trials using low-dose thiazides is not necessarily related to the dose of thiazide as such. It may be related to differences in age, to more effective potassium conservation in these trials or to chance.

In the ALLHAT study involving over 40,000 patients with hypertension, there was no difference in the primary endpoint or mortality between thiazide diuretics, ACE inhibitor and calcium channel blocker.

In the LIVE study, the thiazide-like agent indapamide SR 1.5 mg was compared to enalapril 20 mg over a period of one year. Both agents significantly reduced BP, but only indapamide SR had a significant effect on left ventricular mass, reducing it by 5.8% compared to 1.9% with enalapril (Figure 6.1). The addition of indapamide to the ACE inhibitor perindopril was also associated with significant reductions in recurrent strokes in the PROGRESS study (among patients with previous stroke or TIA).

Hence, thiazide diuretics are effective antihypertensive agents and may be used as first-line treatment in most patients, especially in patients with low renin state (see later).

Adverse effects

Predictably, thiazide diuretics cause hypokalaemia due to renal potassium wasting. Hypokalaemia may result in ventricular arrhythmias and cause adverse drug effects in patients on digoxin or drugs that prolong the QT interval on the ECG (e.g. Class I anti-arrhythmics, tricyclic antidepressants, antihistamines).

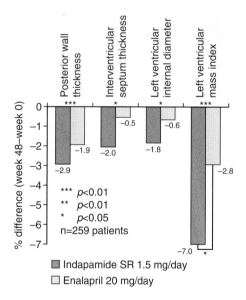

Figure 6.1
Beneficial effects of thiazide on cardiac dimensions; not only do they reduce blood pressure but they can also have a significant effect on left ventricular mass. (Adapted from Gosse *et al. J Hypertens* 2000; **18:** 1465–75.)

Acute gout is another common side-effect of thiazides even when taken in low doses. Hyperuricaemia can be present in about 30% of hypertensives, but is a poor predictor of acute gout.

Thiazide diuretics can increase serum LDL-cholesterol and triglyceride levels, impair glucose tolerance and exacerbate insulin resistance. However, the provocation of overt diabetes is uncommon. Indeed, these adverse metabolic complications are less likely to be a problem at the (low) doses recommended. In hyperlipidaemic and diabetic hypertensive patients, the benefits gained from blood pressure lowering and consequent reduction in cardiovascular risk with low-dose diuretics outweigh these potential metabolic changes. Hence, these metabolic effects should not preclude their use in patients with hypertension.

Rarer side-effects include nausea, headache, rashes, photosensitivity and blood dyscrasias.

> Thiazides can cause metabolic side-effects but are unlikely to pose such problems at low doses

Other diuretics

Loop diuretics act on the ascending limb of the loop of Henle to inhibit the reabsorption of chloride, sodium and potassium. They produce a brisk but short-lived diuresis and are therefore *unsuitable as first-line agents for hypertension* as they lack 24-hour control. They do, however, have a role in those with impaired renal function in whom thiazides are ineffective, and in patients with hypertension resistant to multiple drug therapy who are often fluid overloaded. Furthermore, they may be synergistic with agents such as the ACE inhibitors.

Potassium-sparing diuretics, such as amiloride and triamterene, produce little reduction in BP. They may be useful in combination with other

diuretics to prevent hypokalaemia. Spironolactone is a specific aldosterone antagonist, with a particular role in primary hyperaldosteronism or Conn's syndrome. Eplerenone is also an aldosterone antagonist, albeit with lower receptor affinity (less potent) but higher specificity (fewer anti-androgenic side-effects). The use of aldosterone antagonists is likely to increase with growing recognition of primary aldosteronism (see Chapter 5, 'Primary aldosteronism'). Spironolactone and eplerenone have prognostic benefit in patients with heart failure due to left ventricular systolic dysfunction (RALES study), and heart failure post-myocardial infarction (EPHESUS study) respectively. Serum potassium, however, should be monitored, especially if used in conjunction with ACE inhibitors and in patients with renal failure.

Beta-adrenergic receptor blockers

Beta-adrenergic receptor blockers act by blocking the action of noradrenaline (norepinephrine) at beta-adrenoreceptors throughout the circulatory system and elsewhere. As a class, beta-blockers are heterogeneous with varying selectivity for $beta_1$-adrenoreceptors, their intrinsic sympathomimetic activity and other associated effects on alpha-adrenoreceptors, antioxidative and nitric oxide modulating effects. Their major effect is to slow the heart rate and reduce the force of contraction of the heart. Beta-blockers also cause some reduction in renin release and central sympathetic tone.

The $beta_1$-receptor blockers or cardioselective agents, such as atenolol, have relatively less action on $beta_2$-adrenoreceptors in the bronchi and peripheral vessels, when compared to a non-selective agent such as propranolol. This reduces (but does not totally abolish) $beta_2$-receptor-mediated side-effects. Some beta-blockers, such as pindolol, have intrinsic sympathomimetic activity where they stimulate beta-adrenoreceptors when the background sympathetic nervous activity is low, and block beta-adrenoreceptors when background sympathetic nervous activity is high. They cause less bradycardia and fewer problems with cold extremities than conventional beta-blockers, but in practice are not regularly used in the treatment of hypertension. Labetalol and carvedilol have both alpha-blocking and beta$_1$-blocking properties, leading to a reduction in peripheral vascular resistance as well as slowing the heart rate. They have the disadvantage of possessing the side-effects of both classes of drug. In addition to its beta$_1$-blocking properties, carvedilol also has antioxidant effects, which may have advantages in reducing endothelial damage and lowering levels of highly atherogenic oxidized LDL-cholesterol.

Nebivolol is a highly selective antagonist of the beta$_1$-receptor with vasodilatory properties associated with modulation of nitric oxide production. Studies suggest greater short-term (three months) BP lowering compared to other beta-blockers (metoprolol), ACE inhibitor (enalapril) and calcium channel blocker (nifedipine), with low incidence of beta-blocker-related side-effects.

Efficacy of beta-blockers

Beta-blockers have been used as first-line antihypertensive agents for many years, but recent data are now challenging this practice. Beta-blockers were previously noted to be less effective in the elderly and in Afro-Caribbean patients. Recent meta-analysis suggests that beta-blockers may be ineffective in reducing the risk of myocardial infarction compared to placebo and reduced the risk of stroke by only about half of that expected from previous studies (19% compared to 38%). The efficacy of atenolol in particular has been called into question, with a meta-analysis suggesting higher mortality with atenolol compared to other antihypertensive agents, despite similar reductions in blood pressure. The combination of bendroflumethiazide and atenolol was also shown to be inferior to a regime of amlodipine and perindopril in the recent ASCOT study, raising further doubts about the efficacy of beta-blockers in uncomplicated hypertension.

With potential adverse effects, especially in combination with thiazide diuretics (metabolic effects, see under 'beta-blockers and diabetes'), beta-blockers are now out of favour as a first-line antihypertensive agent in uncomplicated hypertension. Indeed, beta-blockers are now removed as a first-line antihypertensive treatment in uncomplicated hypertension in the recent NICE hypertension guidelines (see later).

However, beta-blockers should not be discarded completely. They have proven symptomatic benefit in stable angina, reduce the incidence of recurrent fatal and non-fatal myocardial infarction (MI) and sudden death in patients following a first MI, and improve prognosis in patients with heart failure due to left ventricular systolic impairment (carvedilol, bisoprolol, nebivolol and extended-release metoprolol).

Therefore, beta-blockers should be used in the presence of these compelling indications, but not as first-line agent in the treatment of uncomplicated hypertension.

Adverse effects and contraindications

Most of the side-effects of beta-blockers are predictable from their pharmacology. For example, beta-blockers slow the rate of conduction at the atrioventricular node and are thus contraindicated in patients with second- and third-degree heart block. Sinus bradycardia is common and is not a reason to stop beta-blockers unless the patient is symptomatic or the heart rate falls below 40 beats/min.

Small doses of beta-blockers can cause bronchospasm due to a blockade of pulmonary beta$_2$-adrenoreceptors, although the problem is less common with cardioselective agents. Even so, all beta-blockers are contraindicated in asthma.

The blockade of beta-receptors in the peripheral circulation causes vasoconstriction at least in the immediate term, and beta-blockers therefore should be used with caution in patients with rest ischaemia of the legs. Nevertheless, they are reasonably tolerated in those with lesser degrees of peripheral vascular disease.

The lipid-soluble beta-blockers (e.g. propranolol and metoprolol) cross the blood–brain barrier more readily and are associated with a higher incidence of side-effects, including sleep disturbances and nightmares. Exercise capacity may be reduced by the beta-blockers and patients may experience tiredness and fatigue. As with most pharmacologically treated patients, impotence has been reported.

> Beta-blocker side-effects can usually be predicted, e.g. slowing the rate of conduction at the atrioventricular node, so they can be contraindicated

Beta-blockers and diabetes

Like diuretics, non-selective beta-blockers can worsen glucose intolerance and hyperlipidaemia. In diabetics prone to hypoglycaemia, beta-blockers could theoretically reduce the awareness of low blood glucose. Nevertheless, many diabetic hypertensive patients have good reasons to be on a beta-blocker, such as a previous myocardial infarction, and should not be denied them because of concerns about such metabolic side-effects.

Beta-blockers may also promote weight gain and in the CAPP study, treatment based on beta-blockers and thiazides resulted in significantly more patients (approximately 21%) developing diabetes over five years when compared to treatment based on the ACE inhibitors. However, body weight and metabolic changes did not adversely influence the efficacy of antihypertensive therapy at reducing cardiovascular morbidity and mortality. Furthermore, in the Atherosclerosis Risk in Communities Study of 12,550 adults 45–64 years old who did not have diabetes, subjects with hypertension who were taking thiazide diuretics were not at greater risk for the subsequent development of diabetes than were subjects with hypertension who were not

receiving any antihypertensive therapy (relative hazard, 0.91; 95% CI, 0.73 to 1.13). In contrast, hypertensive patients who were taking beta-blockers had a 28% higher risk of subsequent diabetes (relative hazard, 1.28; 95% CI, 1.04 to 1.57).

As discussed, the concern about the risk of diabetes should not discourage physicians from prescribing thiazide diuretics to non-diabetic adults who have hypertension. However, the concomitant use of beta-blockers does appear to increase the risk of diabetes. This potential adverse effect must therefore be weighed against the proven benefits of beta-blockers in patients with compelling indications.

Calcium antagonists

Calcium antagonists, otherwise known as calcium channel blockers, act by interfering with the action of voltage-gated calcium channels in the cell membrane, thus reducing the inflow of calcium, smooth muscle contraction and electrical conductivity.

Classes of calcium antagonist

In general, calcium antagonists may be divided into two classes. The dihydropyridines, such as nifedipine and amlodipine, act predominantly by causing peripheral vasodilatation; and the non-dihydropyridines, such as verapamil and diltiazem, which also slow the heart rate and atrioventricular node conduction. The older calcium antagonists, such as nifedipine, have short half-lives and may cause rapid vasodilatation, a reflex tachycardia and catecholamine surges, which increase adverse effects and may aggravate myocardial ischaemia. Certainly, short-acting nifedipine capsules should not be used. The tendency to crush and give them sublingually is illogical, as they are not absorbed from the buccal mucosa, and should never be used. The crushed nifedipine capsule also alters the pharmacokinetics, which can cause erratic falls in BP. Longer-acting agents such as amlodipine or slow-release preparations of nifedipine partially overcome these problems.

The phenylalkylamine calcium channel blocker verapamil is less well studied compared to dihydropyridine calcium blockers. In general, verapamil is a useful alternative to beta-blockers (for example in patients with angina) when the latter are contraindicated because of the side-effect profile or asthma. In one study, verapamil has even been shown to have synergistic effects in combination with the dihydropyridine calcium channel blocker nitrendipine.

> There are two general classes of calcium antagonists: dihydropyridines (e.g. nifedipine and amlodipine) and non-dihydropyridines (e.g. verapamil and diltiazem)

Clinical studies of calcium channel antagonists

In the mid-1990s, a series of pharmacosurveillance case-control studies suggested that the short-acting dihydropyridine calcium antagonists (such as nifedipine capsules) actually increased the risk of coronary events, cancer, bleeding, depression, suicide and other adverse events. There is little biological plausibility for some of the adverse effects proposed.

Recent data from the SYST-EUR trial demonstrated that antihypertensive treatment with the short-acting dihydropyridine calcium antagonist nitrendipine, convincingly reduced strokes and

heart attacks, without an increase in conditions previously attributed to the calcium antagonists (e.g. tumours, bleeding and non-cardiac death) (Table 6.2). Recent trials (INSIGHT, NORDIL) show no significant difference between the calcium antagonists and 'conventional' antihypertensive drugs (diuretics, beta-blockers).

Pahor and colleagues (2000) published a meta-analysis of nine eligible trials that included 27,743 participants, and reported that the calcium antagonists and other drugs achieved similar control of both systolic and diastolic blood pressure. However, compared with patients assigned diuretics, beta-blockers, ACE inhibitors or clonidine ($n=15,044$), those assigned calcium antagonists ($n=12,699$) had a significantly higher risk of acute myocardial infarction (odds ratio 1.26 [95% CI 1.11–1.43], $P=0.0003$), congestive heart failure (1.25 [1.07–1.46], $P=0.005$), and major cardiovascular events (1.10 [1.02–1.18], $P=0.018$). There was no difference for the outcomes of stroke (0.90 [0.80–1.02], $P=0.10$) and all-cause mortality (1.03 [0.94–1.13], $P=0.54$).

In contrast, Staessen and colleagues (2001) published a larger meta-analysis of nine randomized trials comparing treatments in 62,605 hypertensive patients which suggested that calcium-channel blockers provided more reduction in the risk of stroke (13.5%, 95% CI 1.3–24.2, $P=0.03$) and less reduction in the risk of myocardial infarction (19.2%, 3.5–37.3,

Table 6.2
The Syst-Eur Study. (Adapted from Staessen *et al. Lancet* 1997; **350**: 757–64.)

	Rate/1000 patients years (number of events)		
	Placebo (n=2297)	Active (n=2398)	P value
CV events			
Stroke	10.1 (57)	5.7 (34)	0.007
Cardiac endpoints	12.6 (70)	8.5 (50)	0.03
Non-CV events			
Fatal/non-fatal cancer	14.7 (82)	12.4 (73)	0.29
Benign neoplasm	3.0 (17)	4.0 (24)	0.35

$P=0.01$). The recent ASCOT study provides further support for the use of a calcium channel blocker-based antihypertensive regime. In this study of over 19,000 patients with hypertension, amlodipine as first-line, with the addition of ACE inhibitor, was associated with lower all-cause mortality (a secondary endpoint) compared to the atenolol-based regime. Hence, the overall evidence strongly suggests that the benefits of dihydropyridine calcium antagonist treatment clearly exceed any risks.

Dihydropyridine calcium antagonists are an appropriate first-line treatment of hypertension in most cases, especially in low renin states (see later).

Adverse effects

The main side-effect with calcium antagonists is ankle oedema due to vasodilatation, which also causes headache, flushing and palpitation especially with short-acting dihydropyridines. Some side-effects can be offset by combining a calcium antagonist with a beta-blocker.

Verapamil reduces intestinal motility and can cause significant constipation, but more seriously it can cause heart block especially in those with underlying conduction problems. Verapamil should not be prescribed with a beta-blocker owing to the risk of asystole, complete heart block or heart failure. Diltiazem can similarly cause gastrointestinal and conduction problems, although less frequently than verapamil. Verapamil, diltiazem and short-acting dihydropyridines are best avoided in patients with heart failure. In contrast, the long-acting dihydropyridines, such as amlodipine and felodipine, are neutral in heart failure and would be useful for the concomitant treatment of hypertension or angina in these patients.

> The main side-effect of calcium antagonists is ankle oedema, but this can sometimes be offset by combining with a beta-blocker (though not verapamil)

Alpha$_1$-adrenoreceptor blockers

The alpha$_1$-adrenoreceptor blockers cause vasodilatation by blocking the action of noradrenaline (norepinephrine) at post-synaptic alpha$_1$-receptors in arteries and veins, resulting in a fall in peripheral resistance without a compensatory rise in cardiac output. The older alpha$_1$-blocker prazosin is short acting and tends to produce precipitate falls in BP, but the longer-acting doxazosin combines the advantage of a more gentle reduction in BP with once-daily dosing.

Alpha$_1$-adrenoreceptor blockers produce comparable reductions in BP to first-line antihypertensive drugs. They are useful as a third-line drug, producing good falls in BP where using two agents combined has failed.

In contrast to the beta-blockers and diuretics, alpha$_1$-adrenoreceptor blockers modestly improve serum, lipid and glucose tolerance, but whether or not this translates into improved outcomes is unknown, particularly with the lack of data on these agents.

> The alpha$_1$-adrenoreceptor blockers produce vasodilatation by blocking the action of noradrenaline (norepinephrine) in both arteries and veins, leading to a reduction in peripheral resistance without an equivalent compensatory increase in cardiac output

The ALLHAT trial

One worrying analysis from the ALLHAT trial on doxazosin has been highlighted. In January 2000, the independent review committee recommended termination of the doxazosin arm ($n=9067$) of ALLHAT, on account of a 25% higher rate of combined CVD, a major secondary endpoint. After four years, 86% of patients assigned to chlorthalidone were still taking the drug as opposed to 75% in the doxazosin arm, and the mean systolic BP was 135 mmHg in the chlorthalidone group and 137 mmHg in the doxazosin group. Diastolic BPs were similar in the two arms of the trial.

For doxazosin versus chlorthalidone, the relative risk (RR) of developing:

- combined CVD endpoint was 1.25 (95% CI 1.17–1.33; $P < 0.0001$)
- heart failure was 2.04 (95% CI 1.79–2.32)
- stroke was 1.19 (95% CI 1.01–1.4; $P=0.04$).

Thus, it appeared that chlorthalidone, a cheaper drug, was superior to doxazosin for hypertension control, drug compliance and reduction of cardiovascular complications.

Hence, alpha-blockers should not be used as a first-line agent.

Adverse effects

Alpha$_1$-adrenoreceptor blockers are, on the whole, well tolerated, the main side-effect being postural hypotension with the shorter-acting agents. In women, alpha$_1$-adrenoreceptor blockers may cause urinary incontinence, while in men they may improve the symptoms of benign prostatic hypertrophy. Like most antihypertensive drugs, alpha$_1$-adrenoreceptor blockers can cause headache and fatigue.

ACE inhibitors

ACE inhibitors have become increasingly popular antihypertensive agents over the past decade. They work by blocking the renin–angiotensin system, inhibiting the conversion of the inactive angiotensin I to the powerful vasoconstrictor and stimulator of aldosterone release angiotensin II. This results in decreased peripheral vascular resistance and also a reduction in the levels of the sodium-retaining hormone aldosterone.

ACE inhibitors also reduce the breakdown of the vasodilator bradykinin, which may enhance their action but is also responsible for their most troublesome side-effect of coughing. Furthermore, ACE inhibitors may improve endothelial function and reduce central adrenergic tone. They also have beneficial effects on renal haemodynamics, reducing

intraglomerular hypertension and causing improvements in proteinuric renal disease.

> ACE inhibitors work by blocking the renin–angiotensin system, inhibiting the conversion of angiotensin I to angiotensin II

ACE inhibitors and the renin–angiotensin system

Because ACE inhibitors are competitive inhibitors of ACE, the secondary increase in levels of angiotensin I (due to loss of negative feedback) can overcome the ACE blockade. This leads to the return of angiotensin II levels to normal. It is also probable that other non-ACE pathways (involving chymases and tissue plasminogen activator) facilitate the conversion of angiotensin I to angiotensin II and consequent elevation of aldosterone levels. This is termed 'ACE escape' and accounts for the failure of ACE inhibitors to comprehensively block the renin–angiotensin system.

ACE inhibitors as single agents in treatment of hypertension

ACE inhibitors are effective as single agents in hypertension. There is generally little to choose between the large number of ACE inhibitors available. The Captopril Prevention Project (CAPP) study demonstrated that captopril was as effective as traditional antihypertensive agents (mainly thiazides and beta-blockers) in preventing adverse outcomes in hypertension. Other ACE inhibitors, such as fosinopril and trandolapril, have the advantage of hepatic as well as renal excretion. Perindopril, lisinopril and trandolapril are agents with long half-lives, and provide good 24-hour antihypertensive coverage.

Clinical studies of ACE inhibitors

The prognostic benefit of ACE inhibitors is well established in patients with heart failure due to left ventricular systolic dysfunction (CONSENSUS, SAVE and SOLVD trials). Similarly, patients with heart failure post-MI derive significant benefit from ACE inhibition (ramipril in AIRE and trandolapril in TRACE). The positive findings from these early trials led to studies of ACE inhibition in patients at high cardiovascular risk without heart failure.

The HOPE trial randomized 9297 patients at high cardiovascular risk to ramipril or placebo and demonstrated significant reductions in death, MI and stroke. The EUROPA study randomized over 12,000 patients to perindopril or placebo and demonstrated significant reductions in the composite endpoint of cardiovascular death and non-fatal MI. However, there was no significant difference between trandolapril and placebo in cardiovascular death and non-fatal MI in the PEACE trial of 8290 patients. The negative findings in the PEACE trial probably reflect the lower risk profile of the patients in that study (higher use of lipid-lowering treatment and coronary revascularization). Indeed, cardiovascular death and non-fatal MI were highest in the placebo arm of the HOPE study cohort (8.1% and 12.3%), followed by the placebo arm of the EUROPA cohort (4.1% and 6.2%) and lowest in the PEACE cohort (3.7% and 5.3%). Hence, the benefit of ACE inhibitors may be related to the level of cardiovascular risk, with particular benefit in patients with established cardiovascular disease at high risk of further cardiovascular events.

ACE inhibitors are also used in patients with left ventricular dysfunction, and this class is likely to be the most efficacious in LVH regression. The ECG-LVH substudy from the HOPE trial compared baseline and end-of-study ECGs from 8281 patients at high cardiovascular risk who were randomized to ramipril or placebo and followed for 4.5 years in the main HOPE trial. In this analysis, ramipril prevented LVH, or caused a gradual regression of LVH, in 91.9% of patients; interestingly, however, 90.2% of patients assigned to placebo also had regression or prevention of LVH. Patients who experienced regression or prevention of LVH had a reduced risk of the predefined primary outcome

(cardiovascular death, MI, stroke) and of congestive heart failure. Importantly, this effect was independent of hypertension or blood pressure reduction.

ACE inhibitors are also useful in diabetic hypertensive patients, where they slow the progression of diabetic nephropathy (ramipril reduced progression of albuminuria in micro-HOPE study). Reduction in the progression of nephropathy in patients with type 1 diabetes has also been demonstrated (Lewis *et al.* and EUCLID). Furthermore, these agents have shown some benefits in improving diabetic retinopathy and possibly even diabetic neuropathy.

The combination of ACE inhibitor and diuretic has also been shown to reduce the risk of stroke. The PROGRESS study included 6105 patients with a previous history of stroke or transient ischaemic attack and demonstrated significant 43% reduction in the risk of stroke in patients treated with a combination of perindopril and indapamide. The benefit of this combination treatment was associated with significant reduction in blood pressure of 12/5 mmHg. Interestingly, a subgroup analysis of this study found no significant reduction in the risk of stroke with perindopril alone.

Based on these studies, ACE inhibitors are indicated in patients with heart failure from left ventricular systolic dysfunction (including post-MI), high-risk patients with CVD (especially if BP is not adequately controlled to a target of 130/80 mmHg) and patients with diabetes complicated by nephropathy. ACE inhibitors, in combination with a thiazide diuretic, are also indicated in patients with a history of stroke/TIA (secondary prevention). In addition, a number of studies suggest that ACE inhibitors may have additional benefit in reducing the incidence of new-onset diabetes, and may be recommended in patients at high risk of developing diabetes (e.g. glucose intolerance, metabolic syndrome and strong family history of diabetes).

ACE inhibitors may be most useful for treating
patients with heart failure or left ventricular
hypertrophy, as well as diabetic hypertensive
patients

However, the ACE inhibitors tend to be less
effective as antihypertensive agents in Afro-
Caribbean patients and the elderly, owing to the
low renin state of these patients. This relative
ineffectiveness can be overcome by using high
doses or adding a diuretic. The African American
Study of Kidney Disease and Hypertension
(AASK) trial had to be terminated early because
the ACE inhibitor ramipril resulted in a
significant delay in end-stage renal disease
when compared with the calcium antagonist
amlodipine. Patients with a relatively low renin
state should not be deprived of ACE inhibitor
therapy in the presence of a compelling
indication.

Hence, ACE inhibitors may be used as first-line
therapy in patients with higher renin state
(younger and non-Afro-Caribbean patients) or in
the presence of compelling indications described
above.

Adverse effects

Although ACE inhibitors are successful drugs,
they do have some disadvantages. ACE is not a
specific enzyme and is involved in the
breakdown of many other substances, such as
bradykinin. The use of ACE inhibitors results in
increased levels of bradykinin, resulting in the
common side-effect of coughs and the less
common (but serious) complication of
angioedema. Coughing is more common in
women and older patients. Angioedema occurs
in 0.1–0.2% of patients.

Serum urea and creatinine should be checked
before and a few weeks after starting an ACE
inhibitor. As previously described, a rise in
serum creatinine is common with the use of ACE
inhibitors. In general, a rise in serum creatinine

of up to 30% that stabilizes within the first two
months of treatment is acceptable and may in
fact be associated with long-term preservation
of renal function. However, dramatic and
continued deterioration in renal function can
occur in patients with bilateral renal artery
stenosis. Repeated monitoring of renal function
is therefore important to avoid inappropriate
use or withdrawal of ACE inhibitor therapy.

Significant first-dose hypotension is a fairly
uncommon side-effect of ACE inhibitors,
although large doses of short-acting captopril
can cause sudden falls in BP. This first-dose
effect is most common in those with volume
depletion such as heart failure or in patients on
large doses of diuretics. The limited data
available suggest that perindopril is least likely
to cause this initial hypotension.

Because of their effect of reducing aldosterone
and thus potassium excretion, the ACE
inhibitors can also cause hyperkalaemia. Rarer
side-effects of the ACE inhibitors include rash,
taste disturbance, blood dyscrasias and
vasculitis.

Using ACE inhibitors can lead to increased levels
of bradykinin, which has the side-effect of coughs
and the complication of angioedema

Angiotensin II antagonists

Antagonism of the renin–angiotensin system
has become an attractive target for
pharmacological intervention in light of the
impressive record of ACE inhibitors, most
notably with angiotensin II antagonists.
Angiotensin II, an octapeptide derived from its
inactive precursor angiotensin I by the action of
ACE, is the final product of the
renin–angiotensin system. Angiotensin II
antagonists block the action of angiotensin II
at its peripheral receptors, which offers the
prospect of overcoming the 'ACE escape'
phenomenon (see under ACE inhibitors and the
renin–angiotensin system).

Mode of action

Angiotensin II is a significant contributor to the pathogenesis of arterial disease, hypertension, LVH, heart failure and renal disease. Whereas ACE inhibitors work by reducing the conversion of angiotensin I to angiotensin II, the angiotensin II antagonists block the action of angiotensin II at its peripheral receptors, particularly the type I angiotensin II (ATI) receptor. This results in elevated angiotensin II levels via a loss of feedback, which may lead to increased activation of the type II angiotensin II (ATII) receptors as ATI receptors are blocked. Reduced activation of ATI and increased activation of ATII receptors are believed to be the key mechanism of benefit of angiotensin II antagonist therapy. Angiotensin II antagonists also differ from ACE inhibitors in that they do not inhibit bradykinin breakdown, which spares them the ACE inhibitor-related cough but may lack the additional physiological benefits of bradykinin (a vasodilator). Hence, although both ACE inhibitors and angiotensin II antagonists inhibit the renin–angiotensin system, their different mechanisms of action may lead to different physiological effects, which may be of clinical relevance.

Angiotensin II antagonists lower BP by decreasing peripheral vascular resistance without affecting heart rate and cardiac output. Overall, angiotensin II antagonists produce similar falls in BP compared to ACE inhibitors. As with the ACE inhibitors, they are somewhat less effective in patients with low levels of renin, such as Afro-Carribeans and the elderly, but their action may be potentiated by the addition of a diuretic.

Clinical studies of angiotensin II antagonists

The LIFE study, reported in 2002, randomized 9193 patients with hypertension and documented LVH to losartan and atenolol, and followed up for a mean of 4.8 years. This study of high-risk hypertensive patients showed a significantly lower incidence of fatal and non-fatal cardiovascular events in the losartan group, dominated by significant reduction in the incidence of fatal and non-fatal strokes. This study clearly demonstrates the superiority of losartan over atenolol in hypertension (see 'Efficacy of beta-blockers').

The SCOPE study randomized 4964 (older) patients with hypertension (mean age of 76 years) to candesartan or placebo. As this study permitted open-label treatment, antihypertensive treatment was used extensively in the placebo group. Unlike the LIFE study, the incidence of fatal and non-fatal CVD was not statistically significant between the two groups, though the incidence of stroke tended to be lower in the candesartan group ($P=0.06$).

The VALUE trial is the largest trial of angiotensin II antagonists in hypertension to date. This study randomized 15,245 patients to valsartan or amlodipine and followed up over 4.2 years. The primary endpoint of cardiac morbidity and mortality was not significantly different, although more myocardial infarctions ($P=0.02$) and strokes ($P=0.08$) were observed in the valsartan group. The consistently higher BP in the valsartan group may have accounted for these findings. Overall, these studies suggest that angiotensin II antagonists are likely to be as effective as other classes of antihypertensive therapy (probably with the exception of atenolol) and the degree of BP lowering is the key determinant of cardiovascular outcomes.

Angiotensin II antagonists have also been studied in patients with chronic heart failure, post-MI heart failure and diabetic nephropathy. In chronic heart failure, angiotensin II antagonists have not been shown to be superior to ACE inhibitors (valsartan in Val-HeFT, losartan in ELITE II) although candesartan may offer cardiovascular benefits in patients intolerant of ACE inhibitors (CHARM-alternative). Similarly, angiotensin II antagonists have not been shown to be superior to ACE inhibitors in post-MI heart failure (valsartan was not inferior to captopril in

VALIANT, but cardiovascular mortality was higher in losartan compared with captopril in OPTIMAAL). Angiotensin II antagonists have been shown to reduce the progression of (type 2) diabetic nephropathy (losartan in RENAAL, valsartan in MARVAL, irbesartan in IDNT and IRMA-2).

Based on these data, angiotensin II antagonists cannot be recommended over ACE inhibitors in patients with heart failure. However, the data support the use of angiotensin II antagonists in patients with heart failure (after MI), who are ACE inhibitor-intolerant, patients with type 2 diabetes complicated by nephropathy and patients with hypertension with LVH. Indeed, these represent compelling indications for angiotensin II antagonists in the 2004 British Hypertension Society guidelines. Like ACE inhibitors, angiotensin II antagonists appear to reduce the incidence of type 2 diabetes.

Like ACE inhibitors, angiotensin II antagonists may be used as first-line therapy in patients with higher renin state (younger and non-Afro-Caribbean patients) or in the presence of compelling indications described above.

Adverse effects

The main advantage of the angiotensin II antagonists is their apparent lack of side-effects. One study compared losartan with ACE inhibitors, beta-blockers and calcium channel blockers. The results indicated that using losartan, the incidence of any drug-related adverse experience (including cough) was similar to that of placebo. First-dose hypotension occurred in only 0.4% with losartan 50 mg.

Very rarely, however, angioedema has been reported with losartan. Like the ACE inhibitors, the angiotensin II antagonists may cause hyperkalaemia, renal impairment and hypotension, and are contraindicated in patients with renal artery stenosis. Otherwise they are almost as well tolerated as placebo.

> Angiotensin II antagonists are well tolerated and infrequently cause any significant side-effects

Other antihypertensive agents

Other (older) antihypertensive drugs still have a role in some special situations (e.g. pregnancy) and in resistant hypertension. Because they are cheap, they are popular in countries where hypertensive patients on low incomes have to pay for their own medication. *They are not recommended as first-line treatment of uncomplicated hypertension.*

Centrally acting antihypertensive drugs

Centrally acting agents, such as clonidine and methyldopa, have previously been used to treat hypertension. These agents reduce sympathetic outflow by stimulating alpha$_2$-adrenoreceptors in the central nervous system. This effect leads to a fall in both cardiac output and peripheral vascular resistance. Indeed, methyldopa is safe in the hypertensive pregnant woman, and is commonly used in such patients.

Moxonidine represents the first of a new class of centrally acting antihypertensive drugs, the selective imidazoline receptor agonists, and is hoped to have the beneficial effects of centrally acting drugs without their side-effects. By stimulating central imidazoline receptors, moxonidine also reduces central sympathetic outflow, without the dry mouth and sedation of central alpha$_2$-receptor blockade. Moxonidine also reduces peripheral vascular resistance without an increase in heart rate. The drug may also decrease plasma renin activity by direct action on the kidney, and might increase the excretion of sodium and water. Moxonidine has been shown to be superior to placebo and comparable to the main classes of antihypertensive drugs in lowering BP. There are no long-term studies with survival or cardiovascular events as endpoints, and one trial in heart failure (MOXCON) showed an increase in adverse effects compared to placebo, and was stopped early.

Mode of action and side-effects

Side-effects include sedation, a dry mouth and fluid retention. The older agents also suffer from the problem of rebound hypertension on withdrawal. Furthermore, methyldopa can also cause autoimmune hepatic derangement and haemolytic anaemia. Moxonidine causes fewer problems with dry mouth than clonidine, but other side-effects such as sedation, headache, nausea and sleep disturbance may occur. Overall, moxonidine appears to be as well tolerated as the main classes of antihypertensive drugs. Moxonidine also has no adverse effects on plasma lipids and glucose.

Moxonidine stimulates the central imidazoline receptors and reduces central sympathetic outflow, without the dry mouth and sedation side-effects of central alpha$_2$-receptor blockade. However, headache, nausea and interrupted sleep may occur

---

In summary, moxonidine is an effective antihypertensive agent, but although an improvement over clonidine it has not been demonstrated to have major advantages over more well-established drugs.

Direct vasodilators

The direct vasodilators (e.g. hydralazine, minoxidil) act directly to relax vascular smooth muscle, thereby reducing peripheral vascular resistance. The resulting activation of the sympathetic nervous system means that their use is commonly associated with reflex tachycardia and can only successfully be used in combination with drugs that block sympathetic activity. The combination of hydralazine and nitrates has proven of benefit in heart failure due to systolic dysfunction and may be better than ACE inhibitors for hypertensive Afro-Caribbean patients who develop heart failure. Hydralazine use may be complicated by the development of systemic lupus erythematosus, while hypertrichosis may be troublesome with minoxidil (not suitable for women). All these drugs may cause rapid falls in blood pressure.

Adrenergic neuron blockers

Such agents are now rarely used in the UK. Reserpine and guanethidine inhibit the release of noradrenaline (norepinephrine) from peripheral nerves, thus reducing sympathetic tone, peripheral vascular resistance and cardiac output. They cause postural hypotension and central nervous system depression. Where low costs are paramount, especially in the Third World, small doses of reserpine combined with a diuretic form an effective regimen.

Multifactorial interventions to prevent cardiovascular disease

Blood pressure should be managed in the context of overall risk. The importance of considering serum cholesterol, although obvious, has been much neglected. Indeed, hypertensive patients tend to have higher cholesterol levels than the general population and it is well recognized that those with both raised BP and raised cholesterol are at particularly high risk of cardiovascular events. As long ago as 1987, it was found that treating hypertension alone in patients with raised cholesterol had little impact on cardiovascular events.

The treatment of hypercholesterolaemia has been transformed by the introduction of the 3-hydroxy-3-methylgluteryl coenzyme A reductase inhibitors (statins). The value of statins in secondary and primary prevention in high-risk patients has previously been demonstrated. The more recent lipid-lowering arm of the ASCOT study was terminated early due to significant reductions in cardiovascular events with atorvastatin in hypertensive patients with even modestly raised cholesterol levels. This confirms the value of addressing multiple risk factors in the treatment of all patients with hypertension.

The anti-platelet agent aspirin has long been used in the treatment and secondary prevention of many of the complications of hypertension, but until recently, little information has been available on its role in the management of the asymptomatic hypertensive individual. Warfarin has also been found to be useful as a thromboprophylaxis in hypertensive patients with atrial fibrillation, but if BPs remain uncontrolled, such therapy carries significant risks, especially from intracranial haemorrhage.

> The importance of combined interventions has been recognized for some time, although the importance of taking serum cholesterol into account had been ignored

Aspirin

Despite the strong pathophysiological and epidemiological associations between thrombosis and hypertension, there were few or no data on the routine use of antithrombotic therapy in hypertension until the recent publication of the Hypertension Optimal Treatment (HOT) trial.

There are good reasons for treating hypertensive patients with antithrombotic therapy, especially when there have been previous heart attacks and strokes, i.e. secondary prevention. Examples include the use of aspirin following myocardial infarction and cerebral infarction, and warfarin if concomitant atrial fibrillation is present.

HOT trial

There are no trials on the use of warfarin as primary prevention in uncomplicated hypertensive patients as such. The HOT trial was the first study to investigate the use of aspirin as primary prevention in hypertension.

In the HOT trial, 75 mg of aspirin was given daily to treated hypertensive patients aged 50 years or above. This reduced cardiovascular events by 15% and myocardial infarction by 36%, but had no effect on fatal events. This study showed the potential of aspirin to prevent 1.5 myocardial infarctions per 1000 hypertensive patients per year, which was in addition to the benefit achieved by lowering the BP.

The benefit seen in terms of reduced cardiovascular events was at the price of a higher incidence of bleeding events in the aspirin group. There was no increase in the number of fatal bleeding events (seven events in patients taking aspirin, compared to eight in the placebo group). However, there was a 1.8% increase of non-fatal major bleeding events (129 events in patients taking aspirin, compared to 70 in the placebo group) and minor bleeds (156 and 87 respectively). These were mostly gastrointestinal and nasal. This increase in bleeding events was similar to that seen in other studies of aspirin (Figure 6.2).

> Aspirin can prevent up to 1.5 myocardial infarctions per 1000 hypertensive patients each year

Thrombosis prevention trial

In the thrombosis prevention trial of aspirin 75 mg daily for primary prevention, 26% of those studied had treated hypertension. The outcome was similar to that of the HOT trial; a 16% reduction in all cardiovascular events, 20%

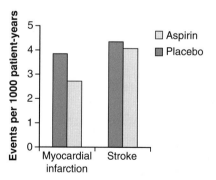

	GI bleeds	Cerebral bleeds
Aspirin	107 (fatal = 5)	14
Placebo	55 (fatal = 3)	15

Figure 6.2
Results from the HOT trial investigating the use of aspirin as primary prevention in hypertension. GI, gastrointestinal.

reduction in myocardial infarction and no effect on fatal events. In both trials, the number of clinically significant bleeding episodes caused by aspirin was similar to the number of cardiovascular events prevented by aspirin, suggesting that the margin between benefit and harm was narrow.

It should also be noted that the HOT trial studied well-controlled hypertensive patients, and in the thrombosis prevention trial, aspirin was withheld when BP was above 170/100 mmHg. Furthermore, those who developed cerebral haemorrhage in the thrombosis prevention trial had significantly higher systolic BP before the adverse event (158 mmHg, versus 135 mmHg in those with no stroke).

Thus, hypertension must be well controlled (BP <150/90 mmHg) before starting aspirin treatment for the primary prevention of CVD.

The British Hypertension Society guidelines state that 'aspirin 75 mg daily' is recommended for hypertensive patients who have:

- no contraindication to aspirin
- secondary prevention of cardiovascular complications:
  —myocardial infarction
  —angina
  —non-haemorrhagic cerebrovascular disease
  —peripheral vascular disease
  —atherosclerotic renovascular disease
- primary prevention:
  —BP controlled to <150/90 mmHg (audit standard)
  —age ≥ 50 years and target organ damage (e.g. LVH, renal impairment or proteinuria)
  —an estimated 10-year CVD risk ≥ 20% by Joint British Societies risk chart.
  This includes patients with type-2 diabetes.

(Source: British Hypertension Society, 2004)

The 2004 British Hypertension Society guidelines make the point that patients with an estimated 10-year CVD risk of ≥ 20% will have their cardiovascular risk reduced by 25% using antihypertensive treatment. The addition of aspirin further reduces the risk of major cardiovascular events by 15%, giving a NNT for five years of about 90 for one cardiovascular complication and 60 for one myocardial infarction prevented by aspirin.

HMG CoA reductase inhibitors (statins)

Several primary and secondary prevention outcome trials have shown that statin treatment for primary and secondary prevention reduces major coronary events by 30%, reduces all-cause mortality significantly, and is safe, simple and well tolerated. Importantly, statin treatment substantially reduces the risk of stroke in patients who have CHD, which is an effect not seen in previous trials of lipid-lowering with non-statin drugs.

Thus, statin treatment should be targeted at a specified threshold of cardiovascular risk and *not just* at thresholds of lipid values. None the less, monitoring of lipid levels is relevant as the benefit of statin therapy is proportional to the reduction in cholesterol, especially LDL cholesterol. The current British Hypertension Society and Joint British Societies guidelines recommend statin treatment for estimated CVD risk of at least 20% and most patients with diabetes. Total cholesterol of <4 mmol/L or LDL cholesterol of <2 mmol/L are the recommended targets.

Resistant hypertension

In view of new BP targets and the need for many drugs to achieve these lower BPs, many patients will be labelled by clinicians as having 'resistant' or 'refractory' hypertension, although careful examination would reveal that such a simplistic approach may be fraught with problems.

A large data review from the USA (the National Health and Nutrition Examination Survey) has demonstrated that only 55% of hypertensive patients are being treated and only 29% have reached a target BP of 140/90 mmHg. Failure to achieve these goals can be attributed to several underlying causes, one of them being refractory hypertension. However, any debate about resistant hypertension is hampered by the lack of a generally approved definition.

One definition for 'resistant' hypertension is when a rational triple combination of antihypertensive drugs in appropriate doses fails to achieve adequate BP control (BP <140/90 mmHg).

The extent of this problem becomes clear when considering that up to 85% of patients referred to specialist hypertension clinics are reported to have 'resistant' hypertension when similar criteria to those above are used.

> Diagnosing resistant hypertension is made more difficult by the lack of a standard definition

Factors contributing to resistance

Several factors contribute to treatment resistance (Table 6.3). In primary care, truly resistant hypertension is most commonly caused by drug non-compliance. This is not an inconsequential problem as non-compliance rates of up to 50% have been reported with antihypertensive therapy. This is particularly a problem in younger patients who do not fully appreciate the need to treat what is usually an asymptomatic disease or risk factor. However, drug side-effects and multiple drug dosing need to be carefully excluded as possible reasons for non-compliance – simple measures such as a change in drug class and the use of once-daily dosing may help. Patient education and greater awareness of the risks associated with hypertension are also needed.

Other causes of resistant hypertension

Other causes of resistant hypertension include concomitant medication, secondary

Table 6.3
Causes of lack of response to therapy

- Non-adherence to therapy:
  —instructions not clear and/or not given to patient in writing
  —inadequate or no patient education
  —lack of involvement of patient in treatment plan
  —cost of medication
  —side-effects of medication
  —organic brain syndrome (e.g. memory deficit)
  —inconvenient dosing
- Drug-related causes:
  —dosage too low
  —inappropriate combinations (e.g. two centrally acting adrenergic inhibitors)
  —rapid inactivation (e.g. hydralazine)
  —drug interactions
  —non-steroidal anti-inflammatory drugs
  —oral contraceptives
  —sympathomimetics
  —antidepressants
  —adrenal steroids
  —nasal decongestants
  —liquorice-containing substances (e.g. chewing tobacco)
  —cocaine or other illicit drugs
  —cyclosporine
  —erythropoietin
- Associated conditions:
  —increasing obesity
  —alcohol intake >1 ounce/day of ethanol
- Secondary hypertension:
  —renal insufficiency
  —renovascular hypertension
  —phaeochromocytoma
  —primary aldosteronism
- Volume overload:
  —inadequate diuretic therapy
  —excessive sodium intake
  —fluid retention from reduction of blood pressure
  —progressive renal damage
- Pseudohypertension
- 'White-coat' effect

(Adapted from Seventh report of the Joint National Committee on Detection, Evaluation, and Treatment of High Blood Pressure (JNC VII). *Hypertension* 2003; **42**: 1206–52.)

hypertension, obesity, alcohol misuse and white-coat hypertension, which may be excluded by thorough clinical assessment and simple laboratory investigations. An approach to resistant hypertension is summarized in Table 6.4.

Table 6.4
Strategies for resistant hypertension

- Are they truly resistant? If no left ventricular hypertrophy, consider ambulatory blood pressure monitoring
- Simplify drug regime
- Check salt, weight, alcohol, exercise
- Check for NSAIDS, steroids, etc.
- Double check for underlying causes
- Remember effects of age and ethnicity

Overall, the prevalence of secondary causes of hypertension amounts to about 5%, but investigations for rare underlying causes should be reserved for those patients whose initial assessment results are indicative of a secondary cause, or in patients with an unusual clinical presentation (e.g. before the age of 20 years, after the age of 50 years, marked end-organ damage, BP >180/110 mmHg). The patient's BP response to treatment can sometimes point to secondary causes. Sudden development of renal failure or dramatic reduction in BP following treatment with an ACE inhibitor or angiotensin II receptor blocker would be consistent with renal artery stenosis.

White-coat hypertension

White-coat hypertension should be suspected in patients with resistant hypertension but no evidence of target organ damage. Some studies have suggested that up to 50% of patients referred to specialized clinics for assessment of their resistant hypertension had normotensive ambulatory BP readings. In hypertensive patients, there can also be a significant difference between office and ambulatory BP, the so-called 'white-coat effect'. If present, the readings in a clinical setting can exceed ambulatory readings by at least 20/10 mmHg.

Obesity, alcohol intake and cigarette smoking

A variety of other patient-related factors can contribute to resistant hypertension. Obesity is a 'pro-hypertensive' condition and weight loss of 10.4 kg reduces the mean arterial BP by 10/8 mmHg. There also seems to be a J-shaped relationship between alcohol and hypertension, where every unit of alcohol in excess of two units a day increases the BP by approximately 1 mmHg. Conversely, a reduction of alcohol intake in regular drinkers lowers BP by 4 mmHg. Another risk factor for resistant hypertension is cigarette smoking, which causes a pressor response and thereby increases the BP.

Pseudohypertension

'Pseudohypertension' might be another underlying cause of resistant hypertension. In pseudohypertension, cuff sphygmomanometer BP readings are falsely elevated when compared to (normal) intra-arterial pressures. This condition is a manifestation of sclerosis of the brachial artery and is more common in the elderly. It should be suspected if the Osler's manoeuvre is positive, i.e. when a palpable radial pulse is present when the cuff is inflated above the systolic BP. However, the only reliable way of proving pseudohypertension is measurement of intra-arterial BP.

Concomitant medication

Concomitant medication is a frequently neglected cause of treatment-resistant hypertension. For example, chronic non-steroidal anti-inflammatory drug (NSAID) use increases the risk of developing hypertension and can impair the success rate of antihypertensive medication. NSAIDs can increase mean BP by about 4–5 mmHg. In addition to this hypertensive property, NSAIDs antagonize the effects of most antihypertensive drug classes. These effects are particularly important as NSAIDs are widely available without needing to be prescribed. Only careful history taking with direct questioning about NSAIDs can reveal this problem.

Response to drug therapy – the renin state

A further important cause of resistant hypertension is a suboptimal antihypertensive treatment regimen. The choice of the first-line drug is very much influenced by the patient's age, ethnicity and coexisting disease(s), and initiation should follow or coincide with non-pharmacological methods, such as dietary advice, exercise and weight loss.

A variable response to the four major antihypertensive drug classes has been noted. In particular, age and ethnic influences on the renin–angiotensin system are of relevance. For example, patients aged <50 years are more likely to respond to ACE inhibitors and beta-blockers, whereas calcium channel blockers and thiazide diuretics are more effective in patients aged >50 years. These age-related differences can be explained by a different activation status of the renin–angiotensin system, with plasma renin activity declining with age.

Thus, blockade of the renin–angiotensin system with the ACE inhibitors, angiotensin II receptor antagonists or beta-blockers tends to be more effective in young patients, who are more likely to have higher renin activity. In contrast, the diuretics and calcium channel blockers are first-line agents in patients with low renin states, such as the elderly and Afro-Caribbeans. This forms the basis for the 'Birmingham Square' and the current British Hypertension Society ABCD algorithm.

> Age and ethnic origin can influence the patient's response to drug therapy

Combination antihypertensive therapy

Many patients will not have their BP controlled by one drug alone. As most antihypertensive agents have fairly flat dose–response curves, using large doses of a single agent will produce significant increases in side-effects without much further lowering of BP. The solution to these problems is to use a combination of two or more drugs. Indeed, the American JNC-VII guidelines suggest that 'when BP is more than 20 mmHg above systolic goal or 10 mmHg above diastolic goal, consideration should be given to initiate therapy with 2 drugs'. In general, about half of hypertensive patients will require two drugs and one-third may require three or more drugs.

In the HOT study, for example, fewer than one-third of hypertensive patients were controlled by monotherapy and more than one-third required a combination of three or more drugs to achieve optimal BP control. The major classes of drug generally have additive effects on BP when they are prescribed together, and most hypertensive people will require combinations of antihypertensive therapy to achieve optimal BP control.

> Combination of submaximal doses of two drugs results in larger BP responses and fewer side-effects than maximal doses of a single drug

Drug combinations

Effective combination therapy will use drugs with different (and complementary) primary modes of action. In general, the combination should include one effective against a high renin state and another for a low renin state. Such combinations include:

- a diuretic with an ACE inhibitor (or angiotensin II antagonist)
- a calcium antagonist with an ACE inhibitor (or angiotensin II antagonist)

As previously discussed, beta-blockers are not recommended for the initial treatment of hypertension in the absence of compelling indications (see under 'Beta-adrenergic receptor blockers').

For third-line drug therapy, commonly used combinations are diuretic, ACE inhibitor and calcium antagonist. Additional antihypertensive therapy beyond these three agents is less established. Alpha-receptor blockers or centrally acting agents such as moxonidine or methyldopa can be considered, but there are few data confirming their effectiveness and possible side-effects in combination therapy. Spironolactone is also increasingly used as 'add-on' therapy, although careful monitoring of renal function and serum potassium is mandatory. Specialist referral should be considered in these patients with 'resistant hypertension'.

Fixed-dose combinations are not widely used in the UK. These combinations are convenient for patients and acceptable provided they are used as second-line treatment when monotherapy is ineffective, the individual drug components are appropriate and there are no major cost implications.

Concomitant disease states should also influence sensible prescribing (Table 6.5). For example, patients with diabetes mellitus should receive ACE inhibitors because of the particularly favourable effects on nephropathy, retinopathy and LVH. Based upon the strength of evidence for reduction of cardiovascular mortality, a sensible choice as first-line drug therapy seems to be:

- ACE inhibitor/angiotensin II antagonist in the young
- a thiazide diuretic (or calcium channel blocker) in elderly or Afro-Caribbean patients

Table 6.5
Useful antihypertensive agents in patients with concomitant conditions

Condition	Possible agents
Benign prostatic hypertrophy	Alpha-blockers
Hyperthyroidism	Beta-blockers
Migraine	Beta-blockers
Atrial fibrillation	Beta-blockers, verapamil, diltiazem
Osteoporosis	Diuretics

- ACE inhibitor in the presence of concomitant heart failure
- beta-blockers or ACE inhibitors in patients with coronary artery disease
- ACE inhibitors in people with diabetes.

> The most effective combination therapy uses drugs with different primary modes of action, so that the side-effects of one drug may be overcome by the action of another

Clinical guidelines

The British Hypertension Society (BHS) amended the 1999 guidelines and published new recommendations in 2004 based on new clinical data. The publication of the ASCOT study in 2005 prompted the National Institute of Clinical Excellence (NICE) to update the recommendations for antihypertensive therapy. Therefore, the 2004 BHS antihypertensive treatment algorithm (ABCD) (see Figure 6.4) is now superseded by the 2006 NICE algorithm (see Figure 6.5). The 2004 BHS treatment algorithm is provided below for reference.

A summary of the 2004 British Hypertension Society guidelines
Threshold for antihypertensive therapy

- Use non-pharmacological measures in all patients with hypertension and people with borderline hypertension.
- Initiate antihypertensive drug therapy in people with sustained systolic BP ≥ 160 mmHg or sustained diastolic BP ≥ 100 mmHg (Figure 6.3).
- Decide on treatment in people with sustained systolic BP between 140 and 159 mmHg or sustained diastolic BP between 90 and 99 mmHg according to the presence or absence of target organ damage, diabetes, established CVD or an estimated 10-year CVD risk of ≥ 20% (according to the Joint British Societies risk assessment chart).

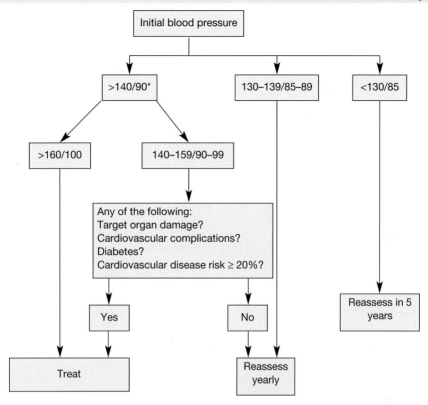

*If initial BP >180/110, confirm over 1–2 weeks unless malignant phase hypertension
If initial BP 160–179/100–109, confirm over 3–4 weeks then treat
If initial BP 140–159/90–99, confirm over 12 weeks then treat

Figure 6.3
Blood pressure threshold for intervention. (Adapted from Williams B, Poulter NR, Brown MJ, *et al*. Guidelines for management of hypertension: report of the fourth working party of the British Hypertension Society. *J Hum Hypertens* 2004; **18**: 139–85.)

Blood pressure treatment targets

- In patients with hypertension but without diabetes, optimal BP treatment targets are systolic BP <140 mmHg and diastolic BP <85 mmHg.
- In patients with hypertension and diabetes, renal disease or established cardiovascular disease, optimal BP targets are systolic BP <130 mmHg and diastolic BP <80 mmHg.

Antihypertensive treatment algorithm

- In the absence of contraindications or compelling indications (Table 6.6) for other antihypertensive agents, first-line therapy for hypertension should follow the ABCD algorithm** (Figure 6.4).
- For most patients, a combination of antihypertensive drugs will be required to achieve the recommended targets for BP

Table 6.6
Compelling indications and contraindications of antihypertensive agents

Class of drugs	Compelling indications	Contraindications
Alpha-blockers	BPH	Urinary incontinence
ACE inhibitors	Heart failure, LV dysfunction or established coronary heart disease, type-1 diabetic nephropathy, secondary stroke prevention (with thiazide)	Pregnancy, renovascular disease
Angiotensin II antagonist	ACE inhibitor intolerance (heart failure), type 2 diabetic nephropathy, hypertension with LVH	Pregnancy, renovascular disease
Beta-blockers	Myocardial infarction, angina, heart failure	Asthma or COPD, heart block
Dihydropyridine calcium channel blocker	Elderly patients, isolated systolic hypertension angina	–
Rate-limiting (non-dihydropyridine) calcium channel blocker	Angina	Heart block, heart failure
Thiazide diretics	Elderly patients, isolated systolic hypertension, heart failure, secondary stroke prevention	Gout

- ACE inhibitors and angiotensin II antagonists should be used with caution in patients with renal impairment; ACE inhibitors and angiotensin II antagonists may be preferred in patients at high risk of developing diabetes (e.g. glucose intolerance, metabolic syndrome and family history of diabetes)
- the use of beta-blockers in heart failure may lead to transient deterioration in symptoms
- thiazides may precipitate gout and concomitant allopurinol should be considered

control. The combination of beta-blocker and thiazide diuretics should be used with caution, especially in patients at high risk of developing diabetes (e.g. family history of diabetes, obesity, patients with glucose intolerance and patients of South Asian and Afro-Caribbean descent).

- Low-dose aspirin (75 mg/day) is recommended for secondary prevention or primary prevention in patients at high CVD risk (estimated CVD risk over 20%) in whom BP is controlled to the audit standard (150/90 mmHg).
- Statins are recommended for all patients with hypertension complicated by cardiovascular disease or patients at high CVD risk (estimated CVD risk over 20%).

(Adapted from William *et al. J Human Hypertens* 2004; **18**: 139–85.)

**Beta-blockers are now not recommended as first-line antihypertensive therapy for uncomplicated essential hypertension. The ACD algorithm should replace the ABCD algorithm by the BHS (see 'NICE guidelines update 2006').*

NICE guidelines update 2006

A number of studies comparing different classes of antihypertensive therapy have now been reported since the publication of the last British Hypertension Society guidelines in 2004. In 2006 the National Institute of Clinical Excellence (NICE) produced a partial update of the initial NICE guidelines published in 2004 to take these studies into consideration.

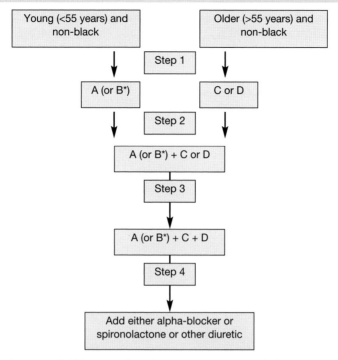

A: angiotensin-converting enzyme inhibitor or angiotensin II antagonist, B: beta-blockers, C: calcium channel blockers, D: diuretic (thiazide)

*combination of B and D may induce more new-onset diabetes compared to other combination therapy

†See Figure 6.5 for the updated treatment algorithm for hypertension (NICE update, 2006)

Figure 6.4
The ABCD algorithm for hypertension (BHS guidelines, 2004).† (Adapted from Williams B, Poulter NR, Brown MJ, *et al.* Guidelines for management of hypertension: report of the fourth working party of the British Hypertension Society. *J Hum Hypertens* 2004; **18**: 139–85.)

The major studies identified include the Anglo-Scandinavian Cardiac Outcomes Trial (ASCOT), the Japanese Multicenter Investigation for Cardiovascular Disease-B study (JMIC-B) and the Plaque Hypertension Lipid-Lowering Italian Study (PHYLLIS). The ASCOT is the largest of these studies, with 19,257 patients followed-up for a median of 5.5 years. This study demonstrated significantly fewer cardiovascular events and all-cause mortality among patients randomized to the amlodipine-based compared to the atenolol-based treatment. The JMIC-B and PHYLLIS are smaller studies, which reported no significant difference between ACE inhibitors versus calcium channel blockers and thiazide diuretic respectively.

Considering the data from these trials with those from earlier studies, the Guideline Development Group noted that beta-blockers were generally less effective than a comparator drug in reducing cardiovascular events, especially stroke. Hence, the group concluded that beta-blockers should *not* be used as first-line treatment of hypertension in the absence of compelling indications.

However, beta-blockers may still be considered in younger patients intolerant of ACE inhibitors or angiotensin II antagonists, of child-bearing potential (potentially teratogenic effects) and patients with high sympathetic drive. If beta-blockers are used in these patients, a calcium channel blocker (not thiazide) should be added if additional antihypertensive treatment is needed to reduce the risk of diabetes. In addition, there is no absolute need to replace beta-blockers if blood pressure is controlled (<140/90 mmHg) on a regimen which includes a beta-blocker.

The other recommendations are as outlined by the British Hypertension Society guidelines 2004. The new algorithm for the treatment of hypertension is illustrated in Figure 6.5. Beta-blockers are the obvious omission from the 2004 British Hypertension Society ABCD algorithm.

In making these recommendations, the group has also highlighted several deficiencies in the data, necessitating several assumptions. These include:

● Beta-blockers as a class, are omitted from the initial treatment algorithm although the majority of the clinical outcome data are derived from atenolol. The generalizability to other beta-blockers is not clear.

● The efficacy of thiazide diuretics is assumed to be a class effect (evidence from outcome trials for the commonly used

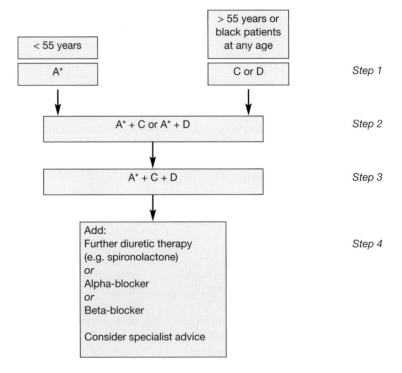

A = ACE inhibitors (*or angiotensin antagonist if ACE inhibitor intolerant), C = calcium channel blocker, D = thiazide diuretic.
Beta-blockers are not preferred initial therapy for hypertension but are an alternative to A in patients < 55 years in whom A is not tolerated or contraindicated (includes women of child-bearing potential).
Black patients are only those of African or Caribbean descent. In the absence of evidence, all other patients should be treated as non-black.

Figure 6.5
Algorithm for the treatment of hypertension (NICE update, 2006). (Adapted from National Collaborating Centre for Chronic Conditions. Hypertension: management of hypertension in adults in primary care: partial update. London: Royal College of Physicians, 2006.)

bendroflumethiazide 2.5 mg daily is lacking).

- The recommendation of ACE inhibitor (or angiotensin II antagonist) in younger patients (<55 years) is based on only limited data.
- The recommendations beyond the three-drug regime (ACE inhibitor, calcium channel blocker and thiazide diuretic) are based on general consensus, as there is little evidence to guide practice.

Further reading

Felmeden DC, Lip GYH. Antihypertensive therapy and cancer risk. *Drug Saf* 2001; **24**: 727–39.

Felmeden DC, Lip GY. Resistant hypertension and the Birmingham Hypertension Square. *Curr Hypertens Rep* 2001; **3**: 203–8.

Lip GYH, Edmunds E, Beevers DG. Should patients with hypertension receive antithrombotic therapy? *J Intern Med* 2001; **249**: 205–14.

National Collaborating Centre for Chronic Conditions. Hypertension: management of hypertension in adults in primary care: partial update. London: Royal College of Physicians, 2006.

Seventh Report of the Joint National Committee on Prevention, Detection, Evaluation and Treatment of High Blood Pressure. *Hypertension* 2003; **42**: 1206–52.

Sever PS, Poulter NR. Hypertension drug trials: past, present, and future. *J Hum Hypertens* 2000; **14**: 729–38.

Williams B, Poulter NR, Brown MJ, et al. Guidelines for management of hypertension: report of the fourth working party of the British Hypertension Society. *J Hum Hypertens* 2004; **18**: 139–85.

Thiazides

ALLHAT Officers and Coordinators for the ALLHAT Collaborative Research Group. Major outcomes in high-risk hypertensive patients randomized to angiotensin-converting enzyme inhibitor or calcium channel blocker vs diuretic: the Anti-hypertensive and Lipid Lowering Treatment to Prevent Heart Attack Trial (ALLHAT). *JAMA* 2002; **288**: 2981–97.

Beevers DG, Ferner RE. Why are thiazide diuretics declining in popularity? *J Hum Hypertens* 2001; **15**: 287–9.

Gosse P, Sheridan DJ, Zannad F, et al. Regression of left ventricular hypertrophy in hypertensive patients treated with indapamide SR 1.5 mg versus enalapril 20 mg: the LIVE study. *J Hypertens* 2000; **18**: 1465–75.

Beta-blockers

Beevers DG. Beta-blockers for hypertension: time to call a halt? *J Hum Hypertens* 1999; **12**: 807–10.

Carlberg B, Samuelsson O, Lindholm LH. Atenolol in hypertension: is it a wise choice? *Lancet* 2004; **364**: 1684–9.

Gress TW, Nieto FJ, Shahar E, et al. Hypertension and antihypertensive therapy as risk factors for type 2 diabetes. *N Engl J Med* 2000; **342**: 905–12.

Lindholm LH, Carlberg B, Samuelsson O. Should beta blockers remain first choice in the treatment of primary hypertension? A meta-analysis. *Lancet* 2005; **366**: 1545–53.

Messerli FH, Grossman E, Goldbourt U. Are beta-blockers efficacious as first-line therapy for hypertension in the elderly? A systematic review. *JAMA* 1998; **279**: 1903–7.

Calcium antagonists

Brown MJ, Palmer CR, Castaigne A, et al. Morbidity and mortality in patients randomised to double-blind treatment with a long-acting calcium-channel blocker or diuretic in the International Nifedipine GITS study: Intervention as a Goal in Hypertension Treatment (INSIGHT). *Lancet* 2000; **356**: 366–72.

Dahlof B, Sever P, Poulter NR, et al. Prevention of cardiovascular events with an antihypertensive regimen of amlodipine adding perindopril as required versus atenolol adding bendroflumethiazide as required, in the Anglo-Scandinavian Cardiac Outcomes Trial-Blood Pressure Lowering Arm (ASCOT-BPLA): a multicentre randomized controlled trial. *Lancet* 2005; **366**: 895–906.

Hansson L, Hedner T, Lund-Johansen P, et al. Randomised trial of effects of calcium antagonists compared with diuretics and beta-blockers on cardiovascular morbidity and mortality in hypertension: the Nordic Diltiazem (NORDIL) study. *Lancet* 2000; **356**: 359–65.

Hansson L, Zanchetti A, Carruthers SG, et al. Effects of intensive blood-pressure lowering and low-dose aspirin in patients with hypertension: principal results of the Hypertension Optimal Treatment (HOT) randomised trial. HOT Study Group. *Lancet* 1998; **351**: 1755–62.

Pahor M, Psaty BM, Alderman MH, et al. Health outcomes associated with calcium antagonists compared with other first-line antihypertensive therapies: a meta-analysis of randomised controlled trials. *Lancet* 2000; **356**: 1949–54.

Staessen JA, Fagard R, Thijs L, et al. Randomised double-blind comparison of placebo and active treatment for older patients with isolated systolic hypertension (SYST-EUR Trial). *Lancet* 1997; **350**: 754–64.

Alpha blockers

Beevers DG, Lip GY. Do alpha blockers cause heart failure and stroke? Observations from ALLHAT. *J Hum Hypertens* 2000; **14**: 287–9.

Major cardiovascular events in hypertensive patients randomized to doxazosin vs chlorthalidone: the antihypertensive and lipid-lowering treatment to prevent heart attack trial (ALLHAT). ALLHAT Collaborative Research Group. *JAMA* 2000; **283**: 1967–75.

ACE inhibitors

Abuissa H, Jones PG, Marso SP, *et al.* Angiotensin-converting enzyme inhibitors or angiotensin receptor blockers for prevention of type-2 diabetes: a meta-analysis of randomised clinical trials. *J Am Coll Cardiol* 2005; **46**: 821–6.

African American Study of Kidney Disease and Hypertension (AASK) Study Group. The effect of ramipril vs amlodipine on renal outcomes in hypertensive nephrosclerosis; a randomised controlled trial. *JAMA* 2001; **285**: 2719–28.

EUCLID Study Group. Randomised placebo-controlled trial of lisinopril in normotensive patients with diabetes and normoalbuminuria or microalbuminuria. *Lancet* 1997; **349**: 1787–92.

Fox KM. Efficacy of perindopril in reduction of cardiovascular events among patients with stable coronary artery disease: randomised, double-blind, placebo-controlled, multicentre trial (the EUROPA study). *Lancet* 2003; **362**: 782–8.

Hansson L, Lindholm LH, Niskanen L, *et al.* Effect of angiotensin-converting-enzyme inhibition compared with conventional therapy on cardiovascular morbidity and mortality in hypertension: the Captopril Prevention Project (CAPPP) randomised trial. *Lancet* 1999; **353**: 611–16.

Heart Outcomes Prevention Evaluation Study Investigators. Effects of an angiotensin-converting-enzyme inhibitor, ramipril on cardiovascular events in high-risk patients. *N Engl J Med* 2000; **342**: 145–53.

Lewis EJ, Hunsicker LG, Bain RP, *et al.* The effect of angiotensin-converting-enzyme inhibition on diabetic nephropathy. *N Engl J Med* 1993; **329**: 1456–62.

Mathew J, Sleight P, Lonn E, *et al.* Reduction of cardiovascular risk by regression of electrocardiographic markers of left ventricular hypertrophy by the angiotensin converting enzyme inhibitor, ramipril. *Circulation* 2001; **104**: 1615–21.

PEACE Trial Investigators. Angiotensin-converting-enzyme inhibition in stable coronary artery disease. *N Engl J Med* 2004; **351**: 2058–68.

PROGRESS Collaborative Group. Randomised trial of a perindopril-based blood-pressure-lowering regimen among 6,105 individuals with previous stroke or transient ischaemic attack. *Lancet* 2001; **358**: 1033–41.

Yusuf S, Sleight P, Pogue J, *et al.* Effects of an angiotensin-converting-enzyme inhibitor, ramipril on cardiovascular events in high-risk patients. The Heart Outcomes Prevention Evaluation Study Investigators. *N Engl J Med* 2000; **342**: 145–53.

Angiotensin receptor antagonists

Brenner BM, Cooper ME, de Zeeuw D, *et al.* Effects of losartan on renal and cardiovascular outcomes in patients with type 2 diabetes and nephropathy. *N Engl J Med* 2001; **345**: 861–9.

Dahlof B, Devereux RB, Kjeldsen SE, *et al.* Cardiovascular morbidity and mortality in the Losartan Intervention For Endpoint reduction in hypertension study (LIFE): a randomized trial against atenolol. *Lancet* 2002; **359**: 995–1003.

Julius S, Kjeldsen SE, Weber M, *et al.* Outcomes in hypertensive patients at high cardiovascular risk treated with regimens based on valsartan or amlodipine: the VALUE randomised trial. *Lancet* 2004; **363**: 2022–31.

Lewis EJ, Hunsicker LG, Clarke WR. Reno protective effect of the angiotensin-receptor antagonist irbesartan in patients with nephropathy due to type 2 diabetes. *N Engl J Med* 2001; **345**: 851.

Lindholm LH, Ibsen H, Dahlof B, *et al.* Cardiovascular morbidity and mortality in patients with diabetes in the Losartan Intervention For Endpoint reduction in hypertension study (LIFE): a randomized trial against atenolol. *Lancet* 2002; **359**: 1004–10.

Lithell H, Hansson L, Skoog I, *et al.* The Study of Cognition and Prognosis in the Elderly (SCOPE): principal results of a randomised double-blind intervention trial. *J Hypertens* 2003; **21**: 875–86.

Parving HH, Lehnert H, Brochner-Mortensen J, *et al.* Effect of irbesartan on the development of diabetic nephropathy in patients with type 2 diabetes. *N Engl J Med* 2001; **345**: 870–8.

Pitt B, Poole-Wilson PA, Segal R, *et al.* The effect of losartan compared with captopril on mortality in patients with symptomatic heart failure: randomised trial – the losartan heart failure survival study ELITE II. *Lancet* 2000; **355**: 1582–7.

7. Hypertension in special patient groups

Diabetes
Coronary artery disease
Cardiac failure
Hypertension following a stroke
Hypertension in the elderly
Renal disease
Peripheral vascular disease
Ethnic groups
Hyperlipidaemia
Oral contraceptives and hypertension
Hormone replacement therapy
Hypertension and anaesthesia
Hypertension in children
Metabolic syndrome

Many patients with hypertension fall into a number of special groups where there are either compelling indications from randomized controlled trials for a particular agent, or good reasons to believe that a particular agent will have favourable effects on a co-morbid condition. These 'special patient groups' are discussed here.

Diabetes

Hypertension and diabetes act synergistically to significantly increase the risk of cardiovascular mortality and morbidity, especially in association with other risk factors such as hyperlipidaemia or smoking (Figure 7.1). Hypertension is present in about a fifth of patients with insulin dependent diabetes and between 30% and 50% of patients with non-insulin dependent diabetes. This proportion may be higher (approximately two-thirds) in patients of Afro-Caribbean or Indo-Asian origin.

Patients with diabetes suffer from both macrovascular complications (e.g. myocardial infarction and peripheral vascular disease) and microvascular disease (e.g. diabetic nephropathy and retinopathy). Diabetes is also linked to an increased risk of heart failure and atrial fibrillation. These complications are further exacerbated by hypertension.

> Diabetes and hypertension combine to significantly increase the risk of vascular mortality and morbidity

In type 1 diabetes, there is clear evidence that angiotensin-converting enzyme (ACE) inhibitors reduce the progression of both retinopathy and nephropathy and possibly even neuropathy. These drugs should be regarded as first-line agents in patients with these complications.

In type 2 diabetes, lower BP targets (BP <130/80 mmHg) improve prognosis. Furthermore, reductions in proteinuria with angiotensin II antagonists, ACE inhibitors, calcium antagonists and, more recently, alpha-blockers have been noted.

Low-dose diuretics have also been found to be as effective in diabetic as non-diabetic patients. Traditionally, drugs such as thiazide diuretics have the potential to exacerbate glucose

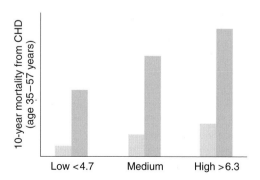

Figure 7.1
Diabetes, lipids and risk of coronary heart disease (diabetes in dark blue).

intolerance and lipid abnormalities, although these metabolic effects are minimal at low doses. However, newer diuretics such as indapamide may be more metabolically neutral. ACE inhibitors or angiotensin II receptor antagonists are probably the first choice for patients with type 2 diabetes and proteinuria, and offer special advantages by reducing the progression of diabetic nephropathy or retinopathy. Indeed, the American Diabetes Association recommends angiotensin II antagonists for patients with type 2 diabetes and proteinuria based on the wealth of clinical studies with this class of drugs (valsartan from MARVAL, losartan from RENAAL, irbesartan from IDNT and IRMA-2). The calcium antagonists and low-dose diuretics are also suitable in uncomplicated type 2 diabetes, with the aim of achieving not just 'good', but 'excellent' BP control. Beta-blockers are generally safe but non-cardioselective agents may theoretically blunt the hypoglycaemic response to insulin. As previously mentioned, beta-blockers are no longer recommended for the initial treatment of hypertension.

Hypertension in type 1 diabetes

In type 1 diabetes, an increased prevalence of hypertension is usually seen in patients with nephropathy (microalbuminuria or proteinuria); otherwise prevalence is similar to a non-diabetic population. None the less, the current British Hypertension Society guidelines regard type 1 diabetes as a high-risk population and recommend intervention with antihypertensive therapy for BP $\geq$ 140/90 mmHg. The optimal BP target of <130/80 mmHg is recommended.

In patients with type 1 diabetes, the development of hypertension may indicate the presence of the nephropathy. Certainly, BP reduction and treatment with ACE inhibitors slows the rate of renal function decline in overt diabetic nephropathy, and delays progression from the microalbuminuric phase to overt nephropathy. These drugs might have a specific renoprotective action in patients with incipient or overt nephropathy and are to be

recommended as first-line therapy. The data for angiotensin II receptor antagonists in type 1 diabetes are scantier and therefore they cannot be regarded as first-line therapy over ACE inhibitors. Indeed, type 1 diabetes with nephropathy represents a compelling indication for ACE inhibitor therapy.

For renoprotection, BP control is crucial, and recommended BP targets should be achieved by multiple drug therapy.

The threshold for antihypertensive treatment in type 1 diabetes with nephropathy is BP $\geq$ 140/90 mmHg, aiming for a target BP <130/80 mmHg, or even lower (BP <125/75 mmHg) if there is proteinuria $\geq$ 1 g every 24 hours. If persistent microalbuminuria or proteinuria is present, these patients may also benefit from ACE inhibitors or angiotensin receptor antagonists, even if BP is normal. As is evident from the recent HOPE trial, the beneficial effects of ACE inhibition (ramipril in the HOPE trial) are independent of the degree of BP reduction (Figure 7.2). In view of the high cardiovascular risk, statin and aspirin therapy are also recommended, the latter when BP is adequately controlled (<150/90 mmHg).

Hypertension in type 2 diabetes

Hypertension is very common in type 2 diabetes, and these patients are frequently obese. In type 2 diabetes, hypertension is prevalent in over 70% of patients and may even precede the onset of diabetes. The presence of hypertension in type 2 diabetes is highly predictive of cardiovascular and microvascular complications, with an overall 10-year cardiovascular event rate of >30%. These are predominantly coronary events.

The threshold for intervention with antihypertensive therapy is BP $\geq$ 140/90 mmHg in type 2 diabetes, irrespective of other risk factors. In the UKPDS (United Kingdom Prospective Diabetes Study), antihypertensive therapy was the only intervention that

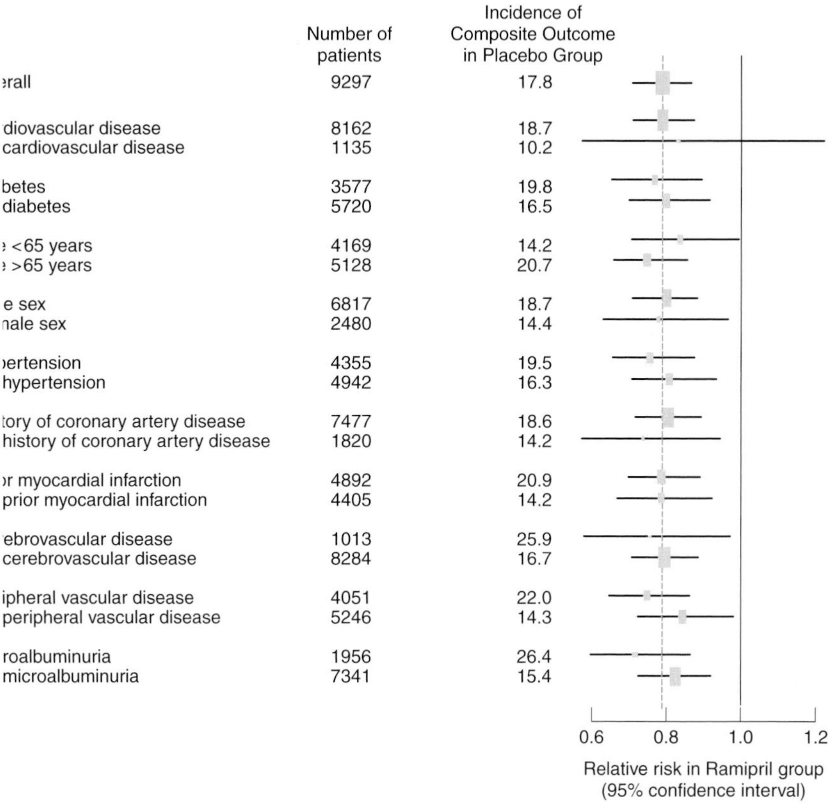

	Number of patients	Incidence of Composite Outcome in Placebo Group
?rall	9297	17.8
diovascular disease	8162	18.7
cardiovascular disease	1135	10.2
betes	3577	19.8
diabetes	5720	16.5
? <65 years	4169	14.2
? >65 years	5128	20.7
e sex	6817	18.7
nale sex	2480	14.4
?ertension	4355	19.5
hypertension	4942	16.3
tory of coronary artery disease	7477	18.6
history of coronary artery disease	1820	14.2
?r myocardial infarction	4892	20.9
prior myocardial infarction	4405	14.2
ebrovascular disease	1013	25.9
cerebrovascular disease	8284	16.7
ipheral vascular disease	4051	22.0
peripheral vascular disease	5246	14.3
roalbuminuria	1956	26.4
microalbuminuria	7341	15.4

Relative risk in Ramipril group
(95% confidence interval)

Figure 7.2
The benefit of ACE inhibition is consistent across various subgroups, including patients without a history of hypertension. (Adapted from Yusuf et al. N Engl J Med 2000; **342**: 145–53.)

decreased mortality rates in patients with type 2 diabetes and proved more effective than tight glycaemic control in protecting against microvascular and macrovascular disease.

In UKPDS, patients with hypertension and type 2 diabetes assigned to tight control of blood pressure, with captopril or atenolol, achieved a significant reduction in risk of 24% for any endpoints related to diabetes and 37% for microvascular disease. In comparison, intensive blood glucose control in the UK prospective diabetes study decreased the risk of any diabetes-related endpoint by 12% (P=0.029) and microvascular disease by 25% (P=0.0099). Those in the Hypertension Optimal Trial (HOT) and the elderly diabetics with isolated systolic

hypertension from the Syst-Eur trial also showed marked benefits after receiving treatment, with a BP target <140/80 mmHg. Specifically, diabetic patients in the HOT study had a 51% reduction in major cardiovascular events in the target group with a diastolic pressure <80 mmHg compared to the group with a target diastolic pressure of <90 mmHg.

In the Irbesartan Diabetic Nephropathy Trial (IDNT), the angiotensin II receptor antagonist irbesartan was compared with amlodipine and with placebo in diabetic patients with overt proteinuria. Both drugs reduced the blood pressure by roughly equal amounts but only irbesartan caused any delay in the progression of diabetic nephropathy.

In the IRbesartan MicroAlbuminuria Type 2 Diabetes Mellitus in Hypertensive patients (IRMA-2) study, irbesartan at two different dose levels (150 mg and 300 mg daily) was compared with placebo in diabetic patients who had microproteinuria. This trial was able to demonstrate a statistically significant dose–response curve, with the 300 mg dose of irbesartan being more effective than 150 mg at reducing microproteinuria or normalizing albumen excretion.

The third study, the Reduction of Endpoints in Non-Insulin Dependent Diabetes Mellitus with the Angiotensin II Antagonist Losartan (RENAAL) trial, losartan was compared with placebo in patients with overt diabetic nephropathy. This trial was able to demonstrate a 16% reduction in the doubling of serum creatinine and a 28% reduction in end-stage renal disease (Figure 7.3). Another finding which was considered as a secondary endpoint was a 32% reduction in hospitalization for heart failure (Figure 7.4).

Suggested drug treatment

The choice of first-line drug for type 2 diabetes favours angiotensin II antagonists and ACE inhibitors (as first-line), with the addition of dihydropyridine calcium antagonists and low-dose thiazide diuretics to achieve target blood pressures. The UKPDS study suggested that regimens based on ACE inhibition (captopril) and beta-blockade (atenolol) were equally effective at reducing macrovascular complications, but the treatment groups were too small to exclude this difference.

In type 2 diabetic subjects with nephropathy, hypertension accelerates the decline of renal function, which is slowed by treatment with antihypertensive therapy. While the ACE inhibitors and angiotensin II receptor antagonists have an antiproteinuric action and delay the progression from microalbuminuria to overt nephropathy, it is less clear whether they have specific renoprotective action beyond BP reduction in overt nephropathy complicating type 2 diabetes. As for patients with type 1 diabetes, statin and aspirin therapy should be offered to all patients with type 2 diabetes and hypertension, as they are considered to be at high cardiovascular disease (CVD) risk.

Coronary artery disease

Hypertension is a risk factor for the development of atheromatous coronary artery

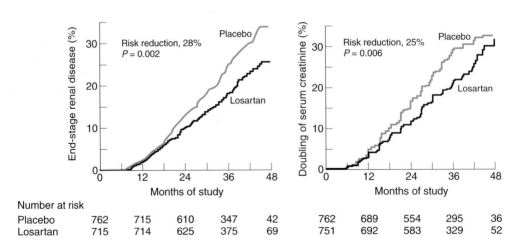

Figure 7.3
The RENAAL study. (Adapted from Brenner et al. N Engl J Med 2001; **345**: 861–9.)

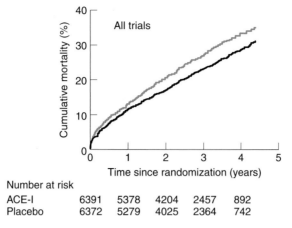

Figure 7.4
A secondary endpoint in the RENAAL study. (Adapted from Brenner *et al. N Engl J Med* 2001; **345**: 861–9.)

disease. Coronary artery disease (CAD), as manifest by angina and myocardial infarction, is more common in patients with hypertension. There appears to be an almost 'dose–response' relationship between coronary risk and increasing BP. While angina usually results from coronary artery atherosclerosis, it can also result from relative ischaemia in severe left ventricular hypertrophy (LVH). In any case, hypertensive patients with overt coronary artery disease are at particularly high risk of further cardiac events. In the peri-infarction state, BP may have fallen so that the diagnosis of hypertension may be missed and only become apparent at subsequent outpatient clinic visits.

Suggested drug treatment

Effective treatment of hypertension may improve the symptoms of angina, regardless of the drugs used. As beta-blockers are useful for secondary prevention after myocardial infarction, they are the first-choice drugs for hypertensive patients who have sustained a myocardial infarct. If beta-blockers are contraindicated, non-dihydropyridine calcium antagonists (e.g. verapamil or diltiazem) may be beneficial provided there is no evidence of

heart failure or left ventricular dysfunction. Verapamil should not be given with a beta-blocker as it can result in asystole, heart block or cardiac failure.

> Beta-blockers are the first-choice drug to treat angina symptoms in hypertensive patients

There is some evidence that diltiazem may be beneficial following non-Q-wave myocardial infarction. The dihydropyridine calcium antagonists (particularly nifedipine) should be avoided both in the immediate period post-infarction and in unstable angina. Short-acting dihydropyridine calcium antagonists (e.g. immediate-release nifedipine) may also exacerbate angina by promoting reflex tachycardia. The presence of heart failure or left ventricular dysfunction post-myocardial infarction is a strong indication for ACE inhibitor therapy.

Patients taking thiazide diuretics who are admitted with myocardial infarction should have their serum potassium concentrations checked; they may have hypokalaemia, which can exacerbate the tendency to cardiac arrhythmia and sudden death.

Cardiac failure

Usually heart failure develops in the hypertensive patient in association with coronary artery disease. Rarely, severe hypertension can be associated with heart failure. Echocardiography can help diagnose structural heart disease and assess cardiac function.

Suggested drug treatment

Many trials have firmly established the role of ACE inhibitors in patients with heart failure and asymptomatic left ventricular dysfunction (Figure 7.5), and the benefits are greater with more severe heart failure. Many such patients have coexisting hypertension. Caution is needed in the use of verapamil or diltiazem for hypertension in patients with heart failure. Long-acting dihydropyridine calcium channel blockers have neutral effect with regard to mortality in heart failure due to systolic dysfunction.

Recent data support the use of angiotensin II receptor antagonists as an alternative to the ACE inhibitors (in ACE inhibitor intolerant patients). Initial subgroup analysis of the Val-HeFT (valsartan) trial suggested potential

adverse effects with the then so-called 'triple therapy' – the addition of angiotensin II antagonist to ACE inhibitors and beta-blockers. However, this has now been refuted by the more recent (and robust) data from CHARM (candesartan), which suggests modest but significant benefit in patients with heart failure secondary to left ventricular systolic dysfunction. Angiotensin II antagonists should therefore be used in ACE inhibitor intolerant patients. The combination of hydralazine and nitrates may be used if ACE inhibitors (and angiotensin II antagonist) are contraindicated or cause side-effects, although this regimen may be better than ACE inhibitors for Afro-Caribbean hypertension patients with heart failure.

In stable patients with chronic heart failure, a beta-blocker (e.g. carvedilol, bisoprolol or nebivolol) added to ACE inhibitors and diuretics has a beneficial effect on mortality and morbidity. Beta-blockers should be initiated in patients with heart failure under specialist advice. Transient deterioration in heart failure symptoms may occur with beta-blocker therapy, and should therefore be started at low-dose and uptitrated slowly ('go low, go slow'). Like ACE inhibitors, beta-blockers are recommended in patients with asymptomatic left ventricular dysfunction.

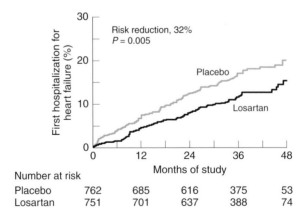

Figure 7.5
Meta-analysis of clinical studies confirms the benefit of ACE inhibitors in heart failure due to left ventricular dysfunction. (Adapted from *Flather et al. Lancet* 2000; **355**: 1575–81.)

Additional blockade of the renin–angiotensin–aldosterone system with the aldosterone antagonist spironolactone also significantly reduces mortality and morbidity in patients established on standard therapy (including the ACE inhibitors) (Figure 7.6). Eplerenone, another aldosterone antagonist, has also been shown to improve clinical outcome when introduced early in patients with post-MI heart failure. Close monitoring of electrolytes is mandatory as the use of spironolactone or eplerenone with ACE inhibitors may lead to dangerous hyperkalaemia.

Hypertension following a stroke

Uncontrolled hypertension in association with cerebrovascular disease is a risk factor for further cerebrovascular events. It is nevertheless unclear whether or not the treatment of mild hypertension post-stroke is of benefit, especially as in the immediate post-stroke period, cerebral blood flow autoregulation is disordered so that rapid reductions in BP can reduce cerebral perfusion and even cause stroke extension. Recent data from the Perindopril pROtection aGainst REcurrent Stroke Study (PROGRESS) trial suggest that treatment with ACE inhibitors in patients who have had a previous (non-acute) stroke significantly reduced mortality and cardiovascular morbidity. In this study, 6105 hypertensive and non-hypertensive patients who had had stroke (haemorrhagic or ischaemic) or transient ischaemic attack (TIA) with no major disability within the past five years, were randomized to perindopril 4 mg daily, with indapamide (2.5 mg daily) added at the

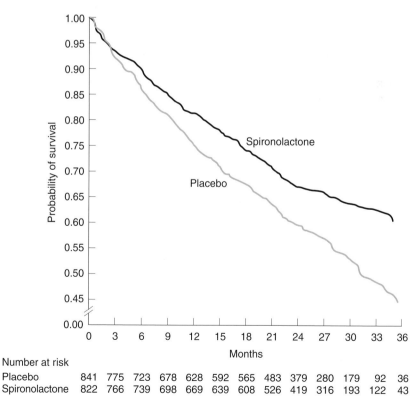

Figure 7.6
Spironolactone reduces mortality in the RALES study. (Adapted from Pitt *et al. N Engl J Med* 1999; **341**: 709–17.)

discretion of the treating physician; or matched placebo. After four years of follow-up, active treatment (60% received both drugs, while 40% received perindopril alone) reduced BP by 9/4 mmHg and stroke recurrence by 28% compared to placebo and that of major cardiovascular complications by 26%. In the subgroup of active treatment patients who received both perindopril and indapamide, BP was reduced by 12/5 mmHg, and the risk of stroke was reduced by 43%. Single-drug therapy with perindopril alone reduced BP by 5/3 mmHg, but produced no significant reduction in the risk of stroke.

In cerebral infarction, low-dose aspirin (75–300 mg) should also be prescribed, although if atrial fibrillation is present warfarin should be considered.

The role of antihypertensive medication during an acute stroke is controversial. Blood pressure is often elevated during the stroke period and this is regarded as a compensatory physiological response to maintain cerebral perfusion. As a result, it is common practice to reduce or withhold antihypertensive treatment. However,

if the BP persistently exceeds 180/110 mmHg, then nifedipine (slow-release) 10–20 mg tablets or 25 mg atenolol may be prescribed with the aim of reducing BP cautiously by 10–15%.

Hypertension in the elderly

It was a widely and incorrectly held myth that a rise in BP with age was inevitable and harmless, and that isolated systolic hypertension was of no consequence. The elderly have a higher prevalence of isolated systolic hypertension (defined as BP $\geq$ 160/<90 mmHg), occurring in >50% of people over 60 years of age. Systolic BP also rises steadily with age. These elderly hypertensive patients have a high risk of cardiovascular complications when compared to younger patients. Treatment with antihypertensive therapy reduces this risk, particularly in very high-risk groups, such as elderly patients with type 2 diabetes and hypertension. Treatment has been shown to reduce heart failure by 50% and possibly reduce dementia (Figure 7.7).

Evidence exists that patients aged up to at least 80 years benefit from antihypertensive treatment.

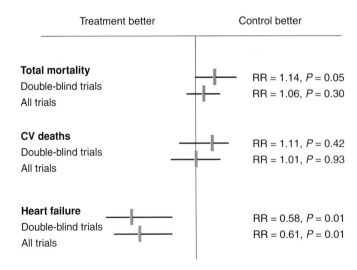

Figure 7.7
Anti-hypertensive treatment effects on cardiovascular outcomes in the elderly. (Adapted from Gueyffier *et al. Lancet* 1999; **353**: 793–6.)

Newly diagnosed hypertension patients aged 80 years or more should be considered for treatment provided they are generally fit and have a reasonable life expectancy.

In the very frail elderly, assessment of the risk:benefit ratio is recommended. One ongoing trial, the Hypertension in the Very Elderly Trial (HYVET), will provide data on treating hypertension in patients aged >80 years. This is likely to be the last placebo-controlled trial and is a double blind study of over 2000 hypertensive patients aged over 80 years. The primary endpoint is stroke events (fatal and non-fatal) and the trial is powered to determine whether there is a 35% reduction in total stroke events between placebo and active treatment. Treatment consists of a diuretic (indapamide SR 1.5 mg daily) and additional ACE inhibitor (perindopril) if required, with a five-year average follow-up. Secondary endpoints include total mortality, cardiovascular mortality, cardiac mortality, stroke mortality and skeletal fracture.

> The elderly are more likely to have isolated systolic hypertension

Elderly hypertensive patients respond to non-pharmacological measures to lower BP as well as younger patients. In a trial of non-pharmacological interventions in the elderly (TONE), reducing sodium intake to less than 2 g/day reduced BP over 30 months and about 40% of those on low-salt diet were able to discontinue their antihypertensive treatment. Low-dose thiazide diuretics and long-acting dihydropyridine calcium antagonists should be considered as first-line drugs for the treatment of hypertension. Beta-blockers are less effective than thiazides as first-line treatment and meta-analyses suggest that beta-blockers decrease stroke but no other cardiovascular events in the elderly. However, the elderly have more co-morbidity and may be open to more polypharmacy and drug interactions. Postural hypotension, defined as a drop in systolic and diastolic BP of > 20 and 10 mmHg respectively,

is more common in the elderly and periodic assessment of lying and standing BP is recommended. Overall, however, the concern that the elderly tolerate antihypertensive drugs poorly is probably exaggerated.

Renal disease

Renovascular disease (renal artery stenosis)

Renovascular disease (renal artery stenosis) is relatively uncommon, but is probably the most frequent curable cause of hypertension. ACE inhibitors may cause or worsen renal impairment in patients with critical renovascular disease. For this reason, they should be used with caution in patients with advanced chronic renal impairment, preferably with specialist supervision.

Clues suggesting renovascular disease are:

- onset of hypertension before the age of 30
- documented sudden onset, or recent worsening, of hypertension in middle age
- accelerated (malignant) hypertension
- resistant hypertension (to a three-drug regimen)
- renal impairment of unknown cause
- elevation of serum creatinine by ACE inhibitor or angiotensin II antagonist treatment
- peripheral vascular disease or severe generalized atherosclerotic disease
- recurrent pulmonary oedema or heart failure with no obvious cause.

Patients with any of these features should be referred for specialist advice because the investigations required to confirm or exclude renovascular disease are complex.

Renal failure

Many patients with renal failure have hypertension, but whether or not the hypertension is the cause of renal failure, or is secondary to it, often remains unclear.

Hypertensive patients with elevated serum creatinine or proteinuria may have parenchymal or obstructive renal disease, and should be referred for specialist evaluation.

Accelerated (malignant) hypertension requires immediate hospital treatment because it causes rapid loss of renal function, which can be irreversible if untreated. Otherwise, there is little evidence that non-malignant essential hypertension causes renal failure. The corollary is that renal impairment, in the absence of previous accelerated phase hypertension, suggests primary renal disease or renovascular disease. In patients with chronic renal impairment, hypertension accelerates the rate of loss of renal function and good BP control is essential to retard this process.

Hypertension treatment in renal failure

Effective treatment of hypertension slows the progression of renal failure. Meta-analysis of all controlled trials showed a 30% reduction in incidence of end-stage renal failure with ACE inhibitors, which may not all be explained by BP reduction alone. ACE inhibitors are renoprotective and delay the progression of both diabetic and non-diabetic nephropathy. Angiotensin receptor antagonists have also been shown to reduce proteinuria and may be a suitable alternative to ACE inhibitors, especially in (type 2) diabetic nephropathy. Hence, ACE inhibitors should be the drugs of first choice for patients with renal disease except in those with bilateral renal artery stenosis (or stenosis in the artery to a single kidney).

The optimal BP should be lower (BP <125/75 mmHg) in patients with renal disease and proteinuria >1 g/24 hours. This lower BP target means that multiple antihypertensive agents are needed in most patients. Thiazide diuretics may be ineffective in patients with renal impairment and loop diuretics (i.e. furosemide), often in high-doses, are frequently required. Calcium channel blockers and alpha-blockers are useful additional agents. The dose of renally excreted antihypertensive drugs may

need to be adjusted. Of note, patients with impaired renal function are particularly salt-sensitive, and dietary salt reduction is important. In addition, patients with renal failure have a very high risk of cardiovascular complications, and may benefit from aspirin or statin treatment in addition to non-pharmacological measures to reduce their cardiovascular risk (Figure 7.8).

Peripheral vascular disease

Hypertension is a common and important risk factor for vascular disorders, including peripheral vascular disease (PVD). Intermittent claudication is the most common symptomatic manifestation of PVD. It is also an important predictor of cardiovascular death, increasing it by three-fold, and increasing all-cause mortality two- to five-fold. Of hypertensive patients at presentation, about 2–5% have intermittent claudication, and this increases with age. Similarly, 35–55% of patients with PVD at presentation also have hypertension. Patients who suffer from hypertension with PVD have a greatly increased risk of myocardial infarction and stroke. Apart from the epidemiological associations, hypertension contributes to the pathogenesis of atherosclerosis, the basic pathological process underlying PVD. Peripheral vascular disease is exacerbated by increases in serum lipid concentrations and by smoking.

> Hypertension is found in one-third to one-half of patients with PVD, and patients with both have a much greater risk of suffering strokes or myocardial infarction

Treatment of hypertension in patients with peripheral vascular disease

None of the large antihypertensive treatment trials have adequately addressed whether or not a reduction in BP causes a decrease in PVD incidence. Treatment of hypertension in patients with PVD should follow the conventional treatment algorithm outlined in the previous chapter. However, ACE inhibitors should be used

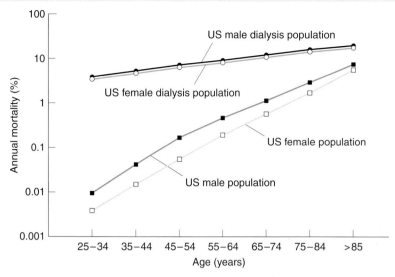

Figure 7.8
Cardiovascular mortality in dialysis patients. (Adapted from *Lancet* 2000; **356**: 147–52.)

with caution as there may be undiagnosed atheromatous renal artery stenosis (see above). In patients with peripheral vascular disease, an 'exquisite' or over-rapid fall in BP in response to ACE inhibitor, or a significant rise in serum creatinine levels, raises a strong possibility of underlying renal artery stenosis. Vasodilators, e.g. calcium antagonists and alpha-blockers, are useful agents in such patients. Calcium channel blockers may modestly improve the symptoms of claudication. There is the misconception that beta-blockers may worsen peripheral vascular disease, but trials comparing beta-blockers with a placebo did not significantly influence claudication distance. Nevertheless, they should be avoided in patients with rest pain or gangrene.

Ethnic groups

The ethnic differences in the incidence, pathophysiology and management of hypertension are particularly pertinent to the Afro-Caribbean population, who have a high prevalence of hypertension and associated complications such as strokes and renal impairment. The lack of large, long-term prospective randomized trials with hard

outcome data has made it difficult to ascertain the precise benefits for the different antihypertensive agents in specific ethnic groups. There is also the difficulty of defining a solely Afro-Caribbean or white population, as many subgroups may exist within a particular ethnic group.

There are clear ethnic differences in cardiovascular disease (CVD) and its risk factors. Despite an increased prevalence of both hypertension and diabetes, the overall risk of coronary artery disease (CAD) in the Afro-Caribbean male population in Europe, in the Caribbean and to a lesser extent in North America, is lower than in white males. By contrast, Indo-Asians have an excess prevalence of CAD. This contrast may be due to a multitude of reasons, and some suggest that the traditional risk factors do not fully explain the ethnic differences in CVD and stroke.

> Ethnic differences are important in how hypertension is managed (especially in Afro-Caribbean people), and also for the risk factors associated with CVD

Afro-Caribbeans

Hypertension is known to occur more frequently in the Afro-Caribbean population and is associated with a higher incidence of cerebrovascular and renal complications. Strokes are more common and hypertension-associated end-stage renal failure is up to 20 times more frequent in Afro-Caribbean patients than in non-Afro-Caribbean patients.

In addition, there is a greater tendency to develop LVH, and Afro-Caribbean patients with mild hypertension have a two-fold higher prevalence of LVH compared to non-Afro-Caribbeans with comparable BP levels. In the West Birmingham malignant hypertension register, there was an excess of Afro-Caribbean patients with malignant hypertension, higher BP and more severe renal impairment at presentation; these patients had a worse overall median survival rate and an increased rate of progression to dialysis. Therefore, Afro-Caribbean patients with malignant hypertension did not do worse simply because they were Afro-Caribbean, but appeared to have poorer BP control and more complications such as renal damage.

> Afro-Caribbean patients are 20 times more likely to develop hypertension-associated end-stage renal failure than white patients

Afro-Caribbean patients with hypertension exhibit enhanced sodium retention with a higher incidence of salt-sensitive hypertension, expanded plasma volume and a higher prevalence of low plasma renin activity. For this reason, hypertension in Afro-Caribbeans is often sensitive to dietary salt restriction. In patients with no evidence of target organ damage, a low salt diet may occasionally be sufficient to control BP. Reduced sodium-potassium ATPase activity is also associated with hypertension in Afro-Caribbean patients, combined with a tendency towards increased intracellular sodium and calcium concentrations. In addition, proteinuria has been observed more frequently in African-Americans compared to white

patients with similar creatinine levels. Control of dietary sodium should be combined with other non-pharmacological measures including weight control, alcohol moderation and regular exercise.

Use of drugs acting on the renin–angiotensin system

Afro-Caribbean patients tend to have lower levels of renin than white patients (Figure 7.9) and tend to respond less well to drugs that act on the renin–angiotensin system, such as beta-blockers, ACE inhibitors and angiotensin II antagonists. In contrast, these patients respond well to calcium antagonists, alpha-blockers and diuretics. Where there are clear indications for these agents, such as post-myocardial infarction or heart failure, these patients should not be denied ACE inhibitors and beta-blockers. Indeed, Afro-Caribbean patients may respond to ACE-inhibition or beta-blockade given in combination with drugs that activate the renin–angiotensin system, i.e. diuretics, calcium channel blockers or alpha-blockers. Of note, angioedema is more common with the use of ACE inhibitors in the Afro-Caribbean population.

South Asians

South Asians (from the Indian subcontinent) have a high prevalence of hypertension, obesity, insulin resistance and type 2 diabetes, giving

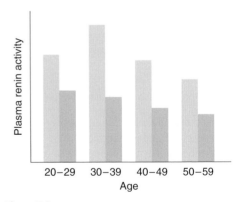

Figure 7.9
Plasma renin in Afro-Caribbean (in dark blue) and Caucasian patients with hypertension.

rise to the so-called 'metabolic syndrome'. This ethnic group is at particularly high risk of CHD. The response to antihypertensive drug treatment in South Asian patients is similar to that in white Europeans although data are limited. Good control of BP is particularly important in those with diabetes, and aspirin and/or statin treatment may be indicated for those at high risk of CHD.

Hyperlipidaemia

The best strategy for patients at high cardiovascular risk with hyperlipidaemia and hypertension is to treat both with different drugs, and not worry too much about small changes in cholesterol. In patients at high risk of CVD, HMG coenzyme A inhibitors (statins) have been shown to reduce cardiovascular events. As the beta-blockers and high-dose diuretics aggravate hyperlipidaemia, they should be avoided in people whose hyperlipidaemia is difficult to control. However, in reality, the clinical effect of these drugs on lipids is small.

Oral contraceptives and hypertension

The combined oral contraceptives (OCs) have a small adverse effect on BP – approximately 5/3 mmHg. The Nurses' Health Study found that current users of OCs had a small but significantly increased risk of hypertension compared to never users. Controlled studies suggest a return of BP to pre-treatment levels within three months of discontinuation, indicating that the BP effect is reversible.

However, the increase in BP may also be idiosyncratic and may occur many months or years after first using a combined OC. In a small proportion of women (approximately 1%) severe hypertension may be induced. As the BP response to any combined OC preparation is unpredictable, and there is a small increase in cardiovascular risk associated with OC use, BP should certainly be measured before starting OC use and then every six months thereafter. It

should not be forgotten that OCs can increase the risk of venous thromboembolism.

If other risk factors for cardiovascular disease (e.g. smoking or migraine) exist, other non-hormonal forms of contraception should be sought. In those women for whom other methods of contraception are unacceptable, careful monitoring of BP is recommended. Antihypertensive therapy should be considered if BP remains elevated.

> Oral contraceptives can affect hypertension slightly although in some cases hypertension can be severe

Hormone replacement therapy

For many years, hormone replacement therapy (HRT) was considered to be contraindicated in postmenopausal women with hypertension. Many such women were excluded from HRT because of concerns that HRT might have an adverse effect on BP. This perception was mainly due to the effects of oral contraceptive drugs, especially the oestrogen component, in increasing BP. Differences exist between the formulation and doses of oestrogen preparations used either as oral contraceptives in premenopausal women (in whom high-dose synthetic oestrogens are used) or as HRT in postmenopausal women (in whom low 'replacement' doses of natural oestrogens are used). This is not inconsequential, as postmenopausal women represent the largest category of women at risk of hypertension.

The Women's Health Initiative, the largest longitudinal study to evaluate the effect of HRT on BP, found an average of 1 mmHg increase in systolic BP over 5.6 years of follow-up among patients randomized to conjugated oestrogen and medroxyprogesterone compared to placebo. This study contrasts with the results of other smaller studies. Overall, the effect of HRT on BP is likely to be modest. However, the question of HRT and BP may be of little clinical relevance in view of the recent reports of adverse cardiovascular outcome associated with the use of HRT and the already well-documented risk of venous thromboembolism.

> The question of hormone replacement therapy and blood pressure may be of little clinical relevance in view of the recent reports of adverse cardiovascular outcome associated with the use of HRT

Treating hypertension in conjunction with hormone replacement therapy

HRT is certainly not contraindicated for women with hypertension. Women with hypertension should not be denied access to HRT as long as BP levels can be controlled by antihypertensive medication. In view of the lack of consensus in the prescribing habits of HRT, suitable guidelines are as follows:

- All clinicians should measure BP before starting HRT.
- In normotensive postmenopausal women, BP should be measured annually following the start of HRT. One exception may be the use of premarin, where a follow-up BP measurement should probably be made at three months (in view of reports of a possible rare idiosyncratic rise in BP).
- In hypertensive menopausal women, BP should at least be measured initially and at six-monthly intervals thereafter. If BP is labile or difficult to control, three-monthly measurements should be taken. If a hypertensive woman on HRT demonstrates a rise in BP, careful monitoring or observation and perhaps an alteration or increase of their antihypertensive treatment should be considered.

Hypertension and anaesthesia

The issues regarding hypertension and anaesthesia can be related to the evaluation of the BP itself (preoperative) and the use of antihypertensive agents (intra- and postoperative). Many non-urgent surgical procedures are postponed unnecessarily when patients are erroneously diagnosed as hypertensive. In fact they are simply exhibiting anxiety-related white-coat hypertension caused by admission to hospital.

Criteria for anaesthesia in the hypertensive patient

If the patient has mild asymptomatic hypertension with no target organ damage, and is otherwise fit and well, then he/she is at no particular risk in the perioperative period. In contrast, patients with severe hypertension, especially those with target organ damage, are at risk of perioperative complications (including arrhythmias or myocardial infarction). If BP >180/110, elective surgery should be postponed in these patients until they have been fully assessed and better BP control has been achieved. Parenteral control of hypertension is rarely needed because patients are usually on bed rest and receiving opioid analgesia, which reduce BP.

Suspension of hypertensive medication before anaesthesia

Care is needed in those patients taking particular antihypertensive drugs as some anaesthetic agents may have a hypotensive effect. The ACE inhibitors may block the response of the renin–angiotensin system, resulting in hypotension following blood loss, while the beta-blockers may block the compensatory rise in heart rate associated with fluid loss. However, beta-blockers should not be stopped in the perioperative period because this class of drug has benefits in preventing postoperative arrhythmias, e.g. including atrial fibrillation. In patients with coronary artery disease, stopping the beta-blocker may provoke myocardial ischaemia. In those cases where antihypertensive drugs have to be stopped, they should be started again as soon as practically possible.

Hypertension in children

Hypertension is a rare problem in children and, where present, it is usually the result of another condition (possibly renal or vasculitic diseases). Children with systemic illness should have their BP checked. It is possible that the origin of adult essential hypertension starts in childhood or even infancy. Children whose BP exceeds the 90th percentile for their age need careful rechecking, and if they exceed the 95th percentile, referral to hospital specialists and detailed investigation is mandatory.

> In children, hypertension is often a symptom of another condition

Measuring BP in children

It is not considered justifiable to screen BP in all children. Children with an initial high BP tend to show a faster rise with advancing age, especially when obese. Under the age of three years, BP measurement can only be achieved with Doppler flow equipment. BP should be measured with the child in a comfortable sitting position (although infants may be supine), with the right arm exposed and supported at the heart level and an appropriate-sized cuff used. However, phase V sounds may be difficult to obtain in children. The guidelines therefore accept the Korotkoff sounds of K4 diastolic BP in the standards for infants and children aged from three years to 12 years, and K5 diastolic BP for adolescents aged from 13 to 18. The fourth and fifth Korotkoff diastolic sounds should still be recorded if both are heard.

Treatment of hypertension in children

As with general management of hypertension, non-pharmacological therapy should be initiated along with salt restriction and diet control. Beta-blockers, calcium antagonists and alpha-blockers are generally safe for use by children. However, thiazides theoretically have long-term metabolic effects and so are best avoided in children. The ACE inhibitors should also be used with caution in children with renal disease.

Metabolic syndrome

Metabolic syndrome describes the frequent coalition of multiple cardiovascular risk factors – abdominal obesity, hypertension, abnormal glucose tolerance (impaired fasting glucose, impaired glucose tolerance or diabetes) and dyslipidaemia (high triglyceride and low HDL cholesterol levels). The World Health Organization and Adult Treatment Panel (ATP)-III diagnostic criteria for metabolic syndrome are summarized in Table 7.1. Metabolic syndrome diagnosed by either of these criteria identifies patients at increased risk of diabetes, CVD and all-cause mortality. The International Diabetes Federation diagnostic criteria build on the ATP-III criteria and include ethnic-specific values for waist circumference (Table 7.2).

Table 7.1
Definition of metabolic syndrome

NCEP definition	WHO definition
At least three of the following: • Fasting plasma glucose >6.1 mmol/L • Waist girth >102 cm (men), >88 cm (women) • Serum triglycerides ≥ 1.7 mmol/L • Serum HDL <1.0 mmol/L (men), <1.3 mmol/L (women) • Blood pressure ≥ 130/85 mmHg	Insulin resistance, impaired glucose regulation or diabetes AND at least two of the following: • Hypertension (blood pressure 140/90 mmHg) • Central obesity (waist–hip ratio 0.9 in men, 0.85 in women or BMI >30 kg/m²) • Dyslipidaemia (serum triglyceride >1.7 mmol/L or HDL <0.9 in men and <1.0 in women) • Microalbuminuria (urine albumin excretion rate ≥ 20 µg/min)

NCEP, National Cholesterol Education Program; WHO, World Health Organization; HDL, high-density lipoprotein; BMI, body mass index.

Table 7.2
International Diabetes Federation definition of metabolic syndrome

- Central obesity
- Waist circumference – ethnic-specific (*see below*)*

Plus any two of the following:
- Raised triglycerides
  >1.7 mmol/L (or specific treatment of this abnormality)
- Reduced HDL cholesterol
  <1.03 mmol/L in men, <1.29 mmol/L in women (or specific treatment of this abnormality)
- Raised blood pressure
  Systolic ≥ 130 mmHg
  Diastolic ≥ 85 mmHg
  (or treatment of previous hypertension)
- Raised fasting plasma glucose
  >5.6 mmol/L or previously diagnosed type 2 diabetes

(glucose tolerance test recommended if fasting glucose >5.6 mmol/L but not required to define this syndrome)

*Ethnic groups
Europids – Men ≥ 94 cm, Women ≥ 80 cm
South Asians – Men ≥ 90 cm, Women ≥ 80 cm
Chinese – Men ≥ 90 cm, Women ≥ 80 cm
Japanese – Men ≥ 85 cm, Women ≥ 90 cm
Ethnic South and Central Americans – Men ≥ 90 cm, Women ≥ 80 cm
Sub-Saharan Africans – Men ≥ 94 cm, Women ≥ 80 cm
Eastern Mediterranean and Middle East populations – Men ≥ 94 cm, Women ≥ 80 cm

Treatment

Lifestyle changes, with the aim of halting weight gain or encouraging healthy weight loss, are the cornerstone for the clinical management of people with metabolic syndrome (see Chapter 6: Non-pharmacological management). Pharmacological adjuncts may be tried, especially in people with clear motivation and in conjunction with appropriate advice, support and counselling, to facilitate weight loss. The National Institute of Clinical Excellence (NICE) guidelines support the use of orlistat (a lipase inhibitor) for people who have lost at least 2.5 kg in weight by non-pharmacological

measures. The novel endocannabinoid receptor antagonist rimonabant has been shown to lower blood pressure and reverse the metabolic abnormalities associated with the metabolic syndrome. Sibutramine, which has an adverse effect on BP, is not recommended in hypertension.

Other cardiovascular risk factors should also be addressed in a multifactorial approach to the management of metabolic syndrome. Blood pressure targets are as outlined previously (see Chapter 6). As patients with metabolic syndrome have an increased risk of developing diabetes, beta-blockers and thiazide diuretics (and especially their combination) are generally not advisable as first-line agents. In contrast, ACE inhibitors and angiotensin II antagonists may be considered as first-line antihypertensive therapy in patients with metabolic syndrome as several clinical trials have shown them to reduce new-onset diabetes.

The Joint British Societies guidelines recommend statin therapy for young (18–39 years) people with type 1 or type 2 diabetes and metabolic syndrome. Indeed, statin and aspirin treatment should be considered in most patients with metabolic syndrome, as the majority of these patients will have CVD risk of over 20%.

Further reading

Adler AI, Stratton IM, Neil HA, *et al*. Association of systolic blood pressure with macrovascular and microvascular complications of type 2 diabetes (UKPDS 36): prospective observational study. *BMJ* 2000; **321**: 412–19.

Alberti KGMM, Zimmet P, Shaw J for the IDF Epidemiology Task Force Consensus Group. The metabolic syndrome – a new worldwide definition. *Lancet* 2005; **366**: 1059–62.

Chung NAY, Lip GYH, Beevers DG. Hypertension in old age. *CPD Journal Intern Med* 2001; **2**: 46–9.

Cohn JN, Tognoni G. A randomized trial of the angiotensin-receptor blocker valsartan in chronic heart failure. *N Engl J Med* 2001; **345**: 1667–75.

Edmunds E, Lip GY. Cardiovascular risk in women: the cardiologist's perspective. *QJM* 2000; **93**: 135–45.

Felmeden DC, Lip GY, Beevers G. Calcium antagonists in

diabetic hypertension. *Diabetes Obes Metab* 2001; **3**: 311–18.

Gibbs CR, Beevers DG, Lip GY. The management of hypertensive disease in black patients. *QJM* 1999; **92**: 187–92.

Grundy SM, Brewer B, Cleeman JI, *et al.* Definition of metabolic syndrome. Report of the National Heart, Lung and Blood Institute/American Heart Association Conference on scientific issues related to definition. *Circulation* 2004; **109**: 433–8.

Lip GY, Beevers M, Beevers DG, Dillon MJ. The measurement of blood pressure and the detection of hypertension in children and adolescents. *J Hum Hypertens* 2001; **15**: 419–23.

PROGRESS Collaborative Group. Randomised trial of a perindopril-based blood-pressure-lowering regimen among 6,105 individuals with previous stroke or transient ischaemic attack. *Lancet* 2001; **358**: 1033–41.

Stratton IM, Adler AI, Neil HA, *et al.* Association of glycaemia with macrovascular and microvascular complications of type 2 diabetes (UKPDS 35): prospective observational study. *BMJ* 2000; **321**: 405–12.

UK Prospective Diabetes Study (UKPDS) Group. Cost effectiveness analysis of improved blood pressure control in hypertensive patients with type 2 diabetes: UKPDS 40. *BMJ* 1998; **317**: 720–6.

UK Prospective Diabetes Study Group. Efficacy of atenolol and captopril in reducing risk of macrovascular and microvascular complications in type 2 diabetes: UKPDS 39. *BMJ* 1998; **317**: 713–20.

UK Prospective Diabetes Study Group. Tight blood pressure control and risk of macrovascular and microvascular complications in type 2 diabetes: UKPDS 38. *BMJ* 1998; **317**: 703–13.

UK Prospective Diabetes Study Group. Intensive blood-glucose control with sulphonylureas or insulin compared with conventional treatment and risk of complications in patients with type 2 diabetes (UKPDS 33). *Lancet* 1998; **352**: 837–53.

Vora JP, Ibrahim HA, Bakris GL. Responding to the challenge of diabetic nephropathy: the historic evolution of detection, prevention and management. *J Hum Hypertens* 2000; **14**: 667–85.

Yusuf S, Sleight P, Pogue J, *et al.* Effects of an angiotensin-converting-enzyme inhibitor, ramipril on cardiovascular events in high-risk patients. Heart Outcomes Prevention Evaluation Study Investigators. *N Engl J Med* 2000; **342**: 145–53.

8. Hypertension in pregnancy

Classification of hypertension in pregnancy
Pre-existing essential hypertension
Secondary hypertension in pregnancy
Pregnancy-induced hypertension
Pre-eclampsia
Eclampsia
Choice of antihypertensive therapy in pregnancy
Treatment of pre-eclampsia and eclampsia
Further pregnancy

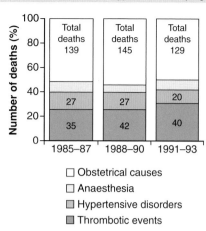

Figure 8.1
Causes of maternal deaths in the UK from 1985 to 1993.

The management of hypertension in pregnancy is a specialist area and a detailed treatise is beyond the scope of this book. Hypertension occurs in around 5% of all pregnancies. However, this covers a wide range of conditions that carry different implications for pregnancy outcome and require different management strategies. Raised blood pressure (BP) may also be a marker of underlying maternal disease or it may be a consequence of pregnancy itself. It is important to remember that hypertension in pregnancy affects the fetus as well as the mother. It can result in fetal growth retardation and, if severe, both maternal and fetal morbidity and mortality (Figure 8.1). If recognized early and managed appropriately, many of these complications can be reduced. Hypertension may be the first sign of impending pre-eclampsia – a potentially more serious condition of the second half of pregnancy and the puerperium. When measuring BP in pregnant women, diastolic BP should be measured at the disappearance of all sounds (phase V) and not at muffling (phase IV) as recommended in the past.

Hypertensive diseases in pregnancy, including pre-eclampsia, remain major causes of maternal and fetal mortality in the UK (the mortality rate is around 2%). Although maternal mortality due to hypertension has fallen markedly over the past three decades, eclampsia remains an important cause of a significant number of deaths. Eclampsia is responsible for one-sixth of all maternal deaths and a doubling of perinatal mortality. Despite accurate figures on the effects of raised BP, the precise causes of hypertension in pregnancy are unknown, and eclampsia has been referred to as the 'disease of theories'.

Classification of hypertension in pregnancy

There have been several attempts at classifying hypertension in pregnancy, although none is entirely satisfactory. This is partly because the diagnoses are often made in retrospect after the pregnancy is over. It is important to understand the different types of hypertension in pregnancy, not least because their prognosis differs widely. The current classification is based on the International Society for the Study of Hypertension in Pregnancy (ISSHP) recommendations (Table 8.1). In 1997, Brown and Buddle published a comparison of the criteria of the Australasian Society for the Study of Hypertension in Pregnancy and the International Society for the Study of Hypertension in 17,657 consecutive pregnancies, of which 1183 (6.7%) were complicated by hypertension (Figure 8.2).

In this above classification the term 'pregnancy-induced hypertension' is abolished. Some of these patients would have chronic hypertension while others have mild early pre-eclampsia (see Brown MA and Buddle ML. *J Hypertens* 1997; **15**: 1049–54).

Table 8.1
A simple classification of the hypertensive disorders of pregnancy

Raised blood pressure (>140/90 mmHg) before 20 weeks gestation
- Known chronic hypertension
  —essential
  —renal (glomerulonephritis, pyelonephritis, polycystic kidney disease)
  —renovascular (fibromuscular dysplasia)
  —adrenal (phaeochromocytoma)
- Presumed chronic hypertension

Raised blood pressure (>140/90 mmHg) after 20 weeks gestation
- Chronic hypertension
- Mild non-proteinuric pre-eclampsia
- Proteinuric pre-eclampsia
- Pre-eclampsia complicating chronic hypertension

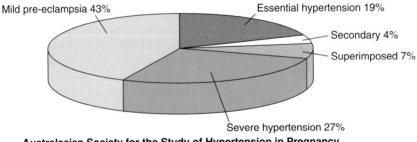

Mild pre-eclampsia 43%
Essential hypertension 19%
Secondary 4%
Superimposed 7%
Severe hypertension 27%

Australasian Society for the Study of Hypertension in Pregnancy

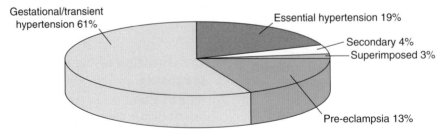

Gestational/transient hypertension 61%
Essential hypertension 19%
Secondary 4%
Superimposed 3%
Pre-eclampsia 13%

International Society for the Study of Hypertension in Pregnancy

Figure 8.2
Classifications of the hypertensive syndromes of pregnancy: the Australasian Society for the Study of Hypertension in Pregnancy classification and the International Society for the Study of Hypertension in Pregnancy classification. (Adapted from Brown et al. J Hypertens 1997; **15**: 1049–54.)

Pre-existing essential hypertension

This is otherwise referred to as chronic hypertension and is present before the 20th week of pregnancy. It is assumed the mother had pre-existing hypertension (although often no data are available). For this reason, chronic hypertension refers to long-term hypertension that is not confined to or caused by pregnancy, but may be revealed for the first time during pregnancy. About 5% of women of childbearing age have chronic pre-existing hypertension, which is usually mild. In women in their late 30s and 40s, this figure approaches 10%. Mild essential hypertension in pregnancy does not appear to carry a bad prognosis for the mother or fetus and its early treatment does not convincingly prevent the onset of pre-eclampsia. The condition is defined by the World Health Organization criteria as BP >140/90 mmHg.

The usual 'cause' of chronic hypertension is essential hypertension. However, there may be other infrequent secondary causes.

> Chronic hypertension is long-term hypertension that is first discovered during the first 20 weeks of pregnancy, but is not caused by the pregnancy

Secondary hypertension in pregnancy

This is uncommon, but is accounted for by causes of secondary hypertension in younger people, such as phaeochromocytoma, renal disease and primary hyperaldosteronism. For example, phaeochromocytoma is well-described in association with pregnancy and is associated with a poor maternal and fetal outcome. Hypertension associated with renal disease may exacerbate renal impairment, resulting in poor outcome of the pregnancy, deterioration of renal function across pregnancy and subsequent subfertility.

Pregnancy-induced hypertension

Pregnancy-induced hypertension usually develops after the 20th week of pregnancy and usually resolves 10 days after delivery. For this diagnosis to be made, BP must be documented to be normal both before and after pregnancy. Therefore, this diagnosis may sometimes only be made retrospectively.

The definitions of pregnancy-induced hypertension vary. The ISSHP defines pregnancy-induced hypertension as a single diastolic (phase V) BP >110 mmHg or two readings of >90 mmHg at least four hours apart, occurring after the 20th week of pregnancy. The US National High Blood Pressure Education Program defines it as a rise of >15 mmHg diastolic or 30 mmHg systolic compared to readings taken in early pregnancy.

A concise clinical definition by Davey and MacGillivray describes the condition as 'the occurrence of a BP of 140/90 mmHg or more on at least two separate occasions a minimum of six hours apart in a woman known to have been normotensive before this time, and in whom the BP has returned to normal limits by the sixth postpartum week'.

The threshold at which drug treatment is recommended is emphatically not 140/90 mmHg. Many young pregnant women may in fact show the BP increase required for the diagnosis of pre-eclampsia without increasing their pressure to 140/90 mmHg. Pregnancy-induced hypertension affects up to 25% of women in their first pregnancy and in 10% of subsequent pregnancies.

> Pregnancy-induced hypertension can be defined as a BP of ≥ 140/90 mmHg measured on at least two separate occasions at least six hours apart, when the patient had been normotensive before pregnancy

If pregnancy-induced hypertension is mild and does not progress to pre-eclampsia or eclampsia, the prognosis is usually good. However, women who develop hypertension early in the second half of pregnancy are more likely to progress to pre-eclampsia. They may develop proteinuria, thrombocytopenia, oedema and may need an early delivery.

Pre-eclampsia

Pregnancy-induced hypertension (BP >140/90 mmHg) after the 20th week of pregnancy that is associated with proteinuria (>300 mg/L), is often referred to as pre-eclampsia. This commonly occurs in primigravidae in the second half of pregnancy and marks a severe, acute change in the mother's condition. Although pre-eclampsia is defined as presenting after 20 weeks, it may often occur earlier or become evident only after delivery. The incidence of proteinuric pre-eclampsia is approximately 1 in 20–30 pregnancies in the UK.

Risk factors for pre-eclampsia

The risk factors for pre-eclampsia include fetal-specific and maternal-specific factors, discussed in detail below (Table 8.2). For example, pre-eclampsia is more common in primigravidae, those aged under 20 years or over 35 years, or in women with previous severe pre-eclampsia. It is thought there is also a genetic predisposition to pre-eclampsia.

Pre-eclampsia is also more common in women who are overweight and of short stature, and in women with chronic hypertension, especially those with associated chronic renal disease. Women with chronic hypertension are three to seven times more likely to develop higher BP and proteinuria (often referred to as 'superimposed pre-eclampsia') than normotensive women.

The patient is usually (not always) symptomatic with frontal headaches and visual symptoms (jagged, angular flashes at the periphery of her visual fields, loss of vision in some areas) due to cerebral oedema. There is often epigastric pain due to hepatic oedema and occasionally an itch over the mask region of the face.

Table 8.2
Pathogenesis of pre-eclampsia – failure of the normal demuscularization of the uterine spiral arteries in early pregnancy

- Predisposing factors:
  —prior hypertension
  —prior diabetes mellitus
  —increased insulin resistance
  —increased testosterone
  —increased triglycerides, decreased HDL and increased small dense LDL cholesterol
  —African origin
  —first pregnancy
  —changed paternity
  —multiple pregnancy
  —hydatidiform mole
  —fetal chromosomal abnormalities
  —placental hydrops
- Pathophysiological and clinical aspects:
  —raised blood pressure
  —proteinuria
  —reduced multi-organ perfusion
  —reduced uterine blood flow
  —increased sensitivity to pressor agents
  —vasospasm
  —reduced plasma volume
  —increased extravascular fluid volume
  —activation of coagulation cascade
  —platelet activation
  —microthrombi formation

> Short, overweight women and women with chronic hypertension are most susceptible to pre-eclampsia

Clinical signs

On examination, BP may be high and there is a sharp increase in proteinuria. Hypertension usually precedes proteinuria but the converse is occasionally encountered. Blood pressures are usually unstable at rest, and circadian rhythm is altered, initially with a loss of physiological nocturnal dipping; in severe cases there is 'reverse dipping' with the highest BP seen at night.

Early papilloedema may be seen on fundoscopy. There may be increased and brisk reflexes and clonus. Oedema is a less reliable diagnostic feature as mild pre-tibial and facial oedema are commonly found in normal pregnancy. Urgent antihypertensive and anticonvulsant treatment is needed. It should be noted that pregnancy-induced hypertension with or without proteinuria may be superimposed on chronic hypertension.

Eclampsia

Eclampsia is a hypertensive emergency associated with a high incidence of both maternal and fetal death. This is a convulsive condition usually associated with proteinuric pregnancy-induced hypertension, occurring in around one in 500 pregnancies.

Clinical signs

The condition resembles other forms of hypertensive encephalopathy, with similar symptoms of headache, nausea, vomiting and convulsions. BP is invariably high and proteinuria >300 mg/L is almost always present. There may be gross oedema and convulsions – if they occur, they usually develop in labour or in the puerperium. Auras, epigastric pain, apprehension and hyperreflexia may precede the convulsions, with little or no warning in many cases.

After intense tonic-clonic seizures, the patient may become stuporose or comatose. Another complication common to eclampsia and hypertensive encephalopathy is cortical blindness, which results from petechial haemorrhages and focal oedema in the occipital cortex. Other complications include pulmonary oedema, renal failure, hepatic failure, retinal detachment and cerebrovascular accidents.

Choice of antihypertensive therapy in pregnancy

Methyldopa remains the antihypertensive drug of choice for idiopathic hypertension or pre-eclampsia because of its long and extensive use without reports of serious adverse effects on the fetus. As a centrally acting anti-

hypertensive agent, methyldopa may be associated with depression and sedation. Autoimmune haemolytic anaemia is also recognized with methyldopa, which necessitates discontinuation of therapy.

Calcium antagonists (especially slow-release nifedipine) and the vasodilator hydralazine are common second-line drugs. Sublingual nifedipine should never be used. Both of these vasodilators may be associated with reflex tachycardia and may work synergistically with beta-blockers. Side-effects are uncommon with short-term use of hydralazine.

Labetalol (alpha-blocker and beta-blocker) is also widely used as a second-line agent, particularly for resistant hypertension in the third trimester. However, ACE inhibitors and angiotensin II antagonists are contraindicated in pregnancy due to adverse effects on the fetus. Beta-blockers such as atenolol may result in small babies (Figure 8.3).

Contraindicated drug therapy

Before 28 weeks' gestation, beta-blockers are not widely used because of concerns that they may inhibit fetal growth. The diuretics may

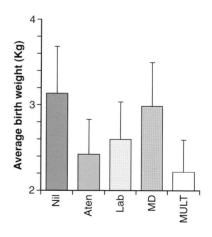

Figure 8.3
Antihypertensive drugs and fetal growth. Aten, atenolol; Lab, labetalol; MD, methyldopa; MULT, multiple drugs. (Adapted from Lydakis *et al. Am J Hypertens* 1999; **12**: 541–7.)

reduce the incidence of pre-eclampsia, although no benefit was shown on fetal outcome. In theory at least, they may reduce the already decreased circulatory blood volume in women with pre-eclampsia and compromise utero–placental circulation.

ACE inhibitors and angiotensin II receptor antagonists should be avoided because they may cause oligohydramnios, renal failure, hypotension and intrauterine death in the fetus. Hypertensive women who are planning a pregnancy or who become pregnant while on antihypertensive treatment should be advised to change their therapy to one of the drugs recommended as safe for the treatment of hypertension in pregnancy (Table 8.3).

Use of prophylactic aspirin

The Australasian Society for the Study of Hypertension in Pregnancy (ASSHP) recommends use of prophylactic low-dose aspirin from early pregnancy in the following groups:

- women with prior fetal loss after the first trimester due to placental insufficiency
- women with severe fetal growth retardation in a preceding pregnancy either due to pre-eclampsia or unexplained causes

Table 8.3
Drug treatments for hypertension in pregnancy

- Contraindicated
  —ACE inhibitors
  —calcium channel blockers in mild hypertension
  —thiazides
  —atenolol, propranolol
- Probably safe
  —methyldopa, particularly in asthmatic mothers
  —alpha-blockers
  —some beta-blockers, e.g. labetalol, oxprenolol, pindolol
  —nifedipine in severe cases
- Emergency
  —intravenous and intramuscular drugs, e.g. hydralazine, labetalol
  —anticonvulsants
  —magnesium sulphate

- women with severe early-onset pre-eclampsia in a previous pregnancy requiring delivery at or before 32 weeks gestation.

Aspirin is not indicated routinely for healthy nulliparous women, women with mild chronic hypertension and women with established pre-eclampsia.

Treatment of pre-eclampsia and eclampsia

Urgent transfer to a specialized maternity unit with an adequate special care baby unit is indicated together with antihypertensive and anticonvulsant therapy. Diazepam and magnesium sulphate prevent fits and reduce BP.

The first line of management is to control the seizures. If at home, the woman should be laid on her side and an airway established. Intravenous diazepam, usually 20–40 mg, is used. Intravenous magnesium sulphate has been shown to improve outcome in eclampsia and is regarded as first-line treatment as an anticonvulsant in eclampsia. Intravenous magnesium also has antihypertensive properties. Occasionally phenytoin is used to prevent recurrence of fits.

Intravenous hydralazine is widely used as an antihypertensive drug of first choice, given as a 5 mg bolus at 20 minutes or as an infusion of 25 mg in 500 ml of Hartman's solution. The dose is titrated against the BP. An alternative is an intravenous infusion of labetalol. If the woman is in labour or induction is considered, an epidural anaesthetic may be helpful both to lower the BP and to reduce the tendency to fit by reducing the pain of uterine contractions. The ultimate treatment of eclampsia is, however, urgent delivery of the baby.

Magnesium sulphate is the first-line drug to treat eclampsia seizures

Further pregnancy

Mothers who have had pre-eclampsia during a first pregnancy should be warned of a 7.5% risk that it might return for their second. A history of spontaneous or induced first trimester abortion in a first pregnancy does not confer the same relative immunity to severe pre-eclampsia in the subsequent pregnancy. Other causes of hypertension should be considered when a patient develops hypertension in pregnancy, especially if there are any unusual features or the hypertension is severe.

Women with previous pre-eclampsia who become pregnant again should be targeted for management in a joint antenatal and BP clinic. Such women are also usually regarded as being more likely to develop essential hypertension in later life and regular screening for hypertension is recommended (Table 8.4). If a woman with a history of hypertension in pregnancy wishes oral contraception (this is not a contraindication), careful BP monitoring is essential. The developmental status of children born to women with pre-eclampsia is usually good.

> Women who develop pre-eclampsia during their first pregnancy have a 7.5% risk of it returning for their next pregnancy, and should be monitored at joint antenatal and BP clinics

The benefits of treating hypertension in pregnancy are summed up in Table 8.5. Clearly the best data are for the treatment of pre-eclampsia/eclampsia, with benefits for both the mother and baby, especially in the presence of severe hypertension. These uncertainties over the benefits of treatment are compounded by a recent meta-analysis suggesting that over-aggressive BP reduction in pregnancy is associated with a greater odds ratio for small-for-gestational-age babies and lower birth weights.

In a paper by von Dadelszen *et al.* (2000), the relation between fetoplacental growth and the use of oral antihypertensive medication to treat mild-to-moderate pregnancy hypertension was assessed using a metaregression analysis of published data from randomized controlled trials. The change in (group) mean arterial pressure (MAP) from enrolment to delivery was compared with indicators of fetoplacental growth. They found that greater mean difference in MAP with antihypertensive therapy was associated with the

Table 8.4
Laboratory tests used for hypertension in pregnancy

Test	Rationale
Full blood count	Haemoconcentration is found in pre-eclampsia and is an indicator of severity Decreased platelet count suggests severe pre-eclampsia
Blood film	Signs of microangiopathic haemolytic anaemia favour the diagnosis of pre-eclampsia
Urinalysis	If dipstick proteinuria of +1 or more, a quantitative measurement of 24-hour protein excretion is required Hypertensive pregnant women with proteinuria should be considered to have pre-eclampsia until proven otherwise
Biochemistry, including serum creatinine, urate and liver function tests	Abnormal or rising levels suggest pre-eclampsia and are an indicator of disease severity
Lactate dehydrogenase	Elevated levels are associated with haemolysis and hepatic involvement, suggesting severe pre-eclampsia
Serum albumin	Levels may be decreased even with mild proteinuria, perhaps owing to capillary leak or hepatic involvement in pre-eclampsia

(Adapted from recommendations of the National High Blood Pressure Education Program Working Group Report on High Blood Pressure in Pregnancy. *Am J Obstet Gynecol* 1990; **163**: 1689–712.)

Table 8.5 (a)
Are there benefits of treating hypertension during pregnancy?

	Mother	Fetus
Pre-existing hypertension	Yes	No
Pregnancy-induced hypertension	No	No
Pre-eclampsia	Yes	Yes

Table 8.5 (b)
Antihypertensive therapy for chronic hypertension during pregnancy

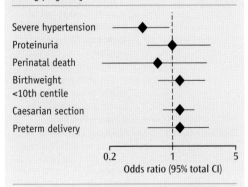

Severe hypertension

Proteinuria

Perinatal death

Birthweight <10th centile

Caesarian section

Preterm delivery

0.2   1   5
Odds ratio (95% total CI)

birth of a higher proportion of small-for-gestational-age (SGA) infants (slope: 0.09 [SD 0.03], r²=0.48, P=0.006, 14 trials) and lower mean birthweight significant after exclusion of data from another paper regarded as an extreme statistical outliner (slope: −14.49 [6.98] r²=0.16, P=0.049, 27 trials). No relation with mean placental weight was seen (slope −2.01 [1.62], r²=0.15, P=0.25, 11 trials). This analysis therefore suggests that treatment-induced falls in maternal blood pressure may adversely affect fetal growth. As discussed above, in view of the small maternal benefits that are likely to be derived from therapy, more information on relative maternal and fetal benefits and risks of oral antihypertensive drug treatment of *mild-to-moderate* pregnancy hypertension may be required.

Further reading

Broughton Pipkin F, Roberts JM. Hypertension in pregnancy. *J Hum Hypertens* 2000; **14**: 705–24.

Brown MA, Buddle ML. What's in a name? Problems with the classification of hypertension in pregnancy. *J Hypertens* 1997; **15**: 1049–54.

Chung NAY, Beevers DG, Lip GYH. Management of hypertension in pregnancy. *Am J Cardiovasc Drugs* 2001; **1**: 253–62.

Dekker G, Sibai B. Primary, secondary, and tertiary prevention of pre-eclampsia. *Lancet* 2001; **357**: 209–15.

Department of Health and Social Security. Report on confidential enquiries into maternal deaths in England and Wales 1982–84. London: HMSO, 1986: 10–19.

Ferrer RL, Sibai BM, Mulrow CD, et al. Management of mild chronic hypertension during pregnancy: a review. *Obstet Gynecol* 2000; **96**: 849–60.

Granger JP, Alexander BT, Bennett WA, et al. Pathophysiology of pregnancy-induced hypertension. *Am J Hypertens* 2001; **14**: 178S–85S.

Lydakis C, Lip GY, Beevers M, et al. Atenolol and fetal growth in pregnancies complicated by hypertension. *Am J Hypertens* 1999; **12**: 541–7.

Sibai BM. Antihypertensive drugs during pregnancy. *Semin Perinatol* 2001; **25**: 159–64.

von Dadelszen P, Ornstein MP, Bull SB, et al. Fall in mean arterial pressure and fetal growth restriction in pregnancy hypertension: a meta-analysis. *Lancet* 2000; **355**: 87–92.

9. Hypertensive urgencies and emergencies

Epidemiology
Malignant hypertension
Pathophysiology
Clinical features
Physical signs
Early management
Summary

Table 9.1
Hypertensive crises

- Hypertensive emergencies
  —hypertensive encephalopathy
  —hypertensive left ventricular failure
  —hypertension with myocardial infarction or unstable angina
  —hypertension with aortic dissection
  —severe hypertension with subarachnoid haemorrhage or stroke
  —acute renal failure
  —phaeochromocytoma crisis
  —recreational drugs (amphetamines, LSD, cocaine, ecstasy)
  —microangiopathic haemolytic anaemia
  —perioperative hypertension*

*This should be given individual consideration given the unique clinical factors present during the perioperative period

A number of different terms have been applied to severe elevations of blood pressure (BP) (>180/110 mmHg). In general, 'hypertensive emergencies' are defined as severe elevations in blood pressure with associated end-organ damage of the central nervous system (CNS), the cardiovascular system and the kidneys. The term 'hypertensive urgencies' is used for patients with severely elevated BP without evidence of acute end-organ damage. Hypertensive encephalopathy, hypertensive left ventricular failure and acute aortic dissection are immediately life-threatening and are considered to be true hypertensive emergencies (Table 9.1). The term 'malignant hypertension' is defined as a syndrome of elevated BP accompanied by encephalopathy or nephropathy.

It is important to have coherent strategies for the diagnosis, investigation and management of hypertensive crises, as the mortality in these patients is high and rapid treatment of hypertension may itself be hazardous. These risks are greatly increased when patients are treated with inappropriate pharmacological agents in the absence of appropriate monitoring.

Epidemiology

There has been a decline in the prevalence of hypertensive crises over the past 20 years, probably as a result of more effective diagnosis and treatment of milder grades of hypertension. Hypertension crises are now reported to be rare in western developed populations, although still reported to be common in some developing countries.

Nevertheless, in Birmingham (UK), the incidence of hypertensive crises does not appear to have fallen substantially over the past 25 years, with an estimated annual incidence of 1–2 per 100,000 population (Figure 9.1). The incidence of hypertensive crises is higher in the Afro-Caribbean population and the elderly. The majority of patients have a history of hypertension and many would have been prescribed antihypertensive therapy with inadequate BP control.

Malignant hypertension

Hypertensive crises may present at any age, including the elderly, and recurrent clinical presentations of malignant-phase hypertension may occur. Severe hypertension in young women

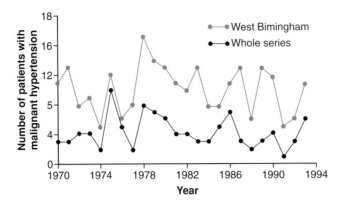

Figure 9.1
Failure of malignant hypertension to decline in Birmingham, UK.

has been related to both the use of the oral contraceptive pill and a history of hypertension in pregnancy. Several studies have also reported an association between cigarette smoking and malignant hypertension.

Demographic and socioeconomic factors appear to be important and may contribute to the failure of malignant hypertension cases to decline in some areas of the world. Malignant hypertension is reported to occur more frequently in patients from lower socioeconomic groups and in subjects with high self-perceived 'stress' levels. Ethnicity may be important, as closer examination of the Birmingham cohort reveals a high prevalence in first-generation migrant groups, including Afro-Caribbeans (mainly from Jamaica) and Asians (mainly from Punjabi-speaking areas of India and Pakistan). In this respect, the Birmingham cohort resembles other series of malignant hypertensive patients from less developed countries (for example, South Africa).

A further reason for the failure of malignant hypertension to decline might be the presence of patients who have limited understanding of the nature and complications of the disease, and the importance of compliance with antihypertensive treatment.

> Hypertensive crises may be found in any age group, including the elderly, and studies have linked them to demographic and ethnic factors

Causes of malignant hypertension

Hypertensive crises are more likely to be associated with an underlying cause (Table 9.2). Conn's syndrome (primary hyperaldosteronism) is reported to be rare in cases of malignant hypertension.

Prognosis

In the modern era, the more effective management of hypertension has led to an improvement in five-year survival rates, in developed countries, from 60% to 75% (Figure 9.2). Nevertheless, in developing countries such as Nigeria, the prognosis continues to be poor with only 40% of patients surviving longer than one year.

Early recognition

Early recognition of malignant hypertension is important as patients tend to develop overt clinical symptoms at a late stage of the disease. In the long term, the most common causes of death in patients with a history of malignant hypertension are chronic renal failure (40%),

Table 9.2
Underlying causes in studies of patients with malignant hypertension

	Glasgow	Leicester	Johannesburg	Birmingham
Follow-up	1968–83	1974–83	1979–80	1970–93
Number of patients	139	100	62	242
Underlying causes (%)				
—essential	60	68	82	56
—renal	18	19	5	28
—renovascular	14	6	3	2
—other	8	7	10	10

cerebrovascular disease (24%), myocardial infarction (11%) and heart failure (10%).

Cigarette smoking exerts an adverse effect on prognosis in patients who continue to smoke following their initial presentation.

Renal function continues to deteriorate in some patients with malignant hypertension despite good BP control during follow-up. Nevertheless, the quality of the BP control does predict the long-term prognosis and BP should be optimized with the target BP of 125/75 mmHg.

> The most common causes of death in patients with a history of malignant hypertension are chronic renal failure, cerebrovascular disease, myocardial infarction and heart failure

Pathophysiology

Malignant hypertension is characterized by fibrinoid necrosis of arterioles in many sites, including the kidneys, eyes, brain, heart and gut. However, this histological feature is not pathognomonic of malignant hypertension. Subintimal cellular proliferation of the interlobular arteries of the kidney is also commonly seen and this may well be important as intimal thickening may lead to luminal occlusion in these small vessels. The occlusion of these small arteries contributes to chronic renal ischaemia, leading to the renal failure that is often seen in malignant hypertension.

Microscopic examination of the arterioles reveals alternating bands of constriction and dilation. These dilated segments are thought to represent focal areas of disruption of the vessel wall related to the rapid rise in intraluminal pressure, and these areas have been shown to be abnormally permeable to plasma proteins. Such disruption of the vessel wall leads to the deposition of fibrin, and therefore fibrinoid necrosis. This process may lead to the further deposition of fibrin in the vessel wall and microcirculation, as well as platelet

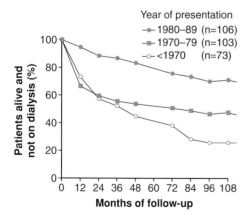

Figure 9.2
Survival of malignant hypertension. (Adapted from Lip *et al.* *J Hypertens* 1995; **13**: 915.)

aggregation, release of growth factors, subintimal cellular proliferation and activation of the coagulation system, which may result in microangiopathic haemolytic anaemia – a recognized feature in some of these patients. In addition, ischaemia of the juxtaglomerular apparatus leads to activation of the renin–angiotensin system with further vasoconstriction and arteriolar damage.

> Malignant hypertension is marked by fibrinoid necrosis of arterioles in sites such as the kidneys, eyes, brain, heart and gut

Cerebral and renal autoregulation

Blood flow and perfusion of the brain and kidneys are maintained over a range of blood pressures – so-called autoregulation. In healthy humans, this autoregulatory mechanism maintains normal cerebral blood flow between a systemic arterial blood pressure of 60 mmHg to 120 mmHg. With chronic hypertension, the pressure-flow autoregulation curve is shifted to the right such that cerebral blood flow is maintained at a higher range of blood pressure.

While this adaptation to chronic hypertension protects the brain and kidneys from chronically elevated BP, a sudden drop in BP (even to 'normal' levels) may result in reduced blood flow to these organs. Cerebral autoregulation is also impaired at extremely high BP levels and in hypertensive encephalopathy, making cerebral perfusion exquisitely sensitive to changes in systemic blood pressure changes. Clearly, these autoregulatory mechanisms have important implications for the practical management of hypertensive emergencies (see below).

Clinical features

Severe hypertension may be an incidental finding in an asymptomatic patient, although associated symptoms may be present. The presenting symptoms of malignant hypertension are variable, although headaches and visual

disturbances are the most common. Initial symptoms are often non-specific and include anorexia, nausea, vomiting and abdominal pain. These non-specific symptoms often lead to delayed diagnosis and treatment. Breathlessness due to left ventricular failure might be present but ischaemic chest pain is less common.

Aortic dissection must be considered in any patient who presents with raised BP and severe pain in the back, chest or abdomen.

Hypertensive encephalopathy is rare and usually occurs in patients with a history of hypertension that has been inadequately treated, or where previous treatment has been discontinued. It may be associated with severe headache, nausea, vomiting, visual disturbances and confusion may also be a feature. However, with the advent of high-resolution CT scanning it has become clear that many patients who are thought to have hypertensive encephalopathy, have actually suffered an acute stroke.

> The most common symptoms of malignant hypertension are headaches and visual disturbances, with non-specific initial symptoms including anorexia, nausea, vomiting and abdominal pain

Physical signs
Retinopathy

Malignant hypertension is confirmed by the presence of advanced retinal hypertensive changes. Clinical decisions, in patients with severe hypertension, should be based on the presence or absence of retinopathy together with the height of the BP.

The Keith, Wagener and Barker classification (see Table 4.7), originally proposed in 1939, remains the most commonly used grading system for hypertensive retinopathy. The strength of this classification is the correlation between the clinical signs and prognosis, although this grading system has a number of limitations. In particular, there is no significant difference in the long-term prognosis between grades III and IV hypertensive retinopathy.

The restrictions of this traditional classification for hypertensive retinopathy have led to the development of a simplified grading system, which is more applicable to modern clinical practice (Table 9.3). In this grading system, arteriolar narrowing and focal constriction, features which correlate with BP levels, age and general cardiovascular status, constitute the first grade (grade I). The presence of retinal haemorrhages or exudates, cotton wool spots (with or without papilloedema) constitute the second and prognostically more significant grade (grade II) (Figure 9.3).

An additional subgroup of patients has been identified who have isolated bilateral papilloedema, in association with severe hypertension (Figure 9.4). The clinical

Table 9.3
Revised grading system for hypertensive retinopathy

Grade	Retinal changes	Hypertensive category	Prognosis
I 'Non-malignant'	Generalized arteriolar narrowing Focal constriction (NB <u>not</u> arteriovenous nipping)	Established hypertension	May depend on height of blood pressure, but age and other concomitant cardiovascular risk factors are equally important
II 'Malignant'	Haemorrhages, hard exudates, cotton wool spots ± Optic disc swelling	Accelerated or malignant hypertension with retinovascular damage present*	Most die within two years if untreated In treated patients, median survival is now >12 years

*To fulfil criteria of Grade II, retinovascular damage should be present in both eyes. Note that if carotid occlusive disease is present, ocular blood flow may be reduced and if asymmetrical this may be sufficient to mask papilloedema or other hypertensive changes in the ipsilateral eye.

(After Dodson *et al*. Hypertensive retinopathy: a review of existing classification systems and a suggestion for a simplified grading system. *J Human Hypertens* 1996; **10**: 93–8.)

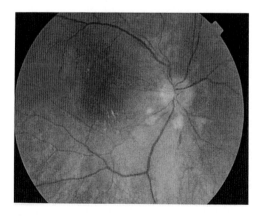 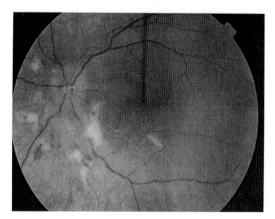

Figure 9.3
Malignant phase hypertension – retinal flame-shaped haemorrhages, cotton wool spots, exudates and papilloedema are visible.

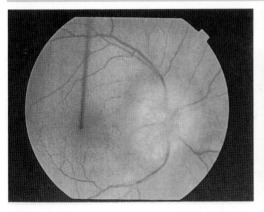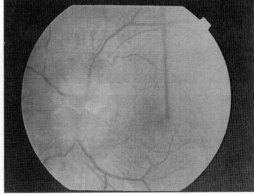

Figure 9.4
Lone papilloedema in a patient with severe hypertension, showing bilateral optic disc swelling and no other significant retinal features.

characteristics of these patients are similar to those with 'conventional' malignant hypertension, although they have been reported to have a shorter median survival. However, care is needed to differentiate such patients from those with benign intracranial hypertension, who are typically young, overweight and female. A CT scan and lumbar puncture may be needed to ascertain the diagnosis.

Other clinical signs

In addition to the retinopathy there may be signs of left heart failure, left ventricular hypertrophy and sometimes anaemia due to associated renal failure. Asymmetrical BP readings, absent pulses, aortic incompetence and neurological signs should raise the suspicion of acute aortic dissection. Fluctuating neurological signs, disorientation, reduced level of consciousness, neurological deficit and focal or generalized seizures are all potential manifestations of hypertensive encephalopathy. Severe injury to the kidneys may result in renal failure with oliguria, proteinuria and even haematuria.

Early management

As previously discussed, patients with chronic hypertension have rightward shifts in their pressure-flow autoregulation curve. In addition, patients with severe malignant hypertension may have abnormal autoregulatory mechanisms. Consequently, over-rapid BP reductions are potentially hazardous and may lead to cerebral, renal or myocardial infarction, while visual loss is also a recognized complication of over-rapid treatment.

Any reduction in BP must be gradual and the approach to treatment governed by the presence (and type) or absence of end-organ damage, i.e. hypertensive emergency or urgency. Parenteral antihypertensive therapy is indicated in hypertensive emergencies, with the aim of lowering diastolic BP by about 15% to 110 mmHg over about 30–60 minutes (with the exception of aortic dissection). Blood pressure should not be lowered to 'normal' levels. Parenteral antihypertensive treatment is not indicated in hypertensive urgencies (without end-organ damage).

In general, parenteral therapy requires high-dependency monitoring and should be restricted to severe emergencies where complications such as hypertensive encephalopathy, left ventricular failure and aortic dissection are present. The choice of parenteral antihypertensive therapy is dependent on the type of end-organ damage.

Hypertensive encephalopathy

Sodium nitroprusside

Sodium nitroprusside is the drug of choice when neurological damage is thought to be imminent. It is a potentially dangerous drug and should only be administered in a high dependency unit with cardiac and BP monitoring.

Nitroprusside is administered as a continuous titrated infusion, which is increased to achieve a diastolic BP of 90–110 mmHg over 2–3 hours. Thiocyanate is the toxic metabolite of nitroprusside and its accumulation is more rapid in patients with renal and hepatic failure.

Labetalol

Parenteral labetalol has been successfully used in the treatment of hypertensive encephalopathy, although it has been reported to cause severe and unpredictable hypotension in some patients. Intravenous nitrates are of limited value in hypertensive encephalopathy because they cause headache at the doses required to bring about a substantial reduction in BP.

Arterial vasodilators

Diazoxide and hydralazine, both arterial vasodilators, were previously popular in the management of hypertensive crises. Diazoxide administered by rapid bolus injection has led to a number of cases of cerebral infarction and death, and it is now rarely indicated in the treatment of hypertensive crises. Hydralazine should also be avoided in hypertensive crises as the antihypertensive effects may be unpredictable, prolonged and not easily titrated.

Reflex tachycardia is associated with both diazoxide and hydralazine and these agents should be avoided in patients with known or suspected coronary disease.

In all cases of suspected hypertensive encephalopathy, if a reduction in BP is not accompanied by clinical improvement, then the diagnosis should be reconsidered.

Hypertensive left ventricular failure

Severe increases in systemic vascular resistance may result in left ventricular failure. In addition to the conventional management with opiates/ opioids and loop diuretics, sodium nitroprusside is used to reduce pre-load and after-load. Nitrates may also be used, but are less potent.

Hypertension with unstable angina or myocardial infarction

In patients with severe hypertension and angina, intravenous nitrates are valuable as they reduce systemic vascular resistance and improve coronary perfusion. Beta-blockers, administered by slow intravenous injection (for example, 5 mg metoprolol repeated at intervals of 20 minutes) may be valuable when the BP is moderately raised, although in severe hypertension an intravenous infusion (for example, labetalol or esmolol) may be necessary. Sodium nitroprusside should be reserved for resistant cases, as it may exacerbate coronary ischaemia.

Aortic dissection

Effective blood pressure control is crucial in the management of aortic dissection. Indeed, prompt and effective BP control is the treatment of choice in type B aortic dissection (descending aorta distal to the subclavian artery). Propagation of the dissection is dependent not only on the elevation in BP but also the velocity of left ventricular ejection. Hence, specific therapy should be aimed at reducing BP and rate of pressure rise. Labetalol, with its beta-blocker effects, is the treatment of choice as it reduces the force of contraction, while sodium nitroprusside may be combined with a beta-blocker if further BP reduction is required. The aim of therapy should be to reduce the systolic BP to 100 mmHg in order to reduce aortic shear stress and limit the size of the dissection.

Stroke and subarachnoid haemorrhage

Cerebral autoregulation is commonly disturbed following an acute stroke. Excessive antihypertensive treatment may only serve to worsen the cerebral damage that results from an intracerebral infarction or haemorrhage. Antihypertensive treatment may lead to rapid and dangerous falls in BP, and should only be administered for severe elevations in BP (diastolic BP >130 mmHg). In these cases, oral therapy with small doses of slow-release nifedipine or atenolol may be indicated, although parenteral treatment is almost always contraindicated.

The calcium antagonist nimodipine has beneficial effects on cerebral vasospasm following subarachnoid haemorrhage, but these effects are not related to the small fall in BP.

Phaeochromocytoma

This condition is a rare cause of acute severe hypertension. The treatment of choice is the orally active short-acting alpha-blocker prazosin or phentolamine (which may also be given by bolus injection or infusion). It is possible to subsequently add a beta-blocker to control heart rate. Labetalol has also been used, while nitroprusside should be reserved for resistant cases.

Alpha-blockade is mandatory in the preoperative management of patients with phaeochromocytoma. It is used to overcome the intense vasoconstriction caused by the high circulating levels of adrenaline (epinephrine) and noradrenaline (norepinephrine).

Recreational drugs

Cocaine, ecstasy, amphetamines and LSD are among the sympathomimetic drugs that can produce severe acute hypertension. Isolated beta-blockade may lead to unopposed alpha-adrenergic effects, which may exacerbate the hypertensive crisis. Although labetalol has both alpha- and beta-blocking effects, controlled studies in animals and humans do not support its use. Nitroprusside, phentolamine or verapamil may be used.

Hypertensive urgencies

In the absence of acute end-organ damage, immediate BP reduction with parenteral drugs is not indicated. Indeed, this form of treatment may place the patient at unnecessary risk, as serious and sometimes fatal complications of treatment have been reported with almost all antihypertensive drugs (Table 9.4).

Table 9.4
Drug treatment in hypertensive crises

Drug	Administeration	Dose	Principal indications
Nifedipine	Oral	Start at 10 mg and repeat after 4–6 hours	Malignant hypertension
	Oral	Maintenance 10–40 mg twice daily	
Atenolol	Oral	Start at 25 mg Maximum 100 mg daily	Malignant hypertension
Sodium nitroprusside	i.v.	0.3–8 µg/kg/min Monitor levels in prolonged use	Hypertensive encephalopathy, left ventricular failure, dissecting aneurysm
Labetalol	i.v.	2 mg/min	Hypertensive encephalopathy, dissecting aneurysm, unstable angina or MI
Nitrates	i.v.	GTN 10–200 µg/min	Left ventricular failure, unstable angina with malignant hypertension

(GTN = glyceryl trinitrate; MI = myocardial infarction; i.v. = intravenous)

Oral therapy

An appropriate first-line oral agent is the slow-release nifedipine (10–20 mg in tablet form), which is a simple, effective and safe treatment and which does not significantly alter cerebral blood flow. Nifedipine capsules and sublingual nifedipine must not be used as their use has been reported to be associated with dramatic and unpredictable falls in BP, leading to cerebral and myocardial infarction.

Intensive care monitoring is not usually necessary. The dose of slow-release nifedipine may be repeated or increased at intervals of 6–12 hours, aiming for a gradual reduction in BP of 20–25% in the first 24 hours and to a diastolic BP of around 100 mmHg over the next few days.

> Slow-release nifedipine in tablet form is a first-line drug that does not alter cerebral blood flow significantly, but sublingual capsules must not be used

Angiotensin-converting enzyme (ACE) inhibitors

ACE inhibitors may produce rapid and dangerous falls in BP (particularly in patients with renovascular disease that might not be diagnosed in the acute situation) and are not recommended as first-line treatment. Diuretics should be restricted to those with evidence of fluid overload as patients with malignant hypertension are often volume depleted, secondary to pressure-related diuresis and activation of the renin–angiotensin system. In severe renal failure, haemodialysis or peritoneal dialysis may be indicated, particularly where there is gross fluid retention.

Combination treatment

Combination treatment is usually required in the long term. In the absence of contraindications, beta-blockers (e.g. atenolol) are an appropriate additional antihypertensive agent. It is sensible to start with small doses, such as atenolol 25 mg daily, increasing as necessary. The combination of atenolol and nifedipine is often a well-tolerated and effective regimen.

Summary

Although hypertensive crises are less common in modern-day medical practice, they are associated with significant morbidity and mortality rates as malignant hypertension remains a disease with a poor long-term prognosis.

In the majority of cases, rapid-onset orally active drugs are sufficient to control BP. Preparations of labetalol or sodium nitroprusside are occasionally necessary in cases of resistant hypertension and true hypertensive crises. However, clinicians should be aware of the hazards of the over-rapid reduction of BP in these patients as well as the complications of hypertension in the first place.

Further reading

Lim KG, Isles CG, Hodsman general practitioner, et al. Malignant hypertension in women of childbearing age and its relation to the contraceptive pill. Br Med J 1987; **294**: 1057–9.

Lip GYH, Beevers M, Beevers DG. The failure of malignant hypertension to decline: a survey of 24 years experience in a multiracial population in England. J Hypertens 1994; **12**: 1297–305.

Lip GYH, Beevers M, Beevers DG. Complications and survival of 315 patients with malignant hypertension. J Hypertens 1995; **13**: 915–24.

Lip GY, Beevers M, Beevers DG. Malignant hypertension in young women is related to previous hypertension in pregnancy not oral contraception. QJM 1997; **90**: 571–5.

Index